# ETHICAL STANDARDS IN
# SOCIAL WORK

# ETHICAL STANDARDS IN SOCIAL WORK

## A CRITICAL REVIEW OF THE NASW CODE OF ETHICS

By

*Frederic G. Reamer*

NASW PRESS

NATIONAL ASSOCIATION OF SOCIAL WORKERS
WASHINGTON, DC

Josephine A.V. Allen, PhD, ACSW, *President*
Josephine Nieves, MSW, PhD, *Executive Director*

Jane Browning, *Executive Editor*

Christina A. Davis, *Senior Editor*

Christine Cotting, UpperCase Publication Services, *Project Manager*

Patricia Borthwick, *Copyeditor*

Louise Goines, *Proofreader*

Robert Elwood, *Indexer*

Chanté Lampton, *Acquisitions Associate*

Heather Peters, *Editorial Secretary*

First impression February 1998

Second impression June 1998

**Library of Congress Cataloging-in-Publication Data**

Reamer, Frederic G., 1953–
    Ethical standards in social work : a critical review of the NASW
code of ethics / by Frederic G. Reamer.
        p.   cm.
    Includes bibliographical references and index.
    ISBN 0-87101-293-6 (pbk. : alk. paper)
    1. Social workers—Professional ethics—United States.
    2. National Association of Social Workers.  I. Title.
HV40.8.U6R43    1998
174'.9362—dc21                            98-9666
                                                    CIP

Printed in the United States of America

For Deborah, Emma, and Leah


Special dedication to Elizabeth DuMez and Charles Levy,
true champions of social work ethics

# Contents

# PREFACE

Ethical standards in social work have been transformed. Like all other professionals, in recent years social workers' understanding of ethical issues has matured dramatically. When the National Association of Social Workers (NASW) published its first code of ethics in 1960, the entire set of 14 guidelines fit on one side of one page. The current *Code*, ratified by the NASW Delegate Assembly in 1996 and implemented in 1997, comprises 155 ethical standards and six broad ethical principles. In the time between, social workers have developed an enriched grasp of the profession's core values, the ways in which core values sometimes conflict in practice, and ethical dilemmas in the profession. In addition, social workers have become more familiar with patterns of ethical misconduct engaged in by a relatively small portion of the profession's members.

The *NASW Code of Ethics*, which constitutes a marked change in the profession's understanding of and approach to ethical issues, reflects this remarkable transformation. It embodies what we have learned about ethics throughout social work's history—much of which has emerged since 1980, when the broader field of applied and professional ethics began to burgeon.

This book has several purposes. First, it provides social workers with a detailed overview and discussion of the *NASW Code of Ethics*. It includes a summary of the evolution of ethical issues in the profession; discussion of the profession's core values, mission, and broad ethical principles; and explanations and illustrations of the profession's more specific ethical standards. My hope is that the material will provide the profession with a useful educational tool for use by both experienced and fledgling practitioners.

In addition, this book should be useful to social workers who seek advice and consultation on ethical issues. Although *Ethical Standards in Social Work* cannot provide formulaic solutions to all ethical issues and should be supplemented by other literature and resources pertaining to social work and professional ethics, it can provide social workers with an overview of relevant guidelines and issues as they sort their way through ethical thickets.

*Ethical Standards in Social Work* should also be useful to social workers and others who rely on the *NASW Code of Ethics* in relation to ethics complaints and lawsuits involving social workers. Members of NASW committees on inquiry and state licensing boards, and those engaged in litigation involving social workers, will find this book helpful in identifying prevailing ethical standards in the profession.

Chapter 1 provides an overview of ethical issues in social work, relevant historical developments, and the purposes and core contents of the *NASW*

*Code of Ethics.* The remaining chapters focus on the *Code's* standards pertaining to social workers' ethical responsibilities to clients, to colleagues, in practice settings, as professionals, to the social work profession, and to the broader society. The chapters on ethical standards provide a summary and analysis of key ethical issues, often including case examples.

During the years that I have paid serious attention to ethical issues in social work, beginning especially in the mid-1970s, I have been amazed by the exponential growth of interest in the subject among social workers. The reasons for this growth are complex, and they are both reassuring and distressing (see chapter 1). The net result, however, is that contemporary social workers have a better understanding of ethical issues in the profession than did any preceding generation, and that is good. Although I have learned a great deal over the years about these issues, I do not claim to have definitive answers to all ethical quandaries. My hope is that the commentary and analysis in this book will provide readers with thoughtful and thought-provoking guidance as they wrestle with difficult ethical questions and issues. (The views and opinions expressed in this book are my own and do not necessarily reflect the views and opinions of the *NASW Code of Ethics* Revision Committee or NASW.)

Serving as chair of the *NASW Code of Ethics* Revision Committee that drafted the code discussed in this book was a genuine privilege. I will always count my work with the esteemed committee members—Carol Brill, Jacqueline Glover, Marjorie Hammock, Vincentia Joseph, Alfred Murillo, Jr., Barbara Varley, and Drayton Vincent—and our principal staff person at NASW, Elizabeth DuMez, among my most treasured professional experiences. This extraordinary group of people spent two years of their professional lives crafting and refining the *Code.* I was awed by and will always appreciate their exceptional dedication, insight, thoughtfulness, and earnestness.

There is no question that the *NASW Code of Ethics* is a vital component of social work's identity and integrity: the *Code* serves as a lodestar for this remarkably diverse profession.

—FREDERIC G. REAMER

CHAPTER

# 1

# ETHICAL STANDARDS IN SOCIAL WORK

## AN INTRODUCTION

One of the hallmarks of a profession is its willingness to establish ethical standards to guide practitioners' conduct (Greenwood, 1957; Hall, 1968; Lindeman, 1947). Ethical standards are created to help professionals identify ethical issues in practice and provide guidelines to determine what is ethically acceptable and unacceptable behavior.

Professions typically organize their ethical standards in the form of published codes of ethics (Bayles, 1986; Kultgen, 1982). According to Jamal and Bowie (1995), codes of ethics are designed to address three major issues. First, codes address "problems of moral hazard," or instances when a profession's self-interest may conflict with the public's interest. Such conflicts can occur in a variety of ways. Examples include whether accountants should be obligated to disclose confidential information concerning financial fraud that their clients have committed, whether dentists should be permitted to refuse to treat people who have an infectious disease such as AIDS, whether physicians should be allowed to invest personally in laboratories or rehabilitation facilities to which they refer patients, and whether social workers should be expected to disclose to law enforcement officials confidential information about crimes their clients have admitted committing.

Second, codes address issues of "professional courtesy," that is, rules that govern how professionals should behave to enhance and maintain a profession's integrity. Examples include whether lawyers should be permitted to advertise and solicit clients, whether psychiatrists should be permitted to engage in sexual relationships with former patients, whether psychologists should be prohibited from soliciting colleagues' clients, and whether social workers should report colleagues who are impaired or who engage in unethical conduct.

Finally, codes address issues that concern professionals' duty to serve the public interest. For example, to what extent should physicians and nurses be expected to assist people when faced with a public emergency? Should dentists donate a portion of their professional time to provide services to low-income people who do not have dental insurance? Should social workers provide services without remuneration to clients whose insurance coverage has been exhausted?

Like other professions—such as medicine, nursing, law, psychology, journalism, and engineering—social work has developed a comprehensive set of ethical standards. These standards have evolved over time, reflecting important changes in the broader culture and in social work's mission, methods, and priorities. They address a wide range of issues, including, for example, social workers' handling of confidential information, sexual contact between social workers and their clients, conflicts of interest, supervision, education and training, and social and political action.

Ethical standards for the social work profession appear in various forms. The *NASW Code of Ethics* (1996; included as an appendix to this book) is the most visible compilation of the profession's ethical standards. Ethical standards also can be found in codes of ethics developed by other social work organizations (for example, the National Association of Black Social Workers [NABSW], the National Federation of Societies for Clinical Social Work [NFSCSW], and the Canadian Association of Social Workers), regulations governing state licensing boards, and codes of conduct promulgated by social services agencies. In addition, the social work literature contains many discussions of ethical norms in the profession (Loewenberg & Dolgoff, 1996; Reamer, 1990, 1994, 1995a, 1995b; Rhodes, 1986).

## ETHICS DURING SOCIAL WORK'S EARLY YEARS

The 1996 *NASW Code of Ethics* reflects major changes in social work's approach to ethical issues throughout its history and the social work profession's increasingly mature grasp of ethical issues. During the earliest years of social work's history, few formal ethical standards existed. The earliest known attempt to formulate a code was an experimental draft published in the 1920s and attributed to social work pioneer Mary Richmond (Pumphrey, 1959). Although several social work organizations formulated draft codes during the profession's early years—including the American Association for Organizing Family Social Work and several chapters of the American Association of Social Workers—it was not until 1947 that the latter group, the largest organization of social workers of that era, adopted a formal code (Johnson, 1955). In 1960 NASW adopted its first code of ethics, five years after the association was formed. Over time, the *NASW Code of Ethics* has come to be recognized in the United States as the most visible and influential code in social work.

The 1960 *NASW Code of Ethics* consisted of 14 proclamations concerning, for example, every social worker's duty to give precedence to professional responsibility over personal interests; respect the privacy of clients; give appropriate professional service in public emergencies; and contribute knowledge, skills, and support to human welfare programs. First-person statements (that is, "I give precedence to my professional responsibility over my personal interests" and "I respect the privacy of the people I serve") were preceded by a preamble that set forth social workers' responsibility to uphold humanitarian ideals, maintain and improve social work service, and develop the philosophy and skills of the profession. In 1967 a 15th principle pledging nondiscrimination was added to the proclamations.

Soon after the adoption of the code, however, NASW members began to express concern about its level of abstraction, its scope and usefulness for resolving ethical conflicts, and its provisions for handling ethics complaints about practitioners and agencies. As McCann and Cutler (1979) noted,

> The sources of dissatisfaction are widespread and have involved practitioners, clients, chapter committees, and, in particular, those persons

directly engaged in the adjudication of complaints in which unethical behavior is charged. At a time of growing specialization and organizational differentiation, a variety of issues have surfaced centering on the nature of the code itself, its level of abstraction and ambiguity, its scope and usefulness, and its provision for the handling of ethical complaints. (p. 5)

In 1977 NASW established a task force, chaired by Charles Levy, to revise the code and enhance its relevance to practice; the result was a new code adopted by NASW in 1979. The 1979 code included six sections of brief, unannotated principles preceded by a preamble setting forth the code's general purpose and stating that the code's principles provided standards for the enforcement of ethical practices among social workers:

> This code is intended to serve as a guide to the everyday conduct of members of the social work profession and as a basis for adjudication of issues in ethics when the conduct of social workers is alleged to deviate from the standards expressed or implied in this code. It represents standards of ethical behavior for social workers in professional relationships with those served, with colleagues, with employers, with other individuals and professions, and with the community and society as a whole. It also embodies standards of ethical behavior governing individual conduct to the extent that such conduct is associated with an individual's status and identity as a social worker. (NASW, 1979, p. v)

The 1979 code set forth principles related to social workers' conduct and comportment, as well as their ethical responsibility to clients, colleagues, employers and employing organizations, the social work profession, and society. The code's principles were both *prescriptive* (for example, "The social worker should make every effort to foster maximum self-determination on the part of clients" [principle II.G] and "The social worker should afford clients reasonable access to any official social work records concerning them" [principle II.H.3]) and *proscriptive* (for example, "The social worker should not exploit relationships with clients for personal advantage" [principle II.F.2] and "The social worker should not assume professional responsibility for the clients of another agency or a colleague without appropriate communication with that agency or colleague" [principle III.K.1]). A number of the code's principles were concrete and specific (for example, "The social worker should under no circumstances engage in sexual activities with clients" [principle II.F.5] and "The social worker should obtain informed consent of clients before taping, recording, or permitting third-party observation of their activities" [principle II.H.5]), and others were more abstract, asserting ethical ideals (for example, "The social worker should maintain high standards of personal conduct in the capacity or identity as social worker" [principle I.A] and "The social worker should encourage informed participation by the public in shaping social policies and institutions" [principle VI.P.7]). Clearly, some of the code's principles—especially those pertaining to social justice and general social welfare—were intended to provide social workers with important aspirations, whereas other principles set forth specific, enforceable standards of conduct, violations of which provided grounds for filing a formal ethics complaint.

The 1979 code was revised twice, eventually including 82 principles. In 1990 several principles related to solicitation of clients and fee splitting were modified after an inquiry into NASW policies by the U.S. Federal Trade Commission (FTC), begun in 1986, that concerned possible restraint of trade. As a result of the inquiry, principles in the code were revised to remove prohibitions concerning solicitation of clients from colleagues or an agency and to modify wording that concerned accepting compensation for making a referral. NASW also entered into a consent agreement with the FTC concerning issues raised by the inquiry.

In 1993 a task force chaired by this author recommended to the NASW Delegate Assembly that it further amend the code of ethics to include five new principles—three related to the problem of social worker impairment and two related to the problem of dual or multiple relationships. This recommendation reflected social workers' growing understanding of the need to address impairment among some social workers and the ways in which blurred or confused boundaries between social workers and clients can compromise the quality of services delivered. The first three of these new principles addressed instances when social workers' own problems and impairment interfere with their professional functioning, and the latter two addressed the need to avoid social, business, and other nonprofessional relationships with clients because of possible conflicts of interest. The 1993 Delegate Assembly voted to incorporate the five new principles and passed a resolution to establish a task force to draft an entirely new code of ethics that would be far more comprehensive and relevant to contemporary practice, for submission to the 1996 Delegate Assembly.

An entirely new code was needed because, since the 1979 code was drafted, a new scholarly field—applied and professional ethics—had emerged. Much of what contemporary professionals in general and social workers in particular have learned about professional ethics had occurred since the ratification of the 1979 code. Social workers had developed a firmer grasp of the wide range of ethical issues facing practitioners, many of which were not addressed in the 1979 code. The broader field of applied and professional ethics, which had begun in the early 1970s, had matured considerably, resulting in the identification and greater understanding of novel ethical issues not cited in the 1979 code. For a variety of reasons, especially during the 1980s and early 1990s, scholarly analyses of ethical issues in all professions burgeoned. First, and perhaps most important, was the emergence of complicated ethical issues in health care (for example, public debate about the ethics of allocating scarce organs, genetic engineering, abortion, and euthanasia). These developments led to the establishment of the bioethics field in the late 1960s and early 1970s. Without question, debate and scholarship in bioethics paved the way for other professions' exploration of ethical issues. With bioethics, all professionals began for the first time to appreciate the useful and complex connections between ethical theory and principles and real-life ethical problems faced by practitioners (Reamer, 1985, 1986, 1991a, 1993b).

Second, at about the same time (the late 1960s and early 1970s), many social work and health professionals were embroiled in sustained debate concerning patients' rights, welfare rights, prisoners' rights, and civil rights. Relevant issues included a patient's right to refuse treatment, the role of informed consent in research, the humane treatment of prisoners, and affirmative action and civil rights protections in the workplace. These concepts, which many professionals now take for granted, were new at the time, and discussion of them helped to shape the emerging field of applied and professional ethics.

Third, professionals began paying more attention to ethical issues because of increased litigation alleging ethical misconduct filed against practitioners in all fields. Lawsuits alleging, for example, breaches of privacy and confidentiality, sexual misconduct, defamation of character, fraudulent billing, and inappropriate termination of services alerted many people in the helping professions to possible ethical problems in their ranks. If for no other reason, practitioners needed to learn more about ethics to prevent malpractice claims and avoid lawsuits (Reamer, 1984, 1995d).

Fourth, increasingly widespread publicity in all media about professional misconduct did much to convince practitioners that they needed to pay more attention to ethics. For example, there were reports of physicians who committed Medicaid fraud, clergy who were sexually involved with minors, lawyers who raided clients' escrow accounts, police officers who accepted bribes, and psychotherapists who developed sexual relationships with clients. Of course, in the midst of this period (the early 1970s) the nation was wrestling with the ethical implications of the Watergate political scandal, an ethical lapse with far-reaching consequences. Watergate and myriad other national and local political scandals have done much to inspire interest in ethical issues.

Finally, interest in professional ethics grew because the professions themselves matured. Like people, professions experience stages of development. It took decades for nearly all the professions to pay serious attention to ethical issues, in part because, during the earlier phases of their development, they tended to be preoccupied with cultivating their technical expertise and proficiency. This is understandable, given the professions' need to establish their credibility with the public.

A clear by-product of this general trend is that social workers as a group have begun to pay much more attention to ethical issues in the profession. For example, presentations on social work ethics at professional conferences sponsored by NASW, the Council on Social Work Education (CSWE), and other social work organizations have increased substantially. In addition, CSWE strengthened the language in its 1992 *Curriculum Policy Statements* requiring instruction on ethical issues and ethical decision making in undergraduate and graduate social work education programs. Moreover, the greatest part of social work scholarship on professional ethics has been published since 1980.

## CURRENT *NASW CODE OF ETHICS*

The *NASW Code of Ethics* Revision Committee was appointed in 1994 and spent two years drafting a new code. This committee, which was chaired by this author and included a professional ethicist and social workers from a variety of practice and educational settings, carried out its work in three phases (Reamer, 1997b). Each phase was designed to provide the committee with the most comprehensive information available on social work ethics and, more broadly, professional ethics, so that the new code would reflect prevailing opinion in the profession.

The committee first reviewed the literature on social work ethics, and applied and professional ethics generally, to identify key concepts and issues that might be addressed in the new code. This was particularly important because so much of the literature on professional and social work ethics had been published after the development of the 1979 code. The committee also reviewed the 1979 code to identify content that should be retained and deleted, and to identify areas where content might be added. We then discussed possible ways of organizing the new code to enhance its relevance and use in practice.

During the second phase, and while the first-phase activities were occurring, the committee also issued formal invitations to all NASW members and to members of various social work organizations (such as NABSW, CSWE, NFSCSW, and the American Association of State Social Work Boards) to suggest issues to be addressed in the new code. The *NASW Code of Ethics* Revision Committee reviewed its list of relevant content areas drawn from the professional literature and from public comment and developed a number of drafts, the last of which was shared with ethics experts in social work and other professions for their review and comment.

In the third phase, the committee made a number of revisions based on the feedback we had received from the experts who reviewed the document, published a copy of the draft code in the January 1996 issue of the *NASW News*, and invited all NASW members to send comments to be considered by the committee as it prepared the final draft for submission to the 1996 NASW Delegate Assembly. In addition, during this last phase various committee members met with each of the six NASW Delegate Assembly regional coalitions to discuss the code's development and receive delegates' comments and feedback. The code was then presented to and ratified overwhelmingly by the Delegate Assembly in August 1996 and implemented in January 1997.

## Social Work's Mission

To enhance the new code's comprehensiveness, accessibility, and practical relevance, the *NASW Code of Ethics* Revision Committee departed from the format of the 1979 code. The 1996 code includes four major sections. The first section, "Preamble," summarizes social work's mission and core values. For the first time in NASW's history, the association has adopted and published a formally sanctioned mission statement and an explicit summary of the profession's core values. The committee members believed strongly that it was time for the profession to codify a widely endorsed mission statement, particularly as social work approached the 100th anniversary of its formal inauguration. The mission statement sets forth several themes key to social work practice.

***Commitment to Enhancing Human Well-Being and Helping Meet Basic Human Needs of All People.*** Social work historically has given particular attention to the needs and empowerment of people who are vulnerable, oppressed, and living in poverty. The concept of this enduring dedication to basic human needs was included to remind social workers of the profession's fundamental preoccupation with people's most essential needs, such as food, clothing, health care, and shelter. (See Towle's seminal work, *Common Human Needs*, 1965, for a discussion of this concept.)

*Client Empowerment.* Especially during the era of charity organization societies in the late 19th and early 20th centuries, many social workers tended to behave paternalistically toward clients. Social workers of that time were inclined to focus on issues of moral rectitude and character in an effort to address people's problems. Over the years, however, as social workers have developed a richer understanding of the ways in which structural problems—such as a weak economy, racial discrimination, poverty, and deindustrialization—can create problems in people's lives, they have promoted client empowerment as a goal (Gutierrez, 1990). *Empowerment* is "the process of helping individuals, families, groups, and communities increase their personal, interpersonal, socioeconomic, and political strength and to develop influence toward improving their circumstances" (Barker, 1995, p. 120). As Black (1994) suggested,

> Social work has found the concept of empowerment useful for deepening the concerns of the generalist by specifying practice objectives that combine personal control, ability to affect the behavior of others, enhancement of personal and community strengths, increased equity in distribution of resources, ecological assessment, and the generation of power through the empowerment process. The helping relationship is based on collaboration and mutual respect and emphasizes building on existing strengths. (p. 397)

*Service to People Who Are Vulnerable and Oppressed.* Historically, social workers have been concerned about the well-being of people living in poverty and who are otherwise oppressed. Throughout the profession's history, however, there has been vigorous debate about the extent to which social work must, by definition, focus on the needs of people who are poor and oppressed. In recent years especially, the profession has seen an increase in the number of people interested in obtaining a social work degree to provide clinical mental health services primarily to those who are affluent or covered by third-party insurers (McMahon, 1992; Popple, 1992; Reamer, 1992a; Siporin, 1992).

The *NASW Code of Ethics* Revision Committee confronted this issue head on, and the committee's conclusion is reflected in the 1996 code. The mission statement stresses social work's "particular attention to the needs and empowerment of people who are vulnerable, oppressed, and living in poverty." This does not mean that social workers are concerned exclusively with poor and oppressed people. However, it does mean that at social work's core is a fundamental interest in and commitment to people who are poor and oppressed. The committee recognized that many legitimate and important forms of social work address the needs of middle- and upper-income people and those who are eligible for third-party coverage, including social work services provided in schools, hospitals and other health care facilities, mental health agencies, private practice settings, work sites, and the military. However, the committee also asserted that a primary commitment to people who are poor and oppressed is an essential ingredient of social work's mission and identity—an ingredient that serves to distinguish social work from other helping professions.

*Focus on Individual Well-Being in a Social Context.* Another defining feature of social work is the profession's earnest attempt to understand and address individuals' problems in a social context. Consistent with the widely embraced ecological perspective (Germain & Gitterman, 1980; Hartman, 1994), social workers pride themselves in their determination to examine people's problems in the context of their environments, including their families, communities, social networks, employment settings, ethnic and religious affiliations, and so forth. As Compton and Galaway (1994) asserted, the ecological perspective

> offers a conceptual framework that shifts attention from the cause-and-effect relationship between paired variables (does the environment cause the person to behave in a certain way, or does the person affect the environment in a certain way?) to the person and situation as an interrelated whole. The person is observed as a part of his or her total life situation; person and situation are a whole in which each part is related to all other parts in a complex way through a complex process in which each element is both cause and effect. These dynamic interactions, transactions, and organizational patterns, which are critical to the functioning of both the individual and the situation, are observable only when we study the whole system. Thus the whole is always more than the sum of its parts. In attempting to understand a problem in social functioning, you cannot achieve understanding by adding together, as separate entities, the assessment of the individual and the assessment of the environment. Rather you must strive for a full understanding of the complex interactions between client and all levels of social systems as well as the meaning the client assigns to these interactions. (p. 118)

***Promotion of Social Justice and Social Change.*** One of social work's hallmarks is its enduring and deep-seated commitment to *social justice* with and on behalf of clients, "an ideal condition in which all members of a society have the same basic rights, protection, opportunities, obligations, and social benefits" (Barker, 1995, p. 354). Throughout the profession's history, social workers have been actively involved in social efforts to address basic human needs and enhance people's access to important social services. Such social action has taken various forms, such as lobbying public officials, undertaking community organizing, changing organizations to be more responsive, and campaigning for political candidates (Weil & Gamble, 1995). Although social workers' social change efforts have ebbed and flowed over time (Gil, 1994, 1998) at both the national and local levels, at least in principle they have understood the importance of social justice and social action. This, too, is one of the features that distinguishes social work from other helping professions.

***Sensitivity to Cultural and Ethnic Diversity.*** Unlike the earlier NASW codes of ethics, the 1996 code emphasizes the need for social workers to understand the role of cultural and ethnic diversity in practice; it also exhorts social workers to strive to end all forms of discrimination, whether related to race, ethnicity, gender, or sexual orientation. Particularly since the 1970s, social workers have enhanced their understanding of the ways in which cultural and ethnic norms and history can affect clients' experiences, perceptions, and life circumstances. In addition, social workers have developed a sound understanding of the ways in which social work interventions and social policies must take into consideration cultural and ethnic diversity (Chau, 1991; Chestang, 1972; Green, 1982; Ho, 1987; Hooyman, 1994; Lister, 1987; Lum, 1986; Pinderhughes, 1994).

The preamble to the 1996 code also sets forth the core values in which social work's mission is rooted.

## Purpose of the Code

The second section of the code, "Purpose of the NASW Code of Ethics," provides an overview of its main functions and a brief guide for dealing with ethical issues or dilemmas in social work practice. This section alerts social workers to the code's various purposes.

*The Code identifies core values on which social work's mission is based.* The preamble identifies six core values: service, social justice, dignity and worth of the person, the importance of human relationships, integrity, and competence. The *NASW Code of Ethics* Revision Committee settled on these core values after a systematic review of literature on the subject. The committee's final list represented a distillation of the numerous lists of social work values proposed by various authors.

*The Code summarizes broad ethical principles that reflect the profession's core values and establishes a set of specific ethical standards that should be used to guide social work practice.* As discussed in more detail later, the code distinguishes between broad ethical principles based on social work's core values and more specific ethical standards designed to guide practice.

*The Code is designed to help social workers identify relevant considerations when professional obligations conflict or ethical uncertainties arise.* The code of ethics is one of many tools social workers can use to address ethical issues that emerge in practice. This section's guide for dealing with ethical issues emphasizes various resources social workers should consider when faced with difficult ethical decisions, such as ethical theory and decision making, social work practice theory and research, laws, regulations, agency policies, and other relevant codes of ethics. Social workers are encouraged to obtain ethics consultation when appropriate, whether from an agency-based or social work organization ethics committee, regulatory bodies (for example, a state licensing board), knowledgeable colleagues, supervisors, or legal counsel.

Ethical theory and decision making are now widely understood to be critically important components of practice. Some ethical issues faced by social workers are clear and straightforward. It is easy for practitioners to agree, for example, that clinical social workers should not have sexual contact with clients, social work administrators should not embezzle agency funds, and social work researchers should not fabricate program evaluation results.

Other issues, however, are ethically complex. They arise in situations in which social workers face conflicting professional duties, such that fulfilling one means violating another (Reamer, 1990, 1998b). Examples include social workers who struggle to decide whether to interfere with a client who is engaging in some form of self-destructive behavior; to withhold troubling information contained in a case record from a particularly vulnerable client; to disclose confidential information against a client's wishes to protect a third party from harm; to report to authorities that a professional colleague is impaired or has engaged in unethical behavior; to exaggerate a clinical diagnosis to help a vulnerable client qualify for service; to participate in a labor strike at a work site, which could have detrimental consequences for clients; or to violate a mandatory reporting law to maintain a therapeutic relationship with a client who has made meaningful progress. In such cases social workers often struggle to reconcile competing and conflicting professional obligations.

Particularly since the early 1970s, when the field of applied and professional ethics emerged, professionals in all fields including social work have developed a better understanding of the role of ethical theory and ethical decision making in circumstances in which practitioners face conflicting ethical duties. During this period social workers began to analyze systematically the ways practitioners make ethical decisions and resolve ethical dilemmas. Although there have been discussions of ethics and values since the profession's formal beginning in the late 19th century, the deliberate, systematic study of ethical dilemmas in the profession is more recent (Joseph, 1989; Keith-Lucas, 1977; Levy, 1972, 1973, 1976; Reamer, 1995a, 1995b).

In recent years, practitioners and scholars in many fields have become interested in examining the ways that principles of ethics and ethical theory—drawn largely from the discipline of moral philosophy and, at times, theology—can be applied to ethical dilemmas in the professions. Much of the inquiry has focused on two key questions: (1) What ethical duties do professionals have in relation to clients, colleagues, employers, the social work profession, and the broader society? and (2) What criteria or guidelines can professionals draw on when their ethical duties and responsibilities conflict? (Bayles, 1981; Callahan & Bok, 1980; Gambrill & Pruger, 1997; Reamer, 1980, 1982, 1983b, 1993a; Reamer & Abramson, 1982; Reid & Popple, 1992).

To approach the analysis of ethical dilemmas deliberately and systematically, social workers and other professionals sometimes draw on theories and principles of ethics. For centuries moral philosophers—sometimes known as "ethicists"—have been developing a wide range of theories and principles concerning issues of right and wrong, the nature of duty and obligation, and justice. Some of these theories focus on issues of metaethics, or debates about whether moral criteria or guidelines can be derived to determine what is ethically right or wrong or good or bad. Some ethicists, known as "cognitivists," believe that "objective" criteria or guidelines can be formulated to assess whether certain actions are or are not ethical; others—"noncognitivists"—assert that ethical judgments will never amount to anything other than subjective opinion or expressions of moral preference (Beauchamp, 1982; Frankena, 1973; Gewirth, 1978; Reamer 1989a, 1993a).

Other theories focus on issues of normative ethics, theories intended to guide real-life decisions in ethically complex situations. Not surprisingly, theories of normative ethics have been of particular interest to professionals who face difficult ethical questions. For example, the deontological view claims that certain actions are inherently right or wrong as a matter of principle. Deontologists might argue, for example, that, as a matter of moral obligation, social workers must always obey mandatory reporting laws related to child abuse, even if doing so would jeopardize a social worker's therapeutic relationship with a client—that is, the law is the law. Similarly, deontologists might argue that clients should always be told the truth, even if knowing the truth might be harmful.

In contrast, the so-called consequentialist, utilitarian, or teleological perspective focuses on the outcome of a course of action and promotes actions that produce the greatest good (Frankena, 1973; Gorovitz, 1971; Smart & Williams, 1973). That is, actions engaged in by professionals are not inherently right or wrong; rather, whether an action is ethical or not is determined by the goodness of its consequences. A proponent of this point of view might argue that although mandatory reporting laws generally should be followed, because of the good consequences such actions produce, social workers who have evidence to suggest that complying with the law in a particular case would produce harmful consequences (for example, undermining a productive therapeutic relationship) should not comply with the law. The ends can justify the means. Similarly, a proponent of a consequentialist, utilitarian, or teleological perspective might argue that although clients usually should be told the truth, a social worker who believes that telling a client the truth would cause more harm than good could, on ethical grounds, not tell the client the truth.

Ethicists and professionals continue to disagree about the merits and demerits of these different points of view. The debate has been healthy in that it has alerted professionals to competing perspectives that need to be considered when they are faced with an ethical dilemma, especially when professional duties conflict and choices must be made. To enhance the quality of their decision making, social workers need to critically examine the strengths and limitations of various schools of thought that can be brought to bear on the diverse challenges that professional practice produces. This is analogous to the need for clinical social workers to understand the strengths and limitations of the diverse conceptual models used to understand individuals' mental health problems and design interventions to assist them.

The code also highlights the role of ethics consultation. In many cases, practitioners should consult with others when they are faced with challenging ethical dilemmas. Social workers well understand the importance of consultation in other practice domains—for example, when they are unsure where to head clinically in a difficult case, how to handle a complicated administrative matter, or how best to promote a legislative proposal to address a critical issue. Two (or more) heads often are better than one, and this holds for those situations in which ethical dilemmas arise.

Ethics consultation can take various forms. First, social workers should always consider examining the professional literature on ethical issues. Scholarship on social work ethics, and on applied and professional ethics generally, has burgeoned in recent years, and practitioners should do their best to keep up with it. Some of the literature addresses broader, and at times more abstract, issues related to ethical theory and decision-making strategies. Much of it, however, concentrates more narrowly on specific ethical issues, such as the limits of confidentiality when third parties are at risk, informed consent, professional boundaries, and impairment.

Second, many agencies have developed their own ethics committees designed to help staff and clients think through the best way to handle an ethical dilemma. The concept of ethics committees (often called "institutional ethics committees" [IECs]) first emerged in 1976, when the New Jersey Supreme Court ruled that Karen Ann Quinlan's family and physicians should consult an ethics committee in deciding whether to remove her from life-support systems. (However, a number of hospitals have had something resembling ethics committees since at least the 1920s.) The New Jersey court based its ruling on an important article by Teel that appeared in the

*Baylor Law Review* in 1975, in which a pediatrician advocated the use of ethics committees in cases in which health care professionals face difficult ethical choices.

Ethics committees typically include representatives from various disciplines and positions, such as nursing, medicine, social work, the clergy, and agency administration. Ethics committees in large agencies often include a professional ethicist, typically someone with formal education in moral philosophy and professional ethics. This expert may be a trained philosopher or theologian or a member of one of the professions (for example, a nurse, physician, or social worker) who has supplemental education related to ethics. Sometimes ethics committees also include an agency's attorney. This is especially controversial because an attorney's obligation is to offer advice intended to protect his or her client (in this case, the agency); some critics believe that all members of an ethics committee should be in a position to think freely without constraint.

Most ethics committees devote the bulk of their time to case consultation (Cohen, 1988; Conrad, 1989; Cranford & Doudera, 1984; Reamer, 1987a). The committee is available to agency staff and perhaps to clients to think through how an ethical dilemma might be handled and to offer nonbinding advice. In health care settings, where ethics committees are particularly prominent, such case consultation might concern the eligibility of a patient for organ transplantation, a patient's right to refuse treatment, and end-of-life decisions. In other settings, such as a community mental health center or family services agency, case consultation might focus on questions concerning the disclosure of confidential information against a client's wishes, whether certain sensitive information should be shared with a particularly fragile client, and how to handle the discovery of some fraudulent activity within the agency. Although ethics committees are not always able to provide clear-cut advice about the complicated issues that come to their attention (nor should they be expected to), they can provide a valuable forum for thoughtful and critical exploration of complex ethical issues.

In addition to case consultation, many ethics committees serve other functions. These include drafting, reviewing, and revising agency policies that pertain to ethical issues, such as confidentiality guidelines or informed consent procedures, and sponsoring staff training on ethics-related matters. Training may include traditional didactic instruction and what has become known in many health care settings as "ethics grand rounds," which are educational sessions offered to staff on various ethics-related topics.

Third, on occasion social workers may want to draw on the expertise of individuals who serve as ethics consultants. These formally educated ethicists can provide useful advice on a case-by-case basis, as well as serve as an advocate or mediator should the need arise. As with ethics committees, ethics consultants are in a position to help practitioners think through difficult ethical choices, acquaint social workers with relevant conceptual tools and practical resources, and offer nonbinding advice (Fletcher, 1986; Fletcher, Quist, & Jonsen, 1989; La Puma & Schiedermayer, 1991; Reamer, 1995c; Skeel & Self, 1989).

Of course, consultation also can be obtained from knowledgeable and thoughtful colleagues and supervisors who do not have formal ethics education. In some instances social workers might find it useful to consult with members of their state licensing or regulatory board or members of their NASW chapter's Committee on Inquiry (the committee charged with reviewing and adjudicating ethics complaints filed against NASW members). Some NASW chapters also provide more formal ethics consultation services, such as an "ethics hotline."

Finally, social workers should keep in mind that many, although certainly not all, ethical issues broach legal questions that should be brought to the attention of an attorney. For example, social workers may want to seek legal advice when they need to decide whether to disclose confidential information to a third party against a client's wishes, comply with a subpoena that requests privileged information, terminate services to a client who has threatened to file a lawsuit against the social worker, or rely on a deceased client's relative for informed consent purposes in a matter pertaining to the former client.

One of the key features of this section of the code is its explicit acknowledgment that circumstances sometimes arise in social work in which the code's values, principles, and standards conflict. The code does not provide a formula for resolving such conflicts and does not specify which values, principles, and standards are most important and ought to outweigh others when they conflict. The 1996 code states,

> Reasonable differences of opinion can and do exist among social workers with respect to the ways in which values, ethical principles, and ethical standards should be rank ordered when they conflict. Ethical decision making in a given situation must apply the informed judgment of the individual social worker and should also consider how the issues would be judged in a peer review process where the ethical standards of the profession would be applied. . . . Social workers' decisions and actions should be consistent with the spirit as well as the letter of this *Code*. (p. 3)

**The** Code *provides ethical standards to which the general public can hold the social work profession accountable.* One of the defining characteristics of a profession is its members' willingness to provide a mechanism through which the general public can hold the profession accountable (Flexner, 1915; Greenwood, 1957). The NASW *Code of Ethics* sets forth specific ethical standards with which the public can expect social workers to comply and to which the public can hold social workers accountable. Members of the public, particularly clients, who believe that social workers have not complied with the code's standards can file an ethics complaint with NASW. The ethics complaint will be reviewed and, if accepted, adjudicated by a Committee on Inquiry (see NASW *Procedures for the Adjudication of Grievances*, 1994b).

The code is particularly relevant in lawsuits involving social workers. Parties that file legal complaints against social workers (former clients or family members, for example) sometimes allege that social workers departed from prevailing ethical standards in social work. A plaintiff in a lawsuit may claim, for example, that a social worker was negligent in failing to obtain informed consent properly before releasing confidential information to a third party, denied a client reasonable access to a case record, failed to protect a third party from harm caused by a client, was sexually involved with a client, or was involved in a harmful business relationship (a conflict of interest) with a client. In these instances, lawyers and judges typically draw on the NASW *Code of Ethics* to establish the standard of care in social work. The *standard of care*—a critically important legal concept in professional malpractice and negligence cases—is defined as how an ordinary, reasonable, and prudent professional would act under the same or similar circumstances (Austin, Moline, & Williams, 1990; Cohen & Mariano, 1982; Hogan, 1979; Meyer, Landis, & Hays, 1988; Reamer, 1994; Schutz, 1982). That is, because of the code's prominence and influence nationally—because it has been ratified by the nation's largest social work organization—the code often serves as the measurement rod of what is ethically appropriate and inappropriate in the profession.

There are various ways in which the general public might use the code as a way to hold social workers accountable. In addition to lawyers, courts of law, and professional liability insurance providers, many licensing and regulatory bodies, agency boards of directors, government agencies, and other professional associations adopt the code or portions of it, or they use the code as a frame of reference.

**The Code *socializes practitioners new to the field to social work's mission, values, ethical principles, and ethical standards.*** The code provides social work educators, including both classroom faculty and field instructors, with an efficient tool that can be used to acquaint students with the profession's mission, core values, broad ethical principles, and specific ethical standards. It is clearly the most visible and widely recognized statement of social work's aims, values, and ethical principles and standards.

**The Code *articulates standards that the social work profession itself can use to assess whether social workers have engaged in unethical conduct.*** The code provides NASW, particularly its committees on inquiry, with specific standards to determine whether social workers have engaged in unethical conduct. Committees on inquiry are required to use the code as their principal source when complaints are filed against members. As mentioned before, many social work licensing and regulatory boards also use the code or portions of it to adjudicate complaints filed against practitioners who fall under their jurisdiction.

## Ethical Principles

The code's third section, "Ethical Principles," presents six broad ethical principles that inform social work practice, one for each of the six core values cited in the preamble. To provide a conceptual base for the profession's ethical standards, the principles are presented at a fairly high level of abstraction. The code also provides brief annotation for each of the principles. It is important to note that the core values on which the ethical principles are based are not listed in rank order. According to the *Code*, "this *constellation* of core values reflects what is unique to the social work profession. Core values, and the principles that flow from them, must be balanced within the context and complexity of the human experience" (p. 1, emphasis added).

The first value, *service*, and the accompanying ethical principle emphasize social workers' commitment to helping people in need. The annotation promotes the concept of altruism, encouraging social workers to "elevate service to others above self-interest" (p. 5). Of special note, social workers are urged but not required to volunteer a portion of their professional skills with no expectation of significant financial return, that is, pro bono service (from the Latin, *pro bono publico*, meaning "for the public good or welfare").

The NASW *Code of Ethics* Revision Committee concluded that it would be inappropriate to require social workers to volunteer a portion of their professional skills because there are pressing professional and personal demands on many practitioners and their often modest salaries. However, the committee did believe that it was important to encourage social workers to provide some pro bono service.

The second value, *social justice*, and the accompanying ethical principle reiterate key points made in the code's mission statement. The annotation makes a special point of emphasizing social workers' obligation to pursue social change with, as well as on behalf of, vulnerable and oppressed individuals and groups of people. That is, social workers should not always act for others; when possible, social workers should engage clients and others as partners in efforts to promote social justice and challenge social injustice.

The third value, *dignity and worth of the person*, and the accompanying ethical principle emphasize the need for social workers to respect people and "treat each person in a caring and respectful fashion, mindful of individual differences and cultural and ethnic diversity" (p. 5). Key elements include promoting clients' "socially responsible self-determination" and enhancing "clients' capacity and opportunity to change and to address their own needs" (pp. 5–6). Thus, although social workers are sensitive to and seek to address structural and environmental determinants of individuals' and social problems, they also understand the important role of individual responsibility. The annotation also acknowledges social workers' dual responsibility to clients and to the broader society and the need for social workers "to resolve conflicts between clients' interests and the broader society's interests in a socially responsible manner" (p. 6).

The fourth value, *importance of human relationships*, and the accompanying ethical principle stress what social workers have long known, that "relationships between and among people are an important vehicle for change" and that social workers need to "engage people as partners in the helping process" (p. 6). This principle is consistent with and reinforces the discussion of empowerment in the code's mission statement.

The fifth value, *integrity*, and the accompanying ethical principle emphasize the role of trust in the helping relationship and the need for social workers to "act honestly and responsibly and promote ethical practices on the part of the organizations with which they are affiliated" (p. 6). That is, social workers are not only responsible for their own professional ethics and integrity; they also must seek to ensure that the agencies and organizations with which they are affiliated act ethically and responsibly.

The sixth value, *competence*, and the accompanying ethical principle assert that social workers should achieve reasonable levels of skill before offering their services to others. This principle exhorts social workers to practice only within their areas of expertise and continually seek to enhance their professional knowledge and skills. The principle also encourages social workers to contribute to the profession's knowledge base.

## Ethical Standards

The code's last section, "Ethical Standards," includes 155 specific ethical standards to guide social workers' conduct and provide a basis for adjudication of ethics complaints filed against NASW members. The standards fall into six categories concerning social workers' ethical responsibilities (1) to clients, (2) to colleagues, (3) in practice settings, (4) as professionals, (5) to the profession, and (6) to the broader society. The introduction to this section of the code states that some of the standards are enforceable guidelines for professional conduct and some are standards to which social workers should aspire. This is a very important distinction. Further, "the extent to which each standard is enforceable is a matter of professional judgment to be exercised by those responsible for reviewing alleged violations of ethical standards" (p. 7).

In general, the code's standards concern three kinds of issues (Reamer, 1994). The first includes what can be described as mistakes social workers might make that have ethical implications. Examples include leaving confidential information displayed on one's desk in such a way that it can be read by unauthorized people or forgetting to include important details in a client's informed consent document. The second category covers issues associated with difficult ethical decisions, for example, whether to disclose confidential information to protect a third party or whether to continue providing services to an indigent client whose insurance coverage has been exhausted. The final category is concerned with issues pertaining to social worker misconduct, such as exploitation of clients, boundary violations, or fraudulent billing for services rendered.

## ETHICAL RESPONSIBILITIES TO CLIENTS

The first section of the code's ethical standards is the most detailed. It addresses a wide range of issues involved in the delivery of services to individuals, families, couples, and small groups of clients. In particular, this section concerns social workers' commitment to clients, clients' right to self-determination, informed consent, professional competence, cultural competence and social diversity, conflicts of interest, privacy and confidentiality, client access to records, sexual relationships and physical contact with clients, sexual harassment, the use of derogatory language, payment for services, clients who lack decision-making capacity, interruption of services, and termination of services.

Unlike the 1960 and 1979 codes, the 1996 NASW Code of Ethics acknowledges that although social workers' primary responsibility is to clients, circumstances can arise when "social workers' responsibility to the larger society or specific legal obligations may on limited occasions supersede the loyalty owed clients" (standard 1.01). For example, this consideration would arise when a social worker is required by law to report that a client has abused a child or has threatened to harm himself or herself or others. Similarly, the code acknowledges that a client's right to self-determination, which social workers ordinarily respect, may be limited when that client's actions or potential actions pose a serious, foreseeable, and imminent risk to himself or herself or others.

Standards for informed consent were added to the 1996 code to specify the elements that should be included when social workers obtain consent from clients or potential clients for the delivery of services; the use of electronic media to provide services (such as computer, telephone, radio, television, and audio- or videotaping clients); third-party observation of clients who are receiving services; and release of information. These standards require the use of clear and understandable language to explain the purpose of services to be provided, risks related to the services, relevant costs, reasonable alternatives, clients' right to refuse or withdraw consent, and the time frame covered by the consent. Social workers also are instructed to inform clients of any limits to services because of the requirements of a third-party payer, such as an insurance or managed care company. This is a critically important provision in light of the growing influence of third-party payers in recent years.

A new section in the code pertains to the subject of cultural competence and social diversity. In recent years social workers have enhanced their understanding of the relevance of cultural and social diversity in their work with clients. Cultural and ethnic norms, for example, may shape clients' understanding of issues in their lives and affect their response to available social services. The code requires social workers to take reasonable steps to understand and be sensitive to clients' cultures and social diversity with respect to race, ethnicity, national origin, color, gender, sexual orientation, age, marital status, political beliefs, religion, or mental or physical disability.

The code's standards concerning conflicts of interest alert social workers to their obligation to avoid circumstances that might interfere with the exercise of professional discretion and impartial judgment. This includes avoiding any dual or multiple relationships with clients or former clients in which there is a risk of exploitation of or other potential harm to the client. Social workers also are urged to take special precautions when they provide services to two or more people who have a relationship with each other. Practitioners who anticipate having to perform in potentially conflicting roles are advised to clarify their obligations with the parties involved and take appropriate action to minimize any conflict of interest (for example, when a social worker is asked to testify in a child custody dispute or divorce proceedings involving clients).

The 1996 code substantially expanded the profession's standards on privacy and confidentiality. Noteworthy details concern social workers' obligation to disclose confidential information to protect third parties from serious harm; confidentiality guidelines for working with families, couples, or groups; disclosure of confidential information to third-party payers; discussion of confidential information in public and semipublic areas (such as hallways, waiting rooms, elevators, and restaurants); disclosure of confidential information during legal proceedings; protection of client confidentiality when responding to requests from the media; protection of the confidentiality of clients' written and electronic records, as well as the confidentiality of information transmitted by use of such devices as computers, electronic mail, fax machines, and telephones; use of case material in teaching or training; and protection of the confidentiality of deceased clients. Social workers are advised to discuss confidentiality policies and guidelines as soon as possible in the social worker–client relationship and then as needed throughout the course of the relationship.

The 1996 code also added considerable detail on social workers' sexual relationships with clients. In addition to prohibiting sexual relationships with current clients, which was addressed in the 1979 code, the current code also generally prohibits sexual contact with former clients. This is a particularly important development because there is intense concern among social workers about practitioners' possible exploitation of former clients. The code also prohibits sexual contact with clients' relatives or other individuals with whom clients maintain a close personal relationship when there is a risk of exploitation of or potential harm to the client. Further, social workers are advised not to provide clinical services to individuals with whom they have had a prior sexual relationship because of the likelihood that such a relationship would make it difficult for the social worker and client to maintain appropriate professional boundaries.

In addition to its greatly expanded detail on sexual relationships, the *NASW Code of Ethics* also comments on other physical contact between social workers and clients. The code acknowledges the possibility of appropriate physical contact (for example, physically comforting a distraught child who has been removed from his home because of parental neglect or holding the hand of a nursing home resident whose spouse has died), but social workers are cautioned not to engage in physical contact with clients, such as cradling or caressing, when there is the possibility that psychological harm to the client could result. Social workers also are admonished not to sexually harass clients.

The 1996 code added a specific provision concerning the use of barter (accepting goods or services from clients as payment for professional service). The code stops short of banning bartering outright, recognizing that in some communities it is a widely accepted form of payment. However, social workers are advised to avoid the use of barter because of the potential for conflict of interest, exploitation, and inappropriate boundaries in their relationships with clients. For example, if a client "pays" a social worker for counseling by performing some service, such as painting the social worker's house or repairing his or her car, and the service is somehow unsatisfactory, attempts to resolve the problem could interfere with the therapeutic relationship and seriously undermine the social worker's effective delivery of counseling services.

In addition to advising social workers to terminate properly with clients when services are no longer required or no longer meet the clients' needs or interests, the code permits social workers in fee-for-service settings to terminate services to clients who have not paid an overdue balance. However, services may be terminated in these circumstances only when the financial arrangements have been made clear to the client, the client does not pose an imminent danger to self or others, and the clinical and other consequences of the client's nonpayment have been discussed with the client.

The code advises social workers who are leaving an employment setting to inform clients of all available options for the continuation of services and their benefits and risks. This is an important standard because it permits a social worker to discuss the advantages and disadvantages associated with a client's decision to continue receiving services from that practitioner in her or his new setting, obtain services from another practitioner in the setting the social worker is leaving, or seek services from a practitioner at some other agency. In addition, the code prohibits social workers from terminating services to pursue a social, financial, or sexual relationship with a client.

# ETHICAL RESPONSIBILITIES TO COLLEAGUES

This section of the code addresses issues concerning social workers' relationships with professional colleagues. These include respect for colleagues; proper handling of shared confidential information; interdisciplinary collaboration and disputes; consultation; referral for services; sexual relationships and sexual harassment; and impaired, incompetent, and unethical colleagues.

The code encourages social workers who are members of an interdisciplinary team, such as in a health care or school setting, to draw explicitly on the perspectives, values, and experiences of the social work profession. If disagreements among team members cannot be resolved, social workers are advised to pursue other ways to address their concerns (for example, approaching agency administrators or board of directors). Social workers are also advised not to exploit disputes between a colleague and an employer to advance their own interests or to exploit clients in a dispute with a colleague.

The 1996 code includes a number of new standards on consultation and referral for services. Social workers are obligated to seek colleagues' advice and counsel whenever such consultation is in the client's best interest, disclosing the least amount of information necessary to achieve the purposes of the consultation. Social workers also are expected to keep informed of colleagues' areas of expertise and competence. In addition, they are expected to refer clients to other professionals when colleagues' specialized knowledge or expertise is needed to serve clients fully, or when they believe they are not being effective or making reasonable progress with clients.

This section of the code also addresses dual and multiple relationships, specifically with respect to prohibiting sexual activities or contact between social work supervisors or educators and those supervised, whether they are students, trainees, or other colleagues over whom they exercise professional authority. In addition, the code prohibits sexual harassment of supervisees, students, trainees, or colleagues.

The 1996 code strengthens ethical standards pertaining to impaired, incompetent, and unethical colleagues. Social workers who have direct knowledge of a colleague's impairment (which may be the result of personal problems, psychosocial distress, substance abuse, or mental health difficulties, and which interferes with practice effectiveness), incompetence, or unethical conduct are required to consult with that colleague when feasible and assist the colleague in taking remedial action. If these measures do not address the problem satisfactorily, social workers are required to take action through appropriate channels established by employers, agencies, NASW, licensing and regulatory bodies, and other professional organizations. Practitioners also are expected to defend and assist colleagues who are unjustly charged with unethical conduct.

# ETHICAL RESPONSIBILITIES IN PRACTICE SETTINGS

This section of the code addresses ethical issues that arise in social services agencies, human services organizations, private practice, and social work education programs. The standards pertain to social work supervision and consultation, education and training, performance evaluation, client records, billing for services, client transfer, agency administration, continuing education and staff development, commitments to employers, and labor–management disputes.

One major theme in this section of the code is that social workers who provide supervision, consultation, education, or training should do so only within their areas of knowledge and competence. Also, social workers who provide these services are to avoid engaging in any dual or multiple relationships in which there is a risk of exploitation or potential harm. Another standard requires social workers who are educators or field instructors to ensure that clients are routinely informed when services are being provided by students.

Several standards pertain to client records. They require that records include sufficient, accurate, and timely documentation to facilitate the delivery of services and ensure continuity of services provided to clients in the future. Documentation in records should protect clients' privacy to the greatest extent possible and appropriate and should include only information that is directly relevant to the delivery of services. In addition, the code requires social workers to store records properly to ensure reasonable future access and notes that records should be maintained for the number of years required by state statutes or relevant contracts.

Social workers who bill for services are obligated to establish and maintain practices that accurately reflect the nature and extent of services provided, and they must not falsify billing records or submit fraudulent invoices.

Social workers are urged to be particularly careful when an individual who is receiving services from another agency or colleague contacts them for services. They should carefully consider the client's needs before agreeing to provide services. To minimize possible confusion and conflict, social workers should discuss with such a potential client the nature of his or her current relationship with other services providers and the implications, including possible benefits or risks, of entering into a relationship with a new provider. If a new client has been served by another agency or colleague, social workers should discuss with the client whether consultation with the previous provider is in the client's best interest.

The 1996 code greatly expands coverage of ethical standards for agency administration. The code obligates social work administrators to advocate within and outside their agencies for adequate resources to meet clients' needs and provide appropriate staff supervision; they also must promote resource allocation procedures that are open and fair. In addition, administrators must ensure that the working environment for which they are responsible is consistent with and encourages compliance with the NASW Code of Ethics, and they should provide or arrange for continuing education and staff development for all staff for whom they are responsible.

The code also includes a number of ethical standards for social work employees. Although social work employees are generally expected to adhere to commitments made to their employers and employing organizations, they should not allow an employing organization's policies, procedures, regulations, or administrative orders to interfere with their ethical practice of social work. Thus, a social worker is obligated to take reasonable steps to ensure that his or her employing organization's practices are consistent with the NASW Code of Ethics. Also, social workers should accept employment or arrange students' field placements only in organizations with fair personnel practices. Practitioners should conserve agency funds where appropriate and must never misappropriate funds or use them for unintended purposes.

A new feature of the code is its acknowledgment of ethical issues that social workers sometimes face as the result of labor–management disputes. Although the code does not prescribe how social workers should handle such dilemmas, it does permit them to engage in organized action, including the formation of and participation in labor unions to improve services to clients and working conditions. The code states that "reasonable differences of opinion exist among social workers concerning their primary obligation as professionals during an actual or threatened labor strike or job action" (standard 3.10[b]).

## ETHICAL RESPONSIBILITIES AS PROFESSIONALS

This section of the code focuses on issues related to social workers' professional integrity. The standards pertain to social workers' competence, obligation to avoid any behavior that discriminates against others, private conduct, honesty, personal impairment, and solicitation of clients.

In addition to emphasizing social workers' obligation to be proficient, the code exhorts practitioners routinely to review and critique the professional literature, participate in continuing education, and base their work on recognized knowledge, including empirical knowledge, relevant to social work practice and ethics.

Several standards address social workers' values and personal behavior. The code states that social workers should not practice, condone, facilitate, or collaborate with any form of discrimination and should not permit their private conduct to interfere with their ability to fulfill their professional responsibilities. Thus, for example, it would be unethical for a social worker who has racist views to campaign for political office, publicize her or his social work credentials, and publicly espouse explicitly racist social policies—this would violate the code's standard on discrimination. In addition, this private conduct would likely interfere with the social worker's ability to fulfill his or her professional responsibilities, assuming that the racist views become well known among clients and colleagues and reflect on the social worker's professional life.

The code further obligates social workers to make clear distinctions between statements and actions engaged in as a private individual and as a social worker. For example, a social work administrator who volunteers to be a spokesperson for a candidate for political office should make it clear that he or she is involved in the political activities in his or her personal, not professional, capacity (unless the social worker's employer or board of directors has authorized him or her to endorse and support the candidate on the agency's behalf).

A prominent theme in the code concerns social workers' obligation to be honest in their relationships with all parties, including accurately representing their professional qualifications, credentials, education, competence, and affiliations. Social workers should not exaggerate or falsify their qualifications and credentials, and they should claim only those relevant professional credentials that they actually possess (for example, a social worker who has a doctorate in physics should not claim to have or create the impression that he or she has a doctoral degree relevant to clinical social work). Also, social workers are obligated to take responsibility and credit, including authorship credit, only for work they have actually performed and to which they have contributed. For example, they should not claim to have had a prominent role in a research project to which they contributed minimally. Also, social workers should honestly acknowledge the work of and the contributions made by others. It would be unethical for a social worker to draw on or benefit from a colleague's work without acknowledging the source or contribution.

The code also requires that social workers not engage in uninvited solicitation of potential clients who, because of their circumstances, are vulnerable to undue influence, manipulation, or coercion. Thus, social workers are not permitted to approach vulnerable people in distress (for example, victims of a natural disaster or serious accident) and actively solicit them to become clients. Further, social workers must not solicit testimonial endorsements (that is, for advertising or marketing purposes) from current clients or from other people who, because of their particular circumstances, are vulnerable to undue influence.

One of the most important standards in the code concerns social workers' personal impairment. Like all people, social workers sometimes encounter personal problems—this is a normal part of life. The code mandates, however, that social workers must not allow their personal problems, psychosocial distress, legal problems, substance abuse, or mental health difficulties to interfere with their professional judgment and performance or to jeopardize others for whom they have a professional responsibility. When social workers find that their personal difficulties interfere with their professional judgment and performance, they are obligated to seek professional help, make adjustments in their workload, terminate their practice, or take other steps necessary to protect clients and others.

## ETHICAL RESPONSIBILITIES TO THE SOCIAL WORK PROFESSION

Social workers' ethical responsibilities are not limited to clients, colleagues, and the public. They also include the social work profession itself. Standards in this section of the code focus on the profession's integrity and social work evaluation and research. The principal theme concerning the profession's integrity pertains to social workers' obligation to maintain and promote high standards of practice by engaging in appropriate study and research, teaching, publication, presentations at professional conferences, consultation, service to the community and professional organizations, and legislative testimony.

In recent years social workers have strengthened their appreciation of the role of evaluation and research. Relevant activities include needs assessments, program evaluations, clinical research and evaluations, and the use of empirical literature to guide practice. The 1996 code includes a substantially new series of standards concerning evaluation and research. These standards emphasize social workers' obligation to monitor and evaluate policies, the implementation of programs, and practice interventions. In addition, the code requires social workers to critically examine and keep current with emerging knowledge relevant to social work and use evaluation and research evidence in their professional practice.

The code also requires social workers involved in evaluation and research to follow widely accepted guidelines concerning the protection of evaluation and research participants. The standards concentrate on the role of informed consent procedures in evaluation and research, the need to ensure that evaluation and research participants have access to appropriate supportive services, the confidentiality and anonymity of information obtained during the course of evaluation and research, the obligation to report results accurately, and the handling of potential or real conflicts of interest and dual relationships involving evaluation and research participants.

## ETHICAL RESPONSIBILITIES TO THE BROADER SOCIETY

The social work profession has always been committed to social justice. This commitment is clearly reflected in the "Preamble" to the *NASW Code of Ethics* and in the final section of the code's standards. The standards explicitly emphasize social workers' obligation to engage in activities that promote social justice and the general welfare of society "from local to global levels" (standard 6.01). These activities may include facilitating public discussion of social policy issues; providing professional services in public emergencies; engaging in social and political action—such as lobbying and legislative activity—to address basic human needs; promoting conditions that encourage respect for the diversity of cultures and social diversity; and acting to prevent and eliminate domination, exploitation, and discrimination against any person, group, or class of people.

## CONCLUSION

Ethical standards in social work—particularly as reflected in the *NASW Code of Ethics*—have changed dramatically during the profession's history. During the late 19th and early 20th centuries, social work's ethical standards were sparse and generally vague.

Along with all other professions, and largely as a result of the emergence of the applied and professional ethics field that began in the 1970s, social work's ethical standards have matured considerably in recent years. The current *NASW Code of Ethics*, adopted in 1996, reflects social workers' increased understanding of ethical issues in the profession and the need for comprehensive ethical standards.

However, ethical standards in social work cannot guarantee ethical behavior. Such standards can guide practitioners who encounter ethical challenges and establish norms by which social workers' actions can be judged. In the final analysis, however, ethical standards in general, and a code of ethics in particular, are only one part of social workers' ethical arsenal. In addition to specific ethical standards, social workers need to draw on ethical theory and decision-making guidelines; social work theory and practice principles; and relevant laws, regulations, and agency policies. Most of all, social workers need to consider ethical standards within the context of their own personal values and ethics. As the *NASW Code of Ethics* states, ethical principles and standards "must be applied by individuals of good character who discern moral questions and, in good faith, seek to make reliable ethical judgments" (p. 4).

# CHAPTER

## 2

# ETHICAL RESPONSIBILITIES TO CLIENTS

The standards in this section of the code concern social workers' relationships with individual clients, couples, families, and small groups. They focus on the nature of social workers' commitment to clients, client self-determination, informed consent, social workers' competence to work with clients, cultural competence and social diversity, conflicts of interest, privacy and confidentiality, client access to records, sexual relationships between social workers and clients (current and former) and clients' relatives or other individuals with whom clients maintain a close personal relationship, physical contact with clients, sexual harassment of clients, social workers' use of derogatory language, client payment for services, serving clients who lack decision-making capacity, interruption of services, and termination of services.

## COMMITMENT TO CLIENTS

### STANDARD 1.01

*Social workers' primary responsibility is to promote the well-being of clients. In general, clients' interests are primary. However, social workers' responsibility to the larger society or specific legal obligations may on limited occasions supersede the loyalty owed clients, and clients should be so advised. (Examples include when a social worker is required by law to report that a client has abused a child or has threatened to harm self or others.)*

Social workers have long recognized that their primary responsibility is to their clients, and their clients' interests are primary. Most often, social workers' responsibility to their clients is clear and straightforward. As this standard suggests, however, instances can arise when social workers find themselves caught between their clients' and the broader society's interests. Here are several common examples:

- A social worker, a caseworker in a family services agency, was told by her client (who was in counseling because she was having difficulty managing her child's behavior) that the client had lost control the day before and injured her child's arm while "dragging her to her room." The client had made impressive progress in treatment after having been referred to the social worker by the county child welfare department, whose staff had received reports of possible child abuse in the home. The client pleaded with the social worker not to report the most recent incident to the child welfare authorities.

- A 17-year-old boy, a client in a residential program for adolescents with emotional and behavioral difficulties, told his social worker during a counseling session, "I'm tired of life's hassles and want to end it all. I know you might think I'm just asking for help, but I'm not. I've had it, and I want to say good-bye. Please don't do anything to stop me." After extensive exploration, the social worker concluded that the client was serious about wanting to commit suicide.

- A social worker in a community mental health center provided counseling to a 32-year-old man who was separated from his wife. According to the client, his wife had had an affair with another man. In a fit of rage, the client told the social worker that he was planning to "really do a number on my wife and her lover. They'll rue the day they decided to ruin my life like this." The client blurted out to the social worker that he had hired someone to physically harm both his wife and her lover. When the social worker pressed the client for details, the client joked and said, "You don't know whether I'm serious or not, do you?" Given the client's well-known penchant for domestic violence, the social worker believed that he could very well carry out the threat.

These examples illustrate how social workers might find themselves torn between their commitment to their clients and their obligation to protect clients from themselves (when there is a threat of injury to self or suicide) or to protect third parties from harm (when clients threaten others). The 1979 *NASW Code of Ethics* stated, "The social worker should make every effort to foster maximum self-determination on the part of clients" (principle II.G). The code did not acknowledge possible conflicts between clients' interests and social workers' responsibility to the larger society or obligation to comply with specific legal requirements. In contrast, the 1996 code recognizes that such conflicts can occur and that clients have the right to be informed about this possibility. This is a fact of professional life, and social workers must accept that circumstances may arise in which they will have to make choices—sometimes difficult choices—that compromise clients' immediate interests.

Social workers have developed considerable understanding of how such conflicts can occur and the ways to deal with them. For example, since the 1960s social workers throughout the United States have been required to disclose confidential information, sometimes against a client's wishes, to comply with mandatory reporting laws on child and elder abuse and neglect. Although many social workers were initially concerned about the possible impact of these reporting requirements, particularly with respect to the possibility that they would erode clients' trust in social workers, in general the profession has come to accept that professional responsibility entails reconciling occasional conflicts between their clients' and others' interests. Certainly such mandatory reporting requirements have the potential to alter clinical relationships between social workers and clients; nonetheless, social workers now recognize the public's compelling interest in this social policy and the need for social workers to balance their commitment to clients with their commitment to the larger society.

Generally speaking, situations involving possible conflict between the interests of clients and others fall into three groups. First, there are circumstances in which clients' interests clearly should prevail—for example, when a client informs his social worker that seven years earlier he committed a relatively minor crime. Although there might be some benefit to the public if the social worker were to disclose this information to law enforcement officials (so the client could be prosecuted), current ethical norms and public policy clearly suggest that, overall, such a disclosure would produce more harm than good, particularly with respect to the public's willingness to trust social workers. Social workers generally agree that in such cases they should not place the public's interests above clients' interests.

Second, there are circumstances in which clients' interests clearly are outweighed by the public's interests or by some legal requirement. An obvious example would involve a client who asks his social worker not to notify child welfare authorities that he has been sexually involved with his 11-year-old stepdaughter. In this case the social worker has an obligation to protect the vulnerable child. Third, sometimes it may not be clear whether the client's or the public's interests, or a legal requirement, should take precedence—for example, when a client informs a social worker that he or she recently committed a moderately serious offense or has been inconsistent in caring for an aged and incapacitated parent (that is, when it is not clear whether the client has been neglectful). In these situations, reasonable social workers may disagree about the nature of their ethical duties to the various parties involved.

These are among the most difficult ethical choices facing social workers. They illustrate why social workers need to be familiar with relevant ethics literature, the role of ethics consultation, and ethical decision-making strategies. Practitioners who encounter such ethical dilemmas would be well advised to check the literature for information about the arguments for and against various courses of action (for example, disclosing confidential information concerning clients' past criminal activity and complying with mandatory reporting laws); consult with colleagues who are knowledgeable about the ethical issues involved (social workers, members of allied professions and, when necessary and appropriate, lawyers); and acquaint themselves with ethical decision-making models to help them organize their thinking, thoroughly consider the key ethical issues (and relevant philosophical or conceptual perspectives), and reach a conclusion (Loewenberg & Dolgoff, 1996; Reamer, 1995a, 1995d).

As an example of this process, consider a social worker whose HIV-positive client has been unwilling to share this information with his sexual partner. The social worker used various clinical approaches in an attempt to bring the client to a point where he was willing to inform his partner about his medical condition. Unfortunately, the clinical strategy failed, and the social worker had to decide whether to disclose confidential information against the client's wishes and alert the client's partner to the potential risk (including the possibility that the partner was already infected).

The practitioner faced a complicated ethical dilemma. The social worker had to decide whether to respect the client's wish for confidentiality and privacy or disclose confidential information to protect a third party—a classic example of conflicting ethical duties. The social worker had exhausted all the clinical options to help the client reach a point where he was willing to share the information with his partner (which are often, but not always, effective ways to address such an issue), so the social worker needed to acquaint himself or herself with the relevant literature on confidentiality of information pertaining to HIV infection and the disclosure of confidential information to protect third parties (see, for example, Francis & Chin, 1987; Gray & Harding, 1988; Kain, 1988; Reamer, 1991a, 1991b). He or she also needed to consult with knowledgeable colleagues and supervisors and an ethics committee, if one was available. An attorney's advice would be especially useful with respect to relevant statutes and case law, particularly concerning the tension between confidentiality rights and professionals' obligation to protect third parties (and associated liability risks for the social worker).

In addition, it would be particularly helpful for a social worker in this situation to be familiar with various ethical theories that might help him or her sort out important conceptual points (for example, comparing and contrasting deontological and utilitarian arguments in this case could be especially useful). Of course, the social worker also should examine all of the relevant standards in the *NASW Code of Ethics* (for example, pertaining to client self-determination and confidentiality limits) and carefully document his or her various decision-making efforts in the case record. In the final analysis, a social worker facing this kind of difficult decision—where professionals in the field disagree about the most appropriate course of action or standard of care—needs to make the ethical decision as carefully and deliberately as possible, taking into consideration as much information as possible. This is the approach that is most likely to protect the social worker's client, third parties, and the social worker himself or herself.

## SELF-DETERMINATION

### STANDARD 1.02

*Social workers respect and promote the right of clients to self-determination and assist clients in their efforts to identify and clarify their goals. Social workers may limit clients' right to self-determination when, in the social workers' professional judgment, clients' actions or potential actions pose a serious, foreseeable, and imminent risk to themselves or others.*

This standard is related to the preceding standard concerned with social workers' commitment to clients. Standard 1.02 makes it clear that, in general, social workers should respect clients' right to self-determination. However, this standard acknowledges explicitly that there are potential limits to clients' right to self-determination, particularly when clients "pose a serious, foreseeable, and imminent risk to themselves or others." As with the standard on social workers' commitment to clients, this standard moves beyond the language of the 1979 code that concerned clients' right to self-determination.

This standard on client self-determination reflects social workers' increased understanding of two key concepts: professional paternalism and protection of third parties. *Professional paternalism* means that situations may arise in which social workers have an obligation to protect clients from themselves. In his classic statement on the subject, Dworkin (1971) defined *paternalism* as "interference with a person's liberty of action justified by reasons referring exclusively to the welfare, good, happiness, needs, interests, or values of the person being coerced" (p. 108).

The most extreme form of self-injurious behavior is, of course, client suicide, and social workers generally agree that professionals have a duty to interfere with clients' efforts to end their lives (although there is some debate among social workers about the ethics of euthanasia and physician-assisted suicide; see Foster, 1995). But there are other, more subtle forms of self-harming behavior that pose difficult ethical dilemmas for social workers. How assertive should social workers be with battered women or men who decide to resume a relationship with an abusive partner? Should social workers interfere with hospital patients who want to return home while they are still in very frail condition and acting against medical advice? To what extent should social workers provide clients with access to information about themselves that is likely to be harmful to the clients?

In these "gray areas," reasonable practitioners may disagree, and it is important for social workers to understand the concept of professional paternalism. The debate concerning the obligation to protect people from themselves is an ancient one, dating back at least to Aristotle's time (Reamer, 1983a). Contemporary debate about the nature and limits of paternalism is especially intense because of widespread concern with civil rights and civil liberties. Controversy about paternalistic treatment of mentally ill people, children, welfare recipients, senior citizens, and prisoners has stimulated much philosophical and judicial speculation about the limits of coercion. This debate demonstrates the tension between social workers who believe in clients' right to identify and pursue their own goals, take risks, and possibly make mistakes and those who believe that at least some degree of coercion or deception is justifiable if it is necessary to protect clients from harming themselves.

Paternalism is such a difficult problem for social workers because most practitioners are drawn to the profession by a sincere wish to help people who are experiencing difficult problems in their lives—for example, people who are clinically depressed, suicidal, living in unsanitary housing, involved in abusive relationships, or addicted to drugs or alcohol. That is, limits on professional paternalism may run counter to many practitioners' instincts to protect vulnerable people from engaging in self-destructive behavior.

Issues involving the protection of third parties are quite different. Here the justification for social workers' placing limits on clients' right to self-determination is based on social workers' explicit concern for other people whose well-being is threatened by a client's actions. Unlike cases involving professional paternalism, when social workers are primarily concerned about the client's well-being, circumstances calling for limits on clients' right to self-determination to protect third parties are those in which social workers must concede that protection and promotion of clients' interests is a secondary consideration.

The concept of interfering with clients' right to self-determination to protect third parties is usually associated with the often-cited case of *Tarasoff v. Board of Regents of the University of California* (1976). This case set the precedent for a number of critically important statutes and court decisions that now influence social workers' decisions when clients pose a threat to third parties.

In 1969 Prosenjit Poddar, an outpatient at Cowell Memorial Hospital at the University of California at Berkeley, informed his psychologist, Dr. Lawrence Moore, that he was planning to kill an unnamed young woman (easily identified as Tatiana Tarasoff) upon her return to the university from her summer vacation. After the counseling session during which Poddar announced his plan, Moore notified the university police and asked them to observe Poddar because he might need hospitalization as an individual who was dangerous to himself or others. The psychologist followed the telephone call with a letter requesting the help of the chief of the university police.

The campus police temporarily took Poddar into custody but released him because there was evidence that he was rational. They also warned him to stay away from Tarasoff. Poddar then moved in with Tarasoff's brother in an apartment near Tarasoff's home, where she lived with her parents. Shortly thereafter, Moore's supervisor and the chief of the department of psychiatry, Dr. Harvey Powelson, asked the university police to return the psychologist's letter about Poddar, ordered that the letter and the psychologist's case notes be destroyed, and directed that no further action be taken to hospitalize Poddar. No one warned Tarasoff or her family of Poddar's threat. Poddar never returned to counseling. Two months later, he murdered Tarasoff.

Tarasoff's parents sued the university board of regents, several employees of the student health service, and the chief of the campus police, along with four of his officers, because their daughter was never notified of Poddar's threat. A lower court in California dismissed the suit on the basis of sovereign immunity of the multiple defendants and the psychotherapist's need to preserve confidentiality. The parents appealed, and the California Supreme Court upheld the appeal and later reaffirmed the appellate court's decision that failure to protect the intended victim was irresponsible. The California Supreme Court ultimately held that,

> When a therapist determines, or pursuant to the standards of his profession should determine, that his patient presents a serious danger of violence to another, he incurs an obligation to use reasonable care to protect the intended victim against such danger. The discharge of this duty may require the therapist to take one or more of various steps, depending upon the nature of the case. Thus it may call for him to warn the intended victim or others likely to apprise the victim of the danger, to notify the police, or to take whatever other steps are reasonably necessary under the circumstances. . . . We recognize the public interest in supporting effective treatment of mental illness and in protecting the rights of patients to privacy, and the consequent public importance of safeguarding the confidential character of psychotherapeutic communication. Against this interest, however, we must weigh the public interest in safety from violent assault. . . . We conclude that the public policy favoring protection of the confidential character of patient–psychotherapist communications must yield to the extent to which disclosure is essential to avert danger to others. The protective privilege ends where the public peril begins. (551 P.2d 334 at 336–337)

Without question, *Tarasoff* changed the way mental health practitioners think about the limits of clients' right to self-determination and confidentiality rights. Since *Tarasoff*, a number of important duty-to-protect cases have influenced courts and legislatures in situations concerning mental health professionals' duty to protect third parties. Many court decisions reinforce the court's conclusions in *Tarasoff*, emphasizing practitioners' responsibility to take reasonable steps to protect third parties when, in the professionals' judgment, clients' actions or potential actions pose a serious, foreseeable, and imminent risk to others. Other cases, however, challenge, extend, or otherwise modify the conclusions reached in *Tarasoff*. I will examine these issues more fully in the discussion of confidentiality (see pages 59–62).

## INFORMED CONSENT

### STANDARD 1.03(a)

*Social workers should provide services to clients only in the context of a professional relationship based, when appropriate, on valid informed consent. Social workers should use clear and understandable language to inform clients of the purpose of the services, risks related to the services, limits to services because of the requirements of a third-party payer, relevant costs, reasonable alternatives, clients' right to refuse or withdraw consent, and the time frame covered by the consent. Social workers should provide clients with an opportunity to ask questions.*

Social workers have always recognized the importance of informed consent, whether it pertains to the release of information, provision of services, medication, or audio or video recording (Bernstein, 1960; Keith-Lucas, 1963; McDermott, 1975; Perlman, 1965; Reamer, 1987b). The new standard concerning informed consent reflects what professionals have learned in recent years about the nature of the consent process, particularly in light of various important court decisions involving parties who questioned the validity of consent obtained by professionals.

The first major legal ruling in the United States on informed consent is found in the 1914 landmark decision of *Schloendorff v. Society of New York Hospital*, in which New York Supreme Court Justice Benjamin Cardozo set forth his opinion concerning an individual's right to self-determination: "Every human being of adult years and sound mind has a right to determine what shall be done with his own body" (cited in Pernick, 1982, pp. 28–29). To do otherwise, Cardozo argued, is to commit an assault upon the person.

Another important decision was handed down in the 1957 case of *Salgo v. Leland Stanford Jr. University Board of Trustees*, in which the term "informed consent" was formally introduced. The plaintiff in this case, who became a paraplegic following a diagnostic procedure for a circulatory problem, claimed that his physician did not properly disclose ahead of time pertinent information concerning risks associated with the procedure.

Although the concept of informed consent has its origins in medicine and health care, over the years it has been applied legislatively, judicially, and administratively to a wide range of other client groups, such as people with mental illness and mental disability, children, senior citizens, people with physical disabilities, prisoners, hospital patients, and research subjects (Schutz, 1982).

States and local jurisdictions have different interpretations of informed consent standards, but there is considerable agreement about a number of key elements, and these are reflected in standard 1.03(a):

- Coercion and undue influence must not have played a role in the client's decision.
- Clients must be mentally capable of providing consent and able to understand the language and terms used during the consent process.
- Clients must consent to specific procedures or actions, not to broadly worded or blanket consent forms.
- The forms of consent must be valid (although some states require written authorization, most recognize both written and oral consent).
- Clients must have the right to refuse or withdraw consent.
- Clients' decisions must be based on adequate information: details of the nature and purpose of a service or disclosure of information; advantages and disadvantages of an intervention; substantial or probable risks to clients, if any; potential effects on clients' families, jobs, social activities, and other important aspects of their lives; alternatives to the proposed intervention or disclosure; and anticipated costs for clients and their relatives. All this information must be presented to clients in understandable language and in a manner that encourages them to ask questions. Consent forms also should be dated and include an expiration date. Social workers should be especially sensitive to clients' cultural and ethnic differences related to the meaning of such concepts as "self-determination" and "consent" (Cowles, 1976; Dickson, 1995; President's Commission, 1982; Reamer, 1987b, 1994; Rozovsky, 1984).

There are various circumstances in which social workers may not be required to obtain informed consent (Dickson, 1995; Rozovsky, 1984). The most important involve emergencies. In genuine emergencies, professionals may be authorized to act without the client's consent. According to many state statutes and case law, an emergency entails a client's being incapacitated and unable to exercise the mental ability to make an informed decision. Interference with decision-making ability might be the result of injury or illness, alcohol or drug use, or any other disability. In addition, a need for immediate treatment to preserve life or health must exist. Many statutes also authorize practitioners to treat clients without their consent to protect the client or the community from harm. Cases involving substance abusers, prisoners, and people with sexually transmitted diseases are examples (Appelbaum, Lidz, & Meisel, 1987; Dickson, 1995; President's Commission, 1982; Rozovsky, 1984).

A special feature of standard 1.03(a) is its reference to social workers' obligation to inform clients of any "limits to services because of the requirements of a third-party payer." This clause empowers social workers who are pressured by third-party payers (insurers) to withhold information from clients about the third-party payers' internal policies concerning covered services, reimbursement for services rendered, and so on. Consistent with social work's long-standing commitment to clients' right to know, this part of the standard enables social workers to resist any efforts on the part of third-party payers to withhold information from clients that concerns limits to services (sometimes referred to as "gag orders").

## STANDARD 1.03(b)

*In instances when clients are not literate or have difficulty understanding the primary language used in the practice setting, social workers should take steps to ensure clients' comprehension. This may include providing clients with a detailed verbal explanation or arranging for a qualified interpreter or translator whenever possible.*

Clearly, clients who are not literate or have difficulty understanding the primary language used in the practice setting would not be able to provide informed consent unless social workers take steps to ensure comprehension. In one case a hospital-based social worker and a doctor spoke with the parents of a two-year-old child who had died during an emergency medical procedure. The parents were Hmong (a Southeast Asian family who emigrated to the United States from Thailand) and had difficulty understanding English. Despite the parents' limited English, the social worker and doctor had the parents sign an informed consent form authorizing the hospital to perform an autopsy on the child. When the parents realized that an autopsy had been performed, they were distraught because the procedure violated their strongly held religious beliefs. The couple ultimately filed a lawsuit alleging that the social worker and doctor had failed in their responsibility to take reasonable steps to ensure that they understood the nature of the informed consent form they were asked to sign.

"Reasonable steps" is a broad term open to varying interpretation. Ordinarily, such steps include providing a detailed oral explanation to someone who is not literate or arranging for a qualified interpreter or translator when clients have difficulty understanding the primary language used in the practice setting. Social workers should be aware that some clients who are able to speak the primary language used in the practice setting reasonably well (expressive language skill) may not be equally capable of understanding the language (receptive language skill).

Social workers also should be aware of cultural and ethnic differences with respect to the concept of informed consent. For example, Hahn stated that "the individualism central in the doctrine of informed consent is absent in the tradition of Vietnamese thought. Self is not cultivated, but subjugated to cosmic orders. Information, direct communication, and decision may be regarded as arrogant" (cited in President's Commission, 1982, pp. 55–56). In contrast, Harwood (cited in President's Commission, 1982) noted that Puerto Rican Hispanics in the mainland United States expect to be engaged in the therapeutic process and want information provided to them without condescension. Social workers should take such cultural and ethnic differences into account when they obtain clients' informed consent; some clients may feel less comfortable with the process than others and thus require more patience and reassurance.

## STANDARD 1.03(c)

*In instances when clients lack the capacity to provide informed consent, social workers should protect clients' interests by seeking*

*permission from an appropriate third party, informing clients con-
sistent with the clients' level of understanding. In such instances
social workers should seek to ensure that the third party acts in a
manner consistent with clients' wishes and interests. Social workers should take reasonable steps to enhance such clients' ability to
give informed consent.*

This standard focuses primarily on clients with diminished capacity to give informed consent, as a result of, for example, mental disability, mental illness, substance abuse, or brain injury. In such cases, social workers should attempt to obtain informed consent from an individual who is authorized to act on the client's behalf. This may be a relative, guardian, or some other individual who has legal authority to provide consent.

Social workers must remember that although clients may lack the capacity to provide informed consent (because of a permanent disability or temporary incapacity), clients retain the right to receive information about the purposes of consent consistent with their level of understanding and comprehension. Consider, for example, a 32-year-old patient in a rehabilitation facility following a serious accident at the construction site where he worked. As a result of the accident, the patient suffered permanent brain damage that severely limited, but did not completely eliminate, his ability to process and retain new information.

During the course of the patient's stay at the rehabilitation center, a social worker received a request from his former employer for information related to the patient's mental impairment (in connection with the former employer's processing of the patient's disability claim). The social worker was required to obtain informed consent before forwarding this clinical information. Because of the patient's disability, she spoke with the patient's wife about providing consent. However, the social worker also sat down with the patient and, in the simplest language possible, explained to him that his former employer had requested information about how he was doing. That is, although the social worker obtained consent from "an appropriate third party," she also informed her client of the request for confidential information in a way that was consistent with the client's level of understanding.

Sometimes it is easy to determine whether a client is sufficiently competent to provide informed consent. Clearly, clients in the midst of a floridly psychotic episode, when there is strong evidence of delusions and hallucinations, would not be considered competent to provide informed consent. Other cases are less clear, however. In general, social workers should not presume that certain client groups—such as children, and mentally ill, elderly, or mentally disabled men and women—are necessarily incompetent (except those who are unconscious). Rather, clients in some categories, such as severely mentally disabled adults or children manifesting psychotic symptoms, should be considered to have a greater probability of incapacity (Reamer, 1994). As Rozovsky (1984) stated, it is important that professionals not assume "that a person who has consumed a moderate amount of alcohol or drugs or who has a history of psychiatric problems is automatically incapable of giving consent: the facts and circumstances of individual cases are essential to such determinations" (p. 89). Rozovsky also noted that clinicians should keep in mind that clients' capacity to provide informed consent may fluctuate over time; individuals who are incompetent at one point may be capable of giving (or withdrawing) consent during a subsequent lucid phase.

Assessments of a client's capacity should include such measures as a mental status examination (evaluation of a person's orientation to person, place, time, situation, mood and affect, content of thought and perception), the ability to comprehend abstract ideas and make reasoned judgments, any history of mental illness that might affect current judgment, and the client's recent and remote memory. When clients are deemed incompetent, social workers should be guided by what is known as the principle of "substituted judgment" or "proxy judgment," according to which an appropriate third party, or surrogate, attempts to replicate the decision that the incompetent client would make if able to make a sound decision (President's Commission, 1982). (For an extensive discussion of these concepts, see Buchanan & Brock, 1989.) According to standard 1.03(c), social workers must seek to ensure that "the third party acts in a manner consistent with clients' wishes and interests." Thus, social workers should be alert to possible conflict of interest when a third party relied on for substituted or proxy judgment places his or her own self-interest above the client's interests.

A social worker who believes that the relative or acquaintance of an incompetent client, who has the authority to consent on the client's behalf, is acting in a manner that is undermining the client's interests, would be obligated to take steps to ensure that this issue is addressed (perhaps by bringing this concern to the attention of the client's attorney). For example, a social worker employed in a nursing home provided casework services to an 82-year-old man who was not able to provide his own informed consent. The client developed several life-threatening health problems, and the medical staff needed to decide how aggressively they should treat his condition. The client's wife, who had the authority to provide consent on his behalf, told the social worker and medical staff that she did not want her husband treated aggressively. The social worker, however, had doubts about the wife's motives. The social worker knew from her conversations with the client that the marriage had been strained for years. In the social worker's judgment, the client's wife might have been eager for her husband to die so that she would be eligible to receive his sizable insurance benefits. The nursing home administrator and the social worker consulted with the nursing home's lawyer about how to handle the possible conflict of interest.

Finally, social workers who need to obtain informed consent from a third party for an incapacitated client also are obligated to enhance the client's ability to provide informed consent. Sometimes, little can be done to improve clients' capacity to provide informed consent—for example, when clients are profoundly mentally disabled or have permanent and extensive brain damage. In other cases, however, social workers may be in a position to enhance clients' ability to give informed consent—for example, when clients are hospitalized as a result of an acute episode of clinical depression or drug overdose. With appropriate services, these clients might very well regain their ability to provide informed consent without the formal involvement of a third party acting on their behalf.

*In instances when clients are receiving services involuntarily, social workers should provide information about the nature and extent of services and about the extent of clients' right to refuse service.*

There are a number of circumstances in which social workers' clients receive services involuntarily. Most notable are clients who are hospitalized involuntarily in a psychiatric facility or who are incarcerated.

There has been extensive debate among professionals, as well as litigation, about involuntary clients' right to refuse service. For example, with respect to life-saving treatment, the recent general trend is that a competent adult has the right to refuse services and treatment, particularly when the client has no dependents and his or her friends or family agree with the decision to refuse treatment; the treatment is highly intrusive or exceptionally painful; the treatment is risky, experimental, or has a small chance of success; the quality of the patient's life will be seriously affected by the treatment or by the medical condition even with the treatment; the treatment will only postpone imminent death; or the client has deeply held religious beliefs opposing the treatment. However, treatment may be mandated against the client's wishes if the client has minor children or other dependents; the treatment would be a relatively minor intrusion or involve a relatively minor invasion of bodily integrity; the proposed treatment is a generally accepted type of treatment; the quality of the client's life would not be adversely affected by the treatment or if the client would not live a limited or painful life following treatment; or the treatment would not merely prolong the client's life for a short time but would actually save the client's life (Saltzman & Proch, 1990).

Courts also may deny a client the right to refuse treatment when the client is a danger to himself or herself or others. In *Rennie v. Klein* (1978), for example, a U.S. District Court ruled that involuntary psychiatric patients may have the right to refuse medication or other forms of treatment in the absence of an emergency, consistent with the constitutional right to privacy. To overrule the patient's refusal four factors should be considered by an objective independent party: (1) the patient's capacity to decide on his or her particular treatment, (2) the patient's physical threat to other patients and staff, (3) whether any less-restrictive treatment exists, and (4) the risk of permanent side effects from the proposed treatment.

When clients receive treatment or services involuntarily for whatever reason, social workers should provide them with as much information as possible about the nature of the treatment or services they will receive and the extent of their right to refuse treatment or service. Consistent with the obligation to respect clients' right to socially responsible self-determination (standard 1.02), social workers should assist clients who wish to assert their right to refuse treatment or services, keeping in mind the simultaneous obligation to protect both clients and third parties from harm. Social workers may need to seek legal advice about any given client's legal right to refuse treatment or services.

*Social workers who provide services via electronic media (such as computer, telephone, radio, and television) should inform recipients of the limitations and risks associated with such services.*

Social workers are now in a position to use various forms of electronic media in their work with clients. Some of these media, such as telephone, radio, and television, have been used in social work for many years. For example, in addition to the many familiar uses of the telephone, some social workers also use radio and television for professional purposes. They are hosts of or guests on radio call-in shows, where listeners call for on-the-air advice about personal or family problems. Similarly, social workers are hosts of or guests on television programs that address mental health issues; these broadcasts also sometimes provide an opportunity for viewers to telephone in for on-the-air advice concerning issues in their lives. Some social workers also use video conferencing to provide services to clients who live far from where the social workers practice.

Social workers also have taken advantage of advances in computer technology to provide professional services, including information and referral services via the Internet. Because of continuing rapid developments in the computer industry, it is likely that social workers' use of computer technology to provide professional services will increase.

Practitioners who provide professional services by use of electronic media must be aware of and routinely inform recipients (who may or may not be formal clients) about the limitations and risks associated with such services. First, recipients should know that the information and advice they receive via electronic media may be superficial. For example, a social worker who hosted a radio call-in show received a call from a man who reported experiencing major anxiety symptoms (heart palpitations, excessive sweating, dizziness, shortness of breath). The social worker talked with the caller on the air about the nature of anxiety disorders and panic attacks. She also described several common therapeutic techniques used to reduce anxiety (for example, systematic desensitization, cognitive therapy). At no time during the conversation, however, did the social worker alert the caller to possible alternative diagnoses (known formally as differential diagnosis), such as substance-induced anxiety disorder or other anxiety and psychotic disorders that have panic attacks as an associated feature. She also did not encourage the caller to seek a local qualified professional for a thorough assessment. As a result, the social worker exposed herself to ethical and legal risk.

A second risk, particularly in relation to the use of computer-linked services, is breach of privacy. Recipients of services provided by social workers on the Internet, for example, should be informed that, given the current state of computer technology, it is possible that computer-based communications will be seen by others who know how to intercept messages or "eavesdrop" electronically. In one case, a social worker who communicated with a client via electronic mail (e-mail) did not realize that he had accidentally selected an option in his software that resulted in sending his message to the client, which contained identifying information, to a list of people in his computer-based address book. Consequently, many people who should not have been privy to the communication had access to it, exposing the social worker to the possibility of an ethics complaint or lawsuit.

*Social workers should obtain clients' informed consent before au-
diotaping or videotaping clients or permitting observation of services to clients by a third party.*

Social workers audiotape or videotape clients, or services provided to them,
in various circumstances. First, they may audiotape or videotape clients for
purposes of supervision. That is, their supervisors, colleagues, or members of
a peer supervision group may listen to or view tapes of work with clients to
provide informed feedback. Second, social workers may audiotape or videotape clients for teaching purposes—for example, to use in a class at a school
of social work or at a professional conference or workshop. Third, clients
may be taped for research purposes. Social workers who conduct in-depth
research interviews, for example, may prefer to audiotape the dialogue for
later transcription to avoid taking copious notes during the interview and
distract the respondent. Fourth, social workers may audiotape or videotape
for clinical purposes. For example, sometimes social workers may want
clients to view videotapes of themselves to obtain feedback on their communication style, behavior, or nonverbal mannerisms. Finally, social workers may audiotape or videotape clients for marketing purposes, that is, to
include in an advertisement, public service announcement, or broadcast
used to publicize a particular agency, program, or service.

In addition to audiotaping and videotaping, on occasion social workers
may want to permit third parties to observe clients, either in person or
through a one-way mirror. Practitioners who administer a residential mental health program, for example, may want to invite local public officials,
media representatives, or financial contributors to tour the facility and see
it "in action."

In all these cases, social workers must be aware of potential violations of
clients' privacy. Some clients may feel strongly about their privacy, and social workers have an obligation to protect it as much as possible. Thus, social workers should always obtain clients' informed consent before taping or
permitting observation of services to clients by a third party. Consistent
with standard 1.03(a), social workers should use clear and understandable
language to inform clients of the purpose of the taping or observation, any
associated risks (for example, who exactly will view the tapes or participate
in the observation), reasonable alternatives (if any), clients' right to refuse
or withdraw consent, and the time frame covered by the consent. Social
workers also should provide clients with an opportunity to ask relevant
questions. In addition, special provisions should be made for clients who
are not literate or who have difficulty understanding the primary language
used in the practice setting (standard 1.03[b]) or who lack the capacity to
provide informed consent (standard 1.03[c]).

# COMPETENCE

*STANDARD 1.04(a)*

*Social workers should provide services and represent themselves as
competent only within the boundaries of their education, training,*

*license, certification, consultation received, supervised experience, or other relevant professional experience.*

Social work is a remarkably diverse profession. It includes clinicians and caseworkers, community organizers, supervisors, administrators, advocates and community activists, policy makers, educators, program evaluators, and researchers. What practitioners have in common is formal social work education and at least one social work degree (undergraduate, graduate, or both).

Social workers must be forthright and clear in their claims about their areas of competence and expertise to colleagues, potential employers, and the public at large. They must not misrepresent their competence for self-serving purposes—for example, to obtain employment or attract clients. There are many examples. A social worker who has been out of graduate school for just one year and has not yet been licensed as an independent clinical social worker should not promote himself or herself as a clinician with years of post-master's-degree experience. Practitioners who have considerable education and expertise related to substance abuse treatment should not claim expertise they do not have in other clinical areas, such as treatment of eating disorders, just as a social worker who has not received formal training in hypnosis techniques should not provide this service to clients. Similarly, a social worker who has never conducted an ambitious program evaluation and has not received extensive training in that area should not claim such expertise in a grant proposal submitted to a foundation to obtain funds.

## STANDARD 1.04(b)

*Social workers should provide services in substantive areas or use intervention techniques or approaches that are new to them only after engaging in appropriate study, training, consultation, and supervision from people who are competent in those interventions or techniques.*

New and interesting innovations that may be relevant to practitioners' work are constantly emerging. Social workers should be aware of and seek education and training about new developments in the field that may be appropriate to incorporate into work with clients. For example, clinical social workers should continually update their knowledge of intervention techniques related to their areas of expertise. Administrators should be aware of new management techniques. Program evaluators should be familiar with new approaches to documenting the outcome and effectiveness of services.

According to standard 1.04(b), social workers who provide substantive services or use intervention techniques should do so only after appropriate study, training, consultation, and supervision. Sometimes independent education may suffice—for example, when a social worker who has considerable experience working with cancer survivors reviews the literature about new clinical social work approaches in oncology treatment, or when an experienced program evaluator learns from a journal article about a new tool to measure client progress.

In other cases, however, social workers may need to obtain formal training, continuing education, consultation, or supervision to begin work in a new substantive area or use a new intervention technique. For example, a clinical social worker who wants to concentrate on "recovered memories" in work with traumatized clients should obtain proper training, consultation, and supervision before doing so. This may involve attending workshops and conferences on the subject and joining a peer consultation or supervision group to learn about the proper use of this approach and to address any clinical risks.

Social workers who obtain training, consultation, or supervision need to ensure that the trainers, consultants, and supervisors themselves are competent. There should be reasonable assurance that they have the requisite substantive expertise the social workers are seeking (specific knowledge about the subject) and the ability to provide effective training, consultation, and supervision. Sometimes, colleagues who are very well informed about a subject are not particularly skilled at teaching others or providing useful consultation or supervision. Social workers should be selective, just as clients should be when they seek out social work services.

For example, a social worker in private practice was interested in the use of hypnosis in work with clients diagnosed with eating disorders. The social worker read several books and journal articles about hypnosis and then began using the technique with selected clients, but he did not attend any workshops, institutes, or continuing education seminars. One of the social worker's clients filed an ethics complaint and lawsuit against the social worker, alleging that the social worker had emotionally abused and traumatized the client during hypnosis sessions. The social worker was vulnerable because he could not demonstrate that he had engaged in proper study before using hypnosis with clients.

### STANDARD 1.04(c)

*When generally recognized standards do not exist with respect to an emerging area of practice, social workers should exercise careful judgment and take responsible steps (including appropriate education, research, training, consultation, and supervision) to ensure the competence of their work and to protect clients from harm.*

Social workers who want to use intervention approaches or techniques that are new to them are the primary focus of standard 1.04(b). In other cases, however, social workers may want to use an intervention approach or technique that is new to the profession. For example, some family therapy conferences have featured presentations on the use of so-called "reparenting therapy" as a treatment for adult survivors of childhood sexual abuse. According to the philosophy behind this treatment approach, clients who were traumatized as children were often neglected by their parents, deprived of appropriate and much-needed nurturing and caretaking. Thus, an important goal of therapy with such clients would be to provide them an opportunity in adulthood to experience being cared for by competent "parents"—that is, a therapist who functions as a surrogate parent. As part of the therapeutic relationship, the counselor may prepare meals or purchase food and clothing for the client, arrange for the client's medical care when the need arises, or take the client out for recreation and entertainment (such as going to a movie or a ballgame). Such activities are intended to help the client experience what it is like to be cared for by a loving parent.

There are no generally recognized standards for this treatment approach. Such an approach would generate controversy among social workers because potential boundary issues might arise (see standard 1.06[c]). Although some social workers may endorse use of reparenting therapy techniques, many others would be reluctant to use them.

Because it remains controversial, social workers who contemplate using this approach would be wise to exercise extraordinarily careful judgment and take responsible steps to protect clients from harm. Before using any techniques that are new to the field, practitioners should spend considerable time reading the relevant literature, consulting with colleagues, attending workshops or continuing education seminars, and obtaining appropriate supervision. In particular, social workers should attempt to locate empirical literature documenting the effectiveness of such an approach (see standards 4.01[c] and 5.02[c]).

Some emerging areas of practice do not raise particularly complicated ethical issues. For example, a social worker interested in the use of a new cognitive therapy technique to address self-esteem issues may not face complex ethical issues. In this kind of situation it may suffice for the social worker to read the relevant literature, consult with colleagues, attend workshops or seminars, and obtain appropriate supervision. In other cases, as in the use of reparenting therapy, social workers need to add another step: exploring in considerable depth the ethical issues connected to the intervention approach. In the case of reparenting therapy, the social worker would need to take a hard look at potential problems pertaining to boundary issues that could emerge and harm the client.

## CULTURAL COMPETENCE AND SOCIAL DIVERSITY

### STANDARD 1.05(a)

*Social workers should understand culture and its function in human behavior and society, recognizing the strengths that exist in all cultures.*

Especially since the 1970s, social workers' understanding of the relevance of cultural competence and social diversity has matured. They have developed an appreciation of the various ways in which clients' cultures, including their ethnic and cultural backgrounds and sexual orientation, affect practice. First, culture and ethnicity may influence how individuals cope with life's problems and interact with each other (Jacobs & Bowles, 1988; Logan, Freeman, & McRoy, 1990). Phenomena such as mental illness, the use of mood-altering substances, and death have different connotations in different cultural and ethnic groups. What is behaviorally appropriate in one culture (talking to deceased relatives, for example) may seem abnormal in another. Accepted practice in one culture (such as shaking hands upon meeting a member of the opposite sex) may be prohibited in another. Active participation in an informed consent procedure in a social services agency may be expected in one culture and considered odd in another. Clearly, to fully understand and appreciate these differences, social workers must be familiar with varying cultural traditions and norms.

Second, clients' cultural backgrounds may affect their interest in seeking professional services in the first place (Lum, 1992). Some cultural groups may have a preference for informal problem solving that takes place within the local ethnic community. For historical or other reasons, some cultural groups may not trust professionals who offer services in the context of formal agencies. Understanding the dynamics of this preference may be helpful to social work administrators and program directors who want to enhance their delivery of services to specific cultural groups.

In addition, the ways in which social services are planned and implemented may affect their effectiveness within particular cultural groups (Boyd-Franklin, 1989; Devore & Schlesinger, 1987). Self-disclosure in the context of a treatment group, placement of a family member in a nursing home, or use of psychotropic medication may be unacceptable or even abhorrent to members of some cultural groups. Social workers must take this variation into account as they plan and deliver services.

It is especially important for social workers to understand how some widely accepted theories of human behavior have fostered destructive stereotypes or have been based on limited samples of people that do not include important cultural and ethnic groups or minorities. Psychodynamic theories (Sigmund Freud), ego psychology theories (Anna Freud, Hartmann, White, Mahler, Erikson), learning theory (Skinner, Bandura), cognitive theory (Piaget), interpersonal theory (Adler, Sullivan), and humanistic theory (Maslow) have been critiqued because of their lack of attention to issues of cultural and ethnic diversity (Beckett & Johnson, 1995).

An important element of this ethical standard concerns social workers' obligation to recognize the strengths that exist in all cultures. Practitioners need a solid understanding of various cultural groups' positive and functional coping patterns, traditions, and customs. Social workers must understand that cultural practices that are different from those of the majority culture are not, by definition, counterproductive or dysfunctional. Rather, differences among cultural groups should be celebrated and accounted for in social work practice (Freeman, 1990; Leashore, 1995; Weick, Rapp, Sullivan, & Kristhardt, 1989). As Devore and Schlesinger (1991) stated,

> As various groups send their children to school, become ill, encounter marital difficulties, and generally live their lives, they bring with them a unique ethnic and class tradition. . . . As they confront "helpers" or "caretakers" they expect . . . that these aspects of their being . . . will be understood [whether or not they are aware that] some of their strengths and tensions are related to this aspect of their lives.
>
> Those charged with the responsibility of . . . helping have the obligation to be sensitive to that possibility. (cited in Devore & Schlesinger, 1995, p. 903)

## STANDARD 1.05(b)

*Social workers should have a knowledge base of their clients' cultures and be able to demonstrate competence in the provision of services that are sensitive to clients' cultures and to differences among people and cultural groups.*

In recent years a number of social work professionals have outlined content related to cultural and social diversity that is essential knowledge for their colleagues. Pinderhughes (1994), for example, recommended that social workers be informed about clients' culture as a factor in problem formation, problem resolution, and the helping process itself, which includes assessment, relationship development, intervention, and evaluation of outcome:

> The specific perspectives, capacities, competencies, and abilities that facilitate such effectiveness, and which are mandatory for cultural competence, include:
>
> 1. knowledge of the specific values, beliefs, and cultural practices of clients;
> 2. the ability to respect and appreciate the values, beliefs, and practices of all clients, including those culturally different, and to perceive such individuals through their own cultural lenses instead of the practitioner's;
> 3. the ability to be comfortable with difference in others and thus not be trapped in anxiety about difference or defensive behavior to ward it off;
> 4. the ability to control, and even change, false beliefs, assumptions, and stereotypes, which means one will have less need for defensive behavior to protect oneself;
> 5. the ability to think flexibly and to recognize that one's own way of thinking and behaving is not the only way; and
> 6. the ability to behave flexibly. This is demonstrated by the readiness to engage in the extra steps required to sort through general knowledge about a cultural group and to see the specific ways in which knowledge applies or does not apply to a given client. These steps take extra time, effort, and energy. (p. 266)

Schlesinger and Devore (1995) have offered a compelling outline of essential knowledge pertaining particularly to ethnicity, which includes knowledge about relevant values (both social workers' and clients'); theories of human behavior that concern cultural and ethnic groups; relevant social welfare policies and services; self-awareness (thinking through and feeling the impact of one's ethnicity on one's perception of self and others); and the impact of the "ethnic reality" on individuals' willingness to seek and receive social services, and the ways in which services are designed and delivered.

This kind of knowledge can be helpful to social workers in various settings and circumstances. For example, social workers in health care settings (hospitals, home health care agencies, nursing homes) need to be familiar with differences among cultural and ethnic groups with respect to blood transfusions, autopsies, and what is assumed to happen to a person following death (such as concepts of the afterlife) and how these differences may affect clients' preferences and choices. Social workers in family services agencies and community mental health centers may need to be familiar with various cultural groups' religious beliefs and observance of religious holidays, particularly as they affect scheduling of programs and services. Practitioners in programs that serve abused and battered women need to be aware of varying cultural norms concerning the role of women in society and in marriage and other intimate relationships. Social workers in treatment programs for children and adolescents may need to be knowledgeable about the perception and treatment of gay men, lesbians, and bisexual men and women by members of different cultural and ethnic groups.

It is not sufficient, of course, for social workers to be knowledgeable about clients' cultures. They also need to be able to demonstrate competence in the provision of services that are sensitive to clients' cultures and to differences among people and cultural groups. In addition to professional experience, such competence can be achieved through formal social work education (both classroom and field education), in-service training in social services agencies, professional workshops and conferences, consultation, and supervision. As Schlesinger and Devore (1995) asserted, culturally sensitive practice "is manifested at the level of daily practice behavior. It represents the capacity to draw on assumptions and facts about diverse ethnic groups in problem solving. Social workers should demonstrate the capacity to move with each client at a pace and in a direction determined by the client's perception of the problem" (p. 906).

## STANDARD 1.05(c)

*Social workers should obtain education about and seek to understand the nature of social diversity and oppression with respect to race, ethnicity, national origin, color, sex, sexual orientation, age, marital status, political belief, religion, and mental or physical disability.*

Social workers' efforts to understand and be knowledgeable about culture and ethnicity should focus especially on the concept of social diversity in all its forms and the role of oppression in the lives of members of culturally diverse groups. This need has been recognized by the Council on Social Work Education (CSWE), particularly with respect to populations at risk. In its *Curriculum Policy Statements*, CSWE (1994) asserted that social work education programs must "provide content about people of color, women, and gay and lesbian persons. Such content must emphasize the impact of discrimination, economic deprivation, and oppression upon these groups."

The concept of oppression is particularly important in social work, especially because of its relevance to the experience of members of ethnic groups, people of color, and members of other socially nondominant groups. According to Gil (1994),

> Oppression refers to relations of domination and exploitation—economic, social, and psychologic—between individuals; between social groups and classes within and beyond societies; and, globally, between entire societies. . . . Oppression seems motivated by an intent to exploit (i.e., benefit disproportionately from the resources, capacities, and productivity of others), and it results typically in disadvantageous, unjust conditions of living for its victims. It serves as *means* to enforce exploitation toward the *goal* of securing advantageous conditions of living for its perpetrators. (p. 233)

As standard 1.05(c) suggests, ideally, social workers obtain education themselves about various forms of diversity, including those related to race, ethnicity, national origin, color, gender, sexual orientation, age, marital status, political belief, religion, and mental or physical disability. This is an impressive amount of knowledge to grasp. Realistically, it may not be possible for social workers to master all this information at the beginning of their careers. What is important is that they recognize the need to obtain this knowledge throughout their careers and take steps to gain it when it is essential for their work (for in-depth discussions of these various forms of diversity, see Black, 1994; Bricker-Jenkins & Gottlieb, 1991; Bricker-Jenkins & Hooyman, 1984; Chau, 1991; Devore & Schlesinger, 1987; Hidalgo, Peterson, & Woodman, 1985; Hooyman, 1994; Longres, 1991; Lum, 1992; Newman, 1994; Pinderhughes, 1989, 1994; Van Den Bergh & Cooper, 1986; Woodman, 1985).

# CONFLICTS OF INTEREST

### STANDARD 1.06(a)

*Social workers should be alert to and avoid conflicts of interest that interfere with the exercise of professional discretion and impartial judgment. Social workers should inform clients when a real or potential conflict of interest arises and take reasonable steps to resolve the issue in a manner that makes the clients' interests primary and protects clients' interests to the greatest extent possible. In some cases, protecting clients' interests may require termination of the professional relationship with proper referral of the client.*

Ethical issues involving actual or potential conflicts of interest are among the most complex faced by social workers. Conflicts of interest occur when a social worker's services to or relationship with a client is compromised, or might be compromised, because of decisions or actions in relation to another client, a colleague, himself or herself, or some other third party. According to Gifis (1991), a conflict of interest involves "a situation in which regard for one duty leads to disregard of another . . . or might reasonably be expected to do so" (p. 88). Conflicts of interest may be actual or potential (when conflicting interests may develop but do not yet exist).

Conflicts of interest can occur in every profession—for example, a lawyer represents two clients charged with the same crime and exposing the guilt of one party may exonerate the other; a physician stands to benefit financially by ordering diagnostic tests for a patient and referring the patient to a laboratory in which the physician has a personal investment; a journalist covers a public scandal in which a close relative is allegedly involved; and a public official is responsible for regulating a utility in which she owns a substantial amount of stock.

Conflicts of interest in social work can take several forms. They may occur in the context of social workers' relationships with clients or in their roles as community organizers, supervisors, consultants, administrators, policy officials, educators, researchers, or program evaluators. Social workers must be careful to avoid conflicts of interest that might harm clients because of their decisions or actions involving other clients, colleagues, themselves, or other third parties. For example, a social worker employed by the state department of corrections administered the prison system's sexual offender treatment program. He conducted treatment groups for inmates convicted of crimes such as child molestation, rape, and other forms of sexual assault. When inmates were eligible for parole, the social worker made recommendations to the parole board concerning each inmate's readiness for parole and, for those deemed ready, services that should be mandated as a condition of parole. These recommendations usually included specific provisions for follow-up counseling.

In addition to his duties as an employee of the state department of corrections, the social worker also was a partner in a community-based group psychotherapy practice. In several cases he recommended to the state parole board that inmates be referred to this group practice after their release from prison, but he did not disclose his own affiliation with the practice. This case involved a conflict of interest because the social worker had an incentive to refer inmates to his group practice, from which he might benefit personally.

In another case a social worker in private practice was married to a man who owned a small manufacturing firm. On occasion the social worker's husband would become aware of his employees' personal problems that were interfering with their work, such as problems related to their marriages or alcohol use. The social worker's husband gave these employees his wife's business card and encouraged them to consult with her about their problems, and he did not provide information about other providers or agencies. These situations involved a conflict of interest in several important ways. First, there was a potential clash between a client's best interests, in a clinical sense, and the employer's (the social worker's husband's) financial interests. That is, the clinical goals could lead to a course of action that would cause a valuable employee to resign from his or her job or ask for a leave of absence, contrary to the needs of the social worker's husband. Second, the social worker might have a financial stake in how she handles the client's employment-related issues. That is, a client's decisions and actions with respect to his or her job with the social worker's husband could have an impact on the family's finances, and this could affect the social worker's judgment. Third, the employees' receipt of social work services provided by their employer's wife may undermine their trust that confidentiality would be respected.

In such circumstances when potential conflicts of interest arise, social workers have an obligation to be alert to and avoid actual or potential conflicts of interest that might interfere with the exercise of their professional discretion and impartial judgment. Practitioners should resolve the conflict in a manner that makes the clients' (or potential clients') interests primary and protects clients' interests to the greatest extent possible. For example, the prison-based social worker who referred sex offenders to the group psychotherapy practice should have disclosed to corrections officials that he was involved in that practice. He should not have referred inmates to the practice because of the possibility that he would benefit from such referrals. It is possible that the social worker would have referred parole-eligible inmates to that practice in part because of the possibility of his own financial gain rather than the inmates' clinical needs. Instead, the social worker should have referred clients to practitioners with whom he was not affiliated, and there would have been no risk of a conflict of interest. If this social worker and his colleagues were the only appropriate local providers of follow-up services for sex offenders, the social worker should have negotiated an explicit agreement with department of corrections officials to avoid any conflict of interest. For example, he could have implemented a comprehensive services delivery plan that included an institutional component and a community-based component, a plan structured in such a way that there would be no financial incentive for the social worker to refer inmates to the practice with which he was affiliated.

The social worker who received referrals from her husband should have explained to him the inappropriateness of such referrals and helped him refer employees to other services providers (perhaps by contracting with an employee assistance program that would screen and refer to providers in the community).

Issues of conflict of interest can be extremely complex, so it is helpful to examine several other examples involving actual or potential conflicts:

- A social worker in community organizing was working with a group of residents in a low-income neighborhood to address affordable housing problems in the area. The social worker, who was very knowledgeable about housing subsidy programs, helped the community group develop a proposal, in partnership with a local developer, that they submitted to the state housing finance agency. The proposal requested funds to subsidize construction costs and a below-market-rate mortgage to finance a new housing development. The social worker did not disclose to his clients or the housing finance agency staff that he was a part-time consultant to the local developer who was a partner in the project and that he would benefit financially if the project were funded.

- A social worker was hired by a nursing home as a consultant. The purpose of the consultation was to conduct a study assessing the adequacy of the nursing home's social services and recommend ways to improve staffing and services delivery. The consultant's final report offered a number of recommendations, including a recommendation that the nursing home consider developing a partnership with a nationally prominent, for-profit home health care agency. The social worker did not disclose that her sister was a partner in the home health care agency and, as a result, she could have an incentive to encourage the nursing home to contract with that agency.

- A social worker served as an assistant director of a county child welfare department. He was primarily responsible for the department's services related to child abuse and neglect (conducting investigations into suspected abuse and neglect; arranging and supervising foster care; and providing preventive, crisis intervention, and counseling services to families). The department received a report that a child placed in one of the department's foster homes had been sexually abused by the foster father. The social worker arranged for and supervised an investigation into the allegation, but the foster father was once a very close friend of the social worker, thus making it difficult for the social worker to be entirely objective.

- A professor of social work maintained a small private practice. One of this social worker's clients, an accountant, decided to make a career change and obtain an MSW, largely because of her successful experience in therapy. The client applied for admission to the local school of social work. The professor, who continued to function as the client's therapist, served on the school's admissions committee and received the client's application for review. She explained to the school's dean that she should not review the application because of a possible conflict of interest, although she did not disclose how she knew the applicant.

- A social worker was retained by a local family services agency to conduct a formal evaluation of the agency's family reunification program, which had the goal of strengthening families when a child had been placed in out-of-home care because of abuse or neglect. With the agency's assistance and cooperation, the social worker designed and conducted an ambitious study of the agency's staff, services, and client outcome. The final report included a number of recommendations for staff to consider.

  Shortly before the project was concluded, the social worker was appointed to the board of a major foundation that had received a proposal from the same family services agency. The foundation staff asked the social worker to review the agency's proposal and recommend whether foundation funding should be approved. The social worker told his foundation colleagues about his prior involvement with the agency and recused himself from the review of the proposal.

Each of these cases requires special efforts to avoid actual or potential conflicts of interest. In the first example, the community organizer who was assisting the neighborhood group with a proposal to develop affordable housing should have disclosed to his colleagues and the staff of the housing finance agency that he was a part-time consultant to the developer involved in the project. He also could have considered drawing on the expertise of another developer with whom he was not affiliated. In the second case, the social worker who was a consultant to a nursing home should not have recommended formation of a partnership with a home health care agency in which her sister was a partner, because such a relationship could be personally beneficial to the social worker's sister but might not be in the nursing home's best interest. She should have disclosed her sister's involvement with the home health care agency to nursing home administrators. In the third example, the social worker in the child welfare department should have removed himself from any involvement in the investigation involving his former friend. He should have explained to colleagues and administrators that it would be inappropriate for him to have any involvement in the case. The fourth case illustrates how the social work professor appropriately explained to the school's dean that she knew the applicant from the community, and therefore it would not be appropriate for her to review the application and make a recommendation (to protect the client's privacy, the social worker should not disclose that the applicant was a client in her practice.) The last example shows how the social worker retained by the family services agency to evaluate its program appropriately explained to his colleagues at the foundation the ways in which he was actively involved with the agency and recused himself from further review of the proposal submitted to the foundation.

## STANDARD 1.06(b)

*Social workers should not take unfair advantage of any professional relationship or exploit others to further their personal, religious, political, or business interests.*

In some, but not all, cases, conflicts of interest arise because social workers are in a position to take advantage of their relationships with clients, as in the case of the prison-based social worker who referred clients to his community-based practice, the social worker who helped a community group draft a proposal for an affordable housing project, and the social worker who consulted with the nursing home in the examples described above. Practitioners need to be particularly careful to avoid exploiting their relationships with clients to further their personal, religious, political, or business interests (or the interests of people close to the social workers). Personal interests involve social workers' own mental health, social, and intimacy needs. For example, a social worker in private practice was counseling a young woman who sought help in addressing marital problems. After a time, the social worker realized that he was attracted to his client. Although the client's clinical needs had been met after 11 counseling sessions, the social worker encouraged her to stay in treatment longer. The social worker eventually disclosed his feelings to the client and explained that he encouraged her to remain in therapy so that he could continue having contact with her. Their relationship deteriorated, and the client filed an ethics complaint with the state licensing board, alleging that the social worker exploited their relationship, at considerable emotional and financial cost to her, to meet his own personal needs.

Religious interests involve the social worker's spiritual or faith needs. Social workers who have strong religious beliefs and convictions may inappropriately introduce religious content into their work with clients who did not ask for or consent to such an approach. Introducing religious content into social work interventions is not, by definition, unethical. A number of social work services are provided under explicitly religious auspices. In such cases, clients understand that the social services are being sponsored by religious organizations or individuals who integrate religion and counseling. This is not unethical as long as clients fully understand the nature of the services they receive, are informed of available alternatives, and consent to such an approach.

Ethical problems arise, however, when social workers use their position of authority to incorporate religious content into their social work without explicitly addressing this issue with clients, who may be vulnerable and susceptible to the social worker's religious influence. For example, a social worker employed by a state psychiatric hospital had very strong religious beliefs and felt obligated to acquaint patients with relevant biblical passages during counseling sessions. On one occasion a colleague accidentally walked into a meeting room where the social worker was kneeling and praying with a patient. The patient later complained to hospital officials about the social worker's emphasis on religion.

Political interests involve social workers' personal political or ideological agendas. Although it is certainly legitimate (and often essential) for social workers to have strong political beliefs, particularly as they pertain to social work's mission and value base, practitioners should not take unfair advantage of their relationships with clients to advance a political agenda.

Not all political activity involving clients is unethical. For example, many social workers and social services agencies actively encourage clients to register to vote. Generally speaking, however, social workers should not take advantage of their relationships with clients to encourage, exhort, or pressure them to support a political agenda that is congruent with their own. For example, a social worker in a community mental health agency who is pro-choice on the abortion issue should not lobby clients to write letters to state legislators opposing a pending bill that would limit women's legal reproductive options. Because of the social worker's position of authority in a client's life, clients who disagree with the social worker's position on the issue may feel pressured to comply with the request just to please the social worker. Similarly, a social worker who supports a particular candidate for public office should not recruit clients to work on or donate their own money to the campaign. Vulnerable clients may find it difficult to say no.

Finally, a social worker's business interests include entrepreneurial or other investment or financial activities in which he or she is involved. A social worker in private practice was a partner in a small restaurant in his community. During one period the social worker and his partner in the restaurant business encountered serious cash flow problems and were having difficulty paying their bills. One of the social worker's clients was a loan officer at a bank. The social worker approached the client about the possibility of obtaining a short-term loan while he and his partner reorganized the restaurant business. Clearly, the social worker was taking unfair advantage of his professional relationship with the client to further his own business interests.

## STANDARD 1.06(c)

*Social workers should not engage in dual or multiple relationships with clients or former clients in which there is a risk of exploitation or potential harm to the client. In instances when dual or multiple relationships are unavoidable, social workers should take steps to protect clients and are responsible for setting clear, appropriate, and culturally sensitive boundaries. (Dual or multiple relationships occur when social workers relate to clients in more than one relationship, whether professional, social, or business. Dual or multiple relationships can occur simultaneously or consecutively.)*

For decades social workers have been aware of the need to maintain clear boundaries in their relationships with clients. Practitioners have understood that, in principle if not always in reality, they should not be sexually involved or maintain intense social relationships with current clients. In recent years, however, social workers, as well as other groups of professionals, have developed a keener understanding of the many subtle issues that can arise in their relationships with clients. The concept of dual and multiple relationships conveys this richer understanding of the complex ways in which boundary issues can emerge in professional–client relationships.

Dual or multiple relationships can assume many forms, not all of which are ethically problematic. At one extreme are dual and multiple relationships that are not typically problematic, for example, when a social worker and client coincidentally attend the same play and have adjacent seats. The boundary issues are temporary and, most likely, manageable. There may be awkward moments, particularly when the client meets the social worker's spouse or partner during intermission, but this kind of unanticipated boundary issue may not unleash complex issues in the therapeutic relationship. This is not to say that an unanticipated social contact should be ignored—it may be useful to address the client's feelings about the encounter. However, in the long run this is not the kind of dual relationship that is likely to have harmful, long-standing consequences. Below are several other examples of dual or multiple relationships that are not likely to be ethically problematic:

- A social worker's client and her nine-year-old daughter canvassed their neighborhood to sell wrapping paper as a fundraiser for the daughter's school. The client was not aware that her social worker, with whom she was in psychotherapy, lived in the neighborhood, and she was surprised to discover that the social worker lived in one of the houses her daughter approached. The social worker purchased some wrapping paper from the client's daughter.

- A school social worker provided counseling services to an 11-year-old student and his parents. The student was referred to the social worker because a teacher was concerned about a sudden deterioration in his school work. Shortly after they began their work together, the social worker and the student's father realized that they were enrolled together in a continuing education class on computer technology.

- A social worker retained to evaluate a local family services agency's substance abuse program discovered that she and the program director were members of the same fitness center. Afterward, the social worker and the program director usually encountered each other once or twice a week at the center.

In each of these situations it may be appropriate for the social workers to talk with their clients about their encounters outside the professional–client relationship to ensure that the encounters will not interfere with or undermine their work together. In all likelihood, superficial contact of this sort will not introduce difficult issues in the professional–client relationship.

At the other extreme are dual or multiple relationships that are clearly problematic, as in these examples:

- A social worker in a residential treatment program for adolescents met regularly with the single mother of a 12-year-old client. The social worker realized that he was attracted to the client's mother and began dating her.

- A clinical social worker had provided counseling to a man who reported that he was dealing with a midlife crisis and possible career change. Counseling ended after 10 months of what both parties regarded as a very successful therapeutic relationship. Three weeks after the termination of the professional–client relationship, the former client telephoned to invite the social worker to become a financial partner in the former client's new business venture. The social worker accepted the very attractive offer.

- A clinical social worker in an outpatient substance abuse treatment program for adults provided counseling to a young man who was struggling with alcohol abuse. As part of the counseling, the social worker encouraged the client to attend Alcoholics Anonymous meetings in the community. The social worker also was a recovering alcoholic. The social worker regularly attended Alcoholics Anonymous meetings and invited the client to accompany her to meetings. The social worker and client attended meetings regularly, during which the social worker often disclosed personal information about her own recovery and substance abuse history.

In these cases the dual or multiple relationships are clearly problematic because of the likelihood of exploitation of or potential harm to the client. The social worker who dated his client's mother was involved in a dual relationship that could be very harmful to the client. The relationship with the client's mother could certainly undermine the client's trust in the social worker and confuse the client about the social worker's role in his life. The social worker's clinical judgment also could be impaired because of his intimate relationship with the client's mother. The therapist who accepted her former client's offer to invest in his new business venture entered into a dual relationship that could be very detrimental to the former client. Dealing with the former client in a new relationship that focused on business and financial decisions could subvert the effectiveness of the former—and very recent—therapeutic relationship, particularly if contentious issues or disagreements were to arise. Over time the former client's perception of and feelings about the social worker might change because of the business relationship, and this could have a detrimental effect on whatever beneficial outcomes were achieved during the course of the professional–client relationship. The social worker who was in recovery and attended Alcoholics Anonymous meetings with her client could harm him as a result of the confused boundary issues. The client might have difficulty distinguishing between the social worker as a professional and the social worker as an acquaintance who is also in recovery. This confusion could interfere with the social worker's professional effectiveness and with the client's recovery.

What these cases have in common is risk of harm to the client. As Kagle and Giebelhausen (1994) observed with respect to the psychotherapeutic relationship:

> Dual relationships involve boundary violations. They cross the line between the therapeutic relationship and a second relationship, undermining the distinctive nature of the therapeutic relationship, blurring the roles of practitioner and client, and permitting the abuse of power. In a therapeutic relationship, the practitioner's influence on the client is constrained by professional ethics and other protocols of professional practice. When a professional relationship shifts to a dual relationship, the practitioner's power remains but is not checked by the rules of professional conduct or, in some cases, even acknowledged. The practitioner and the client pretend to define the second relationship around different roles and rules. Behavior that is incompatible with a therapeutic relationship is made to seem acceptable in the context of the second relationship. Attention shifts from the client to the practitioner, and power appears to be more equally shared. (p. 217)

Not surprisingly, in between these extremes of dual and multiple relationships are "gray areas" where the boundary issues are unclear. In such circumstances reasonable social workers may disagree about the degree of risk for potential harm or exploitation. For example,

- A social worker for a substance abuse treatment program worked with a 28-year-old woman who had a history of cocaine and alcohol abuse. The client claimed that as a result of her work with the social worker, she was "clean and sober" for the first time in her adult life, employed, and in a solid relationship. The social worker received an invitation from the client to attend her upcoming wedding. The client told the social worker how important it was for her to attend the wedding in light of the social worker's major influence in the client's life. The social worker was uncertain about whether to attend the wedding; she did not want the client to feel rejected, but she was uneasy about blurring the boundaries in their relationship.

- A social worker employed by a home health care agency provided services to a terminally ill 72-year-old woman who was receiving hospice services. The social worker visited once each week to provide counseling and support. During one of the visits, the client invited the social worker to join her for lunch. The social worker was torn between politely rejecting the invitation to avoid blurring the boundaries in the relationship and accepting the invitation to avoid hurting the client's feelings and, perhaps, jeopardizing the clinical relationship.

- A social worker in private practice in a rural area provided counseling services to a 32-year-old man who was struggling with self-esteem issues. Three years after the professional–client relationship ended, and primarily as a result of the client's contact with the social worker, the client enrolled in a nearby graduate program in social work. After his graduation, which was six years after the termination of the professional–client relationship, the former client approached the social worker about providing him with clinical supervision. The former client explained that he wanted to learn from the social worker's vast experience and that in their area there were no other MSWs available to provide clinical supervision. The social worker believed that he could manage this new relationship with his former client, especially because several years had elapsed since the termination of the professional–client relationship, but he was unsure this change in roles was appropriate.

When faced with such circumstances, social workers should consult with experienced colleagues and supervisors in an effort to think through their decisions thoroughly and responsibly. Social workers also should document that they obtained such consultation and supervision to demonstrate that they made a diligent effort to handle the situation ethically. In some cases there may not be an obvious "right" answer; however, competent consultation and supervision are essential to minimize the likelihood that clients will be harmed by social workers' decisions to enter into a dual or multiple relationship with a client or former client.

Social workers also should recognize that some dual and multiple relationships are more avoidable than others. For example, they can easily avoid planned social encounters with their clients, such as spending a day together at the beach or going out to dinner. In contrast, it may be difficult for social workers to avoid dual or multiple relationships in small or rural communities where, for example, a former client may marry her social worker's closest friend in town, a current client is elected to the local court in which the social worker's spouse frequently practices, or a social worker and her client are both appointed to the board of their community church.

In such circumstances, according to standard 1.06(c), social workers must "take steps to protect clients and are responsible for setting clear, appropriate, and culturally sensitive boundaries." At a minimum, social workers should discuss the boundary issues frankly with their clients; in addition, they should consult colleagues and supervisors to discuss the most appropriate ways to handle boundary issues that have emerged.

When faced with actual or potential dual or multiple relationships, social workers should critically examine their own motives and needs, which they previously may have failed to do. In many cases involving inappropriate and harmful dual and multiple relationships, social workers are motivated more by self-gratification and their own emotional needs than by a genuine, primary, and deep-seated commitment to the client's needs. Social workers also may find that they are more impulsive in these relationships than in other areas of their lives, because they have placed their own needs above those of their clients. In addition, social workers involved in problematic dual or multiple relationships may find that they have difficulty empathizing with clients—again, because of their preoccupation with their own needs rather than those of their clients.

## STANDARD 1.06(d)

*When social workers provide services to two or more people who have a relationship with each other (for example, couples, family members), social workers should clarify with all parties which individuals will be considered clients and the nature of social workers' professional obligations to the various individuals who are receiving services. Social workers who anticipate a conflict of interest among the individuals receiving services or who anticipate having to perform in potentially conflicting roles (for example, when a social worker is asked to testify in a child custody dispute or divorce proceedings involving clients) should clarify their role with the parties involved and take appropriate action to minimize any conflict of interest.*

Clinical social workers often provide services to two or more people who have a relationship with each other. Common examples include family, marital, or couples therapy; discharge planning for a hospital patient that includes family consultation; and school social work that requires parental involvement. Social workers often provide such services without encountering a potential or actual conflict of interest. However, circumstances sometimes arise in which a serious conflict of interest occurs or might occur:

- A clinical social worker provided individual counseling to a 34-year-old woman who was distressed about her nine-year-old son's behavioral problems. After initially focusing on the child's behavioral issues and strategies for dealing with them, the client brought up some problems related to her marriage. Soon it became clear that the marital issues were contributing to the child's behavioral problems. At first the client's husband was unwilling to participate in the therapy, but eventually, as the marriage deteriorated, he agreed to participate.

    Ultimately, the couple decided to divorce and became involved in a bitter child custody dispute. The husband's lawyer subpoenaed the social worker to testify against the mother about a number of issues related to the child custody dispute.

- A hospital social worker provided services to an 82-year-old woman who was recovering from hip surgery. In addition to her physical problems, the patient also manifested some symptoms of dementia (some modest difficulty learning new information and remembering learned information, performing motor functions, recognizing familiar objects). The client's son, who visited his mother regularly, insisted that the social worker attempt to place his mother in a nursing home. He was very concerned about his mother's dementia symptoms and the risks she faced if she returned to her home to live alone. The client, however, adamantly refused to go to a nursing home and insisted that the social worker arrange home health care; the client said she was willing to assume any risk associated with her living alone.

- A school social worker began counseling a 13-year-old student who was referred by the student's guidance counselor. According to the guidance counselor, the student seemed to be depressed. The social worker and the student met weekly for about two months. With the student's permission, the social worker also met with his parents several times to gather background information about the family's history and relationships and explore the parents' perceptions of their son's difficulties. One afternoon the student's mother telephoned the social worker and asked for an update on his situation at school, but the student was concerned about his privacy and had asked the social worker not to disclose to his parents any information from their counseling sessions.

When social workers provide services to two or more people who have a relationship with each other, they must always think ahead about possible conflicts of interest. Early in any such relationship, social workers should discuss with the parties involved which individuals will be considered clients and the various commitments and obligations the social worker has to all parties involved. For example, social workers who provide marriage or couples counseling should routinely bring up the subject of potential conflicts of interest so that the participants clearly understand the social worker's role and the social worker's effort not to take sides with one person or another. This explanation would not necessarily prevent one party's lawyer from subpoenaing a social worker in a divorce proceeding or custody dispute, but the clients would be fully aware of possible conflicts of interest when they enter their clinical relationship with the social worker.

Similarly, social workers who depend on collateral contacts with family members (or other third parties) to serve their primary clients (for example, social workers in hospitals or schools) should clarify with all parties which individuals will be considered clients and the nature of the social worker's obligations to the various individuals involved. For instance, the hospital social worker in the example above should inform the elderly patient's son and the patient about her primary commitment to the patient, her obligation to respect the patient's right to self-determination, and her simultaneous obligation to take reasonable steps to protect the patient from self-harm. This explanation may not be entirely satisfactory to the son, but it can clarify the social worker's principal obligations and manage potentially conflicting interests as the situation unfolds. The school social worker discussed above should explain to the student and his parents the nature of the social worker's relationship with the student and his policy regarding confidentiality (and the reasons for it). The parents may not agree with this policy, but such an explanation may help manage the parties' diverse agendas and avoid potential conflicts of interest.

## PRIVACY AND CONFIDENTIALITY

### STANDARD 1.07(a)

---

*Social workers should respect clients' right to privacy. Social workers should not solicit private information from clients unless it is essential to providing services or conducting social work evaluation or research. Once private information is shared, standards of confidentiality apply.*

Social workers often have access to sensitive information about intimate aspects of clients' lives, including information about personal relationships, domestic violence, substance abuse, sexual trauma and behavior, criminal activity, and mental illness. Such information is obtained to assess clients' circumstances thoroughly, so that social workers can plan and implement appropriate interventions.

Social workers should be conservative, however, in their efforts to obtain private information from clients. That is, they should seek private information from clients only to the extent that it is necessary to carry out their professional functions. Social workers should constantly distinguish between private information that is essential and private information that is gratuitous. For example, a social worker employed by a residential substance abuse treatment program would have good reasons for asking new clients about their abuse of alcohol, cocaine, amphetamines, and other drugs. However, it would not be appropriate for that social worker to inquire about the client's sexual orientation. A client may wish to bring this subject up if it is somehow related to his or her substance abuse problems, but the social worker should follow the client's lead and respect that person's right to privacy.

Similarly, a social worker in a community mental health center should not routinely ask clients about past criminal activity in which they may have engaged. In this setting social workers may be tempted to ask clients about their past conduct, but unless there is some legally sanctioned mandate to gather such information, they should respect their clients' privacy.

When clients voluntarily share private information or when it is appropriate for social workers to ask for private information to provide services or conduct research, client confidentiality must be protected. The *NASW Code of Ethics* includes a number of standards designed to protect client confidentiality to the greatest extent possible.

### STANDARD 1.07(b)

---

*Social workers may disclose confidential information when appropriate with valid consent from a client or a person legally authorized to consent on behalf of a client.*

There are two kinds of situations in which social workers are in a position to disclose confidential information. First, clients may ask social workers to release confidential information to a third party. For example, a client may ask a social worker to disclose confidential information to another services provider, such as a physician, or to a lawyer who is representing the client in a legal matter, such as a child custody dispute or a lawsuit the client's lawyer filed on the client's behalf against another professional who provided services to the client. Second, social workers may receive requests for confidential information from third parties. For example, a social worker may receive a request for confidential information from law enforcement officials who are investigating a crime that involved the social worker's client or from a lawyer who is defending a party whom the client has sued.

In these situations social workers should disclose confidential information only when they have obtained valid consent from the client or a person legally authorized to consent on behalf of the client. (There are several exceptions to this mandate, particularly ones involving emergency circumstances and court orders to disclose confidential information, which are discussed in standard 1.07[c]). The consent obtained from a client, or a person legally authorized to consent on the client's behalf (such as a relative or friend who has a power of attorney), should conform to the informed consent standards set forth in standards 1.03(a), (b), and (c). That is, in obtaining client consent to disclose confidential information, social workers should use clear and understandable language to inform clients of the purpose of the consent and the disclosure, the risks related to the disclosure, reasonable alternatives (if any), the client's right to refuse or withdraw consent, and the time frame covered by the consent. Social workers also should provide clients with an opportunity to ask questions about the consent to disclose confidential information.

As with any informed consent procedure, when social workers seek client consent to disclose confidential information they must take special precautions when a client is not literate or has difficulty understanding the primary language used in the practice setting (see standard 1.03[b]). Social workers may need to provide such clients with a detailed oral explanation or arrange for a qualified interpreter or translator. If clients lack the capacity to provide informed consent to the disclosure of confidential information, social workers should protect clients' interests to the greatest extent possible by seeking permission from an appropriate third party, informing clients consistent with their level of understanding and comprehension, and attempting to ensure that the third party acts in a manner consistent with the client's wishes and interests (see standard 1.03[c]). Particular care should be taken to ensure that clients do not feel coerced or pressured into consenting to the disclosure.

Many requests for confidential information received by social workers are straightforward. For example, another professional providing services to a client may request confidential information concerning that client; the social worker and the client should discuss the request and consent procedure before the client signs the consent form and the information is shared with the requesting party.

In other cases, however, social workers may be less clear about the appropriateness of a request for disclosure of confidential information. One source of confusion is the extent to which the party requesting the confidential information is legally entitled to it (for example, whether parents are entitled to confidential information concerning their children or whether law enforcement officials are entitled to confidential information about one's client). In such circumstances social workers should consult with knowledgeable colleagues—and, if necessary, a lawyer—about relevant statutes and regulations.

A second source of confusion involves situations in which a social worker questions a client's decision to consent to disclosure of confidential information. For example, a social worker in private practice was asked by her client to disclose confidential information concerning his therapy to the client's employer. The employer had asked the client for this information for reassurance that the client was addressing a mental health problem that affected his job performance. The social worker was concerned about disclosing the amount of information requested by the employer; in her judgment, some of the information in her case notes might be used against the client. Although the social worker shared her concern with the client, the client continued to insist that all the information be shared with the employer. Thus, when social workers believe that complying with a client's request to disclose confidential information would not be in the client's best interest, they should discuss the concerns with the client. If the client continues to insist on the disclosure, social workers should comply with the client's wishes; however, practitioners should document that they discussed the issue with the client. Such documentation helps protect a social worker if questions should subsequently be raised about the appropriateness of the disclosure. As in all cases when social workers are uncertain about how best to proceed, they should consult with knowledgeable colleagues or a lawyer.

There are a number of substantive areas where social workers should clarify when client consent is and is not required for disclosure of confidential information. Numerous authors have discussed these situations, which may be governed by federal, state, or local laws or regulations (Austin, Moline, & Williams, 1990; Dickson, 1995, 1998; Reamer, 1994; Saltzman & Proch, 1990; Wilson, 1978). They include the disclosure of confidential information pertaining to

- protection of third parties who may be at risk (see standard 1.07[c])
- assessment, treatment, or referral of clients to address substance abuse issues
- mandatory reporting of suspected abuse or neglect of a child, senior citizen, or person with disabilities
- coordination of services with other agencies involved with clients (for example, public welfare agencies, psychiatric facilities, school officials)
- the delivery of services within one's own agency (the extent to which staff within an agency should share confidential information with one another)
- peer supervision and consultation with colleagues (see standard 2.05 [c])
- deceased clients (see standard 1.07[r])
- news media (see standard 1.07[k])
- law enforcement officials
- minors' parents or guardians.

*Social workers should protect the confidentiality of all information obtained in the course of professional service, except for compelling professional reasons. The general expectation that social workers will keep information confidential does not apply when disclosure is necessary to prevent serious, foreseeable, and imminent harm to a client or other identifiable person or when laws or regulations require disclosure without a client's consent. In all instances, social workers should disclose the least amount of confidential information necessary to achieve the desired purpose; only information that is directly relevant to the purpose for which the disclosure is made should be revealed.*

The concept of disclosing confidential information contrary to a client's wishes has been considered in the discussion of standard 1.02, which concerns the limits of clients' right to self-determination. Standard 1.02 explicitly acknowledges that circumstances may arise in which social workers are obligated to limit a client's right to self-determination—specifically when, in the social worker's judgment, a client's actions or potential actions pose a serious, foreseeable, and imminent risk to himself or herself or to others.

As discussed under standard 1.02, the *Tarasoff* (1976) case established the most noteworthy precedent concerning the disclosure of confidential information to protect third parties from harm. Since the *Tarasoff* decision, many court cases involving duty-to-protect issues have been litigated, further clarifying social workers' and other mental health professionals' obligations. In addition, in recent years many states have adopted statutes incorporating the guidelines established in *Tarasoff* and other duty-to-warn and duty-to-protect cases (Kopels & Kagle, 1993; Lewis, 1986; Reamer, 1994). Although some court rulings are contradictory or inconsistent, and there is some variation among state statutes, the general trend suggests that, ordinarily, four conditions should be met to justify disclosure of confidential information to protect a third party from harm. First, the social worker should have evidence that the client poses a threat of violence to a third party. As the court asserted in *Tarasoff*, "when a therapist determines, or pursuant to the standards of his profession should determine, that his patient presents a serious danger of violence to another, he incurs an obligation to use reasonable care to protect the intended victim against such danger" (17 Cal. 3d 425 at 431). Although courts have not provided precise definitions of "violence," the term ordinarily implies the use of some kind of force (for example, using a gun, knife, or other dangerous weapon) to inflict harm.

Second, the social worker should have evidence that the violent act is foreseeable—that is, sufficient evidence to suggest that the violent act is likely to occur. Although courts recognize that social workers and other mental health professionals cannot predict violence with absolute certainty, clinicians must be able to demonstrate that they had reason to believe that the client was likely to carry out the violent act (based, for example, on the client's behavior and comments).

Third, the social worker should have reasonable evidence to suggest that the violent act is impending or likely to occur relatively soon. Here, too, the courts have not provided precise criteria or guidelines. "Imminence" may be defined differently by different clinicians; ultimately, the social worker should be able to defend his or her definition, whether it is in terms of minutes, hours, or days.

Fourth, a number of court decisions, but not all, require that a clinician be able to identify the potential victim. The rationale is that the disclosure of confidential information against a client's wishes should be exceptional and should not occur unless the clinician has very specific information about the client's apparent intent to harm a specific probable victim (Lewis, 1986). It also is possible that a duty to protect would exist if a social worker can infer the identity of a foreseeable victim from information available in a case, even if the client has not specifically named the probable victim (Austin et al., 1990; Reamer, 1994).

Although these criteria are fairly straightforward, social workers should be aware that both clinicians and lawyers disagree about their application and "goodness of fit" in individual cases. Most agree that a social worker whose client makes a clear threat to violently harm an identifiable third party within the next day or so has a duty to take steps to protect the potential victim, which may entail disclosing confidential information without the client's consent.

Other cases, however, are not so clear. For example, a social worker at an outpatient mental health clinic was providing clinical services to a young man who had been discharged from a psychiatric hospital after treatment for bipolar disorder. The client was functioning well in the community and complying with his medication regimen; he was employed and involved in a relationship with a woman he had met at work. The client met with the social worker every two weeks.

One afternoon the client telephoned the social worker and said he needed to see her "as soon as possible to discuss some terrible news." The next morning at the social worker's office, the client informed her that, much to his surprise, he was just diagnosed with HIV infection, the virus that causes AIDS. The client explained to the social worker that he had never thought he was in a high-risk category, although he acknowledged that about four years earlier he had been involved in a brief sexual relationship with another man. The social worker and client extensively discussed the implications of the HIV diagnosis, particularly with respect to the client's lifestyle and his relationship with his girlfriend. The social worker soon discovered that the client had not shared with his partner the fact that he had been diagnosed with HIV. The client told the social worker, "She's the best thing that's happened to me in my adult life. My head tells me I should tell her, but my heart is so afraid. I can't bear the thought that I might lose her. But you don't need to worry—the nurse at the health clinic told me how to prevent HIV transmission." The client then described to the social worker all of the precautions he would take to protect his partner, "who I love so very much." He went on to say, "One of these days, I'll get the courage to tell her. I just can't do it now. I'm emotionally paralyzed. Please, please don't say anything to her. You know I wouldn't do anything to harm her."

The social worker discussed the case with her supervisor and several colleagues and tried various clinical interventions to help the client get to a point where he would be willing to share with his partner the news of his HIV diagnosis (offering to role play the conversation with the client's girlfriend, offering to sit in on the actual conversation). Unfortunately, this clinical strategy was not successful. The social worker had to decide whether to honor the client's request for privacy and confidentiality or to take steps to ensure that the client's partner had sufficient information to protect herself. This was especially difficult considering that the social worker's colleagues disagreed about the social worker's obligation.

Circumstances such as these have generated considerable disagreement among social workers and lawyers about the relevance of *Tarasoff* and various duty-to-protect guidelines that have evolved since that precedent-setting decision (Francis & Chin, 1987; Gray & Harding, 1988; Kain, 1988; Reamer, 1991a, 1991b). When the *Tarasoff* case was decided in 1976, no one anticipated its eventual application to AIDS-related cases, because that syndrome did not become well known until 1981. Since the *Tarasoff* decision, some human services professionals have argued that the fact that an HIV-positive individual merely poses a threat to another party is sufficient to rely on the *Tarasoff*-like criteria to protect third parties (Lamb, Clark, Drumheller, Frizzell, & Surrey, 1989). Others, however, claim that *Tarasoff* is not an appropriate precedent because people with HIV infection may not explicitly threaten a third party with an act of violence. In the case discussed above, the client never threatened to harm his partner; in fact, he proclaimed his love for her and his intent to protect her by taking precautions. Moreover, in many cases the risk to third parties may not be demonstrably imminent and a particular potential victim may not be identifiable.

The key point is that circumstances may arise in which social workers are unclear about the extent of their duty to protect third parties in light of prevailing case law and statutes. As Lewis (1986) concluded, "it must . . . be recognized that psychotherapy is an imperfect science. A precise formula for determining when the duty to maintain confidentiality should yield to the duty to warn is, therefore, beyond reach" (pp. 614–615).

Social workers also may be obligated to disclose confidential information when a client poses a threat to himself or herself (VandeCreek & Knapp, 1993). That is, they are obligated to take reasonable steps to prevent a client's suicide, and this may entail disclosing confidential information (for example, to family members or other mental health professionals who may be in a position to prevent a suicide attempt). As Meyer and colleagues (1988) noted,

> While the law generally does not hold anyone responsible for the acts of another, there are exceptions. One of these is the responsibility of therapists to prevent suicide and other self-destructive behavior by their clients. The duty of therapists to exercise adequate care and skill in diagnosing suicidality is well-established. . . . When the risk of self-injurious behavior is identified an additional duty to take adequate precautions arises. . . . When psychotherapists fail to meet these responsibilities, they may be held liable for injuries that result. (p. 38)

Specific laws and regulations may require social workers to disclose confidential information without a client's consent. Perhaps the most common are mandatory reporting laws pertaining to suspected abuse or neglect of a child, senior citizen, or disabled person. Especially since the widespread establishment in the 1960s and 1970s of statutes on mandatory reporting of child abuse and neglect, social workers have come to accept their responsibility to disclose confidential information in some exceptional circumstances.

Here too, however, social workers' ethical decisions are not always clear. Sometimes social workers may be reluctant to comply with a mandatory reporting statute because of their concern about jeopardizing their therapeutic relationship with a client; social workers in this situation may believe that they can manage the risk themselves (Besharov, 1985; U.S. National Center on Child Abuse and Neglect, 1981). Practitioners who decide not to comply with mandatory reporting statutes should recognize that they assume considerable risk in the form of potential ethics complaints and lawsuits. Child welfare officials and other interested parties who become aware that a social worker had reason to suspect abuse or neglect and yet failed to report this concern may file an ethics complaint or lawsuit against the social worker. This could occur, for example, if the social worker's client subsequently neglects or abuses the party at risk and an investigation reveals that the social worker failed to report the suspected abuse or neglect.

An important element of standard 1.07(c) is its requirement that, when social workers are obligated to disclose confidential information, they should disclose "the least amount of confidential information necessary to achieve the desired purpose; only information that is directly relevant to the purpose for which the disclosure is made should be revealed." Although extraordinary and compelling circumstances may require social workers to disclose confidential information, practitioners should be conservative about which and how much information is shared. Only information that is absolutely essential for the recipient to have (for example, to protect a third party from harm or to prevent a suicide) should be disclosed. Thus, if a client threatens to harm his estranged spouse, law enforcement officials notified by the social worker should be given the least information possible to enable the police to prevent harm (for example, the identity of the party at risk, the nature of the threat the client poses, recommendations for the most effective way to intervene with the client). It should not be necessary for the social worker to share extensive details of clinical history, particularly facts that are extraneous to the threat.

### STANDARD 1.07(d)

---

*Social workers should inform clients, to the extent possible, about the disclosure of confidential information and the potential consequences, when feasible before the disclosure is made. This applies whether social workers disclose confidential information on the basis of a legal requirement or client consent.*

In those extraordinary circumstances that require social workers to disclose confidential information, they should attempt to inform clients about the disclosure before it is made. Common courtesy requires that clients be told when important information about them is going to be shared with others (such as child welfare officials, when a social worker suspects possible abuse or neglect, or law enforcement officials, when a social worker is concerned that a client is planning to harm a third party), especially when the disclosure will be made without the client's consent.

Also, informing clients about the disclosure may affect the circumstances that led to the need for the disclosure. In some, although not all, cases, clients who are reluctant to consent to the disclosure of information may change their minds when they learn that the social worker is serious about his or her decision to disclose confidential information. For example, a social worker in a home health care program was concerned that the son of her elderly client, a 79-year-old man diagnosed with Alzheimer's disease, was physically abusing his father. The son adamantly denied the abuse and warned the social worker not to share this information with anyone, "or there will be trouble you don't want to have." The son's threat added to the social worker's concern. She decided that she had to report her concern to the state department of elderly affairs, as required by law. She also decided that she would tell her client's son before she made the report. Once the social worker explained her concern and obligation to the son—as diplomatically as possible—the son began to cry and admitted that he had "lost control a few times." He then talked at length about "how unbearable it is to take care of someone with this disease." This clinical breakthrough enabled the social worker to provide genuine assistance and support to the son, who was then eager to learn about ways to cope with his situation and his father's disease. The social worker's informing the son of her plan to notify the department of elderly affairs was the catalyst needed to help him acknowledge his frustration and abusive behavior. Later the social worker and the son together called the department of elderly affairs and described their plan to address the son's frustration and coping mechanisms. The protective services worker at the department commended the son for his willingness to address the issues he was facing and approved the plan.

Note that standard 1.07(d) states that clients should be informed about the disclosure of confidential information and the potential consequences "to the extent possible" and "when feasible" before the disclosure is made. The *NASW Code of Ethics* Revision Committee recognized that in some circumstances it may not be feasible or realistic to inform clients in advance—or at all—about the disclosure. For practical reasons under no one's control, it may not be possible to reach a client before a disclosure is made. For example, a social worker at a family services agency was telephoned by his client's wife, who also met with the social worker occasionally. According to the wife, her husband, with whom she had just had a serious fight, "just stormed out of the house with the children and said I'd never see them again, except at their funeral. The kids were screaming at the top of their lungs, they were so afraid. I know he's going to do something awful to them just to get back at me. He'll really do it." The husband had a history of violence, having physically abused both his wife and their children. After consulting with his supervisor, the social worker decided to notify local child welfare and law enforcement officials and discuss with them the most appropriate way to intervene to protect the children. This involved disclosing confidential information without notifying the client ahead of time. In the circumstances, it was not feasible to notify the client in advance.

It also may not be wise or possible to inform the client of the disclosure when the social worker would be at risk of harm. For example, in the case involving the son who had abused his father, it is conceivable that the social worker would have been physically afraid of the client, who had warned her not to talk to anyone about her concerns, "or there will be trouble you don't want to have." Such risk is difficult to assess, but situations can arise when social workers conclude, quite reasonably, that the physical risk they face from informing clients of the impending disclosure of confidential information is too great. Social workers should be careful to obtain proper consultation in such situations and document their concerns and rationale.

Not all decisions by social workers to disclose confidential information stem from a legal requirement such as an obligation to protect third parties from harm or to report suspected abuse or neglect of a child, senior citizen, or person with a disability. Often social workers disclose confidential information based on clients' consent, for example, when information is shared willingly with other services providers. In such cases, social workers should be sure that a client is informed about the timing of the disclosure, its purpose and content, the client's right to refuse or withdraw consent, the time frame covered by the consent, and any potential consequences (see standard 1.03[a]). It is always wise to document that clients were given this information.

### STANDARD 1.07(e)

*Social workers should discuss with clients and other interested parties the nature of confidentiality and limitations of clients' right to confidentiality. Social workers should review with clients circumstances where confidential information may be requested and where disclosure of confidential information may be legally required. This discussion should occur as soon as possible in the social worker–client relationship and as needed throughout the course of the relationship.*

Clients have the right to know how social workers will handle confidential information. Social workers have a responsibility to inform clients about their policies concerning confidentiality, particularly those related to any limitations. Social workers should draw on relevant statutes, regulations, and ethical standards of the profession when developing confidentiality policies.

Ideally, social workers should inform clients of their confidentiality policies early in the social worker–client relationship. In most cases this can occur during the first meeting with a client. There are some times, however, when this may not be practical—for example, when a new client is in a state of crisis or when the social worker provides services in an emergency. In these situations, social workers should inform clients of their confidentiality policies as soon as possible. Also, occasions arise during the course of their work with clients when it is appropriate to reacquaint them with confidentiality policies (for example, when a social worker receives an unusual request for confidential information or is particularly concerned about protecting a third party from harm).

It is most often preferable for social workers to inform clients of their confidentiality policies both orally and in writing. A written summary of a social worker's confidentiality policies can help clients retain the information over time. Clients may be so overwhelmed during their first meeting with a social worker that they find it difficult to remember all the information that the social worker presented. In addition, a written summary signed by the client provides documentation that the social worker conveyed this information to the client.

A social worker's explanations of confidentiality policy should address a number of topics. Depending on the setting, these topics can include

- the importance of confidentiality in the social worker–client relationship (a brief statement of why the social worker treats the subject of confidentiality so seriously)

- laws, ethical standards, and regulations pertaining to confidentiality (relevant federal, state, and local laws and regulations; ethical standards in social work)
- measures the social worker will take to protect clients' confidentiality (storing records in a secure location, limiting colleagues' and outside parties' access to records)
- circumstances in which the social worker would be obligated to disclose confidential information (for example, to comply with mandatory reporting laws or a court order, to protect a third party from harm or the client from self-injury)
- procedures that will be used to obtain clients' informed consent for the release of confidential information and any exceptions to this (a summary of the purpose and importance of and the steps involved in informed consent)
- the procedures for sharing information with colleagues for consultation, supervision, and coordination of services (a summary of the roles of consultation, supervision, and coordination of services and why confidential information might be shared)
- access that third-party payers (insurers) or employee assistance program (EAP) staff will have to clients' records (social workers' policy for sharing information with managed care companies, insurance company representatives, utilization review personnel, and staff of EAPs)
- disclosure of confidential information by telephone, computer, fax machine, e-mail, and the Internet
- access to agency facilities and clients by outside parties (for example, people who come to the agency to attend meetings or participate in a tour)
- audiotaping and videotaping of clients.

## STANDARD 1.07(f)

*When social workers provide counseling services to families, couples, or groups, social workers should seek agreement among the parties involved concerning each individual's right to confidentiality and obligation to preserve the confidentiality of information shared by others. Social workers should inform participants in family, couples, or group counseling that social workers cannot guarantee that all participants will honor such agreements.*

Social workers who provide counseling services to families, couples, or groups face special confidentiality issues. In addition to the usual exceptions to confidentiality found in individual counseling (such as social workers' obligation to disclose information in certain exceptional circumstances involving threats to harm third parties, prevention of suicide, and compliance with mandatory reporting laws and court orders), participants in family, couples, and group counseling also face the possibility that other participants will not respect the right to confidentiality. Social workers should inform clients that they cannot guarantee that other participants will not share information from family, couples, or group counseling with third parties.

Social workers who provide such clinical services have an obligation to seek agreement among the parties involved in counseling concerning each individual's right to confidentiality and the obligation to respect the confidentiality of information shared by others. Practitioners should consider preparing forms that explain the importance of confidentiality and request each participant's agreement to honor the others' right to confidentiality. For example, "I understand that confidentiality and privacy are basic to building trust among group members. I agree to keep confidential what other group members share, and I will not talk about what is shared during the group with others outside the group" (Houston-Vega, Nuehring, & Daguio, 1997, p. C-56).

There is no consensus in the legal profession as to whether clients who disclose confidential information in the context of family, couples, or group counseling forfeit their right to have this confidentiality protected during legal proceedings (such as lawsuits involving personal injury or malpractice claims and custody or paternity disputes). Some lawyers argue that a client who discloses information to third parties in family, couples, or group counseling forfeits the right to have confidentiality protected because of his or her clear willingness to share this information with others. Others argue, however, that this sort of disclosure should not invalidate this right (Meyer et al., 1988).

Some courts have ruled that group therapy involves an expectation of privacy and that confidential information should be protected during legal proceedings (Meyer et al., 1988; Reamer, 1994). In a case involving marital therapy, the Connecticut Appeals Court rejected the husband's argument that confidential information shared by the wife with the couple's therapist was not privileged and should have been disclosed in court. The husband had appealed the outcome of divorce and custody proceedings and wanted to introduce the therapist's testimony to support his arguments. He claimed that the disclosures made by his wife occurred during marital counseling rather than "psychological counseling" and therefore were not privileged. The appeals court held that the wife's communications were privileged and, because she had not waived the privilege, the therapist could not testify about her sessions with the wife or her sessions with the couple ("Psychologist–Patient Privilege," 1991). Because laws vary from state to state and case law is sometimes inconsistent, social workers should consult a lawyer to determine the current status in their state of clients' right to privileged communication in family, couples, and group counseling (VandeCreek, Knapp, & Herzog, 1988).

### STANDARD 1.07(g)

*Social workers should inform clients involved in family, couples, marital, or group counseling of the social worker's, employer's, and agency's policy concerning the social worker's disclosure of confidential information among the parties involved in the counseling.*

Social workers who provide family, couples, marital, or group counseling should develop policies on sharing confidential information among the parties involved in the counseling. First, social workers who provide family, couples, or marital counseling need to clarify their policy (or their employer's or agency's policy) concerning the handling of "family secrets," particularly when a family member, a partner, or a spouse approaches the social worker to discuss an issue that he or she does not want shared with the others involved in the counseling. For example, a social worker who provided marital counseling to a couple received a telephone call from the husband, who requested an opportunity to meet with the social worker individually to discuss "a very personal matter that I don't feel comfortable discussing with my wife during counseling." It turned out that the husband was having an extramarital affair and wanted to discuss with the social worker how to end the affair. The social worker had to decide whether to meet with the husband individually and whether she would respect the husband's request for confidentiality.

Social workers' policies on this issue vary. Many practitioners, perhaps the majority, will not provide individual counseling to clients they are seeing in family, couples, or marital therapy because this can introduce clinical complexity (for example, problems related to confidentiality, the need for couples and family members to address their issues in therapy openly as a family or couple, or perceptions by clients that the social worker favors one party over another or is colluding with one party against another). These social workers explain to clients at the beginning of the therapeutic relationship that the family or couple is the client and they will not meet with the participants individually; any participant who wants individual counseling can ask for a referral to another practitioner. This may be accompanied by a statement that the social worker does not keep secrets and that it is important for the participants to be able to raise issues openly in the context of the counseling.

Some practitioners are willing to meet individually with participants in family, couples, or marital counseling sessions if—and only if—all the participants agree at the beginning of the counseling that this is an acceptable policy. Social workers who favor this approach typically explain that anyone who is seen individually will be regarded as a separate client with a separate case record and with an individual client's customary rights to confidentiality. That is, other participants in the family, couples, or group counseling will not have access to the case record involving the individual counseling, and any information shared within the context of the individual counseling will be considered confidential.

This is a complex and controversial issue. At present social workers disagree about the most appropriate way to handle requests for individual counseling made by participants in family, couples, or group counseling. In light of practitioners' different perspectives on the issue, they are, at the very least, obligated to explain to clients their policy (or their employer's or agency's policy) concerning the disclosure of confidential information among all parties involved in the counseling.

The second consideration concerning confidential information involves social workers who provide family counseling with minor children. As part of family counseling, social workers may spend time individually with a child. They should explain to clients how they will handle information shared by children during such individual counseling sessions. Many practitioners explain to family members, and especially to parents, that discussions they have with children in the parents' absence will be considered confidential, subject to the customary limitations (the obligation to disclose information if a child talks about harming himself or herself or others, in response to a court order, or to comply with a local law). Although the child will be encouraged to discuss his or her concerns in the context of family counseling, ordinarily the social worker will not share information disclosed during an individual counseling session. Parents who have legal custody, however, may have a legal right to inspect case records pertaining to their children unless there is compelling evidence that the children would be at risk of serious harm or the child is considered under the law to be a "mature" or "emancipated" minor.

Finally, social workers who provide group counseling typically have a firm policy that they will not talk individually with any group member about any other group member. This policy enhances trust among group members and avoids any perception of favoritism on the social worker's part or special alliances between the social worker and certain individual clients. There may be an occasional exception to this policy—for example, when a group counseling client also is receiving individual counseling from the social worker facilitating the group and the client feels the need to talk to the social worker about how to handle some troubling interpersonal dynamics in the group. Social workers are obligated to explain to group counseling participants how they handle such situations; under what, if any, circumstances other group members would be discussed in individual counseling sessions; and the extent to which this information would be considered confidential.

## STANDARD 1.07(h)

*Social workers should not disclose confidential information to third-party payers unless clients have authorized such disclosure.*

Social workers routinely receive requests from third-party payers such as insurance and managed care companies for information about clients. Such information may include details of clients' mental health symptoms, psychiatric and other mental health treatment history, clinical diagnosis, and treatment plan. Ordinarily, third-party payers ask for this information to review requests for mental health and other social services for which clients may be eligible under their health insurance coverage.

Social workers should obtain clients' informed consent before disclosing confidential information to third-party payers. Consistent with standards 1.03(a), (b), and (c), social workers should provide clients with a clear explanation of the purpose of the consent, risks related to it (for example, office staff who serve the third-party payer would have access to the confidential information), reasonable alternatives (for example, limiting the amount of detail shared with the third-party payer or bypassing the third-party payer entirely by paying for services out of pocket), clients' right to refuse or withdraw consent, and the time frame covered by the consent. Some social workers also include statements in the informed consent form used for this purpose indicating that the client understands that the social worker cannot be responsible for the protection of the client's confidential information once it is shared with the third-party payer, and that the client releases the social worker from any liability connected with a breach of confidentiality by a third-party payer (sometimes called a "hold harmless" clause).

## STANDARD 1.07(i)

*Social workers should not discuss confidential information in any setting unless privacy can be ensured. Social workers should not discuss confidential information in public or semipublic areas such as hallways, waiting rooms, elevators, and restaurants.*

Ideally, social workers would discuss confidential information only in sound-proofed settings where eavesdropping cannot occur. In reality, they sometimes find themselves in circumstances in which confidential information needs to be discussed, or it would be convenient to discuss, but there is a risk that the conversation would be overheard by others. This can occur, for example, when social workers suddenly and unexpectedly encounter in a hallway or elevator a colleague with whom they need to consult but have been unable to reach. It is understandable that the colleagues would want to take advantage of this opportunity to discuss pressing issues.

In one case a relatively inexperienced social worker in a family services agency had been providing counseling to an adolescent who was using drugs. When the social worker learned that the client had made an unsuccessful suicide attempt, he was eager to consult with his supervisor, whom he had not been able to locate. The social worker unexpectedly encountered his supervisor in the agency's hallway, told her about the client's suicide attempt, and asked for advice about how best to proceed. Unbeknown to the social worker, another of the agency's clients, who knew the client from school, was sitting in a nearby office and overheard the entire conversation.

In some situations social workers have control over privacy for their discussions of confidential information. With some effort, they can avoid discussing confidential information in agency hallways, waiting rooms, and elevators; in restaurants; at professional conferences; and so on. In other settings, however, it is difficult for social workers to protect the privacy of their discussions of confidential information. For example, some agencies do not provide social workers with individual or private offices. Staff may share an office or have unenclosed or only semipartitioned office space. Although social workers may not have the administrative authority to alter such architecture and office design, they should at least bring their concerns to the attention of appropriate administrators in an effort to have the issue addressed properly (see standards 3.09[c] and [d]).

## STANDARD 1.07(j)

*Social workers should protect the confidentiality of clients during legal proceedings to the extent permitted by law. When a court of law or other legally authorized body orders social workers to disclose confidential or privileged information without a client's consent and such disclosure could cause harm to the client, social workers should request that the court withdraw the order or limit the order as narrowly as possible or maintain the records under seal, unavailable for public inspection.*

There are many circumstances in which social workers may be asked or ordered to disclose confidential information, especially in the context of civil or criminal proceedings. Examples include social workers who are subpoenaed to testify in

- malpractice cases in which a client has sued another services provider (for example, a physician). The defendant's lawyer may subpoena the client's social worker to have him or her testify about comments the client made during counseling sessions. The defense lawyer may attempt to produce evidence that the lawsuit merely reflects the client's emotional instability, irrational tendencies, or vindictiveness; the defense also may try to show that the client has a history of mental health problems that preceded the mental health problems the client has alleged were caused by the defendant in the case. Defense lawyers may use this same strategy in other tort cases in which a social worker's client claims to have been wronged or injured by the actions of another party (for example, as a result of a workplace injury or automobile accident).

- divorce proceedings in which a social worker is subpoenaed by one spouse who believes that the social worker's testimony about confidential communications will support his or her claims against the other spouse.

- custody disputes in which one parent subpoenas a social worker who has worked with one or both parents, believing that the social worker's testimony will support his or her claim (for example, testimony concerning comments made during a counseling session about one parent's allegedly abusive behavior).

- paternity cases in which, for example, the child's birth mother subpoenas the putative father's social worker, believing that the social worker's testimony concerning the client's comments made during a counseling session about the couple's sexual relationship may support the birth mother's claim.

- criminal cases in which a prosecutor or defense attorney subpoenas a social worker to testify about the defendant's comments during counseling sessions.

Social workers may be asked to disclose confidential information during the discovery phase of a legal case or during the court hearing itself. Discovery is a pretrial procedure by which one party obtains information (facts and documents, for example) about the other. For example, during discovery a social worker may be asked to testify in a deposition under oath. In a deposition an attorney poses questions in the same form used in court. Depositions, known as "interrogatories," also may be taken in written form.

Social workers are obligated to protect clients' confidentiality during such legal proceedings to the extent permitted by law. To do so, they need to understand the concepts of privileged communication and subpoena. The concept of privilege concerns the admissibility of information in court, especially the extent to which courts may compel disclosure of confidential information during legal proceedings. The right of privileged communication—which assumes that a professional cannot disclose confidential information during legal proceedings without a client's consent—originated in British common law, under which no "gentleman" could be required to testify against another individual in court. Among professionals the attorney–client privilege was the first to be recognized, then the courts and various state legislatures eventually granted the right of privileged communication to clients of other groups of professionals, such as physicians, psychiatrists, psychologists, social workers, and clergy (Meyer et al., 1988; Reamer, 1994; Wilson, 1978).

Many states have enacted legislation granting the right of privileged communication to social workers' clients during proceedings in state courts. Further, in the landmark case of *Jaffe v. Redmond* (1996), the U.S. Supreme Court ruled that clinical social workers and their clients have the right to privileged communication in federal courts as well (Alexander, 1997).

In general, courts insist that four conditions be met in order for information to be considered privileged (Wigmore, 1961):

1. The communication must originate in a confidence that it will not be disclosed;
2. The element of confidentiality must be essential to the full and satisfactory maintenance of the relationship between the parties;
3. The relation must be one which in the opinion of the community ought to be sedulously fostered; and
4. The injury that would inure to the relationship by the disclosure of the communication must be greater than the benefit thereby gained for the correct disposal of litigation. (p. 52)

Social workers who receive a subpoena to produce records or testify concerning confidential information should attempt to protect clients' confidentiality to the greatest extent possible. If the social worker is subpoenaed in a federal case or by a state court in a state that recognizes the social worker–client privilege, protecting client confidentiality may be easier.

Social workers must understand that it can be a mistake to disclose the information requested in a subpoena. Often social workers can legitimately argue that the requested information should not be disclosed (perhaps because the client has not provided consent or because of the damage this will cause to the social worker–client relationship) or can be obtained from some other source. A subpoena itself does not require a social worker to disclose information. Rather, a subpoena is a request for information, and the request may not be an appropriate one. Lawyers can issue subpoenas very easily, sometimes as a form of harassment, and may request the disclosure of information that they have no legal right to command (Grossman, 1978; Wilson, 1978).

Social workers who face subpoenas should follow several guidelines (Austin et al., 1990; Reamer, 1994):

- Social workers should not release any information unless they are sure they have been authorized to do so (for example, in writing or in response to a court order).
- If it is unknown whether the privilege has been waived, social workers should claim the privilege to protect the client's confidentiality.
- If a social worker employs an assistant or trainee, the claim of privilege should extend to this individual, although the court might rule that unlicensed practitioners are not covered by the privilege.
- At a deposition, when no judge is present, social workers may have their own attorney present or choose to follow the advice and direction of the client's attorney.

- If a social worker's information about a client is embarrassing, damaging, or immaterial, written permission can be obtained to discuss the information with the client's attorney.

- Unless required to produce records or documents only (as with a *subpoena duces tecum*), social workers must appear at the location specified in the subpoena.

- If social workers are asked to appear in court to disclose confidential information and lack a signed release from the client, they should write a letter to the judge stating their wish to comply with the request but that the client has not waived the privilege. The court may or may not order disclosure of the information.

Several strategies can be used in an effort to protect clients' confidentiality during legal proceedings. If social workers believe that a subpoena is inappropriate (for example, because it requests information that should be considered privileged under state law), they can arrange for a lawyer (or perhaps the client's lawyer) to file a motion to quash the subpoena, which is an attempt to have the court rule that the request contained in the subpoena is inappropriate. A judge may issue a protective order explicitly limiting the disclosure of specific privileged information during the discovery phase of a case. In addition, social workers, perhaps through a lawyer, may request an in camera review (a review in the judge's chambers) of records or documents they believe should not be disclosed in open court. The judge can then decide whether the information should be revealed in open court and made a matter of public record.

### STANDARD 1.07(k)

*Social workers should protect the confidentiality of clients when responding to requests from members of the media.*

There are various circumstances in which social workers might be asked for confidential information by members of the media (newspaper, television, or radio reporters and staff):

- A newspaper reporter was investigating the arrest of a prominent elected official for domestic violence. A relative of the victim told the reporter that the official "has had a problem for a long time and has been in counseling" and mentioned the name of his social worker. The reporter contacted the social worker and asked her for information about the official's history of domestic violence.

- A television reporter was preparing a series on sexual abuse of children. The reporter contacted a local social worker who specialized in the treatment of perpetrators of childhood sexual abuse. During a recorded interview with the social worker, the reporter asked the social worker to describe in detail the types of perpetrators with whom she had worked.

- A nationally syndicated television talk show host and his staff were preparing a show on eating disorders. One of the show's producers contacted a social worker who specializes in the treatment of eating disorders and asked him to consider appearing on the show with one or two of his clients.

Social workers who are approached by members of the media must protect the confidentiality of their clients. If a reporter discovers that a person who is the subject of a story has been in treatment with a social worker and asks the social worker for specific information about the client, the social worker should respond by informing the reporter that, because of confidentiality requirements, he or she is not permitted to confirm or deny that the individual is or ever has been a client. If a social worker is asked by a reporter to talk about the types of clients she has worked with (for example, perpetrators of childhood sexual abuse), the social worker should speak only in very general terms, without disclosing any details or specific information that might enable the reporter or members of the public to identify individual clients.

Social workers may discuss specific clients or cases with the media only when clients have provided informed consent. In the example above, the elected official in treatment with a social worker to address domestic violence issues may want the social worker to talk somewhat openly with members of the media about the progress he has made in an effort to reassure the public during a political campaign. In the third example, the client may want to appear on a television talk show to discuss her clinical issues and may want the social worker to accompany her and participate in the discussion. In such exceptional circumstances, social workers must be especially careful to obtain truly informed consent. They should discuss with clients in detail the possible risks involved in having the social worker talk openly with members of the media (for example, the risk of public embarrassment or harassment or of undermining clinical progress) as well as possible benefits (the possible therapeutic value of discussing one's issues openly, the opportunity to educate the public about an important issue).

## STANDARD 1.07(l)

*Social workers should protect the confidentiality of clients' written and electronic records and other sensitive information. Social workers should take reasonable steps to ensure that clients' records are stored in a secure location and that clients' records are not available to others who are not authorized to have access.*

It is essential for social workers to ensure that clients' confidential written and electronic records are protected. There are several possible risks. With respect to written records, social workers should not leave case files in public or semipublic areas, available to people who are not authorized to have access to them. In agencies and offices, records should be stored in a secure location under lock and key.

- A clinical social worker in a community mental health center was scheduled to see five clients during the workday. He placed the clients' files on top of his desk at the beginning of the day, on the side closest to the chair in which clients typically sat. One of the clients glanced at the social worker's desk during the counseling session and read the names of the other clients that appeared in large letters on the tab of each case file.

- A clinical social worker in a group private practice was preparing a letter describing the progress a client was making in substance abuse counseling. The letter was to be sent to the client's employer, with the client's consent. At the end of the day the social worker had not finished the letter. She placed her notes in the case record and placed the record on top of her desk to remind her to resume work on the letter the following morning. Later that evening, a custodian entered the office to do his work. When the custodian picked up the wastepaper basket under the social worker's desk, he glanced at the desk and recognized the client's name on the outside of the case record. The client was the custodian's brother-in-law. The custodian then read the entire confidential case record.

- A clinical social worker in private practice in a large city took the commuter train home at the end of the day. The social worker took a client's case record with him so that he could review his notes that evening in preparation for a court hearing the following morning. During the long train ride, the social worker pulled out the case record and began reading it. He was unaware that the passenger next to him furtively read portions of the case notes.

- A social worker who was a case manager for an EAP took home two case records so she could finish some paper work. After dinner, she sat at the kitchen table to work on the project. Later that evening, she and her spouse went to a party. While the couple was out, the baby-sitter went to the kitchen for a snack, found the case records, and leafed through them.

As a general rule, social workers should not remove case records from the workplace (except, for example, when the case record must be brought to court in response to a court order or subpoena). Within the workplace, social workers should always place case records in a secure location, unavailable to people who do not have authorized access to them.

Social workers also need to be vigilant about the protection of clients' electronic records. Access to computer-based files must be restricted (for example, by secure passwords). In addition, social workers should take steps to ensure that confidential information displayed on computer monitors cannot be seen by members of the public or other unauthorized people. Monitors on secretaries' or social workers' desks, for example, should be positioned so that unauthorized people cannot view the screen.

## STANDARD 1.07(m)

*Social workers should take precautions to ensure and maintain the confidentiality of information transmitted to other parties through the use of computers, electronic mail, facsimile machines, telephones and telephone answering machines, and other electronic or computer technology. Disclosure of identifying information should be avoided whenever possible.*

Technological developments have made it possible for social workers to transmit confidential information quickly and efficiently via various electronic media. Along with this convenience and efficiency come considerable risks, primarily involving the inappropriate disclosure of confidential information. For example, social workers who use the Internet for professional purposes need to be careful to protect clients' privacy and confidentiality. Practitioners who plan to use the Internet to communicate confidential or other sensitive information should first obtain clients' informed consent and inform clients about the potential risks involved (such as security breaches).

Similarly, social workers should be aware of several risks associated with the use of fax machines. The confidentiality of faxed communications can be breached in several ways. The receiving fax machine may not be in a secure location (out in the open in a secretary's office, for example); unauthorized parties thus may have access to faxed confidential communications. In addition, the receiving fax machine's telephone number could be misdialed inadvertently, sending the confidential communication to an inappropriate destination.

Social workers should avoid sending confidential information via fax machine. When faxing confidential information seems necessary (as in an emergency), social workers should notify the recipient by telephone that a fax is being sent and obtain the recipient's agreement to go to the fax machine immediately to await the document's arrival. Ideally, social workers should obtain clients' informed consent authorizing them to convey information via fax. Further, the cover sheet should include a statement to alert recipients to the confidential nature of the communication, along with the sender's telephone number—for example,

> The documents accompanying this fax transmission may contain confidential information. The information is intended for the use of only the individual(s) or entity(ies) named above. If you are not the intended recipient, you are advised that any disclosure, copying, distribution, or the taking of any action based on the contents of this information is prohibited. If you have received this fax in error, please notify us immediately by telephone at the above number to arrange for return of the documents.

Telephones and telephone answering devices also can be problematic. Social workers should not discuss confidential information on cellular telephones, for example, because of possible scanner eavesdropping by third parties. Social workers also should be careful not to include confidential information in a message on a telephone answering device when it is possible that the message could be heard by a third party (for example, another member of a client's household or an office mate of a colleague for whom a social worker leaves a message). In fact, social workers should discuss with clients what kind of information should be left on the clients' telephone answering devices. In one case a social worker in private practice left a detailed message on a client's answering machine, including information about where to seek additional help related to the client's substance abuse problem. The client's partner was unaware of the client's problem until she listened to the social worker's message before the client arrived home. In another case a social worker employed in a public child welfare agency left a detailed message concerning a client on a colleague's home answering machine; the colleague was under contract with the public child welfare agency to provide clinical services to the child in the agency's custody. The colleague's spouse arrived home first that evening and listened to the message, which contained considerable confidential information.

### STANDARD 1.07(n)

*Social workers should transfer or dispose of clients' records in a manner that protects clients' confidentiality and is consistent with state statutes governing records and social work licensure.*

Social workers who transfer a case record to another practitioner should take steps to ensure that unauthorized individuals do not have access to confidential information. Delivery services should be selected based on their ability to protect the confidentiality of the information.

Social workers should dispose of records, when appropriate (see standard 3.04[d]), in a manner that protects client confidentiality. Records should be shredded or otherwise destroyed so that unauthorized individuals cannot gain access to confidential information. In one case an agency disposed of old client files by placing them, unshredded, in the trash. The trash hauler had a collision with an automobile on the way to the local dump and portions of case records were strewn over the highway.

### STANDARD 1.07(o)

*Social workers should take reasonable precautions to protect client confidentiality in the event of the social worker's termination of practice, incapacitation, or death.*

Social workers need to anticipate the possibility that at some point they may not be able to continue working with clients because of illness, disability, incapacitation, or death. To ensure continuity of service and to protect client's confidential records, social workers should make arrangements with colleagues to assume at least initial responsibility for their cases in the event they are unable to continue practicing. This may take the form of oral or written agreements with colleagues or stipulations that appear in a plan the social worker develops with the assistance of a lawyer (for example, designating a personal representative who will handle the social worker's professional affairs). Many experts recommend that social workers prepare a will that includes plans for the transfer or disposition of cases in the event of the practitioner's death or incapacitation. The will can provide for an executor or trustee who will maintain records for a certain period (30 days, for example), at the end of which the social worker's practice and all records will be sold to a designated colleague (typically for a nominal fee). A major advantage of such arrangements is that they limit unauthorized persons' access to confidential information.

Social workers who expect to retire or move to another community should give clients as much notice as possible and make arrangements to respond to telephone calls or other inquiries from clients (such as arranging for a colleague to respond). Social workers who plan to refer clients to other providers should always give clients several names to avoid the appearance that they are actively "steering" clients. Selected colleagues, supervisors, and administrators should be acquainted with details concerning the handling of the social worker's affairs in the event that he or she terminates practice or becomes unavailable.

In one case a social worker in private practice in a rural community died without having made any arrangements for a colleague to step in and handle clients' matters. Several of the social worker's clients were in crisis at the time of the death and did not know where to turn for assistance. In desperation, a member of the social worker's family looked through the clients' files in an effort to provide them with help, thereby breaching the clients' confidentiality.

## STANDARD 1.07(p)

*Social workers should not disclose identifying information when discussing clients for teaching or training purposes unless the client has consented to disclosure of confidential information.*

Social work educators and trainers often use case material to illustrate conceptual points, a widely used and respected pedagogical approach in all professions. When presenting case material in classroom or agency settings or at professional workshops or conferences, social workers must be careful to protect clients' confidentiality—identifying information should not be disclosed without clients' informed consent. Social workers who present case illustrations during a lecture, class discussion, workshop, or conference presentation should not mention clients' names and should disguise or alter case-related details to ensure that the audience cannot identify the clients or other individuals involved. One common strategy is to change details concerning clients' gender, age, ethnicity, clinical history, geographic setting, and family circumstances in a way that does not detract from the educational or training point or interfere with the educator's or trainer's goal. Any written case material that a social work educator or trainer distributes should be similarly disguised.

Sometimes social work educators or trainers present videotaped or audiotaped material, especially taped clinical sessions. Such material should not be presented unless clients have provided informed consent to the taping itself (see standard 1.03[f]) and to the presentation of the tape to an audience. With videotapes, it may be possible to protect client confidentiality by taping clients from an angle that limits their visibility or using technological devices to blur distinguishing characteristics or disguise voices, but in some instances (group or family therapy, for example) this may be difficult.

Social workers who seek clients' informed consent to disclose identifying information during teaching or training must use their best judgment as to the clients' ability and competence to make a sound decision. Clients who are asked for their consent may be vulnerable for clinical or other reasons; they may feel pressured to provide their consent to the disclosure when it is not in their best interest to do so. Social workers must be careful not to exploit clients or take advantage of their vulnerability.

Social work educators' responsibility also extends to their students. That is, social work educators who arrange for or encourage students' presentation of case material must inform the students about their obligation to protect client confidentiality. Social work educators should discuss with their students methods they can use to disguise case material and avoid disclosing identifying information without client consent.

## STANDARD 1.07(q)

*Social workers should not disclose identifying information when discussing clients with consultants unless the client has consented to disclosure of confidential information or there is a compelling need for such disclosure.*

Social workers encounter many situations in which consultation with colleagues may be helpful or necessary. A social worker who specializes in the treatment of eating disorders may be working with a client who has a serious substance abuse problem. She may want to consult with a colleague with expertise in the treatment of substance abuse problems to discuss how these issues might be addressed effectively within the context of treatment for an eating disorder. A social worker in a nursing home who is providing services to a clinically depressed elderly client may want to consult with a psychiatrist about effective treatment approaches.

Two important confidentiality issues can arise during consultation. First, clients routinely should be informed, ideally at the beginning of treatment, that social workers sometimes find it useful or necessary to consult with colleagues to provide the most effective services possible. Clients have the right to know that this is how a professional social worker functions. Second, whenever possible, social workers who find it necessary to disclose identifying information to a consultant should obtain clients' informed consent in advance. This may not always be possible, particularly in a crisis or emergency, but every effort should be made to obtain a client's consent before disclosing any identifying or other confidential information.

Social workers often can obtain consultation without disclosing identifying information. To provide useful feedback and advice, consultants may need to know only basic, nonidentifying demographic and clinical information. Social workers can often obtain valuable consultation without disclosing clients' names and by limiting their description of clients to clinically relevant details of clients' age, ethnicity, family circumstances, clinical issues, and so forth. Identifying information should not be disclosed unless there is a compelling reason to do so (see standard 2.05[c]). There are times, however, when consultants would be able to provide more useful feedback or advice if they were to know clients' names, particularly when the consultant has had prior contact with the client. Ordinarily, social workers should obtain clients' consent before disclosing such identifying information to consultants, but exceptions may be necessary during a genuine crisis or emergency.

## STANDARD 1.07(r)

*Social workers should protect the confidentiality of deceased clients consistent with the preceding standards.*

Social workers sometimes receive requests for confidential information about former clients who have died. Surviving family members of a client who has committed suicide may ask for information to help them cope with their loss, or social workers may be subpoenaed in a legal case involving a dispute among family members concerning the former client's will. A reporter or law enforcement official may request information about a deceased client who was the victim of a serious crime, or an Internal Revenue Service agent may seek information about a deceased client's lifestyle.

Social workers must be diligent in their efforts to protect the confidentiality of deceased clients. They should not disclose confidential information unless they have received proper legal authorization to do so (for example, from the legal representative of the client's estate or by a court order). Disclosure of confidential information without such authorization would constitute a violation of the former client's confidentiality rights.

In a highly publicized case, a clinical social worker was approached by a reporter after a client's death. She made the mistake of disclosing confidential information to the reporter and was subsequently sanctioned by her state licensing board. As part of the sanction, the social worker was required to write a comprehensive guide on confidentiality issues in social work and mail it to all licensed social workers in the state where she practiced. The preface to the guide included the following statement (some details have been altered to protect the social worker's privacy):

> I am a clinical social worker in private practice specializing in treating people with substance abuse problems. Most of my 15 years of experience has been in substance abuse treatment programs. I serve a large suburban area of about 70,000 people.
>
> Two years ago I thought confidentiality ended at death and spoke to news reporters about a dramatic incident involving a case. I soon realized that this had breached the confidentiality of a client. This booklet is written as part of a sanction for that ethical misconduct.

Social workers who receive requests for confidential information about deceased clients may need to seek legal advice before disclosing any information. When disclosure of confidential information has been authorized or is considered appropriate, practitioners should disclose the least amount of information necessary to achieve the purposes of the disclosure (see standards 1.07[c] and 2.05[c]).

## ACCESS TO RECORDS

### STANDARD 1.08(a)

*Social workers should provide clients with reasonable access to records concerning the clients. Social workers who are concerned that clients' access to their records could cause serious misunderstanding or harm to the client should provide assistance in interpreting the records and consultation with the client regarding the records. Social workers should limit clients' access to their records, or portions of their records, only in exceptional circumstances when there is compelling evidence that such access would cause serious harm to the client. Both clients' requests and the rationale for withholding some or all of the record should be documented in clients' files.*

On occasion clients ask their social workers if they can see copies of their clinical record. Clients may be curious about the language or terms their social workers have used to describe their situations or symptoms, or they may be concerned about how other individuals or agencies that have access to the records (courts of law or insurance providers, for instance) might interpret entries in the records.

- A 38-year-old man, a social worker, sought counseling from another social worker to help him deal with what he described as "overwhelming anxiety." With the exception of a small copayment, the counseling was paid for by the client's health insurance provider. The client was concerned that a colleague of his who worked for the health insurance provider approving mental health benefits would see some of the paper work in his case. The client asked the therapist to let him see the case record.

- A 42-year-old woman was referred to a social worker by the court, which had placed the woman on probation after her third arrest for shoplifting. The judge expected a progress report from the social worker at the conclusion of counseling. After five weeks of counseling, the client asked the social worker whether she could read his clinical notes.

- The parents of an 11-year-old boy with serious behavioral issues arranged for their son to receive counseling from a social worker. According to the parents, the boy had suddenly become "very hard to manage" and was "beginning to hang out with a tough crowd." The parents said they were concerned that their son was starting to experiment with drugs. After two months of counseling, the parents informed the social worker that they would like to see a copy of the record.

As a general rule, social workers are obligated to provide clients with reasonable access to their records. Practitioners have come to recognize that clients have a right to know what social workers record about their life circumstances, mental health symptoms, treatment plans, and progress. Earlier in the profession's history, relatively few social workers believed that clients should have the right to examine their own records, and records were typically viewed as agency property. More recently, this thinking has evolved: Social workers now understand why clients may want or need to see their records and that such disclosure can be therapeutically beneficial if handled properly. Shortly before the ratification of the 1979 NASW *Code of Ethics*, Wilson (1978) noted,

> Only a few short years ago, the social work profession simply assumed that a record was the private property of the professional or the agency, and that was that. A few therapists occasionally advocated client participation in recording as part of the therapeutic process, and others began using the video-recorded interview as a means of allowing the individual to study how he communicates and to provide feedback regarding the therapist's effectiveness. However, such procedures were considered experimental rather than routine. . . . There will be increasing pressure from consumers (and also as a result of the ethical philosophy of the social work profession) for all settings to be more open in sharing record materials with clients. (pp. 83, 85)

At times social workers may be concerned that clients' access to their records could be harmful or cause serious misunderstanding. This may occur because, in the social worker's judgment, the client is too fragile emotionally to handle reading the social worker's notes about the clinical situation, or the client is likely to misunderstand what the social worker has written. With few exceptions, even in these circumstances social workers have an obligation to provide clients with access to their records. When practitioners are concerned that access could be harmful or lead to some misunderstanding, they should talk with the client about the records' content and help him or her interpret the records. Only in the most extreme circumstances—when there is compelling evidence that a client's access to the records would cause serious harm—should social workers withhold records (or portions of records). This could occur, for example, when a social worker has evidence that a client is suicidal or homicidal and that providing the client with access to specific information in the case record would likely lead to serious harm. In such exceptional circumstances, both the client's request to see the record and the social worker's rationale for withholding some or all of it should be documented. Consultation with colleagues, supervisors, and legal counsel may be important in these situations, because there is widespread presumption that clients should have access to their records. Clients who are denied access to their records may have grounds for a lawsuit or ethics complaint.

Social workers should explore whether relevant regulations or statutes permit them to use professional discretion in deciding whether to provide clients with access to case records. For example, the federal Freedom of Information Act (1996) and similar laws in all states provide for client access to records maintained by the government, including public social work agencies. According to Saltzman and Proch (1990), "these laws usually allow people to obtain any records maintained by a public agency, whether or not they relate to them, unless access to one's own records would be harmful or access to records which relate to others is precluded by a confidentiality law" (p. 409).

Social workers should always explore clients' reasons for requesting access to their records. The reasons for these requests vary; clients simply may be curious about the social worker's perceptions and opinions, or they may be unhappy about the quality of some aspect of the treatment and want information that can be used against the social worker or agency in a lawsuit. Social workers routinely should inform clients of the emotional risk that can be associated with reading material in their records.

In one case a clinical social worker for a family services agency provided crisis intervention services to a woman who was depressed because of work-related problems. The client, who had been referred to the social worker through her company's EAP, said she was depressed because she faced racial discrimination at work. The social worker met with the client four times to help her address her symptoms and discuss various longer-term treatment options.

After the third session, the client contacted the social worker and asked to see his case notes. The client explained that she was suing her employer for racial discrimination she had experienced and wanted to give her lawyer a copy of the notes. The social worker was concerned that some of the entries would confuse or upset the client and told her that he had retained only the demographic information required by the EAP. The client ultimately filed an ethics complaint against the social worker, and the social worker was sanctioned for not providing his client with reasonable access to the clinical record. The social worker might have prevented the ethics complaint had he reviewed the *NASW Code of Ethics* and consulted with colleagues about the client's initial request.

Social workers who provide services to minor children need to be particularly careful to respond appropriately when parents or legal guardians request access to a child's clinical record. Many social workers explain to their minor clients and to their parents or guardians that the case record will be considered confidential, subject to the customary exceptions (for example, when a case record is subpoenaed during legal proceedings or there is a court order mandating disclosure of all or parts of a case record). This explanation often suffices and discourages parents and guardians from requesting access to the case record. Occasions may arise, however, when a parent or guardian insists on having access to the case record. In the absence of a local statute governing parents' and guardians' access to confidential information about their children, many lawyers argue that parents and guardians have a legal right to confidential information. That is, parents or guardians who have legal custody have a legal right to inspect case records pertaining to their children unless there is compelling evidence that the children would be at risk of serious harm or the child is considered under the law to be a mature or emancipated minor. As Saltzman and Proch (1990) concluded, "Generally parents are entitled to their children's records if the children would be entitled to the records themselves if they were adults. Records related to birth control, treatment for substance abuse, or treatment for venereal disease are generally excepted from this rule, however" (p. 409). Social workers should keep in mind that details they include in case records about children may be seen by their parents or guardians; the obligation to document the issues addressed and the services provided to children must be balanced with the obligation to protect children's privacy.

## STANDARD 1.08(b)

*When providing clients with access to their records, social workers should take steps to protect the confidentiality of other individuals identified or discussed in such records.*

It is not unusual for case records to contain confidential information about third parties. Whenever clients request access to their records, social workers should review the records to ensure that information shared with the client does not violate other individuals' right to confidentiality. This includes information in the case records obtained from third parties, for example, other service providers or clients' relatives. Confidential information about third parties should not be shared with clients unless the third parties have consented to such disclosure.

In one case a clinical social worker provided marriage counseling to a couple. With the clients' consent, the social worker occasionally met individually with each spouse. The social worker's case notes summarized both the marriage counseling and the individual counseling sessions.

Eventually the husband decided to seek counseling elsewhere. The husband's new counselor asked for a copy of the first social worker's case notes, which contained confidential references to the wife. The social worker obtained the wife's consent before forwarding a copy of the notes to the new practitioner. At the wife's request—and consistent with standard 1.08(b)—the social worker withheld several details in the case notes, specifically concerning the wife, that the wife did not feel comfortable disclosing to the new practitioner.

## SEXUAL RELATIONSHIPS

### STANDARD 1.09(a)

*Social workers should under no circumstances engage in sexual activities or sexual contact with current clients, whether such contact is consensual or forced.*

As discussed in the section on dual and multiple relationships, social workers must be vigilant in their efforts to maintain clear boundaries in their relationships with clients. This includes avoiding any sexual activities or contact with current clients. Any form of sexual activity or contact with clients is generally considered self-serving and exploitative regardless of the social worker's motives. Clients who become sexually involved with their social workers are likely to be confused about the nature and purposes of the relationship, and this is likely to be detrimental to them.

- A social worker at a neighborhood health center provided counseling to a woman who was being treated for a serious kidney ailment. The social worker and the client met weekly for about six weeks. The client often talked about how alone she felt and how eager she was for companionship. The social worker, who was attracted to his client, asked her if she would like to have dinner with him later in the week. The client accepted the invitation. Within three weeks, the social worker and the woman, who continued to be the social worker's client, began a sexual relationship.
- A social worker in private practice provided counseling to a man whose marriage was ending. After several months, the social worker—whose own marriage was in trouble—found herself fantasizing about having an affair with her client. Within two weeks the social worker and the client became sexually involved. At the ethics committee hearing, the social worker claimed that the client was not harmed by this consensual relationship.
- A school social worker provided counseling to a 17-year-old student who was having difficulty in her relationship with her parents. According to the social worker, he "gave into temptation when the student began behaving seductively." "I know what I did was wrong," he said. "At the time I managed to convince myself that this student was unusually mature and could handle this sort of relationship."

Allegations of sexual misconduct are among the most common made by clients who file ethics complaints against social workers (Reamer, 1997b). These complaints often allege that a social worker and client had sexual contact during the course of the professional–client relationship. On occasion social workers who have had complaints filed against them have argued that the sexual contact was a consensual and legitimate form of therapeutic intervention—that is, the social worker claims to have attempted, with the client's consent, to "help the client address intimacy issues" or "accept the fact that she is lovable." An alternative argument has been put forth that the sexual relationship was conducted independently of the professional–client relationship, that the social worker and client were able to distinguish between their sexual and professional relationships. Neither argument is credible. Social workers have an obligation to avoid sexual contact with clients whether such contact is consensual or forced.

## STANDARD 1.09(b)

*Social workers should not engage in sexual activities or sexual contact with clients' relatives or other individuals with whom clients maintain a close personal relationship when there is a risk of exploitation or potential harm to the client. Sexual activity or sexual contact with clients' relatives or other individuals with whom clients maintain a personal relationship has the potential to be harmful to the client and may make it difficult for the social worker and client to maintain appropriate professional boundaries. Social workers—not their clients, their clients' relatives, or other individuals with whom the client maintains a personal relationship—assume the full burden for setting clear, appropriate, and culturally sensitive boundaries.*

A social worker's sexual relationships with a client's relative or another person to whom the client is close may cause the client to feel betrayed and can undermine confidence in the social worker and the social work profession. Social workers are obligated primarily to protect clients' interests (see standard 1.01) and must avoid conflicts of interest that may be harmful to clients (see standards 1.06[a] and [b]).

In some cases social workers' relationships with clients' relatives or other individuals with whom clients have a close personal relationship are clearly inappropriate:

- A school social worker provided counseling to an 11-year-old student who was referred by a teacher. The student was having difficulty establishing and maintaining friendships and asked his teacher for help. After meeting with the student, the social worker arranged to meet with the student's mother, a single parent. During the course of the social worker's professional relationship with the student, the social worker began a sexual affair with the student's mother that continued after the termination of the social worker's professional relationship with the student.

- A social worker for a home health care agency provided casework services to an elderly woman who was recovering from heart surgery. During one of the home visits, the social worker met the client's adult son. Several weeks later, the client's son contacted the social worker and invited her to join him for dinner and a play. The social worker accepted the invitation, and the two began dating regularly and then began a sexual relationship. The social worker continued to provide professional services to the elderly woman during the course of her relationship with the client's son.

- A social worker in a community mental health setting provided counseling to a 27-year-old woman who was having difficulty in her relationship with her parents. About eight weeks after the professional–client relationship began, the social worker happened to meet the client's sister at a party in the community. Eventually the social worker and the client's sister began a sexual relationship, which began while the social worker was providing services to the woman's sister.

In each of these examples it is easy to imagine how the client might feel betrayed by the social worker's sexual relationship with the client's relative and how this relationship could interfere with the social worker's effectiveness. In other cases, however, social workers may disagree about whether a sexual relationship with a client's relative or other individual to whom a client is close is inappropriate. Below are examples that may generate disagreement among practitioners:

- A social worker employed by a state prison provided occasional counseling to an inmate serving a three-year sentence for assault with a deadly weapon. The social worker happened to meet the inmate's second cousin at a friend's party. The social worker and the inmate's cousin began dating and considered beginning a sexual relationship. The social worker learned from the inmate that he and his cousin had not had contact with each other in seven years and had no plans to resume contact.
- A social worker in a vocational training program provided supportive services to a 22-year-old man with a mental disability. The client participated in a sheltered workshop and had contact with the social worker every other week. The social worker also met occasionally with the client's parents. At a holiday dinner the social worker met a woman who was a "good friend" of the client's mother. The social worker and the woman began to date and planned to enter into a sexual relationship.

When social workers disagree or are unsure about the appropriateness of a sexual relationship with a client's relative or an individual to whom a client is close, it must be clear that the social worker assumes the full burden and considerable risk should he or she decide to enter into such a relationship. When faced with uncertainty, social workers who are considering entering into such a relationship should consult with knowledgeable colleagues and supervisors.

### STANDARD 1.09(c)

*Social workers should not engage in sexual activities or sexual contact with former clients because of the potential for harm to the client. If social workers engage in conduct contrary to this prohibition or claim that an exception to this prohibition is warranted because of extraordinary circumstances, it is social workers—not their clients—who assume the full burden of demonstrating that the former client has not been exploited, coerced, or manipulated, intentionally or unintentionally.*

The general presumption in social work is that practitioners should not enter into sexual relationships with former clients. First, it is not unusual for former clients to face challenging issues in their lives after the formal termination of the professional–client relationship. New emotional issues, relationship problems, or developmental crises, for example, may emerge, and former clients may find it useful to contact the social worker for assistance. The social worker's familiarity with the client's circumstances and the established relationship between the social worker and client may be especially helpful in such cases; "starting from scratch" with a new provider may be both inefficient and intimidating. Clearly, however, a social worker and former client who have entered into a sexual relationship could have difficulty resuming an effective professional–client relationship. Social workers and former clients who enter into sexual relationships after the termination of their professional–client relationship essentially forfeit resuming that relationship, and this may not be in the client's best interest.

Second, former clients may encounter less challenging new issues or problems in their lives and still may find it helpful to speculate about what their former social worker would have said about the matter. The former client may not feel the need to resume a formal relationship with the social worker; however, the client might find it helpful merely to reflect on the social worker's perspective. A sexual relationship between the social worker and the former client presumably would interfere with the former client's ability to draw on what he or she has learned from the social worker's professional expertise, given the shift from a professional to an intimate relationship. Thus, social workers should consider their clients as "clients in perpetuity": once a client, always a client.

In some exceptional circumstances, a sexual relationship with a former client may be permissible because of unusual and extraordinary circumstances:

- A social worker who earned a living as a researcher and program evaluator had a contract to evaluate a home-based, family intervention program. The social worker's primary contact at the agency was the executive director. Five years after the evaluation was completed, the social worker and the agency executive director happened to encounter each other at the home of a mutual friend. They discovered that each was "available" and decided to go out on a date; eventually they engaged in a sexual relationship. In their judgment a sexual relationship was not inappropriate because of the nonclinical nature of their original professional–client relationship and the amount of time that had passed since they had worked together.

- A hospital social worker had two relatively brief conversations with a patient who was being treated for a serious orthopedic problem. The social worker helped the patient arrange home-based health care to begin after discharge from the hospital. The social worker and patient spent a total of 30 minutes together during the patient's hospital stay and exclusively discussed logistical details of the discharge plan. About three years after the patient's hospital discharge, the social worker and former patient met each other at a swim club to which both belonged. They began dating and eventually began a sexual relationship. The social worker concluded that the sexual relationship was permissible because of the brief nature of their professional–client relationship and the fact that their professional–client relationship was concerned with discharge planning issues and not emotional or psychotherapeutic issues.

There is virtual consensus in the social work profession that practitioners involved in clinical relationships with clients (providing counseling or psychotherapeutic services) should not enter into sexual relationships with those clients after termination of the professional–client relationship. In some extraordinary circumstances, a sexual relationship with a former client may be permissible, but social workers who reach such a conclusion should be aware that they assume the full burden of demonstrating that the former client has not been exploited, coerced, or manipulated, intentionally or unintentionally.

Social workers who believe that an exception to this prohibition may be warranted should take several important factors into consideration:

- How much time has passed since termination of the professional–client relationship? Clearly, a sexual relationship that begins shortly after termination is more suspect than one that begins long after the social worker's services to the client have ended. This question is difficult to answer because there is no magical length of time that must elapse so that a sexual relationship can be "appropriate."
- To what extent is the client mentally competent and emotionally stable? A sexual relationship with a former client who has a lengthy history of emotional instability and vulnerability is a greater cause for concern than a relationship with a former client who is clearly competent and emotionally stable.
- What issues were addressed in the professional–client relationship? A sexual relationship after a professional–client relationship that involved discussion or examination of emotionally sensitive and intimate issues is more problematic than a relationship limited to such activities as program evaluation, fundraising, and political action.
- How long did the professional–client relationship last? Should a sexual relationship develop, a professional–client relationship that lasted for many months is a greater cause for concern than a relationship that lasted for 30 minutes.
- What circumstances surrounded the termination of the professional–client relationship? Was it terminated so that the social worker and the client could begin a sexual relationship, or did it come to a natural conclusion because the requisite work was done? The social worker must carefully examine the motives and circumstances surrounding the termination of the professional–client relationship (see standard 1.16[d]).
- To what extent is there foreseeable harm to the client or others as a result of a sexual relationship? How likely is it that the client could

be harmed by a sexual relationship, especially if that relationship ends unpleasantly? Could those who are close to the client—such as a spouse or partner—be harmed by a social worker's sexual relationship with the client? To what extent could the client's ability to trust social workers be harmed by the relationship? Is it likely that rumors about the relationship would undermine the profession's integrity?

Certainly these are difficult questions to answer. Social workers may answer them differently based on their particular education and training, professional experience, and personal philosophy. In the final analysis, social workers must recognize that there is a general proscription against sexual involvement with any former client and that, should they decide that exceptional circumstances justify a sexual relationship with a former client, social workers assume the full burden of responsibility.

## STANDARD 1.09(d)

*Social workers should not provide clinical services to individuals with whom they have had a prior sexual relationship. Providing clinical services to a former sexual partner has the potential to be harmful to the individual and is likely to make it difficult for the social worker and individual to maintain appropriate professional boundaries.*

Obviously, social workers have personal lives that may involve sexual relationships. Ideally, such relationships involve mutually intimate sharings of information and feelings. In its purest form, an intimate relationship between two people is not hierarchical in nature, with one person assuming more authority, power, or control than the other.

Moving from an intimate sexual relationship to a professional–client relationship can be detrimental to the client. Former lovers who become clients may find it difficult to shift from the role of an egalitarian partner in a relationship to a party who, to some degree, is in a dependent or subordinate position. No matter how much a social worker believes in empowering clients and engaging clients as equal partners in the helping relationship, clients are, by definition, in the position of someone asking for or required to receive assistance (a form of dependency), and the social worker is in the position of authority charged with providing assistance. This inescapable dynamic places clients in a vulnerable position that reflects the power imbalance in the relationship.

Confusion about the nature of the relationship could cause a client who was sexually involved with a social worker before the onset of the professional–client relationship to be unable to benefit fully from the social worker's expertise. The client may have difficulty distinguishing between the social worker's professional and personal roles in his or her life. The couple's interpersonal history and dynamics may interfere with the client's ability to receive help and the social worker's ability to provide help. The social worker's influence and credibility might be undermined because of the client's intimate familiarity with the social worker's personal life and issues.

In psychodynamic terms, the transference and countertransference involved in such a relationship are likely to limit the social worker's effectiveness and the ability of both client and practitioner to maintain appropriate professional boundaries. Transference is a frequent phenomenon in psychotherapy: A client's emotional reactions in the current relationship with the social worker may be stimulated or triggered by former experiences, relationships, or developmental conflicts in his or her life. Given the possibility of transference, a client's feelings about and reactions to a social worker may be complicated by emotional experiences in the sexual relationship with the social worker that preceded the professional–client relationship. In countertransference a social worker's emotional reactions to a client may have originated in the social worker's own prior experiences, relationships, or developmental conflicts (Barker, 1995). In this context the practitioner's feelings about and reactions to the client may be affected by the intimate relationship with the client that occurred before the professional–client relationship.

For example, a social worker in private practice was contacted by a former lover about 18 months after the end of their intimate relationship. The couple had been sexually involved for a little more than a year and had ended the relationship amicably. They had agreed to remain friends and had had sporadic contact since. The former lover told the social worker that he "really needed to talk to someone about some issues" and she was "the person who knows me best and the person I trust the most." After seeing the social worker professionally for eight sessions, the client discovered that he had strong, unresolved, romantic feelings for the social worker, and these feelings were distracting. The client felt that he had not accomplished very much in his therapy and his confusion about his relationship with the social worker was hindering his progress. The client shared this realization with the social worker, who acknowledged that she, too, was finding the client–professional relationship difficult to manage. "In retrospect," the social worker told her client, "I shouldn't have agreed to be your therapist. That was a mistake." Consistent with standard 1.09(d) (see also standard 1.16[a]), the social worker recommended that the client see another therapist for assistance.

## PHYSICAL CONTACT

### STANDARD 1.10

*Social workers should not engage in physical contact with clients when there is a possibility of psychological harm to the client as a result of the contact (such as cradling or caressing clients). Social workers who engage in appropriate physical contact with clients are responsible for setting clear, appropriate, and culturally sensitive boundaries that govern such physical contact.*

Social workers must always be careful to distinguish between appropriate and inappropriate physical contact with clients. Appropriate physical contact may take various forms—its essential feature is that it is not likely to cause clients psychological harm:

- A social worker was employed by a residential program for children with serious emotional and behavioral problems. One of the residents was an 11-year-old boy who often engaged in self-destructive behaviors. He had been severely abused by his father. One day a police officer informed the social worker that the boy's mother, to whom he was very attached emotionally, had died of a drug overdose. The social worker broke the news to the boy, who was distraught and cried uncontrollably. The social worker sat down beside the boy, put her arm around him, and rested her head against his as he sobbed.

- A social worker for a home health care agency provided services to a 42-year-old woman who was dying of breast cancer. The social worker sat at the patient's bedside and listened while she talked about the end of her life and her concern about how her husband and young children would handle her death. The woman cried intermittently as she talked about her grief and speculated about her family's uncertain future. The patient held out her hand for the social worker to hold. The social worker held and stroked the patient's hand and arm as they talked.

- A social worker at a family services agency provided counseling to a college student who was struggling with self-esteem issues. The counseling lasted for four months. According to the client, the counseling was enormously helpful, and she was deeply grateful for the social worker's insight and skill. The client reported that her "entire world view had changed as a result of this intense experience." At the end of the last session the client thanked the social worker and initiated a good-bye hug that lasted about three seconds.

In these three situations the social workers had brief and limited physical contact that is generally considered acceptable. None of these clients would likely be psychologically harmed by the contact. To the contrary, most likely they would find the physical contact psychologically comforting, as a form of consolation or "therapeutic touch."

In contrast to these situations are those involving physical touch that has more potential to cause clients psychological harm. In general, inappropriate physical touch occurs when the nature of the touch might exacerbate the client's transference in harmful ways, thus confusing or troubling the client; or perhaps the touch might suggest that the relationship between the social worker and client extends beyond the formal professional–client relationship. For example,

- A social worker in private practice provided counseling to a young woman who reported being depressed ever since acknowledging that, as a young child and teenager, she had been sexually abused by her stepfather. The social worker and client focused mostly on the client's self-esteem issues and her difficulty sustaining intimate relationships with men. Toward the end of one particular counseling session, which took place about 10 months after the start of the therapy, the client began to cry about the trauma she had endured. The social worker got up from his chair and sat next to the client on the sofa to comfort her, and he put his arms around the client while she leaned against him. He held her tight, rocking her back and forth while she cried. The social worker continued to hold and stroke the client after her crying had subsided.

- A social worker in private practice specialized in providing group therapy to women who had been physically and sexually abused. As a routine part of therapy, the social worker asked group members to sit in a circle on the floor ("to get down low, on the same level, and as a way to get in touch with the small child within themselves," the social worker said), then she lowered the office lights and turned on soothing music. In the course of this part of the therapy, each client had an opportunity to experience being nurtured by the social worker: the social worker sat on the floor with her legs spread open, and the client sat with her back against the social worker's chest and the social worker's arms wrapped around her. The social worker rocked the client and spoke soothingly and softly to the client's "inner hurt child." At times, the social worker would wipe away the client's tears and gently stroke her hair. The social worker said this provided clients with "a corrective emotional experience" and "constructive reparenting."

- A clinical social worker had a long-standing interest in the therapeutic effects of massage. She had not received formal training as a massage therapist but had learned a number of massage techniques from a close friend. The social worker was providing counseling to a recently divorced 52-year-old woman. The client explained that she had divorced her husband after realizing that she was a lesbian and had sought counseling to address her difficulty coping with the dissolution of her marriage and the dramatic changes in her life. During a session the client commented that in recent weeks she had been feeling unusually "tense and tight," a reflection of the anxiety she had been experiencing. The social worker suggested that some massage might be helpful and offered to rub the client's shoulders, neck, head, face, arms, and back during their therapy session.

These situations can be problematic because the social worker's conduct has the potential to confuse clients about the nature of the professional–client relationship and introduce complex boundary issues into the relationship. Some forms of touch—especially cradling and caressing, which typically have a sexual connotation—are likely to distract both social workers and clients from their therapeutic agenda and thus jeopardize the client's well-being. Other than brief contact for therapeutic purposes—such as a quick hug to say good-bye or to console a distraught client—physical touch is likely to cause psychological harm and interfere with the professional–client relationship.

## SEXUAL HARASSMENT

### STANDARD 1.11

*Social workers should not sexually harass clients. Sexual harassment includes sexual advances, sexual solicitation, requests for sexual favors, and other verbal or physical conduct of a sexual nature.*

Not only is social workers' sexual contact with clients unethical, sexual harassment in any form is unethical as well. According to Conte (1990), sexual harassment can take three forms: verbal (pressure for sexual activity, comments about a person's body, sexual boasting, and sexist or homophobic comments), nonverbal (suggestive looks or sounds or obscene gestures), and physical (touching, patting, pinching, kissing, and rape).

Sexual harassment of clients can be psychologically harmful. It can cause emotional stress and trauma, guilt, and shame. As Singer (1995) noted, "these afflictions result from the double bind of abuse—giving in to the abuse to avoid penalty and facing the indignities or fighting the abuse with the resultant threat of retaliation. Some victims report symptoms characteristic of those with posttraumatic stress disorder—that is, recurring nightmares, nonspecific fears, and anger years after the event" (p. 2152). In addition to its impact on clients, sexual harassment also can undermine the social work profession's integrity and credibility with the public:

- A social worker employed by a women's prison provided individual and group counseling to inmates. He met regularly with one inmate who was serving a three-year sentence for possession and distribution of drugs. During one of the counseling sessions, the social worker told the inmate that she had a "great figure."

- A clinical social worker in private practice provided counseling to a 32-year-old woman who was separated from her husband. The client sought counseling to address several issues related to the end of the marriage. The client's managed health care company refused to authorize more than six counseling sessions. Toward the end of the fifth session, the client said she felt the need for more counseling but did not have the funds to pay for it. The social worker, who felt attracted to the client, suggested that they "might be able to work something out" and asked the client whether she would be interested in spending "some time with me away from the office, just the two of us."

- A female social worker in the military provided counseling to an 18-year-old male soldier. The soldier reported feeling depressed because he was away from his home and family for the first time. At the conclusion of the second counseling session, the social worker patted the soldier on the buttocks as he was leaving her office.

Social workers are obligated to avoid any behaviors that constitute sexual harassment. They should not make sexual advances toward clients, solicit sexual favors, or make comments or gestures of a sexual nature.

## Derogatory Language

### STANDARD 1.12

*Social workers should not use derogatory language in their written or verbal communications to or about clients. Social workers should use accurate and respectful language in all communications to and about clients.*

Social workers must be careful to avoid disparaging or pejorative language in their comments to or about clients simply because it is disrespectful. Below is an excerpt with inappropriate language from a case record in a child protective services agency; the entry was written by a social work student who was completing a field placement in the agency (details have been altered to protect the client's privacy):

> I visited the Smith home to investigate allegations of child neglect. I was met at the door by Mrs. Smith, a single parent. I was surprised by her size; she was morbidly obese and smelled as if she hadn't showered in weeks. Rolls of fat hung out of Mrs. Smith's shirt, and portions of her legs were covered with dirt. Mrs. Smith's slovenly appearance suggests that she is unable to care for herself, much less her children.

In addition to being disrespectful, certain forms of derogatory language can expose social workers to legal risk, as when there is evidence of defamation of character. Defamation occurs as a result of "the publication of anything injurious to the good name or reputation of another, or which tends to bring him into disrepute" (Gifis, 1991, p. 124). It can take two forms: libel and slander. Libel occurs when the publication is in written form—for example, in a social worker's progress report about a client that is read by a judge or employer concerned with the client's circumstances. Slander occurs when the publication is in oral form—for example, when a social worker testifies about a client in a court of law or provides an oral report about the client's progress to a probation officer.

Social workers can be legally liable for defamation of character if they say or write something about a client that is untrue, if they knew or should have known that the statement was untrue, and if the communication caused some injury to the client (for instance, the client was terminated from a social services program or fired from a job). In one case a hospital social worker referred to a newborn infant as a "cocaine baby" because of a number of symptoms manifested by the baby at birth. Based in part on the social worker's assessment and report, the baby was placed in foster care against the mother's wishes. Subsequent laboratory tests confirmed that although the baby manifested symptoms similar to those found in infants delivered by mothers who had used cocaine, in this particular case the baby suffered from a syndrome unrelated to cocaine use. The mother ultimately filed a lawsuit alleging defamation of character against the hospital and the social worker. As a result of this experience, the social worker learned that he must characterize clients very carefully, avoiding any terms or labels that might not be true or accurate. In this case, for example, the social worker might have written at the time of the birth: "baby seems agitated; Dr. X suspects baby may be experiencing withdrawal symptoms from mother's drug use; awaiting results of toxicology screen."

In another case a social worker in a child welfare agency was responsible for screening prospective foster parents. As part of the process of screening prospective foster parents for licensing, the social worker conducted personal interviews with applicants, ran criminal background checks, and contacted personal references. The social worker rejected an applicant's request to be a foster parent after reviewing his criminal record. According to the case notes, the applicant had been convicted two years earlier of assault with a deadly weapon; the incident apparently arose from a violent argument between the applicant and a neighbor. Based on this information, the social worker concluded that the applicant would not be a fit foster parent.

The applicant sued the social worker for defamation of character (among other claims related to the rejection of his application). He was able to demonstrate that, in fact, he had not been convicted of assault with a deadly weapon, as reported by the social worker. Rather, the criminal charges had been dismissed. The social worker had misinterpreted the documents he examined and concluded, wrongly, that the applicant had been convicted of the offense when he had only been charged with the offense.

The best way for social workers to prevent defamation of character claims is to report information about clients accurately. The best defense against such an allegation is that the written or oral statement was true (Schutz, 1982).

## PAYMENT FOR SERVICES

### STANDARD 1.13(a)

*When setting fees, social workers should ensure that the fees are fair, reasonable, and commensurate with the services performed. Consideration should be given to clients' ability to pay.*

Many factors are considered in social workers' determination of professional fees. Practitioners typically are influenced greatly by the marketplace—the fees charged by other professionals for comparable services. As a result, most private practitioners charge clients an hourly rate similar to that charged by colleagues with comparable education in that geographic area. Per diem rates for such services as residential treatment and day treatment programs tend to be similar, if not identical, within geographic areas; agencies in locations with a higher cost of living may charge higher fees. Similarly, fees charged by agencies for services such as adoption home studies, geriatric assessments, and clinical evaluations are usually influenced by market forces. Social workers, like most other professionals, usually want to be in line with the industry standard, so they do not price themselves out of the market or earn substantially less than their colleagues.

Other factors also influence social workers' fees. As part of a managed care program, insurance providers may negotiate specific reimbursement rates with social workers for mental health and other social services. Some social workers set their fees above the field's norms to influence the kinds of people who seek their services; social workers who charge fees above the norm may do so to limit their clientele to affluent clients who can afford to pay all or part of the fee out of pocket. Other social workers may set their fees below the field's norms so that access to services will be enhanced, particularly for low-income people.

On occasion ethical questions are raised about social workers' fees. For example, a couple interested in adopting a child consulted with a family services agency that had just started to provide adoption services (conducting home studies, facilitating placements, providing pre- and postadoption counseling). The agency director, a social worker, knew that prospective adoptive parents often feel desperate and are willing to pay large sums of money to adopt an infant. The agency director told the assistant director that by setting high fees, the agency—the only one in the area providing adoption services—had a "golden opportunity to generate substantial revenue." The assistant director told the agency director that she felt this would be exploitative and unethical.

Standard 1.13(a) explicitly encourages social workers to take clients' ability to pay into account when they set fees. Historically, the social work profession has been concerned about the well-being of low-income people. The preamble to the 1996 *NASW Code of Ethics* asserts, "The primary mission of the social work profession is to enhance human well-being and help meet basic human needs of all people, with particular attention to the needs and empowerment of people who are vulnerable, oppressed, and *living in poverty*" (p. 1, emphasis added). To the extent possible, then, social workers should make their services available to people of little or modest means. Of course, this is more feasible in some cases than in others. Some social workers and agencies are not in a financial position to reduce their fees or otherwise underwrite the costs associated with delivering services. Thus, the code does not require social workers to set fees based on clients' ability to pay; rather, it exhorts social workers to be sensitive to clients' ability to pay. According to the code's summary of ethical principles, "Social workers are encouraged to volunteer some portion of their professional skills with no expectation of significant financial return (pro bono service)" (p. 5).

## STANDARD 1.13(b)

*Social workers should avoid accepting goods or services from clients as payment for professional services. Bartering arrangements, particularly involving services, create the potential for conflicts of interest, exploitation, and inappropriate boundaries in social workers' relationships with clients. Social workers should explore and may participate in bartering only in very limited circumstances when it can be demonstrated that such arrangements are an accepted practice among professionals in the local community, considered to be essential for the provision of services, negotiated without coercion, and entered into at the client's initiative and with the client's informed consent. Social workers who accept goods or services from clients as payment for professional services assume the full burden of demonstrating that this arrangement will not be detrimental to the client or the professional relationship.*

The majority of clients (or their insurance providers) pay fees for social services, but in a relatively small number of cases, social workers participate in barter arrangements when clients are unable to pay for services and offer goods or services as a substitute. Bartering also occurs in some communities where there are established norms involving such nonmonetary exchange of goods and services.

On the surface, barter may not seem to pose ethical problems if the parties participate willingly. In actuality, though, barter may lead to troubling ethical questions, as in this example: A social worker in private practice provided counseling services to a young man who manifested symptoms of mild depression. In general, the client functioned well in the community; he was involved in a long-term relationship and earned his living as a house painter. With the social worker's help, the client began exploring a number of family issues that seemed to be related to his depression.

The client's managed care provider authorized six counseling sessions. The company was not willing to authorize additional sessions, despite the social worker's detailed explanation of the client's wish for additional assistance. In an effort to be helpful to the client, the social worker, whose office badly needed painting, suggested that they work out an arrangement by which the client would paint the social worker's office in exchange for counseling services. The client agreed to the proposal and, after some initial disagreement about the fair market value of the paint job, the two determined the number of counseling sessions that would be traded for it (fair market value for the paint job divided by the social worker's customary hourly fee).

About three weeks after the painting was completed, while the client was still in counseling with the social worker, a wall in the social worker's office began to peel. She brought this to the client's attention, but the client said it would be some time before he could repair the wall because he had other commitments. The social worker was concerned about the appearance of her office and began to lose patience with the client. She ultimately admitted that her feelings about the client's handling of the defective paint job affected her professional relationship with him.

This case illustrates what can be ethically problematic in barter arrangements. Negotiations about the fair market value of the goods or services to be exchanged and, in particular, about the handling of defects in a product or service can interfere with the social worker–client clinical relationship in a way that is harmful to the client. In addition, the services the social worker provides to the client may be determined by the market value of the goods or services provided by the client rather than the client's clinical needs. Especially because the client may be dependent on the social worker, and because of the unequal power relationship between the parties, the client may be vulnerable to exploitation, conflicts of interest, or coercion.

Some social workers argue, however, that barter is ethical, particularly in communities where it is an accepted practice (for example, where farmers commonly exchange hay or corn for plumbing or carpentry services). In light of this argument, the NASW *Code of Ethics* Revision Committee concluded that it would not be appropriate categorically to prohibit barter arrangements between social workers and clients. Rather, the committee took the position that social workers should avoid bartering and that they should accept goods or services from clients as payment for professional services only in very limited circumstances when certain conditions are met. First, to what extent are such arrangements an accepted practice among professionals in the local community? The widespread use of barter in the local community can strengthen a social worker's contention that this was an appropriate practice in a particular case. Second, to what extent is barter essential for the provision of services? Is it used merely because it is the most expedient and convenient form of payment available, or is it used because it is the only reasonable way for the client to obtain needed services? As a general rule, barter should be considered as a last resort only when more conventional forms of payment have been ruled out and only when it is essential for the provision of services. Third, is the barter arrangement negotiated without coercion? Social workers should not pressure clients to agree to barter. For example, feeling some coercion, a client may agree reluctantly to give a social worker a treasured work of art from the client's personal collection, primarily because the social worker has commented on how much he or she would like to own such a work. Clients who agree to participate in a barter arrangement must do so freely and willingly, without any direct or indirect coercion from the social worker. Fourth, was the barter arrangement entered into at the client's initiative and with the client's informed consent? To avoid coercing clients or the appearance of such impropriety, social workers should not take the initiative to suggest barter as an option. Such suggestions should come from clients, with their fully informed consent. Social workers should explain the nature and terms of the arrangement in clear and understandable language and discuss risks associated with barter (for example, how the professional–client relationship could be adversely affected, particularly if there is a defect in the goods or services provided by the client in exchange for the social worker's services), reasonable alternatives for payment (for example, a reduced monthly payment rather than payment in full or by credit card), the client's right to refuse or withdraw consent, and the time frame covered by the consent (see standard 1.03[a]).

Social workers must recognize that even when all these conditions have been met, they assume the full burden of demonstrating that bartering will not be detrimental to the client or the professional relationship. Their principal responsibility is to protect clients: practitioners must exercise sound judgment when considering the risks associated with barter.

### STANDARD 1.13(c)

*Social workers should not solicit a private fee or other remuneration for providing services to clients who are entitled to such available services through the social workers' employer or agency.*

Many social workers provide services in more than one setting. They may have two or more part-time jobs, for example, or a practitioner who is employed full-time in a social services agency also may have a part-time private practice. Social workers who provide services in more than one setting must maintain clear boundaries between the settings, particularly with respect to payment for services.

In one case a social worker was employed as a caseworker in a public child welfare agency. His responsibilities included supervising children in foster care and providing counseling to parents who were trying to regain custody of children who had been abused or neglected. In addition to his full-time position, the social worker maintained a part-time private practice.

In his position at the child welfare agency, the social worker provided casework and counseling services to a family whose eight-year-old child was in foster care; the child had been placed in foster care after he was physically abused by his father. In the social worker's judgment, the family would benefit from more counseling than he could provide in his position at the child welfare agency. He shared his views with the family and offered to see them in his private practice. The family agreed, and paid him a reduced out-of-pocket fee.

This arrangement is unethical because there was a conflict of interest. The social worker stood to benefit personally from seeing the clients in his private practice. He did not attempt to arrange for the child welfare agency to provide more in-depth counseling under its own auspices; rather, he essentially referred his clients to himself. To avoid this conflict, the social worker should have conferred with supervisors or administrators at the child welfare agency to arrange for additional counseling services for the family to be provided by staff of the child welfare agency or by another professional in their local community.

## CLIENTS WHO LACK DECISION-MAKING CAPACITY

### STANDARD 1.14

*When social workers act on behalf of clients who lack the capacity to make informed decisions, social workers should take reasonable steps to safeguard the interests and rights of those clients.*

Social workers sometimes provide services to clients who lack the capacity to make informed decisions as a result of, for example, a brain injury, mental illness or disability, or a drug overdose. Ordinarily, a person is deemed incompetent when, because of age, mental illness, mental disability, excessive use of drugs or alcohol, or some other form of mental or physical incapacity, he or she is incapable of either managing his or her property or caring for himself or herself (Dickson, 1995; Saltzman & Proch, 1990).

To protect such clients, social workers should be knowledgeable about their legal rights. In general, adults in the United States are presumed to be legally competent and entitled to make all decisions for themselves. They can be deprived of this right only if they have been determined to be incompetent by a court that considers evidence concerning mental or physical impairment. It is possible that a person is considered to have a mental illness, a developmental disability, or alcoholism, for example, but competent to make decisions, manage money, and care for himself or herself; that is, impairment or disability does not, by itself, imply incompetence (Saltzman & Proch, 1990). As Saltzman and Proch (1990) asserted, the presumption of competency

> should only be overcome if a person is incapable of making certain or all decisions and it is necessary to have another make the decisions to protect the incapable person. The presumption should not be overcome merely because a person might make unwise decisions or decisions that could cause harm to himself or herself. Adults have a right to be wrong. The state may intervene to protect a person incapable of making a rational decision on a certain matter or any rational decisions under the doctrine of *parens patriae,* but . . . the breadth and vagueness of the definition of incompetence in many statutes, as well as the lack of procedural protections in guardianship proceedings, may result in findings of incompetence that are not justified. (pp. 329–330)

Social workers who provide services to clients who lack the capacity to make informed decisions should be knowledgeable about these clients' legal rights in a number of key areas. As discussed under standard 1.03(c), social workers should protect clients' interests by seeking informed consent on a client's behalf, when necessary, from an appropriate third party (proxy or substituted judgment). This person is usually a spouse, partner, or other relative who is likely to act in the client's best interests or who has been appointed as the client's legal guardian. To the extent possible, a social worker should explain to such a client, in a manner consistent with the client's level of understanding, what services are being provided, what options are available, and what decisions are being made. This may not be possible with some clients (for example, clients with profound mental disability or serious brain injury), but it is possible with many (for example, certain clients with moderate mental disability or who are recovering from a serious drug overdose).

Social workers also should be aware that many states now require that judicial decisions concerning an individual's incompetence should focus narrowly on specific issues or circumstances rather than take the form of a broad determination that an individual is incompetent for any and all purposes. Thus, a client may be considered incompetent to make sound decisions about handling a large inheritance yet competent to make a decision about where to live. A court might then appoint a guardian to handle only the client's financial matters; the guardian would not have the authority to determine where the client will live. Many states recognize the concept of "least-restrictive alternative" as a guiding principle, which states that a person considered incompetent should lose only those rights that he or she cannot properly exercise (Dickson, 1995; Saltzman & Proch, 1990).

In these situations a number of important issues arise with respect to health care decisions. Generally speaking, competent adults have a right to refuse medical treatment. When an individual is incompetent, a court may appoint a legal guardian to make a decision on that individual's behalf. A court also may use a substituted judgment test by which it attempts to determine what the client would want. This subjective test contrasts with an objective test by which the court attempts to determine what a reasonable person would want. Some courts have recognized an incompetent individual's prior expression of wishes and desires concerning medical treatment, even when such wishes and desires were not documented in writing, as in a living will (Dickson, 1995; Saltzman & Proch, 1990).

Although in most cases minor children are not considered competent to consent to their own medical treatment, exceptions do exist. In many states minor children are permitted to consent to medical treatment in cases of genuine emergency or if they want assistance with birth control or treatment for substance abuse or a sexually transmitted disease.

Social workers in mental health settings should be familiar with laws and regulations concerning clients' right to treatment, right to refuse treatment, and right to humane treatment in the least-restrictive manner (particularly with respect to religious freedom, freedom of speech, privacy and visitation rights, the right to be free of restraints and seclusion, and the right to personal property). With the exception of certain rights that are federally protected such as civil rights and the right to privacy, the rights of incompetent individuals and related laws and regulations can vary from jurisdiction to jurisdiction. Agencies would be wise to develop written guidelines and policies that reflect local laws and regulations.

## INTERRUPTION OF SERVICES

### STANDARD 1.15

*Social workers should make reasonable efforts to ensure continuity of services in the event that services are interrupted by factors such as unavailability, relocation, illness, disability, or death.*

Social workers' services to clients are sometimes interrupted, expectedly or unexpectedly. For example, a social worker may have to leave town—suddenly and temporarily—to care for an ill parent, or may move to a new city or state for professional or personal reasons. A social worker could also be unavailable because of a planned vacation, retirement, a sudden illness, disability, or death.

Social workers should anticipate the possibility that they may not be available to clients who are in need of assistance and arrange for adequate coverage. Different circumstances require different contingency plans. Social workers who know ahead of time that they will be unavailable because of vacation or personal leave (for planned surgery or maternity leave, for example) should arrange for a colleague to provide coverage. The colleague should be selected carefully, to ensure that the individual who will provide coverage has the requisite education and expertise to assist one's clients. For example, a social worker in private practice who specializes in services to elderly clients should arrange for a colleague with comparable expertise to provide coverage, not a colleague who specializes in treatment of adolescent substance abusers.

As discussed above with respect to standard 1.07(o), social workers who know that they will be leaving a work setting for another position, retiring, or moving away also should take steps to ensure continuity of services. When leaving an agency for another work setting, a practitioner should be sure that a qualified colleague in the former workplace will assume responsibility for his or her clients. The social worker should spend time in conference with the colleague to ensure that he or she has sufficient information to meet clients' needs. Of course, social workers should inform clients of their plans as soon as possible (ideally at least several months in advance) and make clear that the clients have the option to obtain services elsewhere. Similarly, social workers who are retiring should inform clients as soon as possible and discuss referral possibilities. Social workers in private practice who plan to move out of the geographic area should help active clients select another services provider and inform clients of their new location, in case the clients or other authorized parties need to have access to information in case records.

Because illness, disability, and death are unpredictable, social workers also should identify colleagues who will provide coverage in the event that they are suddenly and unexpectedly unavailable. Social workers in private practice should consider consulting with a lawyer to develop a plan that names a personal representative authorized to handle client matters, referrals to new services providers, and client records.

Ethical problems can arise when social workers are not available when they are needed by clients. In one case a social worker in part-time private practice left town suddenly to care for a disabled relative. He did not arrange back-up coverage until one week after his departure. Before coverage was arranged, however, one of his clients became suicidal and attempted to contact the social worker for assistance. After several failed attempts to reach the social worker, the client jumped from a highway overpass and killed himself.

In another case an independent social worker died suddenly after a heart attack. She had not contacted a lawyer to plan for the appointment of a personal representative and had not consulted a colleague about providing emergency coverage. Several of the social worker's clients became distraught when they discovered that she had died and had left no contingency plan.

# TERMINATION OF SERVICES

## STANDARD 1.16(a)

*Social workers should terminate services to clients and professional relationships with them when such services and relationships are no longer required or no longer serve the clients' needs or interests.*

Social workers use a variety of criteria and data to determine when it is appropriate to terminate services to clients and professional relationships with them. In some circumstances social workers and clients may agree in advance to work together for a specific length of time. For example, clinical social workers and their clients may contract for a specific number of counseling sessions, or a social worker retained as an organizational consultant may have a contract to work on a project for a specified period of time. This may occur at the initiative of the social worker, the client, or some third party, for example, an insurance or managed care company that authorizes a specific number of sessions.

In other circumstances social workers terminate services when clients reach specific goals. For example, a client may wish to continue seeing a social worker until a divorce is finalized or until a child's behavior shows marked improvement, or social work consultants may provide services until certain project goals are reached.

Some social workers provide services to clients in a relatively open-ended fashion. Certain clients who want counseling may not feel comfortable agreeing to a specific number of sessions; they may prefer to see where the sessions go and what they achieve, making decisions along the way about the length of service. A social worker who is a community organizer may not have a structured time frame in work with residents of a particular neighborhood, preferring instead to follow the community's lead (assuming there is ample funding to support the activities).

No matter how social workers approach the delivery of services, whether closed- or open-ended, they must terminate services to clients and professional relationships with them when such services and relationships are no longer required or no longer serve the clients' needs or interests (that is, if the services were not terminated because of the client's uncooperativeness or lack of compliance with program requirements, or because of a client's failure to pay for services). If, in the social worker's judgment, a client has accomplished what he or she has set out to achieve, the social worker has a responsibility to talk with the client about terminating the professional–client relationship.

Ethical issues arise when social workers do not terminate services to and relationships with clients even though the services are no longer needed or no longer serve the clients' needs and interests. This most often occurs for one of two reasons. First, social workers who are particularly concerned about their income may discourage clients from terminating or fail to broach the subject of termination because they wish to maintain the revenue that these clients provide. In one case an independent social worker provided counseling to an affluent man who reported struggling with a midlife crisis. The client was considering abandoning his lucrative business career to pursue an uncertain career as an artist. After the 13th clinical session the social worker believed that the client had adequately addressed the clinical issues. However, the social worker, who had a number of serious financial concerns, was worried about losing the income generated by this self-paying client. As a result, he was much more assertive than usual in his effort to have the client identify other issues in his life that might require counseling. The social worker soon realized that, for self-interested reasons, he was trying much too hard to hold on to the client.

Second, to meet their own emotional needs, social workers may extend services beyond what is clinically appropriate or necessary. A social worker may find working with a particular client to be unusually satisfying and rewarding or may, unconsciously perhaps, want to encourage the client's dependency. In the case discussed above of the client who was contemplating a career change, the social worker discovered that working with the client was also helping him explore his own ambivalence about a possible career change. Through his work with the client, the social worker achieved a number of useful insights into his own goals and circumstances.

Social workers need to be careful not to place their own interests above those of their clients. As one of the code's ethical principles states, "social workers elevate service to others above self-interest" (p. 5). Social workers must be sure not to let the financial and emotional rewards associated with their work guide their decisions about termination of services to clients and professional relationships with them.

## STANDARD 1.16(b)

*Social workers should take reasonable steps to avoid abandoning clients who are still in need of services. Social workers should withdraw services precipitously only under unusual circumstances, giving careful consideration to all factors in the situation and taking care to minimize possible adverse effects. Social workers should assist in making appropriate arrangements for continuation of services when necessary.*

Social workers need to be concerned about terminating services prematurely and not being available when a client needs assistance. On occasion, practitioners terminate services to clients who are not making adequate progress; whose behavior toward the social worker is hostile, resistant, or uncooperative; who have needs that require services outside the social worker's areas of expertise; who threaten a social worker's safety or file a complaint or lawsuit against him or her; who do not comply with a treatment plan or provisions of a contract; who have exhausted their insurance coverage; or who do not pay an overdue balance (see standard 1.16[c]).

In one case an ethics complaint was filed against a social worker at a community mental health agency by a former client who alleged that the social worker had terminated services abruptly. The client, who had a severe disability, had sought counseling to help her develop skills to cope with her chronic impairment. After several months of intervention, the social worker began having difficulty working with the client. According to the social worker, the client was "demanding, resistant, and aggressive." She reported that the client telephoned her incessantly, often leaving angry messages concerning the social worker's lack of responsiveness.

During one intense exchange with the client, the social worker became irritated and told the client that she "would be much better off with another counselor." The social worker terminated services shortly thereafter. The client sent the social worker a registered letter asking for a detailed explanation of her decision to terminate services, but the social worker refused to accept the letter. In addition, the social worker made no attempt to provide the client with names of other practitioners whom she could contact for assistance. Although the social worker's frustration in this case may be understandable, she clearly violated ethical standards by not terminating services properly.

Social workers who terminate services to clients who are still in need of assistance or who are not available when needed (for example, when they go on vacation or resign their job), risk allegations of abandonment. Abandonment is a legal concept that pertains to instances when a professional is not available to a client when needed. Once a social worker begins to provide services to a client, she or he incurs a legal responsibility to continue those services or properly to refer a client to an alternative services provider (see standards 2.06[a] and [b]).

Social workers should take a number of steps to avoid abandoning clients (Austin et al., 1990; Reamer, 1994; Schutz, 1982):

- Consult with colleagues and supervisors about a decision to terminate services. In some cases termination can be prevented by addressing relevant issues. For example, social workers may be able to address a client's reason for not paying an overdue balance and develop a workable payment plan. Social workers whose clients are not making reasonable progress may be able to modify their intervention to enhance the clients' progress.

- Give as much advance warning as possible to clients who will be terminated.

- Provide clients with the names, addresses, and telephone numbers of at least three appropriate referrals when it is necessary to terminate services.

- When clients announce their decision to terminate prematurely, explain to them the risks involved and offer suggestions for alternative services. Include this information in a follow-up letter.

- In cases involving discharge of clients from a residential facility, be sure that a comprehensive discharge plan has been formulated and significant others have been notified of the client's discharge (clients should be informed of this). In cases involving court-ordered clients, seek legal consultation and court approval before terminating care.

- Follow up with a client who has been terminated. If she or he does not go to the referral, write a letter to the client about the risks involved should she or he not follow through with the referral.

- Provide clients with clear instructions to follow and telephone numbers to use in case of emergency. Include a copy of these instructions in their case records. Ask clients to sign this copy, indicating that they received the instructions and the instructions were explained to them.

- When away from the office for an extended time, call in regularly for messages. Social workers who are away from the office should leave an emergency telephone number with a secretary, an answering service, or an answering device. Social workers who anticipate that certain clients may need assistance during their absence should refer those clients to a colleague with appropriate expertise.

- Carefully document in the case record all decisions and actions related to termination of services.

## STANDARD 1.16(c)

*Social workers in fee-for-service settings may terminate services to clients who are not paying an overdue balance if the financial contractual arrangements have been made clear to the client, if the client does not pose an imminent danger to self or others, and if the clinical and other consequences of the current nonpayment have been addressed and discussed with the client.*

Some clients are unwilling or unable to pay an overdue balance for professional services rendered by a social worker. Social workers should first discuss with such clients the reasons for nonpayment and take reasonable steps to help clients meet their financial obligations without terminating services. For example, if a client does not pay her overdue balance because she is angry or upset about some aspect of the services received, the social worker should discuss that dissatisfaction with her and attempt to address her concerns. If a client does not pay his overdue balance because of sudden unemployment, the social worker should consider trying to work out a reasonable payment plan, which might include reducing the fee to an affordable level.

If attempts to address a client's reasons for nonpayment of an overdue balance fail, the social worker may terminate services, but only when two conditions have been met. First, the social worker should be confident that the client does not pose a danger to himself or herself or others. It would be unethical to terminate services to an actively suicidal or homicidal client, even though the client has an unpaid balance.

Second, a social worker who is considering terminating services should first discuss with the client the possible clinical and other consequences of the nonpayment and termination of services. What clinical risks would the client face if he or she stopped receiving services? What emotional and psychological implications might there be? How might family members and other friends and acquaintances be affected by the termination of services? Social workers should document their impressions in the case record, which can help ensure that these issues are addressed with clients and protect social workers, should questions later be raised about the decision to terminate services.

In one case a social worker in private practice provided counseling services to a young woman who was distraught after the break-up of a long-term relationship. Under the terms of the client's insurance coverage, she was responsible for a 50 percent copayment for each counseling session. After three months, she had accumulated a $550 outstanding balance. The social worker terminated services, and the client filed an ethics complaint and a lawsuit alleging that the social worker terminated services inappropriately. The social worker was unable to provide documentation indicating that she had discussed with the client how the nonpayment might be addressed or the possible clinical implications of the nonpayment. Also, the social worker was vulnerable because she had allowed the client to accrue such a large outstanding balance, one that the social worker knew the client was not likely to be able to pay off.

In another case a social worker provided clinical services to a client who had been diagnosed with dysthymia (an affective disorder involving symptoms of depression). The client reported to the social worker that occasionally he had fleeting thoughts about committing suicide. The social worker assessed the client for suicide risk by use of a standardized suicide assessment protocol, and he concluded that the client did not pose an imminent risk of suicide. Eventually the social worker terminated services to the client because the client had not paid his large overdue balance. Two weeks after the termination of services, the client attempted unsuccessfully to commit suicide; as a result of the attempt he suffered grave physical injuries (brain injury due to loss of blood). The client filed a lawsuit and an ethics complaint against the social worker, alleging that he had terminated services without properly assessing the client's suicide risk. At issue was the timing of the suicide assessment that the social worker had conducted and on which he based his judgment; the client claimed that the suicide assessment was conducted at the beginning of the professional–client relationship and was out of date by the time the social worker decided to terminate services. The social worker was vulnerable because he did not have documentation in the case file confirming that he had properly assessed for suicide risk at the time services to the client were terminated.

## STANDARD 1.16(d)

*Social workers should not terminate services to pursue a social, financial, or sexual relationship with a client.*

During the course of their work with clients, social workers may be tempted to become involved with clients socially, financially, or sexually. The code of ethics proscribes dual and multiple relationships (standard 1.06[c]), and such relationships are not permissible even if the professional–client relationship has been terminated. However, some social workers may be tempted to terminate a professional–client relationship to pursue a social, financial, or sexual relationship, as in these examples:

- A social worker for a family services agency provided individual counseling to a woman, a single mother, who wanted advice about managing her son's behavioral problems. The social worker provided counseling services to the mother and, on occasion, her son over a period of three months. During the third month, the social worker and the mother acknowledged that they were attracted to each other. Knowing that an intimate relationship with a client is prohibited by the code of ethics, the social worker referred the client to a colleague for further counseling, terminated the professional–client relationship, and began dating her shortly thereafter.

- A social worker in private practice provided counseling to a man who was having difficulty coping with some problems at work. After working together for some time, the client told the social worker that he was planning to start his own business in an effort to get away from his problems at work. The client told the social worker about his plans to start a restaurant supply business (a field in which he had considerable expertise and experience) and how he needed to raise capital to get the business off the ground. The client asked the social worker if he would like to become a financial partner in the new business. The social worker found the investment opportunity appealing and talked to his client about how they would need to terminate their professional–client relationship if they became business partners. The client and social worker agreed to terminate the professional–client relationship and soon thereafter entered into a business relationship.

It is unethical for social workers to terminate a professional–client relationship to pursue a social, financial, or sexual relationship. As in the case of standard 1.09(c), which concerns sexual involvement with former clients, entering into dual and multiple relationships after the termination of the professional–client relationship can exploit and harm clients. Because of the unequal power in the relationship, clients may be particularly susceptible to social workers' suggestions or influence concerning post-termination social, financial, or sexual relationships. In addition, as discussed elsewhere in this chapter, entering into such a dual or multiple relationship after termination can confuse a client about the social worker's role in his or her life and can interfere with the client's ability and opportunity to draw on the social worker's expertise should issues arise that would warrant professional social work assistance.

### STANDARD 1.16(e)

*Social workers who anticipate the termination or interruption of services to clients should notify clients promptly and seek the transfer, referral, or continuation of services in relation to the clients' needs and preferences.*

There are legitimate and understandable reasons why social workers might terminate services to clients who still need some form of assistance. These include planned retirement, resignation to assume a new position, evidence that clients are not making appropriate progress or cooperating with an intervention plan, lack of expertise to assist clients with specific needs, being threatened or sued by clients, and clients' failure to pay an overdue balance. Social workers who anticipate the termination or interruption of services to clients for such reasons should work with them to develop a plan to address their needs. As discussed in relation to standard 1.16(b), social workers should take several steps to protect clients:

- Give clients as much advance notice as possible.

- Provide clients with the names, addresses, and telephone numbers of at least three appropriate referrals when it is necessary to terminate services.

- When clients announce their decision to terminate prematurely, explain to them the risks involved and suggestions for alternative services. Include this information in a follow-up letter.

- In cases involving discharge of clients from a residential facility, be sure that a comprehensive discharge plan has been formulated and significant others have been notified of the client's discharge (clients should be informed of this). In cases involving court-ordered clients, seek legal consultation and court approval before terminating care.

- Follow up with a client who has been terminated. If she or he does not go to the referral, write a letter to the client about the risks involved should she or he not follow through with the referral.

- Provide clients with clear instructions to follow and telephone numbers to use in case of emergency. Include a copy of these instructions in their case records. Clients should be asked to sign this copy, indicating that they received the instructions and the instructions were explained to them.

- Carefully document in the case record all decisions and actions related to termination of services.

Here is an example of appropriate termination: A social worker who was the clinical director for a community-based psychiatric program (a group home) provided services during a four-month period to a 46-year-old man who had a dual diagnosis of substance abuse and clinical depression. During his stay in the program, the client had difficulty complying with a number of program rules. On several occasions he had sexual contact with another resident, was found with contraband (medications that contained alcohol), and failed to attend several mandatory group meetings. The social worker and other staff worked with the client to enhance his compliance with program rules. Despite these efforts, the client repeatedly violated the rules. Eventually the staff decided that they would need to ask the client to leave the program.

The social worker took a number of steps in an effort to meet this client's needs. First, she informed him of the staff's decision to discharge him from the program and of their reasons; she also gave him as much notice of the termination as possible given the circumstances (three weeks). Second, she consulted with the client about other possible services providers and explored several options. The social worker gave the client the names, addresses, and telephone numbers of three appropriate referrals and offered to help the client contact these services providers. Third, she prepared a comprehensive discharge plan and, with the client's consent, notified his wife of the pending discharge. Because the client had been admitted to the program as a condition of probation after an arrest for shoplifting, the social worker sought legal consultation and court approval before terminating services. Once the court had approved the discharge and referral to a new program, she followed up with the client to ensure that he had contacted the new services provider. Because the client did not make immediate contact with the new provider, the social worker wrote him a letter about the risks involved should he not follow through with the referral. The social worker also carefully documented in the case record all decisions and actions related to the discharge from the residential program and the termination of services. Thus, ethical practice also is humane care for the client and may provide the social worker with some protection should the client file an ethics complaint or a lawsuit alleging that the social worker mishandled the termination process.

## STANDARD 1.16(f)

*Social workers who are leaving an employment setting should inform clients of appropriate options for the continuation of services and of the benefits and risks of the options.*

As do all professionals, social workers sometimes leave positions of employment for new opportunities. This may occur for a variety of reasons, such as wanting to pursue a new professional challenge, an increase in responsibilities, a change in client population, increased compensation, or a new group of colleagues. Sometimes social workers leave employment settings for "positive" reasons—for example, to develop new skills and to take on more challenging responsibility—but they may also leave employment settings for "negative" reasons—for example, because of conflict with an administrator or dissatisfaction with the tasks required by the job.

Social workers who leave an employment setting should be sure to terminate with clients properly. As discussed concerning standard 1.16(b), social workers should take specific steps to avoid abandoning clients (such as giving clients as much advance warning as possible and thoroughly discussing the implications of the impending departure, providing clients with detailed information about their options for continuing to receive services, and documenting in the case record all decisions and actions related to arranging continued services for clients who are in need of assistance).

In this discussion with clients, social workers should review all appropriate options for the continuation of services. Ordinarily there are four options. First, clients may choose to terminate services if they feel their needs have been addressed adequately. Second, they may choose to continue receiving services in the social worker's current agency. In this case the social worker and the client should work together to identify another professional in the agency who would assume responsibility for the client's case. The social worker would then consult with the colleague to ensure a smooth transfer (see standard 2.06[b]). Third, clients may choose to obtain services from another agency or a private provider. Here, too, the social worker and the client should work together to identify another agency or professional in the community with whom the client can feel comfortable. Again, the social worker would consult with the new provider to ensure a smooth transfer.

A fourth option, when feasible, is for clients to continue working with the current social worker in her or his new employment setting. For example, a social worker at a family services agency provided individual counseling to a woman who was having marital difficulties. After working together for nine weeks, the social worker informed the client that in two months she would be leaving the agency and establishing a private practice. The social worker informed the client that she could choose to remain at the family services agency and receive assistance from another staff member or obtain services from another agency or practitioner. The client was reluctant to interrupt the continuity of the counseling, give up her rapport with her current social worker, and establish a relationship with a new practitioner. The social worker then explained to the client that she also could choose to continue working with her as a client in the new private practice.

Social workers who inform clients that they may choose to continue working with them in the new employment setting must be exceedingly careful to ensure that the clients are fully aware that this is merely an option; social workers should not pressure or coerce clients to follow them to their new employment setting. A social worker could stand to benefit if clients choose to follow them to a new employment setting, for example, when clients choose to leave their current agency and continue working with the social worker in a new private practice. Practitioners must avoid the appearance of impropriety and actual conflicts of interest that may harm clients (standards 1.06[a] and [b]). A social worker's primary goal should be to meet clients' needs (standard 1.01) and respect clients' right to self-determination (standard 1.02). They should carefully discuss with the client all available and reasonable options and assess their benefits and risks. Clients who choose to follow their social worker to a new employment setting should do so because continuing to work with that social worker is the best way to meet their needs.

In one case a social worker at a community mental health center provided counseling to a man with alcoholism who was in recovery. After they had worked together for four months, the social worker informed the client that he had decided to leave the agency and establish a private practice. The social worker was very anxious about the financial risk he was taking because he was trading a secure, predictable income for an uncertain one. He knew that it would take some time for him to establish a sufficient clientele and a steady income. The social worker actively encouraged the client to follow him to his new private practice. He spent considerable time pointing out why it would be best for the client to continue working with him and little time discussing other resources available at the community mental health center and elsewhere in the community. Although there may have been sound clinical reasons for the client to follow the social worker to his new private practice, it was unethical for the social worker to actively encourage the client to pursue this option without thoroughly exploring with him—as objectively as possible and without attempting to steer the client toward his private practice—all available and reasonable options.

# CHAPTER

## 3

# ETHICAL RESPONSIBILITIES TO COLLEAGUES

The standards in this section of the code concern social workers' relationships with professional colleagues, particularly other social workers. They concern treating colleagues with respect, handling shared confidential information, interdisciplinary collaboration, disputes involving colleagues, consultation, referral for services, sexual relationships with and sexual harassment of colleagues, impairment and incompetence of colleagues, and unethical conduct of colleagues.

## RESPECT

### STANDARD 2.01(a)

*Social workers should treat colleagues with respect and should represent accurately and fairly the qualifications, views, and obligations of colleagues.*

Social workers often collaborate with colleagues in various ways and settings. Those who work in agency settings frequently collaborate with colleagues within and outside of their agencies. Social workers in private practice collaborate with colleagues employed in other settings. Such collaboration occurs for many reasons, including case consultation, peer supervision, coordination of services, referral for services, agency audits, quality assurance reviews, program evaluations, and inter- and intra-agency task forces.

Most interactions among social workers occur without conflict. As with all human beings, however, conflict sometimes occurs between practitioners during their professional encounters. Social workers may have professional disagreements concerning a joint task—for example, a decision about how best to intervene with a client or whether services to a client should be terminated. Such conflict may result from legitimate differences of opinion. Social workers also may have personality clashes with one another—they simply do not get along. Even social workers who see eye to eye ideologically may find that their personal styles clash; one practitioner may be easy-going and a colleague much more intense and assertive. In addition, conflict between social workers can arise for what might be called "political" reasons. Social workers within an agency who are vying for a particularly attractive administrative opening may become resentful of each other. Practitioners who head competing agencies in a community may find themselves involved in a "turf battle" of sorts.

Recognizing that conflict with colleagues can arise, social workers always should treat them with respect. In particular, social workers should not undermine colleagues or misrepresent colleagues' views or qualifications to gain a competitive edge. Below are several examples of unethical conduct:

- A social worker employed in a family services agency informed his supervisor that he would be leaving the agency to establish a private practice. For some time the social worker and supervisor had not gotten along. The supervisor contacted the social worker's clients to discuss how the family services agency might best continue to meet their needs. In each of these conversations, the supervisor told the clients that they would receive more competent care from other staff at the agency than from the social worker who was leaving to establish a private practice. The supervisor intimated to each of the clients that the social worker's skill was not up to the agency's standards, which was the reason for his leaving.

- Two social workers for a public welfare agency applied for the open position of assistant department director. Both were eager to be offered the position. One of the social workers sent an anonymous letter to the department director informing the director that, over a two-year period, his colleague had embellished her travel expenses vouchers and overstated the number of overtime hours she had worked. These claims were wildly exaggerated and intended to cast aspersions on the colleague.

- A social work administrator employed in a hospital also served on the board of directors of a local shelter for battered women. The board was in the process of reviewing several ambitious proposals from social workers in the community who wanted to conduct a program evaluation at the shelter. The proposals were submitted in response to a request for proposals (RFPs) issued by the shelter director several months earlier.

  Years earlier, one of the social workers who submitted an RFP had worked with the social work administrator who served on the board of directors. The two had had a great deal of conflict when they worked together at a local psychiatric hospital. At a board meeting to discuss the various proposals, the social work administrator told his colleagues that the applicant who was his former colleague was "remarkably inept and unskilled." The administrator then tried to convince his colleagues that they would be making a big mistake if they awarded the contract to this particular applicant. In fact, the administrator knew little about the applicant's program evaluation skills; he was simply determined to see that his former "nemesis" did not get the program evaluation contract.

Social workers may encounter situations in which it is tempting to misrepresent colleagues' qualifications, views, or professional duties. Ethically, however, social workers are obligated to "take the high road" and always treat colleagues professionally and with respect.

## STANDARD 2.01(b)

*Social workers should avoid unwarranted negative criticism of colleagues in communications with clients or with other professionals. Unwarranted negative criticism may include demeaning comments that refer to colleagues' level of competence or to individuals' attributes such as race, ethnicity, national origin, color, sex, sexual orientation, age, marital status, political belief, religion, and mental or physical disability.*

It is unrealistic to expect that social workers should never criticize colleagues in their communications with clients or other professionals. In some relatively rare cases, criticism is warranted. For example, a social worker employed by a public child welfare agency was arrested for having sexual contact with one of the agency's clients. The social worker was convicted of first-degree sexual molestation and sentenced to 20 years in prison. At a meeting of senior staff at the child welfare agency, several social workers spoke critically of their colleague. Although they understood that their colleague's conduct might be explained by serious psychological impairment, the social workers were upset that their colleague would engage in such unconscionable behavior. They were particularly angry because of the damage caused by their colleague to their agency's reputation. Their criticism was legitimate.

In another case a social work administrator who headed a consortium of residential programs for adolescents with emotional disturbances was terminated by the agency's board of directors after their accountant discovered that the administrator had skimmed a substantial amount of agency funds for his own use. As a result of the social worker's misconduct, several large referral sources suspended referrals to the agency, thus forcing the agency to lay off a number of staff. The social workers at the agency met to discuss the crisis; during the conversation several social workers criticized the former administrator for his self-serving behavior. Here, too, the negative criticism was warranted.

It is important for social workers to distinguish between warranted and unwarranted negative criticism of colleagues. Criticism may be warranted when a colleague has engaged in egregiously harmful or unethical behavior. It is generally unwarranted when it takes the form of demeaning, gratuitous, inaccurate, discriminatory, or unfair comments about a colleague's competence or about the colleague's personal attributes related to race, ethnicity, national origin, color, gender, sexual orientation, age, marital status, political beliefs, religion, or mental or physical disability. Below are several examples of unwarranted negative criticism:

- A social worker employed at a high school referred one of the school's students to a social worker at a local community mental health center for counseling. A month after making the referral, the social worker in the high school contacted his colleague at the mental health center and asked for an update on the student's progress. The social worker at the mental health center told her colleague that she could not disclose any information about the student without the student's signed release of information, which was required by law. The high school social worker became angry at his colleague and said, "Aw, come on—give me a break! I'm the one who referred [the student]! Who do you think you are, keeping information from me?" At lunch that day with a colleague from the high school, the high school social worker shared the story and said, "Can you believe that kike [a derogatory term for a person of Jewish descent]? Who does she think she is—holier than thou?"

- A social worker in a group practice provided counseling to a woman who had just terminated her professional–client relationship with another social worker. According to the client, the social worker she had been seeing "wasn't terribly helpful. I never felt as if I was accomplishing much." Several years earlier, the client's new social worker and the social worker she had been seeing for counseling had been lovers; however, the relationship ended bitterly. Even years later, both harbored considerable resentment. After hearing the client's comment about the social worker she had first seen, the new social worker said, "Yeah, I've had several clients over the years who have had problems with her. It's just as well you got out of there. She can be trouble."

- A social worker for a state juvenile correctional facility was a member of a very conservative religion. The religion's adherents were deeply opposed to homosexuality, believing that homosexuality was immoral and forbidden by the Bible. One of the social worker's colleagues at the correctional facility was openly gay and walked with a severe limp that was caused by an injury from a serious automobile accident. During a group therapy session run by the social worker, one of the participants made a snide remark about the gay man's disability. The social worker laughed along with the other youths and said, "You know, that could very well be God's way of punishing him for his sinful behavior."

## STANDARD 2.01(c)

*Social workers should cooperate with social work colleagues and with colleagues of other professions when such cooperation serves the well-being of clients.*

Although social workers occasionally may have conflict with colleagues, they must be careful not to let such conflict interfere with their obligation to meet clients' needs (see standard 1.01). Interpersonal conflict, ideological clashes, and "turf battles" may occur; however, social workers are obligated to ensure that their own personal issues and agendas do not compromise the quality of care they provide to clients. In one case, for example, a social worker in a drug and alcohol treatment program worked with a client who, in addition to having a serious substance abuse problem, was diagnosed with an eating disorder. The social worker needed to refer the client to a professional who had expertise treating eating disorders, particularly someone who had some understanding of the relationship between eating disorders and substance abuse. In this moderately sized community there was only one professional who had this expertise; unfortunately, this was the social worker's former spouse, from whom he was estranged and with whom he had chosen not to have contact. After giving the matter considerable thought, the social worker concluded that his former spouse was the best person for his client to see professionally, so he contacted his former spouse to arrange the referral. He and his former spouse talked openly and candidly about their obligation to separate their personal differences in relation to their obligation to meet the client's needs.

In another case a social worker for an employee assistance program (EAP) was contacted by a local psychologist, who was interested in receiving referrals from the EAP. The psychologist had expertise that would be a useful resource for the program. However, the psychologist did not know that he had supervised the social worker's closest friend in another agency. The social worker often had heard from her friend that the psychologist was "brilliant with clients but could be difficult as a colleague." Because of her friend's reports, the social worker was initially reluctant to refer to the psychologist, but then she realized that she might be shortchanging the agency's clients as a result. The social worker decided that both she and colleagues at the EAP should interview the psychologist and reach their own, independent conclusions about him.

## CONFIDENTIALITY

### STANDARD 2.02

*Social workers should respect confidential information shared by colleagues in the course of their professional relationships and transactions. Social workers should ensure that such colleagues understand social workers' obligation to respect confidentiality and any exceptions related to it.*

Social workers often receive confidential information from colleagues. Most commonly, colleagues in other agencies and within one's own agency or work setting share confidential information about clients to plan and coordinate services.

Social workers who receive confidential information from colleagues in the course of a professional relationship must treat this information responsibly. They should not disclose such confidential information to other parties without proper authorization. For example, a social worker in a grade school provided counseling to a nine-year-old child because her teacher thought she might be depressed. The social worker met with the child's father, a single parent, and learned that the child's home life was chaotic. Her mother was in prison on a drug-related charge, and her father was being treated for alcoholism.

With the father's consent, the social worker obtained confidential information from the father's counselor at a local alcoholism treatment center. Several days later, the teacher asked the social worker for an update about the child's situation. The social worker shared several details about the father that were contained in the confidential report he had received from the father's alcohol treatment counselor without the father's explicit consent. Later, during a parent–teacher conference, the father learned that these details had been shared with the teacher. He was terribly upset about the unauthorized disclosure and filed an ethics complaint against the social worker.

Social workers also should ensure that their colleagues understand the professional obligation to respect confidentiality, as well as any exceptions related to it. For example, a social worker at a nursing home was contacted by the nursing home's physical therapist. The physical therapist provided services to an elderly man who was admitted to the nursing home following a short hospital stay for a fractured hip. The physical therapist had learned from the man that his son had gotten angry with him one afternoon and pushed his father down several steps in a fit of rage. According to the nursing home resident, his son often became violently angry and abusive. He told the physical therapist about several times when his son had abused him physically, but said, "I don't want you to say a word to anyone about this. My son would kill me if he knew I told anyone."

The physical therapist contacted the social worker to discuss how to handle the situation. She told the social worker that the resident insisted that no one else know about the abuse. The social worker then explained that she was obligated by law to report the staff's concerns to the protective services division of the state department of elderly affairs. Although the physical therapist was initially upset that the social worker was not willing to respect the resident's wishes concerning confidentiality and worried that the resident would feel betrayed by her disclosure to the social worker, she ultimately understood the social worker's obligation. As a result of the incident, the social worker organized a two-hour training session for all nursing home staff on confidentiality and exceptions related to it.

## INTERDISCIPLINARY COLLABORATION

### STANDARD 2.03(a)

*Social workers who are members of an interdisciplinary team should participate in and contribute to decisions that affect the well-being of clients by drawing on the perspectives, values, and experiences of the social work profession. Professional and ethical obligations of the interdisciplinary team as a whole and of its individual members should be clearly established.*

Many social workers are members of interdisciplinary teams, particularly in settings such as schools, medical and psychiatric hospitals, nursing homes, rehabilitation facilities, community mental health centers, family services agencies, substance abuse treatment programs, correctional programs, and the military. In such settings social workers often collaborate with colleagues from other disciplines to plan, deliver, coordinate, and evaluate social services.

Interdisciplinary collaboration can be fruitful because it provides the opportunity to share expertise from diverse perspectives. In the clinical field, for instance, the quality of services provided to clients can be enhanced by an exchange of ideas among social workers, psychologists, psychiatrists, psychiatric nurses, and other counselors. Discussion and debate among various professionals about the merits and limitations of different intervention approaches can provide a useful system of checks and balances.

As seasoned social workers know, however, interdisciplinary collaboration also can be stressful. In some interdisciplinary settings, social workers find that ideological differences of opinion, "turf" issues, and an informal "pecking order" among different professions can lead to intra-agency strife. Members of one profession may not fully appreciate the values and perspectives of other professions, or they may feel threatened by their colleagues from other professions.

In this challenging context, social workers should be diplomatically and constructively assertive about their profession's unique perspectives, values, and methods. This is not to say that social workers' perspectives are necessarily always distinctive—or even unique—and the most cogent; often, for example, social workers' views are similar to those of practitioners affiliated with other professions. At times, however, social workers bring a unique perspective to interdisciplinary collaboration. They should do their best to present and apply the profession's world view when opportunities arise, especially when ethical issues are at stake.

In one case a social worker was employed at a private counseling agency. The mental health staff at the agency had been trained in various disciplines, including social work, psychology, psychiatry, and counseling. During a staff meeting, the agency executive director—a psychologist by training—announced that the agency was experiencing a serious revenue shortfall. The administrator explained that the number of new intakes was down considerably. He went on to say that the agency would have to eliminate its counseling program for low-income people without full insurance coverage and limit new clients to those who had adequate insurance coverage or who paid full fees for service.

Of all the staff, only the social worker openly objected to the plan. She delivered an impassioned plea for the agency administrators to rethink their decision. The social worker felt strongly that the agency had a moral obligation to provide at least some mental health services to low-income people, especially because the agency was in a low-income community. The social worker explained that her profession has a long-standing commitment to helping low-income people and that, for her, it would be "unethical to abandon this segment of the population." The social worker urged the agency administration to appoint a task force to consider various alternatives. As a result of this suggestion, the agency director appointed a task force that quickly identified several viable, money-saving options for the agency that would allow it to continue serving low-income people. The social worker's assertiveness, based in large part on the profession's values, had an important impact on this interdisciplinary program.

Opportunities for social workers to influence ethical decisions in interdisciplinary settings have been much more numerous since the advent of interdisciplinary ethics committees (IECs) (see chapter 1), which often provide case consultation and opportunities for staff to develop ethics-related guidelines and policies. Typical hospital-based IECs may include, for example, some combination of physicians, nurses, hospital administrators, social workers, clergy, and members of allied health professions (physical and occupational therapists, for instance). Such committees provide ideal opportunities for social workers to share their social work perspectives, expertise, and values when ethical issues arise.

For example, a social worker at a pediatric hospital served on the IEC. A hospital nurse referred to the committee a case that involved an infant born with several serious, possibly life-threatening problems, including hydro-cephalus (an accumulation of serous fluid within the cranium, attributable to obstruction of the movement of cerebrospinal fluid). After thorough assessment of the infant's condition, the hospital's medical staff concluded that it would be inadvisable to treat the infant aggressively. In their judgment the infant's quality of life, if it survived, would be so impaired that the humane course of action would be to allow a "natural death."

The baby's single mother, however, insisted that the medical staff "do everything possible to save the baby." She explained that her religious beliefs required her to do everything possible to save the baby's life, no matter what kind of impairment or disability the baby faced. "He is here as an expression of God's will," the mother said. "It is not up to us to take his life. I want everything possible done for him."

The hospital IEC explored various medical alternatives. No one, however, suggested the possibility that a skilled social worker spend some time with the mother to explore her beliefs and feelings about the baby's medical predicament. The social worker on the IEC encouraged her colleagues to "put things on hold for a day or two and have one of my colleagues from the social work department spend some time with the baby's mother." The IEC accepted this recommendation, and one of the hospital's experienced social workers spent several hours talking with the mother. The social worker also brought the mother's pastor in, with the mother's consent, to participate in a portion of the discussion. After two days, during which the mother had an opportunity to talk openly about her grief and guilt ("Is God punishing me for getting pregnant before marrying?") and consult with her pastor, the mother agreed with the medical staff's recommendation to withhold aggressive medical treatment. The social worker's clinical skill and insights concerning the mother's emotional needs and the role of her religious beliefs were important in resolving what was initially a serious disagreement between the medical staff and the mother. Having a social worker's perspective was critically important in this case.

Another example of the value of a social worker's perspective in an interdisciplinary setting involved a social worker assigned to a hospital's outpatient pediatric clinic. One of the clinic's patients was a nine-year-old Southeast Asian girl, whose family had recently emigrated to the United States. According to the case notes, the girl was referred to the clinic after a school nurse noticed a large growth behind one of her ears. The physician who examined the child, a pediatric oncologist, wanted to biopsy the growth to determine whether it was cancerous. Much to the physician's surprise, the girl's parents refused to consent to the biopsy. The physician contacted the clinic's social worker and asked her "to do something—talk some sense into these parents."

The social worker sat down with the parents to explore their reactions to the physician's recommendation. He quickly discovered that the parents did not consent to the biopsy because their culture and religion prohibited any medical procedure involving penetration of the head. The parents explained that, according to their beliefs, penetration of the head with a biopsy needle would release the child's spirit, which would have devastating effects on the child and other family members.

The physician felt strongly that the child's medical condition and the parents' reaction required the hospital to go to court immediately and file a medical neglect petition against the parents to override their refusal to consent to the biopsy. However, based on his familiarity with the family's cultural heritage and religious traditions (see standards 1.05[b] and [c]), the social worker argued that there might be an alternative way to intervene. With the parents' permission, he contacted a shaman of their faith (a healer or priest who acts as an intermediary between the natural and supernatural worlds) who lived in the community and knew the family, and consulted with him about the situation. The shaman spoke with the family and was able to interpret the medical circumstances in such a way that a biopsy would be permissible. The social worker's skillful understanding of the role of culture and religion—and use of a community leader important to the family—helped resolve this complex ethical dilemma.

## STANDARD 2.03(b)

*Social workers for whom a team decision raises ethical concerns should attempt to resolve the disagreement through appropriate channels. If the disagreement cannot be resolved, social workers should pursue other avenues to address their concerns consistent with client well-being.*

Disagreements and conflicts sometimes occur among members of an interdisciplinary team who face ethical issues. In many cases these disagreements and conflicts can be resolved through discussion and skillful management of group dynamics (such as addressing interpersonal relationships and "turf" issues).

On occasion, however, such disagreements and conflicts are not easily resolved. Social workers sometimes feel obligated to take a stand on an ethical issue that is contrary to the views of other team members. For example, a social worker at a high school provided counseling to many students with substance abuse problems (typically involving alcohol and cocaine abuse). She received referrals regularly from teachers, guidance counselors, and administrators when they became aware of individual students' substance abuse. Over time the social worker became aware that several of the school's guidance counselors were regularly sharing confidential information about the students' substance abuse problems with teachers—without the students' consent. Although the social worker understood why the teachers wanted such information about their students, she knew that sharing confidential information with teachers without students' consent violated both federal and state regulations. The social worker raised this concern at a staff meeting and was criticized by several guidance counselors and teachers, who believed that she was taking the guidelines much too seriously. In the counselors' and teachers' view, the teachers had a right to know about their students' problems and progress and, as one teacher stated, "I'm not about to let some silly regulations stand in the way."

The social worker felt strongly that the regulations had to be enforced, in part because of the protection they provide to students and in part because of the serious penalties that can be imposed on those who violate the regulations. The social worker expressed her concerns assertively but did not succeed in convincing her colleagues that the de facto practices at the school should be changed. The school principal was silent throughout the discussion, but the social worker decided to find other avenues to pursue for addressing this ethical issue.

Social workers who are unable to resolve disagreement among team members about an ethical issue are obligated to find alternatives to address their concerns. In this particular case, the social worker might have consulted with a school department attorney, who might have been able to convince her colleagues of the importance of adhering to the confidentiality regulations. If necessary, the social worker could have contacted other school department administrators in positions of authority or members of the city's school board.

These situations can become complicated and stressful, both politically and interpersonally. Ideally, social workers can address such disagreements amicably and quietly by facilitating group discussion and, when necessary, involving individuals in positions of authority who may be able to resolve the disagreements constructively. If this is not possible, social workers who are convinced that an interdisciplinary team is not handling an ethical matter responsibly have an obligation to address it through other channels.

## DISPUTES INVOLVING COLLEAGUES

### STANDARD 2.04(a)

*Social workers should not take advantage of a dispute between a colleague and an employer to obtain a position or otherwise advance the social workers' own interests.*

Social workers sometimes have disagreements with their employers, as do all professionals. These may concern such matters as salaries, working conditions, promotions, organizational policies or regulations, or the delivery of services to particular clients. Some disputes are resolved relatively smoothly; others, however, are not and may lead to chronic strain in social workers' relationships with their employers and, possibly, termination of employment.

Social workers who are colleagues of individuals involved in disputes with their employers should not manipulate or exploit this opportunity to obtain a position or otherwise advance their own interests. This is not to say that social workers who are interested in an employment opportunity created by a dispute between a colleague and his or her employer should not apply for the position or should refuse an offer to fill it; rather, standard 2.04(a) requires that social workers avoid calculated or deliberate attempts to engineer employment opportunities for themselves by exploiting colleagues.

In a case involving a community action program, for example, a social worker who was an assistant director became embroiled in a dispute with the agency director. According to the social worker, the agency director was mismanaging grant funds and jeopardizing the agency's future. The director and the social worker had not gotten along for years and were often involved in one disagreement or another.

The director often confided in one of the agency's program directors, also a social worker. They had developed a solid friendship over the years, including a social relationship outside the agency. After hearing about the latest dispute between the assistant director and the director, the program director began to fantasize about replacing the assistant director, a position he very much wanted. He met with the agency director to summarize a litany of concerns he had about the assistant director, primarily about the assistant director's shortcomings as a supervisor. The program director embellished some of his concerns in an effort to convince the agency's director that it was time to terminate the assistant director's employment. He thought that the timing was right because of the most recent dispute between the director and the assistant director.

It is normal, of course, for social workers, like any other professionals, to wish and even yearn for certain employment opportunities and promotions throughout their careers. Social workers must be careful, however, not to scheme or manipulate in a manner that takes advantage of a dispute between a colleague and an employer to advance their own employment opportunities. Earnest pursuit of available employment opportunities is entirely appropriate; exploitation of colleagues to obtain a coveted position is not.

## STANDARD 2.04(b)

*Social workers should not exploit clients in disputes with colleagues or engage clients in any inappropriate discussion of conflicts between social workers and their colleagues.*

Ideally, social workers should resolve disputes with colleagues through open and frank discussion. Unfortunately, some disputes between social workers are not resolved so easily, and they may linger and fester. When such disputes occur, social workers must be careful not to involve clients, try to force them to take sides, or engage them in any inappropriate discussion about colleagues.

For example, a social worker in private practice was contacted by a potential client. The potential client explained that she had been in therapy with one of the social worker's colleagues and that "the relationship just didn't work out. Over the two months I saw her, I never really felt comfortable with her style." The social worker arranged to meet with the potential client so they could explore the possibility of working together. Their rapport was good, and they began a long-term professional–client relationship. During a number of the early counseling sessions, the client spoke openly and passionately about her former therapist and the problems in their relationship.

The client's current social worker was involved in a long-standing dispute with this former therapist. They had once been partners in a large group practice that was dissolved after several partners, including the client's current social worker, had become increasingly concerned about the apparently unethical practices of the client's former therapist. The client's current social worker and the client's former therapist had ended their relationship abruptly and bitterly. On several occasions when the client talked about her unsatisfactory relationship with her former therapist, the social worker commented that she knew from personal experience how incompetent and unethical the former therapist was. For some time, the social worker did not realize that she was taking advantage of her client's dissatisfaction with her former therapist to work through her own anger and frustration. Eventually, when some comments about the social worker's former partner were made during a peer supervision group, the social worker realized that she had engaged in some inappropriate discussion with her client.

After encouragement from members of her peer supervision group, the social worker brought this issue up with her client, apologized for her inappropriate comments, and talked candidly about her obligation to separate her own personal issues with her former partner from the client's experience with her.

In another case a social worker at a family services agency provided counseling to a man who sought help to address his long-standing substance abuse problem. The client reported that he drank excessively and "dabbled in cocaine." The client also told the social worker that he had been in counseling for six weeks with another social worker, who, according to the client, terminated services abruptly and inappropriately. He told his current social worker that his former social worker "seemed very moody and impatient with me. One day, without warning, [the social worker] told me I wasn't working hard enough in therapy and he wouldn't see me anymore. Can you believe that?"

The client's current social worker had once been fired by this former therapist from a job at a residential substance abuse treatment program. The client's current social worker shared the client's perception that his colleague was unstable and, at times, irrational, although the current social worker did not share these opinions with his client. However, after hearing the client's comments about his former social worker (the current social worker's former supervisor), the current social worker decided to encourage the client to file a formal ethics complaint against him, alleging abandonment and unethical termination of services. The client replied, "I don't know. I really don't think I want to get involved with something like this. You know how these things can get out of hand. Yeah, I'm angry about the way things ended, but I'm not really interested in going after the guy. Frankly, I've got enough on my own plate to deal with. Let him take care of his own problems." Despite the client's reluctance, his current social worker continued urging him to file a complaint against the former social worker.

This social worker failed to realize that he was exploiting his client's dissatisfaction with another professional because he wanted to retaliate for the way he believed he had been mistreated by that colleague some time earlier. The social worker had an obligation to avoid entangling his own personal issues with the client's; rather than take advantage of the client's discontent to meet his own needs, the social worker should have explored with his client how he wanted to handle his relationship with his former social worker, keeping in mind only what was in the client's best interests. This course of action is consistent with social workers' commitment to clients (standard 1.01) and their obligation to respect clients' right to self-determination (standard 1.02).

## CONSULTATION

### STANDARD 2.05(a)

*Social workers should seek the advice and counsel of colleagues whenever such consultation is in the best interests of clients.*

Every social worker encounters circumstances in which it is appropriate to consult with colleagues. Common examples include issues in work with a client that require knowledge or skills outside the social worker's areas of expertise and situations in which a social worker and client seem to be "stuck," and the social worker is unsure about where to head with the client clinically. When such challenges arise, social workers should consult with knowledgeable colleagues to ensure that clients receive the most competent assistance possible.

The nature of consultation in social work has changed over time (Kadushin, 1977; Reamer, 1994; Rieman, 1992; Shulman, 1995). Consultation was not formally recognized as an important component in social work practice until after World War II. The earliest forms of consultation in social work, particularly in the 1950s, involved social workers as consultees, often with psychiatrists who provided case consultation and education about psychiatric phenomena encountered in clinical social work. More recently, social workers have broadened their use of consultation to include a wider range of professionals, including other social workers. Social workers employed in substance abuse treatment programs may consult colleagues about the treatment of anxiety disorders. Practitioners in residential programs for children may consult colleagues about the treatment of eating disorders or post-traumatic stress. Social work administrators may seek consultation in relation to conducting needs assessments or program evaluations. According to Kadushin's (1977) classic definition,

> Consultation is regarded as an interactional helping process—a series of sequential steps taken to achieve some objective through an interpersonal relationship. One participant in the transaction has greater expertise, greater knowledge, greater skill in the performance of some particular specialized function, and this person is designated *consultant.* The *consultee,* generally a professional, has encountered a problem in relation to his job which requires the knowledge, skill, and expertise of the consultant for its solution or amelioration. Consultation is thus distinguished from other interpersonal interactional processes involving the giving and taking of help, such as casework, counseling, psychotherapy, by virtue of the fact that its problem-solving focus is related to some difficulties encountered in performing job-related functions and by virtue of the fact that the identity of the consultee is generally restricted to someone engaged in implementing professional roles. (pp. 25–26)

In one case a social worker for a residential program for battered women provided counseling to a client who was diagnosed with major depression. The social worker, who had considerable skill providing services to women with major depression, began to suspect that her client might have an eating disorder as well. Although she did not have any specialized training or education related to eating disorders, she raised her concern with the client and began to address the issue during counseling sessions. The social worker did not consult any colleagues who had expertise in the area. Three weeks after she began talking with the client about the eating and food issues, the client was rushed from her home to the emergency room because of severe malnutrition. She was admitted to the hospital when the medical staff discovered extensive organ damage related to the eating disorder. Ultimately the client filed a lawsuit against the social worker, alleging that the social worker failed to obtain proper consultation that was needed to provide the client with skilled help. The client claimed that her hospitalization and injuries might have been prevented had the social worker obtained appropriate consultation.

Consultation in social work also includes the obligation to notify law enforcement or other public welfare authorities when necessary (Besharov, 1985). For example, social workers who do not comply with mandatory reporting statutes pertaining to abuse and neglect could be found not only in violation of the *NASW Code of Ethics* but also liable for damages or even guilty of committing a crime for failure to consult with a specialist. In one case a social worker at a family services agency provided counseling to a young man whose wife had threatened to divorce him if he did not get help with his violent temper and abusive behavior toward her and their children. The family was involved with the county child welfare agency because of concerns about possible abuse in the home. For some time the client seemed to be making progress in treatment. During one family counseling session, however, he started screaming at one of his children. The child screamed back at her father, and the father slapped the child in the face.

The father realized immediately what he had done, and he pleaded with the social worker not to notify the child welfare authorities about the incident. The social worker decided not to alert the authorities, as required by law, and continued to counsel the family; he later said that he "was trying to preserve the therapeutic relationship." Two weeks after the incident, the father strangled the child to death. The social worker was eventually charged with a criminal offense because, according to the indictment, the social worker "failed to consult with child welfare authorities as required by the general laws of the state."

Social workers should also seek consultation when their work with a client does not seem effective or productive. Clients who are frustrated with their progress in treatment may be particularly likely to file a complaint against a social worker. As Schutz (1982) argued,

> When therapy reaches a prolonged impasse, the therapist ought to consider consulting another therapist and possibly transferring the patient. Apart from the clinical and ethical considerations, his failure to seek another opinion might have legal ramifications in the establishment of proximate cause in the event of a suit. While therapists are not guarantors of cure or improvement, extensive treatment without results could legally be considered to have injured the patient; in specific, the injury would be the loss of money and time, and the preclusion of other treatments that might have been more successful. To justify a prolonged holding action at a plateau, the therapist would have to show that this was maintaining a condition against a significant and likely deterioration. Consultation at this point would establish the reasonableness of one's approach and help establish criteria for when to terminate one's efforts to treat a patient. (p. 47)

## STANDARD 2.05(b)

*Social workers should keep themselves informed about colleagues' areas of expertise and competencies. Social workers should seek consultation only from colleagues who have demonstrated knowledge, expertise, and competence related to the subject of the consultation.*

It is not enough for social workers merely to obtain consultation when it is necessary to address clients' needs. Social workers also need to be selective when they use consultants. That is, social workers should take steps to ensure that the consultants they use have the requisite knowledge and expertise needed for the subject of the consultation. Social workers who need consultation concerning intervention with elderly clients manifesting symptoms of dementia, for example, should seek colleagues who have extensive training and education in this area. Similarly, social workers who need consultation about the design and execution of a comprehensive program evaluation should seek colleagues who are knowledgeable and skilled in this area. Practitioners should not rely on consultants who do not have specialized, relevant expertise, no matter how willing or available the potential consultants may be. Relying on advice from such consultants would be unethical and risky—a form of negligent consultation. When consultants are needed, social workers should obtain information about colleagues' areas of expertise and competence.

For example, a social worker in a program for adolescents at high risk worked with a 15-year-old girl who had been arrested for illegal drug use. In the course of counseling, the social worker learned that the girl was having dreams about having been sexually abused by her father. The social worker had read an article in a popular magazine about the use of "recovered memory" techniques in counseling with trauma victims. The social worker approached a colleague who worked with trauma victims to find out more about these techniques. The colleague the social worker consulted did not have specialized training in this area, yet the social worker relied on her colleague's advice about the implementation of this technique.

Shortly after the social worker's use of the recovered memory technique with her client, the client went to the police with specific allegations of sexual abuse by her father. The father denied the allegations and filed an ethics complaint and a lawsuit against the social worker, claiming that the social worker had "planted" these ideas in his daughter's mind. One of the father's allegations was that the social worker had used a treatment technique without having obtained proper training in the approach and had relied on a consultant who did not have specialized expertise in the approach.

## STANDARD 2.05(c)

*When consulting with colleagues about clients, social workers should disclose the least amount of information necessary to achieve the purposes of the consultation.*

When social workers consult with colleagues about clients, they must be mindful of clients' right to confidentiality. Although clients may consent to social workers' use of consultants, they may not be comfortable having their social workers share certain confidential information with the consultants. First, social workers should obtain clients' informed consent when they need to share confidential information with consultants. As a general rule, practitioners may want to inform clients in writing at the beginning of their working relationship that social workers occasionally consult with colleagues. When feasible, social workers should specify to clients exactly what information they would like to disclose to consultants and why, along with a description of any possible risks (see standard 1.03). Second, social workers who obtain clients' permission to disclose confidential information to consultants should share the least amount of information necessary to accomplish the purposes of the consultation. This protects clients' confidentiality to the greatest extent possible.

In one case a social worker was a member of a peer consultation group. During one group meeting, the social worker asked his colleagues for help with respect to a particularly challenging case, which involved a client who was having an affair without his spouse's knowledge. The social worker wanted some feedback about how best to handle several clinical issues presented by the client. He had obtained the client's general permission to consult with colleagues about the case in a way that would minimize the disclosure of confidential information; that is, the social worker would share background information concerning the client's clinical issues without divulging the client's identity.

When the social worker presented the case to his colleagues in the peer consultation group, the social worker mentioned the client's age, job, marital status, and neighborhood, but no name. One of the other group members quickly realized that the client being described was the husband of a couple to whom she was providing marriage counseling. The social worker who was providing the marriage counseling was stunned by the revelation concerning the client's affair; in the sessions with her, the client had adamantly denied his wife's allegations that he was having an affair. This social worker was concerned about the clinical implications of the husband's disingenuous participation in the marriage counseling. After consulting with a psychologist whose judgment she respected, the social worker who was providing the marriage counseling decided to confront the husband. The husband was outraged that the marriage counselor knew of the affair and that this information had been divulged by the social worker who was providing him with individual counseling. He filed an ethics complaint against the social worker who was providing him with individual counseling, alleging that the social worker had shared confidential information beyond that authorized by the client.

In another case a social worker at a junior high school needed to consult with a psychiatrist about a student's behavioral problems. The social worker gave the psychiatrist the relevant demographic and clinical information, such as the student's age, ethnicity, family situation, clinical history, and current behavioral problems. She appropriately withheld some sensitive information about the student's mother's trauma history, which the mother had shared with the social worker in passing, albeit confidentially, some time earlier. The social worker reasoned that the mother's trauma history was not relevant to the student's issues and, therefore, should not be disclosed to the psychiatrist. That is, the social worker disclosed the least amount of information necessary to achieve the consultation purposes.

## REFERRAL FOR SERVICES

### STANDARD 2.06(a)

*Social workers should refer clients to other professionals when the other professionals' specialized knowledge or expertise is needed to serve clients fully or when social workers believe that they are not*

*being effective or making reasonable progress with clients and that
additional service is required.*

There are various circumstances in which social workers should refer clients to other professionals. Sometimes clients may require specialized assistance that is outside their social workers' areas of expertise. For example, a social worker who provided counseling services to a young man with a substance abuse problem found that the client was manifesting classic symptoms of attention deficit disorder (ADD). The social worker had no specialized training or education related to the treatment of ADD and, with the client's consent, referred the client to a colleague experienced in that area. As a result, for a short time the client received services from two social workers whose areas of expertise complemented each other.

In some circumstances a social worker and a client may conclude that it would be best for the client to terminate the relationship with the social worker and begin work with another professional. This may occur when a client does not seem to be making satisfactory progress with the social worker or when the client's needs require knowledge and skills outside the social worker's areas of expertise. In one case a social worker provided long-term counseling services to a man with a physical disability who was having difficulty coping with his declining health. Over time the client began to manifest symptoms of a serious anxiety disorder, and the social worker sensed that the anxiety disorder was inhibiting the client's progress in counseling. The social worker was especially concerned because she did not have much experience treating people with major anxiety symptoms. With the client's consent, the social worker referred the client to a colleague who specialized in the treatment of anxiety disorders. The social worker and the client left open the possibility that they would resume their professional–client relationship when the client's anxiety symptoms improved.

Social workers should be especially alert to clients' health care needs and the possibility that they may need to be referred for medical assistance. Of course, social workers cannot be expected to be fully knowledgeable about organic and other medical problems their clients may have. They are, however, obligated to be alert to the possible need for a medical referral. As Meyer et al. (1988) observed with respect to psychologists' comparable obligation,

> Failure to refer is a type of negligence if it leads to some injury to the client. For example, a client consulting a psychologist who describes a recent blow to the head followed by recurrent headaches, personality changes, and difficulty with memory and concentration, may have sustained a neurologic injury. Alternatively he may be displaying a conversion syndrome. The psychologist would be expected to ascertain whether a neurologist or other physician was involved in the case, and either consult with that person or make an appropriate referral to help in the diagnostic process. If the psychologist proceeded on the assumption that no organic damage was present, he could be held liable for negligently failing to refer the patient to a practitioner capable of treating his problem. (p. 50)

As with social workers' obligation to consult with colleagues when necessary to address clients' needs, social workers who refer clients to other professionals must exercise due care in the referral process they use. Practitioners should be selective when they refer clients to other professionals. Referrals should be limited to colleagues who have solid reputations, who have legitimate and recognized credentials, and in whom the referring social worker has confidence. Otherwise, the practitioner may risk allegations of negligent referral. In one case a social worker was disciplined for referring a client to an unlicensed and unqualified counselor who practiced alternative forms of psychotherapy. The client claimed to have been injured emotionally by the unlicensed counselor's methods and alleged that the social worker was unethical and negligent when he referred the client to the counselor. As Cohen (1979) observed, "if a referral is indicated, the professional has a duty to select an appropriate professional or institution for the patient. Barring any extraordinary circumstances, the professional making the referral will not incur any liability for the acts of the person or institution that he refers the patient to, provided that the person or institution is duly licensed and equipped to meet the patient's needs" (p. 239).

### STANDARD 2.06(b)

*Social workers who refer clients to other professionals should take appropriate steps to facilitate an orderly transfer of responsibility. Social workers who refer clients to other professionals should disclose, with clients' consent, all pertinent information to the new service providers.*

Social workers who refer clients to other professionals should follow certain procedures. First, it is important to discuss with clients the reasons for the referral to ensure that both parties agree that the referral makes sense. Social workers should be prepared to respond to a client's possible concerns about the need for or appropriateness of a referral. Second, assuming that choices are available locally, several possible professionals to whom clients might be referred should be carefully considered and discussed with the client. Providing clients with a choice of new providers enhances their options and self-determination (see standard 1.02) and avoids any suggestion that the social worker is trying to steer the client to particular practitioners (see standard 1.06[a]). Social workers might offer clients the opportunity to meet jointly with the new provider to coordinate and enhance the continuity of the services. Third, social workers who refer clients to other professionals should disclose, with clients' consent, all pertinent information to the new practitioners. Social workers should discuss with clients which information from the case record is relevant and should be shared with the new service provider. The possible benefits (for example, to facilitate delivery of services) and risks (for example, disclosure of private information) associated with such disclosure should be explained to clients. Finally, a social worker should follow up with the client once the referral is made to ensure that the client contacted the new provider. Although social workers cannot force clients to contact the new provider, following up with the client demonstrates that the social worker has made an earnest effort to ensure that the client's needs were met.

Such steps to facilitate an orderly transfer of responsibility are often carried out smoothly, but this is not always the case. In one case, for example, a social worker provided counseling to a couple experiencing serious relationship problems. After a number of counseling sessions, the couple informed the social worker that they were not pleased with the quality of the social worker's counseling skill. The social worker and the couple ended their relationship on a sour note after exchanging a number of unpleasant comments. In addition, the couple refused to pay the social worker for the final counseling session. To his credit, the social worker gave the couple the names of several colleagues they could approach for counseling.

Two weeks later the couple informed their former social worker that they were going to begin working with a new therapist and asked the social worker to forward a number of important documents from the case record to the new provider. The social worker told the couple that he would not forward the documents to the new provider until they paid their outstanding balance. He thus violated his ethical obligation to take appropriate steps to facilitate an orderly transfer of responsibility for services provided. The social worker may have had reasonable concerns about the couple's outstanding balance; however, he should not have held the material in the couple's case record hostage pending receipt of the overdue payment—he should have handled these two matters separately.

## STANDARD 2.06(c)

*Social workers are prohibited from giving or receiving payment for a referral when no professional service is provided by the referring social worker.*

Social workers who refer clients to other professionals must not receive "kickbacks" for such referrals. Payment for referrals may create the impression that the referring social workers steered clients to particular providers because those colleagues were willing to compensate the referring social worker for the referrals, not because of the providers' qualifications and expertise as they pertain to the particular client's needs. For example, a social worker in private practice had a contract with a small college to provide assessment services for students experiencing emotional or mental health problems. According to the contract's terms, when students appeared to require counseling beyond crisis intervention, the social worker was expected to refer clients to one of several social workers and other mental health professionals who practiced in the community. The social worker worked out an agreement with the professionals to whom she referred students that they would pay her the equivalent of their customary hourly fee for each referral. This was unethical because of the potential conflict of interest (see standard 1.06[a]).

Such financial arrangements became an issue for NASW. The 1979 code of ethics stated, "The social worker should not divide a fee or accept or give anything of value for receiving or making a referral" (principle II.I.1, p. 6). However, in 1986, the U.S. Federal Trade Commission began an inquiry into NASW policies concerning possible restraint of trade. As a result of the inquiry, in 1990 NASW agreed to modify the wording of this principle to "the social worker should not accept anything of value for making a referral" (p. 6).

The *NASW Code of Ethics* Revision Committee responsible for drafting the 1996 code decided to clarify the wording further by specifying that social workers are prohibited from giving or receiving payment for a referral when no professional service is provided by the referring social worker. In some communities, for example, social workers operate referral services. Such social workers conduct a professional service, initiate clinical assessments for individuals seeking social work services and, based on the findings, provide those individuals with the names of appropriate social work providers. The referring social workers then receive a one-time payment of part of the client's fee for the professional services the providers render.

Social workers should consider the following when sharing fees (for more detail see *NASW Guidelines on the Private Practice of Clinical Social Work*, Robertson & Jackson, 1991):

- The client should receive specific services from all parties sharing in the fee paid by the client. In addition to referral services, examples of legitimate services include information, treatment, problem solving, supervision and consultation, use of facilities, administrative support, and participation in program activities. Social workers should not accept a fee when they make a referral if they do not provide any professional services.

- The division of income among professionals should take into consideration the value and costs for specific services provided, such as office space and administrative services. These costs may be factored into the decision about the division of income.

- Fees paid and received should be commensurate with the value of the services provided. That is, the income should be divided in a fair and proportionate manner, reflecting the extent of services provided by the professionals involved. A social worker who provided minimal service should not receive the bulk of the fee.

- Social workers participating in fee sharing should inform clients of the relevant financial arrangements and consider the potential clinical implications. Social workers should be certain that clients are comfortable with the fee sharing and that there are no untoward clinical consequences. The practitioners involved should be sure that clients do not feel exploited by the arrangement and do not perceive any conflict of interest.

## SEXUAL RELATIONSHIPS

*STANDARD 2.07(a)*

*Social workers who function as supervisors or educators should not engage in sexual activities or contact with supervisees, students, trainees, or other colleagues over whom they exercise professional authority.*

Not only are social workers obligated to avoid sexual relationships with clients, but they also must avoid sexual relationships with staff they supervise, students, trainees, and other colleagues over whom they exercise some form of authority. In relationships with clients, social workers must avoid sexual contact because of the likely deleterious clinical consequences. In relationships with supervisees, students, trainees, and other colleagues, social workers must avoid sexual contact because of the potential for exploitation and other forms of emotional harm. Supervisees, for example, are typically dependent on their supervisors and could feel pressured to accede to a supervisor's initiation of a sexual relationship out of fear of jeopardizing the supervision being provided.

In one case, a social worker who had just completed her MSW degree arranged to receive clinical supervision from an experienced social worker in the community. The recent graduate needed to accumulate a certain number of clinical supervision hours to be eligible for licensure in her state. For several months the supervisor and supervisee met weekly in the supervisor's office to discuss clinical issues that arose in the supervisee's job at a family services agency. Then the supervisor, who was married, found that he was becoming attracted to the supervisee. He suggested that they begin to socialize together at the end of their supervision sessions: "Why don't we spend some time really getting to know each other, if you get my drift. I'd really like to have you be part of my life." Before long the supervisor suggested that the two begin a sexual relationship.

The supervisee felt confused and overwhelmed by the supervisor's sexual overtures. She was reluctant to resist his advances, in part because she found him attractive and in part because she did not want to jeopardize the valuable supervision she was receiving from him. The supervisee agreed to become sexually involved with her supervisor, although she felt somewhat exploited by him. In this case the supervisor was unethical because he took advantage of his position of authority to enter into a sexual relationship with his supervisee. The supervisee was emotionally troubled by the situation and worried that her sexual involvement with her supervisor eventually could injure her reputation and hurt her career.

Both students and trainees are similarly vulnerable to exploitation. Social workers who function as field instructors for social work students, for example, maintain control over their students' lives and careers in much the same way that supervisors have control over their supervisees' lives and careers. Field instructors have considerable influence on the grades students receive for their field internships, and students may feel that their educational and professional careers would be jeopardized if they were to resist field instructors' attempts to get involved with them sexually. Trainees may feel similarly vulnerable when social workers have authority over them in the context of continuing education or professional development programs. Thus, social workers should not engage in sexual relationships with any colleague over whom they exercise professional authority: the risk of exploitation and conflict of interest because of the power imbalances in these relationships is too great.

### STANDARD 2.07(b)

*Social workers should avoid engaging in sexual relationships with colleagues when there is a potential for a conflict of interest. Social workers who become involved in, or anticipate becoming involved in, a sexual relationship with a colleague have a duty to transfer professional responsibilities, when necessary, to avoid a conflict of interest.*

Not only are social workers obligated to avoid engaging in sexual relationships with colleagues over whom they exercise professional authority (standard 2.07[a]), but they also must avoid engaging in sexual relationships with any colleague where there is a potential for a conflict of interest. For example, a social worker employed as a grants officer at a major philanthropic foundation was responsible for monitoring a large refugee resettlement program run by a local community action agency with funds provided by the foundation. As part of her duties, the social worker met periodically with the community action agency director. Over time the two individuals were attracted to each other and began dating, and they talked frankly about engaging in a sexual relationship. The social worker handled the situation responsibly by informing her supervisor at the foundation of the developing relationship and her wish to avoid any conflict of interest. The social worker's supervisor agreed that she should be reassigned to new duties that did not involve the community action agency and another foundation staff member should be assigned to monitor the foundation's grant for the refugee resettlement program.

In another case two hospital social workers were asked by their department director to develop a new outpatient mental health program. The social workers collaborated for several months in planning services, recruiting staff, and working out a budget. The department director explained to both social workers at the beginning of the project that she intended to have one of them—the current head of the department's pediatric social work unit—appointed as head of the new outpatient mental health program and the other social worker (who was then working in the hospital's oncology unit) appointed as the new program's clinical supervisor.

While the two social workers collaborated on the project, they began a sexual relationship. They did not, however, disclose this fact to the department director, despite the potential for a conflict of interest because of the formal authority the new program director had over her partner, the assistant director. These social workers had an obligation to take steps to avoid a conflict of interest, which might have included discussing the situation with the department director and having one of the social workers request a transfer to another position in the hospital that would not involve an actual or potential conflict of interest.

## SEXUAL HARASSMENT

### STANDARD 2.08

*Social workers should not sexually harass supervisees, students, trainees, or colleagues. Sexual harassment includes sexual advances, sexual solicitation, requests for sexual favors, and other verbal or physical conduct of a sexual nature.*

Not only are social workers prohibited from sexually harassing clients (standard 1.11), they also are prohibited from sexually harassing supervisees, students, trainees, or colleagues. As with the standards concerning sexual relationships, sexual harassment is prohibited because of the exploitation, coercion, and emotional injury that could ensue. In one case a social worker for a senior center supervised an agency caseworker. The supervising social worker, who had many years of experience providing services to elderly clients, and the caseworker met weekly to discuss clinical issues the case-worker encountered in her work. At the conclusion of one of their meet-ings, the supervisor, a single man, invited the caseworker to join him for a swim that evening at his home swimming pool. After issuing the invita-tion, the supervisor said, "I hope you can make it. I've often wondered what you'd look like in a sexy bathing suit." The caseworker was upset by the comment but was afraid to make an issue of it. She thought that her super-visor, who was considerably older, was simply from a different generation and unaware of the inappropriateness of such comments. The caseworker also worried about causing trouble at work.

In another case a part-time social work educator taught an undergradu-ate course on research methods and statistics at a local college. One of the students was having difficulty with the material and arranged to meet with the instructor during his office hours for tutoring. After their third meeting, the student confessed to the instructor that she was terrified of possibly fail-ing the course. The instructor, who found the student attractive, rested his hand on her knee for about one minute and attempted to reassure her. He told her that he did not mind spending time with her and would do what-ever he could to help her get through the course. Although the instructor did not explicitly proposition the student, the student felt uncomfortable during the interaction, especially when the instructor allowed his hand to linger on her knee. Only after she graduated did the student disclose the in-cident to her academic advisor at the college. The student explained that she had been afraid to disclose the incident at the time it occurred; her ma-jor concern, she said, was that the instructor would not help her pass the course if she told anyone about the sexual harassment.

These cases illustrate an all-too-common problem: social workers in po-sitions of authority making inappropriate sexualized comments to people over whom they have authority. Supervisees, students, trainees, and other colleagues may be reluctant to confront the issue for fear of jeopardizing their jobs or careers. The power imbalance between the harasser and the victim thus exacerbates the exploitation.

To prevent such sexual harassment, social workers, particularly adminis-trators, should offer education and training in their work settings concern-ing sexual harassment. All social workers should be introduced to material on the nature of sexual harassment, forms it can take, disciplinary proce-dures and penalties for engaging in sexual harassment, and possible preven-tion strategies. Agencies also should develop clearly stated policies pro-hibiting sexual harassment in any form.

## IMPAIRMENT OF COLLEAGUES

### STANDARD 2.09(a)

*Social workers who have direct knowledge of a social work col-league's impairment that is due to personal problems, psychosocial distress, substance abuse, or mental health difficulties and that in-terferes with practice effectiveness should consult with that col-league when feasible and assist the colleague in taking some reme-dial action.*

As in all professions, social work includes some practitioners whose personal problems interfere with their ability to provide competent services and perform professional duties. Social workers sometimes become aware that a colleague's mental health, marriage or intimate relationship, family, physical health, financial, legal, substance abuse, or job-related problems are clouding the colleague's judgment or otherwise compromising the quality of his or her professional work (Reamer, 1992a).

In recent years social workers, like most professionals, have begun to pay increased attention to the problem of impaired practitioners (Reamer, 1992c, 1994). Social work's first major acknowledgment of the problem of impaired practitioners occurred in 1979, when NASW released a public policy statement on alcoholism and alcohol-related problems (NASW, 1987). By 1980 a small nationwide support group for chemically dependent practitioners, Social Workers Helping Social Workers, had formed. In 1982 NASW created the Occupational Social Work Task Force, which was charged with developing a "consistent professional approach for distressed NASW members" (NASW, 1987, p. 7). In 1984 the NASW Delegate Assembly approved a resolution on impairment, and in 1987 the organization published the *Impaired Social Worker Program Resource Book*, prepared by the NASW Commission on Employment and Economic Support, to help practitioners design programs for impaired social workers. The introduction to the 1987 resource book stated,

> Social workers, like other professionals, have within their ranks those who, because of substance abuse, chemical dependency, mental illness or stress, are unable to function effectively in their jobs. These are the impaired social workers. . . . The problem of impairment is compounded by the fact that the professionals who suffer from the effect of mental illness, stress or substance abuse are like anyone else; they are often the worst judges of their behavior, the last to recognize their problems and the least motivated to seek help. Not only are they able to hide or avoid confronting their behavior, they are often abetted by colleagues who find it difficult to accept that a professional could let his or her problem get out of hand. (p. 6)

In 1993, based on recommendations made by an NASW committee chaired by this author, the NASW Delegate Assembly amended the 1979 code of ethics to include three new principles related to social worker impairment. The subject also received substantial attention in the 1996 code.

Impairment among social workers takes various forms. It may involve failure to provide competent care because of a social worker's alcohol problem or ethical misconduct (for example, boundary violations involving a client that occur because of a social worker's troubled marriage or primary relationship). Lamb et al. (1987) have provided a useful definition of *impairment* among professionals:

> Interference in professional functioning that is reflected in one or more of the following ways: (a) an inability and/or unwillingness to acquire and integrate professional standards into one's repertoire of professional behavior; (b) an inability to acquire professional skills in order to reach an acceptable level of competency; and (c) an inability to control personal stress, psychological dysfunction, and/or excessive emotional reactions that interfere with professional functioning. (p. 598)

Social workers have an ethical obligation to be alert to signs of impairment among colleagues and to consult with those colleagues when feasible about possible remedial action, particularly when the impairment appears to interfere with the colleagues' practice effectiveness. Although there are no precise predictors of impairment among professionals and reasons for impairment vary considerably, data have suggested that patterns exist. Freudenberger (1986), for example, concluded with regard to warning signs:

> I have worked with at least 60 impaired professionals, psychologists, social workers, dentists, physicians, and attorneys during the past ten years and have found certain personality characteristics to be common. For the most part, impaired professionals are between 30 and 55 years of age. . . . Early childhood impoverishment is another common characteristic. . . .
>
> Most, if not all, of the patients I worked with led consistently unhealthy lifestyles. They tended to be masochistic, to have low self-images, and to be self-destructive in their personal and professional lives. Eighteen of the 60 had been married more than one time, 10 were bachelors, and the remainder were separated or divorced. Those who were married had frequent extramarital affairs. They all worked excessively long hours. . . . All tended to be perfectionists and were usually never pleased with their work. "I know I can be better, I'm not good enough, I could have done more" are frequently heard refrains. They tended to conduct their lives, both at home and in the office, in such a way that they found little, if any, relief from their chores. They had a desperate need to be needed and rationalized taking drugs as doing something for themselves. . . . They rationalized, denied, and overcompensated to an excessive degree. While expressing a sense of dedication and commitment, they denied that abusing drugs or alcohol or sexually abusing clients might eventually lead to their destruction. As a group they were risk takers with their own as well as their patients' lives. (pp. 137–138)

Social workers' primary obligation is to address colleagues' impairment when there is evidence that it interferes with the colleagues' practice effectiveness (consistent with social workers' primary commitment to clients as set forth in standard 1.01). For example, when a social worker's colleague who is clinically depressed has begun to miss appointments with clients or abuse clients verbally, the social worker must take steps to address the impairment.

There may be times, however, when a social worker is concerned about a colleague's impairment, but there is no evidence that the impairment affects his or her work. For example, a social worker in a state prison was concerned that one of his colleagues was abusing alcohol, based on the colleague's self-reports and the social worker's observations of the colleague at several social gatherings. There was no evidence, however, that the colleague's work was affected in any way by the apparent alcohol abuse. In such cases social workers must use their best judgment about the appropriateness and likely effectiveness of sharing their concerns with colleagues.

One other important element in standard 2.09(a) concerns the feasibility of consulting with a colleague about his or her impairment. The *NASW Code of Ethics* Revision Committee was aware that there are circumstances in which it may not be feasible for a social worker to consult directly with a colleague. This can occur when, for example, the colleague seems to be emotionally unstable and dangerous or when the social worker would be putting himself or herself in an especially vulnerable position (for example, if the impaired colleague is the social worker's boss). These exceptional circumstances do not absolve social workers of their responsibility; they may mean only that direct consultation with one's colleague may not be feasible, and some alternative course of action may be appropriate (for a discussion of options, see standard 2.09[b]).

## STANDARD 2.09(b)

*Social workers who believe that a social work colleague's impairment interferes with practice effectiveness and that the colleague has not taken adequate steps to address the impairment should take action through appropriate channels established by employers, agencies, NASW, licensing and regulatory bodies, and other professional organizations.*

Sometimes social workers who consult with an impaired colleague about their concern find that the colleague is able to address the problem on his or her own and no further action is needed. Unfortunately, this approach is not always successful. In some cases impaired social workers are unable or unwilling to address their problem; in others, it is not feasible to consult with impaired colleagues because of possible risks, and social workers need to consider other options to address their concerns about possible harm to clients.

Ideally, social workers' efforts to address impairment among colleagues would include several components (Fausel, 1988; Schoener & Gonsiorek, 1988; Sonnenstuhl, 1989; VandenBos & Duthie, 1986):

- Social workers need to be able to recognize and acknowledge impairment when it exists.
- Social workers should have some understanding of the causes of impairment.
- When feasible, social workers should be willing to approach colleagues who appear to be impaired and discuss their concerns and possible remedies (what Sonnenstuhl, 1989, called "constructive confrontation").
- If efforts to work with an impaired colleague are not successful, social workers should take action through appropriate channels established by employers, agencies, NASW (committees on inquiry), licensing and regulatory bodies, and other professional organizations (such as professional associations that certify social workers to use particular treatment approaches or work with particular groups of clients).

If there is evidence that a social worker is impaired, that practitioner's colleague, supervisor, or local regulatory body should make specific recommendations to help the colleague address his or her problems. These recommendations should include a course of corrective action to remediate and rehabilitate. When such attempts at corrective action do not succeed, or the impaired social worker is unwilling to acknowledge or address the problem, the relevant authorities (for example, regulatory or licensing boards or an NASW committee on inquiry) may need to impose sanctions. Possible sanctions include censure, limitations placed on the social worker's practice (for example, concerning clientele who can be served), mandatory supervision or consultation, or suspension or revocation of a license and NASW membership. Sometimes members of the profession and the public may be notified through a notice published in professional newsletters and general circulation newspapers.

As an illustration of this process, consider Anne, a social worker in a nursing home, who noticed that one of her social work colleagues, Barbara, occasionally came to work with alcohol on her breath. Anne was friendly with Barbara and knew that she was experiencing serious family problems. Barbara had told Anne about the impending break-up of her marriage and the overwhelming responsibilities she faced in caring for her daughter, who had severe disabilities. Anne also knew that Barbara was a recovering alcoholic who had been sober for nearly six years.

Anne also noticed that Barbara was beginning to have difficulty performing all her tasks at work. Barbara was reprimanded by her supervisor for failing to complete paperwork in a timely fashion. In addition, Anne overheard several other members of the nursing home staff talking about overhearing Barbara apparently being verbally abusive to one of the residents.

Anne decided to invite Barbara out to lunch to discuss her concerns. During their lunch, Anne told Barbara that she was concerned about how she was functioning, particularly in light of her problems at home. Anne described in detail what concerned her and asked Barbara whether she was able to cope with the stress in her life. Barbara began to cry and disclosed to her friend that "things are really falling apart. Not only has my marriage failed; my kid's problems are getting worse and, to top it off, I've started drinking again—I've relapsed."

The two social workers talked candidly about how to address the problems. Barbara said that she was going to contact a therapist she had seen previously and resume attending Alcoholics Anonymous meetings. Eventually her job performance got back on track and she was able to cope more effectively with the acute and chronic stress in her life. The constructive confrontation was effective.

In another, less successful, case a social worker for a family preservation program was summoned by his supervisor, who was concerned about several aspects of the social worker's job performance. The supervisor had been contacted by three of the social worker's clients—all from different families—who complained that the social worker occasionally missed appointments, was often hostile, and was not very helpful.

The supervisor invited the social worker to comment on the complaints and explored whether he was having difficulty in his personal life. The social worker reacted defensively and said that the family members who complained were unusually difficult clients who did not like his professional style. The supervisor and social worker spent time discussing how the social worker might improve his relationship with these clients.

Over the next two months the supervisor continued to receive similar complaints about the social worker, some from the same clients and some from other clients. Once again the supervisor called in the social worker to discuss the problems. During this conversation he acknowledged that he had been under a lot of stress lately because of some serious financial problems; he said he understood that this stress might be affecting his work.

When the social worker's job performance did not improve, the supervisor told him that he was being placed on probation for three months. They worked out a plan to help the social worker improve his performance (mainly by increasing the frequency of supervision); the plan included several specific goals related to improved job performance that the social worker would need to achieve to retain his job. During this period the social worker disclosed to the supervisor that his work-related problems stemmed from cocaine addiction, and he agreed to enter an outpatient substance abuse treatment program. After only one month, however, he dropped out of the treatment program; in the meantime, his job performance continued to deteriorate. The supervisor then consulted with the agency director and the agency's lawyer and recommended that the agency terminate the social worker's employment. The agency director also notified the state licensing board about her concerns, concluding that she had an obligation to protect the public from the clearly impaired social worker. The licensing board initiated proceedings to review the case. This course of action was necessary because of the social worker's difficulty in addressing his impairment and because of the risk he posed to clients.

## INCOMPETENCE OF COLLEAGUES

*STANDARD 2.10(a)*

---

*Social workers who have direct knowledge of a social work colleague's incompetence should consult with that colleague when feasible and assist the colleague in taking remedial action.*

Social workers sometimes encounter colleagues whose professional competence is questionable. This may result from inadequate education, poor training, or limited skill or aptitude. Unlike the preceding standards concerning practitioner impairment, which focus on social worker dysfunction, standard 2.10(a) focuses primarily on the adequacy (or inadequacy) of social workers' basic professional knowledge and skill. For example, social workers who work with elderly clients but lack basic education concerning the aging process and intervention models relevant to elderly people may be incompetent in their work. Social workers who conduct suicide assessments or program evaluations ineptly because they have not yet learned these skills may be incompetent in these areas. Clinical social workers who lack basic assessment and interviewing skills may be incompetent.

Social workers who have direct knowledge of a colleague's incompetence should consult with that colleague when feasible and assist the colleague in taking remedial action. In formal terms, social workers are considered to be incompetent when their job performance falls below what is known as the "standard of care" in the profession. The standard of care requires a professional to do what the "reasonable person of ordinary prudence" would do in similar circumstances (Gifis, 1991, p. 460).

For many years courts defined the standard of care by comparing a practitioner's actions with those of similarly trained professionals in the same community (the locality rule). The underlying assumption was that levels of training, education, and skill varied from community to community because of differences in available educational programs and opportunities, teaching technology, and intervention approaches.

Now, however, the locality rule has been replaced in many jurisdictions either by judicial decision or legislation (Schutz, 1982). These more recent guidelines are based on the availability of modern technological developments that enable professionals nationwide to have access to similar education, training, and information. For example, book and journal publishing, dissemination of information through computer networks, teleconferencing, and videotapes enable practitioners all over the United States to gain access to similar information. As a result, the standard of care now typically refers to national rather than local norms.

Incompetence can be defined in two ways. First, an incompetent social worker may perform specific actions or duties in a flawed manner, inconsistent with the prevailing standard of care. These are called "acts of commission." Examples include social workers who conducted suicide assessments but did not do so thoroughly, referred clients to other providers but did not properly screen the providers' areas of expertise or qualifications, documented insufficient services provided to clients, or disclosed confidential information to third parties without proper authorization. Second, social workers may fail to perform their expected duties in light of the prevailing standard of care. These are called "acts of omission" or "nonfeasance." Examples include social workers who failed entirely to conduct a suicide assessment that needed to be conducted, failed to notify clients about what to do in case of emergency, or failed to notify child welfare authorities when they had information indicating that the child of clients had been physically abused by the parents.

Often the standard of care in social work is clear. For example, practitioners agree that competent social workers conduct suicide assessments when their clients appear to be suicidal, obtain clients' consent before videotaping or audiotaping them, notify clients about what to do in case of emergency, and refer clients to other providers when the social workers do not have the skills or knowledge required to assist those clients.

Occasionally, however, the standard of care in social work is not clear. At times even experienced practitioners disagree among themselves about the most appropriate approach or course of action. Social workers sometimes disagree about the appropriateness of intervention approaches in general (for example, the use of hypnosis or recovered memory techniques) or about how specific clinical circumstances should be handled. For example, in a case discussed elsewhere in this book, social workers disagreed about the nature of a practitioner's obligation to disclose a client's HIV-positive status to his sexual partner when the client was unwilling to do so himself and, in the practitioner's judgment, the sexual partner was at risk of infection. In another case also discussed elsewhere in this book, a hospital-based social worker was told by colleagues that the parents of a Southeast Asian child who had a possibly cancerous growth behind her ear had refused for religious reasons to consent to a biopsy of the growth. Hospital staff disagreed about the core ethical obligation in this case. Some argued that the hospital lawyer should file a petition in court requesting authorization for the hospital to biopsy the growth against the parents' expressed wishes. Others argued that the hospital was obligated to respect the parents' wishes and religious beliefs, even though the child's life was at risk.

Courts recognize that professionals subscribe to various, sometimes competing, schools of thought (Austin et al., 1990; Reamer, 1994). Rather than try to determine which school of thought is superior, courts have generally acknowledged the legitimacy of different perspectives as long as they are supported by a "respectable minority of the profession" (Hogan, 1979, p. 9). In cases in which it is difficult to determine whether a particular school of thought is endorsed by at least a respectable minority of a profession, a judge is likely to explore whether relevant standards of practice and ethical guidelines exist.

Thus practitioners' competence is judged according to the principles and doctrine endorsed by the school of thought to which they subscribe. As Slovenko (1978) noted with respect to court decisions concerning psychotherapists' competence,

> The courts tend not to pass judgment on the appropriate therapy or the efficacy of different forms of treatment (except sterilization, electroshock, and psychosurgery), a reflection of Judge Cardozo's observation that the law treats medicine with diffidence and respect. Thus, the court has refused to consider which "of two equally reputable methods of psychiatric treatment"—psychoanalysis as against a physiological approach—would prove most efficacious in a particular case. In *Tribby v. Cameron*, for example, the U.S. Court of Appeals for the District of Columbia said: "We do not suggest that the court should or can decide what particular treatment this patient requires. The court's function here resembles ours when we review agency action. We do not decide whether one agency has made the best decision, but only make sure it has made permissible and reasonable decision in view of the relevant information and within a broad range of discretion." (pp. 61–62)

In the final analysis, social workers must use their own best judgment as to their colleagues' competence. If social workers have reason to believe that a colleague is incompetent, they should consult with the colleague, if feasible, and help him or her address the concerns. As with impaired colleagues, it may not always be feasible to consult with the colleague who appears to be incompetent, perhaps because the colleague would respond in a hostile manner or the concerned social worker would be placed in a vulnerable position. Often, however, colleagues' incompetence can be addressed, for example, by arranging for increased supervision, consultation, and continuing education.

## STANDARD 2.10(b)

*Social workers who believe that a social work colleague is incompetent and has not taken adequate steps to address the incompetence should take action through appropriate channels established by employers, agencies, NASW, licensing and regulatory bodies, and other professional organizations.*

As with impaired colleagues, social workers sometimes find that colleagues are not able or willing to address their incompetence. Social workers who are incompetent in some way may be in denial about their limitations or unwilling to take the time and make the effort to enhance their knowledge and skills. When social workers are concerned about the possible impact of a colleague's incompetence on clients, they must take steps to prevent harm, and this may result in bringing those concerns to the attention of supervisors or administrators. In extreme cases, social workers may need to bring their concerns to the attention of NASW, licensing and regulatory bodies, or other relevant professional organizations.

For example, Jack, a social worker on the staff of an outpatient adolescent treatment program, discovered that his colleague at the agency, also a social worker, was not very astute clinically. He had noticed over time that the other social worker, Bill, was unfamiliar with many relevant and commonly used assessment and diagnostic tools, had not read much literature related to work with troubled adolescents, had difficulty engaging clients, and often seemed lost or confused in staff case conferences concerning clinical dynamics. Eventually Jack concluded that Bill was "in over his head clinically." Jack did not feel comfortable sharing his concerns with Bill, given that they were colleagues in similar positions at the agency. Instead, Jack shared his concerns with his supervisor, explaining that he was uneasy about discussing these issues with her, but that he felt an obligation to the agency and its clients.

Shortly thereafter, the supervisor, who also was concerned about Bill's competence, arranged to meet with him and discussed her concerns about his performance. During their meeting, Bill told the supervisor that he knew he was not doing as well as he was capable of doing; he explained that he had been feeling overwhelmed by his responsibilities and recognized that he needed to strengthen his clinical skills. He and the supervisor then developed a plan to help him enhance his skills, primarily by enrolling in continuing education courses and professional seminars and increasing the amount of time spent in supervision. Within six months, the quality of Bill's work improved substantially.

## UNETHICAL CONDUCT OF COLLEAGUES

### STANDARD 2.11(a)

*Social workers should take adequate measures to discourage, prevent, expose, and correct the unethical conduct of colleagues.*

One of the characteristics of being a member of a profession is willingness to establish, maintain, and enforce high ethical standards. Most social workers embrace social work's values and practice ethically, but a relatively small percentage of social workers violate ethical standards of the profession. Examples include social workers who become sexually involved with clients, disclose confidential information without proper authorization, use derogatory or defamatory language to describe clients, discriminate against members of ethnic subgroups, falsify records, submit fraudulent invoices to insurance carriers for reimbursement, or abandon uncooperative clients. Regrettably, for decades social workers were reluctant to take on the difficult task of openly acknowledging unethical behavior by another practitioner; only in recent years have social workers come to understand the importance of alerting the profession's members to unethical behavior and to strategies to prevent it.

There are various ways in which social workers can discourage, prevent, expose, and correct colleagues' unethical behavior. Unethical conduct is most effectively discouraged by teaching social work students about the phenomenon and offering in-service training sessions and continuing education workshops or seminars on the subject to social workers already in the field. All kinds of social services agencies can offer systematic overviews of ethical problems that sometimes arise in practice and ways to address them. Professional conferences also are an ideal venue for such presentations.

Professional and continuing education concerning unethical behavior should be organized around several important points. First, social workers and students should be informed about the pattern of unethical conduct found in the profession; such knowledge may help practitioners be more alert to risk areas in the profession. Publicly available aggregate data summarizing the pattern of ethics complaints filed against social workers with NASW and with state licensing and regulatory boards should be presented, along with data on the pattern of lawsuits filed against social workers that alleged some form of ethical misconduct.

Second, information—preferably empirical—about the myriad causes of unethical behavior should be easily accessible to social workers and social work students. Although many unethical social workers are impaired or incompetent, not all are. Some social workers are unethical because of greed, not because of some demonstrable impairment. Others are unethical but impressively talented and competent as administrators, organizers, clinicians, instructors, and so forth. Thus, although impairment, incompetence, and unethical conduct are sometimes correlated, this is not always the case. There are many exceptions.

Third, social workers and social work students should be well informed about ways to respond to unethical behavior—for example, in what circumstances it is appropriate to consult with the colleague whose behavior appears to be unethical and in what circumstances it is appropriate to bring one's concerns about a colleague's ethical misconduct to the attention of an administrator, the board of directors, regulatory bodies, or professional associations. In-depth discussion of appropriately disguised case examples can be helpful in clarifying these situations.

Unfortunately, there is no foolproof way to discourage and prevent unethical behavior among social workers. Professional and continuing education can help enormously; however, they cannot guarantee virtue. It would be difficult to prevent ethical misconduct among the small percentage of social workers who are not predisposed toward ethical conduct in the first place. As Kass (1990) concluded, "Perhaps in ethics, the true route begins with practice, with deeds and doers, and moves only secondarily to reflection on practice. Indeed, even the propensity to *care* about moral matters requires a certain *moral disposition*, acquired in practice, before the age of reflection arrives. As Aristotle points out, he who has 'the that' can easily get 'the why'" (p. 8).

There are times when social workers' efforts to discourage and prevent unethical behavior do not succeed. In such cases, a social worker must consider whether to expose the unethical behavior to those in a position to address it—for example, agency administrators and boards of directors, NASW committees on inquiry, state licensing or regulatory boards, or even the media. Such actions, often referred to as "whistle-blowing," are among the most challenging faced by social workers and will be discussed below with respect to standard 2.11(d).

Social workers also are obligated to attempt to correct colleagues' ethical misconduct. This can occur in several ways. When feasible, social workers should consult with colleagues who have or are engaged in unethical conduct to try to discourage the behavior, address whatever issues may be causing it, and prevent future occurrences. Similar steps should be taken by agency supervisors and administrators and by bodies in positions of authority when social workers over whom they have authority have or are engaged in ethical misconduct (see standard 2.11[c]). This prescription does not assume that all unethical behavior can be stopped. Although constructive and skillful intervention can be effective, some social workers may resist efforts to discourage, prevent, or end unethical behavior or be unsuccessful in their attempt to address the underlying issues. In extreme cases, individuals or organizations in positions of authority may have to take steps to terminate an unethical social worker's employment and authority to practice, either temporarily or permanently (see standard 2.11[d]).

## STANDARD 2.11(b)

*Social workers should be knowledgeable about established policies and procedures for handling concerns about colleagues' unethical behavior. Social workers should be familiar with national, state, and local procedures for handling ethics complaints. These include policies and procedures created by NASW, licensing and regulatory bodies, employers, agencies, and other professional organizations.*

Many organizations and professional associations have standards concerning social workers' unethical behavior, including the *NASW Code of Ethics* and codes of ethics promulgated by the Canadian Association of Social Workers, the National Association of Black Social Workers, and the National Federation of Societies for Clinical Social Work. Social workers also should be familiar with codes of ethics that are relevant to their particular areas of interest or practice, such as those developed by the American Association of Marriage and Family Therapists and the Feminist Therapy Institute.

In addition, social workers should be familiar with the specific procedures that these national organizations have to address social workers' unethical conduct. NASW, for example, has developed procedures for filing ethics complaints and handling complaints against social workers. Ethics complaints filed against NASW members are processed initially by professional peers in local chapter committees on inquiry. The chapter committee may accept or reject a complaint filed against an NASW member and, when appropriate, conduct quasi-judicial hearings during which the complainant, respondent, and witnesses have an opportunity to present testimony. After deliberation and discussion, the committee prepares a report for chapter officers that summarizes their findings and recommendations. Recommendations may include sanctions or various forms of corrective action, such as suspension from NASW membership, mandatory supervision or consultation to address problems related to the social worker's practice, censure in the form of a letter, or instructions to send complainants a letter of apology. In some cases the sanctions may be publicized, for example, in the NASW News or chapter newsletters. The parties involved have various rights of appeal (for further detail see standard 2.11[d] and NASW Procedures for the Adjudication of Grievances, 1994b).

Social workers also should acquaint themselves with policies and procedures established by state and local bodies for handling concerns about colleagues' unethical behavior. State licensing and regulatory boards typically have detailed policies and procedures for processing complaints filed against social workers under their jurisdiction. As with NASW committees on inquiry, these bodies follow quasi-judicial procedures to determine whether there is sufficient evidence to suggest that a social worker has violated standards adopted in the particular state. Also like NASW, licensing and regulatory boards can impose a range of sanctions and requirements for corrective action, such as suspending a social worker's license to practice, mandatory supervision or continuing education, censure, and probation. Many employers, such as public and private social services agencies, also follow explicit policies and procedures concerning ethical misconduct. Administrative hearings may result in termination of employment, probationary status, mandatory supervision or counseling (often through an employee assistance program), or continuing education, among other sanctions and requirements for corrective action. Finally, some professional associations related to particular areas of expertise (for example, family therapy, group work, school social work) may have policies and procedures related to unethical conduct.

### STANDARD 2.11(c)

*Social workers who believe that a colleague has acted unethically should seek resolution by discussing their concerns with the colleague when feasible and when such discussion is likely to be productive.*

As in the case of colleagues who appear to be impaired or incompetent in some respect, social workers who are concerned about a colleague's unethical behavior are obligated to consider discussing such concerns directly with that colleague. As a matter of principle, social workers should attempt to help colleagues address unethical behavior. However, as this standard acknowledges, direct discussion with a colleague about possible unethical behavior is not always feasible. Social workers may find that colleagues who have engaged or are engaging in ethical misconduct are in denial about or unwilling to address the problem. Also, practitioners who are aware of a colleague's unethical behavior may feel threatened by the colleague and, consequently, reluctant to discuss their concerns directly with that person. For a variety of reasons, a social worker who is concerned about a colleague's apparent misconduct may feel as if direct discussion with the colleague is not likely to be fruitful.

In one case, Dora, a social worker for a neighborhood health care program, discovered that Phil, her social work colleague who provided services in the agency's mental health unit, was spending time socially with one of his clients. The client was a single parent who had come to the agency to seek help dealing with her school-age son, who was engaging in a number of problematic behaviors at home and in school. As part of the counseling, Phil met with the child's mother, in part to obtain background information and periodic updates concerning the child and in part to provide the mother with counseling services to help her cope with the child's behavioral difficulties.

Entirely by coincidence, Dora, who had once provided services to the client, bumped into Phil and the client at a local movie theater. It was clear to Dora that her colleague and his client were at the theater on a date. The next morning at the agency, Dora met with Phil and, as diplomatically as possible, told him that she was concerned about his decision to see the client socially. Fortunately, the two social workers had a good working relationship. Phil acknowledged that he had gone out on a date with his client and explained to Dora that, the week before, he and the client had decided that they would soon terminate their professional–client relationship. He explained further that he had already taken steps to transfer responsibility for the client and her son to another agency. Dora alerted him to provisions in the *NASW Code of Ethics* concerning dual and multiple relationships with clients (standards 1.06[a], [b], and [c] and 1.16[d]), relevant agency policies concerning such relationships, and the possible harm to both the client (in the form of emotional injury) and the social worker's career that could result from the relationship. After much discussion, Phil acknowledged that he had made an error in judgment and he would need to talk to his client about the situation as soon as possible to decide on a way to end the relationship. This is a good example of a case in which it was feasible for a social worker to discuss with a colleague her concern about the colleague's apparently unethical conduct.

In contrast, in another case a social worker at a substance abuse treatment program met with the program director, also a social worker, to discuss an upcoming site visit by an important accrediting agency. The site visit—which included an assessment of the program's physical facilities, interviews with staff, and an examination of agency and client records—was a critical component of the program's attempt to be accredited.

At the meeting the program director instructed the social worker to review all her case records from the past two years to be sure that no information was missing. The program director gave the social worker a list of the information that the accrediting agency would be looking for, including assessment data, treatment plans, progress notes, and discharge notes. According to the social worker, the director then told her, "If you find anything's missing, just fill in the information as best you can. If you need to, invent details that sound right—and don't indicate that you made any late entries."

The social worker was appalled that the director would ask her to alter and possibly falsify client records. When she tactfully expressed her concern, the director pointed a finger at her and said angrily, "Now listen. It's not your job to second-guess me. I know what I'm doing. This accreditation is vitally important to this agency, and I'm not about to let some goody two-shoes like you jeopardize it. If you don't want to play by my rules, you may want to look for employment elsewhere. Do we understand each other?"

The social worker quickly realized that it was not feasible for her to discuss the matter further with the director. After some discussion with two trusted colleagues at the agency, she decided to bring the matter to the attention of the chair of the agency's board of directors. The board's chair was dismayed by the social worker's report of the incident and quickly looked into the matter. Shortly thereafter, the agency's board of directors terminated the director's employment. In this case, the social worker concluded that it was not feasible for her to continue to discuss her concerns about a colleague's ethical misconduct directly with the colleague and it was necessary for her to bring this serious matter to the attention of the agency's board of directors.

## STANDARD 2.11(d)

*When necessary, social workers who believe that a colleague has acted unethically should take action through appropriate formal channels (such as contacting a state licensing board or regulatory body, an NASW committee on inquiry, or other professional ethics committees).*

As the last example illustrates, there are times when social workers are obligated to alert people or organizations in positions of authority to colleagues' unethical behavior. When efforts to resolve unethical behavior through direct discussion with colleagues who appear to have behaved unethically do not succeed, social workers must bring their concerns to the attention of bodies such as state licensing or regulatory boards, an NASW committee on inquiry, or another professional ethics committee.

Decisions about whether to "blow the whistle" on a colleague are exceedingly difficult. Social workers generally understand that their obligation to protect clients and the public from unethical social workers may necessitate such action, but they also understand that it can have serious detrimental repercussions for colleagues whose behavior is reported and, as well, for the social workers who report the unethical behavior. On occasion whistle blowers are themselves suspect; their motives may be questioned and their reputations sullied.

Social workers who contemplate reporting colleagues' unethical behavior should ask themselves several questions (Barry, 1986; Reamer, 1992b). First, what are my motives? Am I considering blowing the whistle on my colleague because of a genuine wish to protect clients and the public, or am I seeking some sort of revenge or retribution? For whistle blowing to be justifiable, social workers must satisfy themselves that their motives are honorable and sincere rather than self-interested or retributive.

Second, how compelling and valid is the evidence of wrongdoing? Clearly, greater weight should be given to evidence that is strong, reliable, and substantiated. The evidence should suggest that prevailing ethical standards in the profession, as reflected in the *NASW Code of Ethics* and other relevant guidelines, have been or are being violated. Less weight should be given to evidence that is circumstantial, unverified, or based on hearsay.

Third, have I pursued every reasonable alternative in an effort to adequately address the ethical issues? Reasonable alternatives include direct discussion with the involved colleagues (standard 2.11[c]) and other colleagues, such as trusted agency staff. Notification of outside bodies (such as an NASW committee on inquiry or state licensing board) should occur only when other feasible internal mechanisms have been considered and exhausted. Intermediate steps and mediation can be productive, although they are not always successful.

Finally, how likely is it that bringing a colleague's unethical behavior to the attention of outside authorities will be effective? Is this form of whistle blowing likely to resolve the matter satisfactorily and in a manner that protects clients and the public?

In a case involving a small, rural family services agency, one caseworker, David, learned that another caseworker, Helen, was falsifying invoices submitted to the state for mental health services provided to low-income clients. According to the state's contract with the agency, the agency was to provide counseling services only to those low-income clients who met strict eligibility criteria. David discovered that in her invoices submitted to the state, Helen was consistently underreporting clients' income, inflating the number of clinical sessions that had occurred, and exaggerating clinical diagnoses to qualify for reimbursement (under the contract's terms, only services for certain clinical diagnoses were reimbursable). David was especially concerned because both he and the agency's other staff could be implicated in Helen's fraudulent activity. He confronted Helen, who became defensive and denied that she was submitting fraudulent bills. She acknowledged that she may have made a few "innocent mistakes or clerical errors on the form," but denied any intentional or systematic wrongdoing. David, however, was certain that she was actively committing fraud.

Before taking action through formal channels, David carefully considered his own motives, the quality of the evidence of wrongdoing, whether he had exhausted all other options, and the likely effectiveness of notifying formal authorities. He concluded that he was not considering blowing the whistle for self-serving reasons; to the contrary, he liked Helen and was very reluctant to cause trouble for her. His main concerns were to ensure that public funds reached the clients who most needed them and that the agency's other social workers would not be implicated in one colleague's ethical misconduct.

David also concluded that he had solid, incontrovertible evidence that Helen was submitting fraudulent bills because he was the staff member responsible for overseeing the agency's finances. In addition, he believed that he had done as much as possible to resolve the situation by direct discussion with Helen. Unfortunately, the direct discussion had not worked. Finally, David believed that there was reasonable likelihood that bringing this matter to the attention of the agency administrator and, if necessary, the agency's board of directors, the state licensing board, and the local NASW chapter's committee on inquiry would put a stop to his colleague's unethical behavior.

In contrast, in another situation, a social worker for a community mental health center concluded, reluctantly, that it would be a mistake for him to notify authorities about a colleague's clearly unethical behavior. This social worker was providing counseling to a woman who had been the victim of domestic violence, focusing mainly on issues related to the client's tendency to get involved in abusive relationships. The client explained that she had just been in counseling with another social worker but decided that she "wasn't really getting anywhere in that therapy. I had heard good things about you from a friend and decided to switch." After several months the client disclosed to the social worker that she had been sexually involved with her former social worker while they had a professional–client relationship. The client brought up the issue, she said, because she was "feeling terribly guilty and dirty." In addition to dealing with the clinical issues surrounding the client's sexual relationship with her former social worker, the current social worker informed the client that she could file an ethics complaint against the former therapist, with the state licensing board or the local NASW chapter's committee on inquiry. The current social worker and the client spent a lot of time discussing the reasons for and against filing such a complaint. On one hand, the client might find filing the complaint to be useful therapeutically and an empowering experience, especially in light of her past victimization. On the other hand, filing such a complaint and seeing it through the adjudication process could be stressful and traumatic and would perhaps exacerbate the client's symptoms.

After much thought, the client informed the current social worker that she had decided not to file a complaint against her former social worker. She explained that she was preoccupied with her own clinical issues and did not "have room left over to deal with an ethics complaint." She also said that she was not sure she could handle the added stress, and that she "would probably feel very guilty about going after [the former social worker]. I know what he did was wrong, but, after all, there are lots of things about him that I liked, and he really did help me in some ways."

The current social worker explored the client's feelings and conclusions thoroughly and ultimately decided to respect his client's wishes. The social worker then had to decide whether to file an ethics complaint himself in an effort to hold his colleague accountable for his apparent ethical misconduct. The social worker had no reason to doubt the validity of his client's claims; in addition, he had heard rumors over the years from other social workers about his colleague's sexual involvement with clients. The social worker felt strongly that he had an obligation to file a complaint. He did not question his motives: he knew that his primary objective was protecting clients and the public at large from an unethical colleague. Moreover, he did not believe that sharing his concerns with his colleague would be effective.

The social worker encountered a major problem, however, when he considered the strength of his evidence against the client's former social worker and the likelihood that filing a complaint would be effective. Without the client's direct testimony, the social worker would have difficulty providing convincing, valid, and reliable evidence that his colleague had been sexually involved with clients. All the information would be hearsay and unsubstantiated. It would be inappropriate for the social worker to pressure his client to testify about her former therapist because of the client's expressed wish not to be involved; the social worker would have an obligation to respect his client's wishes and right to self-determination (standards 1.01 and 1.02). Without compelling evidence of the colleague's unethical behavior or the colleague's admission of wrongdoing, it was unlikely that a state licensing board or NASW committee on inquiry could find the colleague in violation of ethical standards. Thus, filing an ethics complaint against the colleague was not likely to be effective (except, perhaps, to put the client's former social worker on notice that colleagues were aware of his misconduct). In such situations, however, social workers have an obligation to protect clients from harm, respect clients' right to self-determination, and take action against unethical conduct through appropriate formal channels only when the available evidence is valid, reliable, and likely to lead to a productive outcome.

*Social workers should defend and assist colleagues who are unjustly
charged with unethical conduct.*

It is certainly possible that social workers would be unfairly charged with
ethical misconduct by clients, colleagues, or other parties. Although many
ethics complaints are legitimate and well founded, some are frivolous or
gratuitous. For example, a former client could file an ethics complaint to
seek revenge against a social worker who did not forgive the client's unpaid
bill, or a colleague who has had a disagreement with a social worker may
seek revenge by filing an unwarranted complaint.

Social workers should do their best to defend and assist colleagues who
have been charged unjustly with unethical conduct. This may take the
form of offering to be a witness on a colleague's behalf, when appropriate,
or providing support and counsel to colleagues who have been charged unfairly. In one case a social worker at a public welfare agency was concerned
about proposed cuts in public assistance benefits. Believing she was protected by her civil service status, the social worker used her personal time to organize both staff and clients to protest the proposed cuts. She circulated petitions and helped stage a march and rally that was covered extensively by
the local media.

The public welfare department director summoned the social worker to
his office and told the social worker how upset he was by her active involvement in the protests. The department director asked the social worker
to stop her activities. The social worker, who had been involved in various
forms of community organizing and social activism for many years, politely
told the department director that she felt an obligation to organize protests
against the proposed cuts in benefits and did not plan to stop. Shortly
thereafter the department director filed a complaint with the state licensing board alleging that the social worker was unethical in a variety of ways,
even though she was within her legal rights to continue her organizing activities as long as they did not occur during working hours.

Word about the ethics complaint spread quickly throughout the local
social work community. Members of the social worker's local NASW chapter organized an ad hoc committee to object to the department director's
allegations and come to their colleague's defense. The committee offered to
be a witness on her behalf with respect to social workers' obligation to engage in social action to address clients' basic human needs (see standard
6.04[a] and the ethical principles in the code that concern social workers'
obligation to challenge social injustice).

In another case a social worker's former client filed an ethics complaint
alleging that the social worker was incompetent. It appeared that the former client, who had been diagnosed with borderline personality disorder,
was disgruntled when his clinical symptoms did not disappear after several
months of treatment. The social worker, who was widely respected in the
professional community, was distraught about the ethics complaint. Two
colleagues in the social worker's mental health agency agreed to testify as
witnesses on his behalf (as allowed by adjudication procedures) about his
professional competence and expertise.

Unfortunately, it is not always easy for social workers to determine
whether charges of unethical conduct brought against colleagues are

warranted or unwarranted. Social workers may sometimes be inclined to assist colleagues who have been appropriately charged with unethical conduct or may be asked by colleagues or their lawyers to testify (perhaps as a paid expert witness) on colleagues' behalf. In such circumstances, social workers should not come to their colleagues' defense in any way that would attempt to justify unethical behavior. Defending or testifying to ethical aspects of a colleague's conduct is appropriate; colluding or conspiring with an unethical colleague and fabricating supportive testimony to protect him or her is not.

# CHAPTER

## 4

# ETHICAL RESPONSIBILITIES IN PRACTICE SETTINGS

T he standards in this section of the code concern social workers' relationships in social services agencies and other work settings. They concern issues related to supervision and consultation, education and training, performance evaluation, client records, billing, client transfer, administration, continuing education and staff development, commitments to employers, and labor–management disputes.

## SUPERVISION AND CONSULTATION

### STANDARD 3.01(a)

*Social workers who provide supervision or consultation should have the necessary knowledge and skill to supervise or consult appropriately and should do so only within their areas of knowledge and competence.*

Supervision and consultation have always been central in social work. Social work supervision, for example, has historical roots in the charity organization society of the 19th and early 20th centuries, which subscribed to the philosophy that the master exercised control over the tasks and activities of the apprentice. The "paid agents" of the charity organization society's agencies provided what was essentially supervision of the large numbers of "visitors" who provided direct services. Over time the profession has generated its own body of knowledge concerning the nature of competent supervision and consultation, the administrative and clinical responsibilities of the supervisor and consultant, and unique challenges involved in moving from practitioner to supervisor and consultant (Kadushin, 1992; Rieman, 1992).

Social work supervision takes many forms. Many social workers provide clinical supervision in family services agencies, community mental health centers, schools, hospitals and health care facilities, residential treatment programs, and other direct practice settings. Social workers also provide supervision to staff involved in administration, community organizing, policy and planning, and research and evaluation. Supervisors perform a wide range of tasks, including monitoring and overseeing clinical interventions; teaching clinical, administrative, policy, planning, and research and evaluation skills; and evaluating social workers' professional performance. As Miller (1987) observed, "Supervision has remained the principal method—with the individual conference as its keystone—by which knowledge and skill are transmitted from the experienced to the inexperienced, from the trained to the untrained, and in professional education, from the teacher and field instructor to the student" (p. 749).

In recent years the social work profession has developed various norms for supervision. In 1994, for example, NASW published *Guidelines for Clinical Social Work Supervision* (1994a). According to these guidelines,

> Supervision is the relationship between supervisor and supervisee that promotes the development of responsibility, skill, knowledge, attitudes, and ethical standards in the practice of clinical social work. The priority in the supervision process is accountability for client care within the parameters and ethical standards of the social work profession. During supervision, the supervisee provides information to the supervisor regarding the assessment, diagnosis, and treatment of each client. In a reciprocal dialogue, the supervisor provides oversight, guidance, and direction in assessing, diagnosing, and treating clients, and evaluates the supervisee's performance. The supervisor balances the establishment of a safe place in which the supervisee can discuss mistakes with the need to intrude into the supervisee's work to ensure quality service. (p. 2)

In addition to monitoring supervisees' job performance and promoting professional growth and development, supervision also may help social workers fulfill licensing, credentialing, third-party reimbursement, administrative, regulatory, and accreditation requirements. In some cases supervision may be required as part of corrective action recommendations or sanctions arising from the adjudication of ethics complaints.

Social workers who provide supervision should have the necessary knowledge and skills to supervise appropriately and should do so only within their areas of knowledge and competence. Practitioners who provide administrative or research supervision, for example, should have substantial experience as administrators and researchers. In clinical social work, NASW (1994a) has stipulated that supervisors should have various qualifications pertaining to educational background and social work degrees attained, licensure and certification, and professional experience (including supervision experience and training) and affiliations. NASW guidelines also address issues related to frequency, methods, and duration of supervision; use of learning plans; accountability; documentation and recording; and compensation.

Social work supervisors should be especially familiar with the legal concept of *respondeat superior*, which means "let the superior reply" (Gifis, 1991, p. 416). This doctrine also is known as "vicarious liability," because supervisors may be found liable for the actions or inactions of supervisees in which the supervisors were involved only peripherally, if at all. According to the principle of vicarious liability, supervisors are responsible for the actions or inactions of their supervisees that were conducted during the course of employment and over which the supervisor had some measure of control (Cohen, 1979; Reamer, 1993b). In one case a social work supervisor in a family services agency was named as a defendant in a lawsuit filed by a former client. According to the client, who injured herself badly during an unsuccessful suicide attempt, her caseworker failed to properly assess her risk of attempting suicide. Under the doctrine of vicarious liability, the client also alleged that the caseworker's supervisor was negligent because the supervisor did not meet regularly with the caseworker for supervision or talk to the caseworker specifically about suicide assessment procedures.

To provide competent supervision, especially in clinical settings, social work supervisors should have knowledge and skill in various areas (Austin et al., 1990; Reamer, 1994; Schutz, 1982; Wilson, 1978):

- providing information for supervisees to obtain proper informed consent (see standard 1.03)
- identifying errors made by supervisees (for example, misdiagnosis of suicidal risk or dangerousness)
- overseeing supervisees' efforts to develop and implement thorough treatment and intervention plans
- knowing when supervisees' clients need to be reassigned, transferred, or have their treatment terminated (see standards 1.06[a]; 1.16[a], [b], and [e])
- knowing when supervisees should arrange for consultation (see standards 2.05; 3.01[b], [c], and [d])
- monitoring supervisees' competence and addressing any issues concerning incompetence, impairment, and unethical behavior (see standards 2.09, 2.10, 2.11, and 4.05)
- monitoring proper boundaries between supervisees and their clients (see standards 1.06[c]; 1.09[a], [b], and [c])
- reviewing and critiquing supervisees' case records and paperwork (see standards 3.04[a], [b], and [c])
- providing supervisees with regularly scheduled supervision
- documenting supervision provided
- maintaining proper boundaries in relationships with supervisees (see standards 2.07[a] and 3.01[c])
- providing supervisees with timely and informative performance evaluations and feedback (see standards 3.01[d] and 3.03).

Social work consultants also need to ensure that they have the necessary knowledge and skill to consult appropriately. As with supervisors, social work consultants should provide only services within their areas of competence and expertise. Consultants, however, have less direct control over the social workers to whom they provide services because they offer advice that those who have consulted them can either accept or reject. As Miller (1987) noted, consultation "consists of structured advice giving and problem clarification about clients and professional practice; [it] becomes more or less equivalent to supervision, with all the pleasures and few of the headaches" (p. 749).

### STANDARD 3.01(b)

*Social workers who provide supervision or consultation are responsible for setting clear, appropriate, and culturally sensitive boundaries.*

As in relationships with clients and colleagues, social work supervisors and consultants must maintain proper boundaries in their relationships with supervisees and consultees. In addition to avoiding problematic dual and multiple relationships (see standard 3.01[c]), supervisors and consultants should clarify the extent and nature of contact they will have with supervisees and consultees. An effective way to spell this out is for supervisors and consultants to prepare written understandings and agreements to be signed by the parties. According to NASW's *Guidelines for Clinical Social Work Supervision* (1994), such agreements should address several key issues:

- *Supervisory context:* Spell out the purposes and objectives of the supervision, which staff will provide supervision, and any unique supervision methods that will be used (for example, audio or video recording).

- *Learning plan:* Identify specific learning goals. Identify any specific bodies of knowledge and skills that will be a priority.

- *Format and schedule:* Clarify how often supervision will take place, as well as the location, duration, and format (for example, whether individual or group supervision will be provided, whether the supervisor will be available by telephone or e-mail, and whether specific supervision techniques will be used, such as process recordings, role playing, viewing through one-way mirrors, or audio or video recordings). Take into consideration any relevant cultural, ethnic, and religious issues (for example, scheduling to avoid conflicts with special events or holidays, or avoiding video recording for religious reasons).

- *Accountability:* Spell out the nature of the supervisor's authority within the context of supervision. For example, will the supervisor be expected to prepare performance evaluations, provide recommendations for licensure, or sign case records or claim forms?

- *Conflict resolution:* Summarize procedures to be used to address conflicts or disagreements between supervisors and supervisees. This may include details concerning possible use of mediation and appeals.

- *Compensation:* If supervisors will be paid for their services, state who is responsible for payment, the terms of payment, and the mutual obligations and rights of each party.

- *Client notification:* Include provisions for notifying clients that supervision is taking place, the nature of information that is to be shared, and the supervisor's name and affiliation (or the name and affiliation of someone with administrative authority). This is necessary in order to protect clients' right to confidentiality and to give informed consent.

- *Duration and termination:* Indicate over what period supervision will be provided (for example, beginning and ending dates) and procedures for termination of the supervision.

## STANDARD 3.01(c)

*Social workers should not engage in any dual or multiple relationships with supervisees in which there is a risk of exploitation of or potential harm to the supervisee.*

This is an extension of the other standards concerning dual and multiple relationships (standards 1.06[c]; 1.09[a], [b], [c], and [d]; 1.10; and 2.07[a] and [b]). Like social workers' clients and colleagues, supervisees can be exploited or harmed by dual and multiple relationships. By definition, supervisors exercise some form of authority over supervisees, and this imbalance of power can lead to exploitation or harm if supervisors do not handle it properly.

Dual and multiple relationships between supervisors and supervisees can take various forms, including personal, religious, political, or business relationships. Supervisors should not become sexually involved with supervisees, attempt to exert inappropriate influence on supervisees' religious practices or political involvement or preferences, or engage in business relationships that are unrelated to the supervision. In addition, friendships with supervisees can be problematic. Such relationships have the potential to interfere with the quality and objectivity of supervision provided, as well as the supervisees' learning, delivery of services, and skill. For example, a social worker in private practice provided clinical supervision to a relatively inexperienced social worker employed at a community mental health center. The supervisee had arranged for the supervision to satisfy licensing requirements. The supervisor was actively involved in his church, which opposed reproductive rights. During one supervision session the supervisee brought up a case involving a pregnant adolescent who was trying to decide whether to terminate the pregnancy. The supervisor talked at length about "the immorality of abortion" and, according to the supervisee, pressured her to share these views with the client. She also reported that the supervisor "talked me into attending services at his church. I didn't really want to go, but I felt like I had to. After all, I can't afford to get on [the supervisor's] wrong side." The supervisee clearly felt pressured and exploited.

In another case a state licensing board required that a social worker obtain supervision to address issues raised by a former client who had filed a complaint against her. The former client claimed that the social worker did not provide him with proper access to his case record, which the client wanted to see in relation to a lawsuit he had filed against his former employer. The licensing board agreed that the social worker did not respond properly to the client's request, reprimanded the social worker, and required her to obtain time-limited supervision concerning the issue. The supervisor was expected to provide the licensing board with a final report of the supervisee's progress. With the licensing board's approval, the social worker began meeting with an experienced social worker in her community. The supervisor and the supervisee were scheduled to meet four times. After the second meeting, they had an informal chat about the current state of funding for clinical social work, trends in managed care, and their respective plans for retirement. The supervisor told the supervisee that he was beginning a side business unrelated to social work (landscape design), which he planned to pursue full-time in two years. It happened that the supervisee also had a long-standing interest in landscape design. The supervisor offered her an immediate opportunity to become an investor and partner in his new business.

This dual relationship was problematic because of the authority the supervisor had over the supervisee in relation to the state licensing board. In principle, the supervisee may have felt pressured by the supervisor to invest in his new business. In addition, the supervisor's eagerness to recruit the supervisee as an investor could interfere with his objectivity and impartiality in the supervision and final recommendations concerning the supervisee's progress. Because of the potential for harm and exploitation, the supervisor should have avoided establishing any dual relationship with the supervisee.

### STANDARD 3.01(d)

*Social workers who provide supervision should evaluate supervisees' performance in a manner that is fair and respectful.*

Supervisors evaluate supervisees' performance for various reasons. These include customary and routine performance reviews (such as annual evaluations), assessments for licensure or credentialing, and reports to licensing boards or ethics committees that have mandated supervision as part of adjudication or disciplinary proceedings.

Because of the considerable consequences often associated with evaluations, supervisors should evaluate supervisees' performance in a manner that is fair and respectful. This protects both supervisees and clients and the public. Evaluations that exaggerate a supervisee's skills, for example, could lead to unwarranted promotions and, ultimately, could place that social worker in a position for which she or he is not qualified, thus exposing clients to risk. Evaluations that are unfairly critical of supervisees could interfere with job opportunities and career advancement.

In one case a social worker in private practice agreed to provide supervision to another social worker who recently received his MSW degree. The supervisee was employed at a small family services agency as the sole social worker in the agency's family reunification program. The agency director agreed to pay the supervisor for her services as an employment benefit for the supervisee and to help him satisfy licensure requirements.

The supervisor and supervisee met weekly. The supervisor found the supervisee to be pleasant and receptive; over time, however, the supervisor became concerned about his clinical skills, especially those related to assessment and relationship building.

Several months after their relationship began, the supervisee applied for a higher-level clinical position at the family services agency and asked the supervisor to write a reference letter commenting on his clinical skills. The supervisor wrote the evaluation but exaggerated the supervisee's strengths and glossed over his weaknesses. Based largely on the supervisor's evaluation, the promotion was granted. Before long, however, it became clear to the agency director and other staff that the supervisee was not qualified to handle his new responsibilities. He was demoted and eventually left the agency. Clearly, in this case the supervisor's behavior was unethical.

In another case a social worker who was the clinical director in a day treatment program at a psychiatric hospital provided supervision to a social worker on the hospital staff. Over time the two found that their ideas clashed on various clinical issues, in part because of their different ideological perspectives. In addition, according to the social worker on staff, the two experienced "personality conflicts almost from day one."

The staff social worker eventually filed a grievance at work alleging that her supervisor's annual evaluation was "unjustifiably critical and unfair" in a number of respects. The social worker claimed that the supervisor "was determined to make my life miserable in this job" and "went out of her way to paint a false picture of my job performance." The social worker arranged for coworkers to testify about her competence and proficiency at the grievance hearing. The hearing officer ultimately concluded that the social work supervisor's evaluation had been "unfair, contradictory, and overly critical. The evidence presented by [the social worker] and her coworkers' testimony refuted [the supervisor's] conclusions about inferior job performance."

Social workers who provide supervision thus need to be careful to be fair and respectful when evaluating supervisees' performance and professional expertise. Constructive criticism is appropriate, warranted, and necessary at times. Such critical feedback should always be worded in terms of concrete, observable, and specific behaviors that indicate below-par performance. Examples include documentation of meetings missed by supervisees; supervisees' lack of knowledge in specific relevant areas; incidents of insubordination or offensive language directed toward administrators, staff, or clients; and failure to complete paperwork on time. Social work supervisors who have conflicts with supervisees must be careful to avoid criticizing them unjustly. Whatever conflict exists should be addressed directly and forthrightly, always using respectful language.

Social work supervisors also should avoid gratuitously positive evaluations of supervisees. Hyperbolic and unwarranted praise can be damaging as well, particularly to clients and the public, who depend on competent and skillful social workers for assistance. Social workers need to have a realistic grasp of their limitations, as well as their strengths, to provide the best service possible.

## EDUCATION AND TRAINING

### STANDARD 3.02(a)

*Social workers who function as educators, field instructors for students, or trainers should provide instruction only within their areas of knowledge and competence and should provide instruction based on the most current information and knowledge available in the profession.*

Many social workers have opportunities during the course of their careers to serve as classroom instructors, field instructors, or trainers. Classroom instruction typically occurs in undergraduate and graduate social work education programs. Field instruction occurs in many social services and social welfare settings, including community mental health and family services agencies, government offices, public policy organizations, research institutes, philanthropic foundations, health care facilities, substance abuse treatment programs, programs for senior citizens and for people with disabilities, schools, correctional facilities, law enforcement agencies, and the military. Training and continuing education occur in all these settings as well, sometimes provided by in-house staff and sometimes by professionals recruited from the field. Training and continuing education also are offered by professional associations, companies offering continuing education, and consortiums of agencies.

Social workers should agree to serve as educators, field instructors for students, and trainers only in areas in which they have demonstrated knowledge, expertise, and competence. They should never mislead employers and audiences (such as social work students and employees and practitioners who attend training programs) about these areas of experience.

- The director of a master's degree program at a school of social work needed to recruit adjunct faculty from the community to teach several sections of required courses in which too many students were enrolled. The program director contacted a local practitioner who earlier had sent the school a letter indicating his interest in teaching clinical courses at the school part-time. The program director told him that she was recruiting faculty to teach a second section of a course on clinical social work with elderly clients. The social worker, who was eager to work at the school, knowingly misled the program director by telling her that he had "quite a bit of experience working with elderly people" through his prior experience at a family services agency. However, he actually had little experience working in the area and was not familiar with the literature on the subject. He figured he could "bone up" on the topic before and during the semester.

  The director hired the social worker to teach the course. As the semester proceeded, it became clear to the students that the instructor was not knowledgeable about clinical social work with elderly men and women; he often read directly from books and other publications and scheduled many guest speakers. The students' end-of-semester evaluations were critical; many complained that they had not learned what they needed to learn.

- A social worker for the adult unit of a small psychiatric hospital was told by her supervisor that she would have to take over in midcourse as a social work student's field instructor. The student was completing a field placement in the hospital's adolescent unit, but his instructor unexpectedly had resigned from her position.

  The social worker was uncomfortable about serving as the student's field instructor because she had never worked with adolescents before. At the same time, the social worker, who was eager to receive a positive performance evaluation at work and be an effective team player on the staff, was reluctant to turn down her supervisor's request to serve as a field instructor. With misgivings, she agreed to serve as a field instructor. She confided in a colleague, however, that she felt "completely fraudulent. I just know deep down that this student isn't getting what he needs from me. What do I know about working with adolescents? How did I let myself get talked into this?"

- A social worker in private practice received a telephone call from an administrator of a national continuing education firm. The administrator explained that he had obtained the social worker's name from one of his colleagues and that the continuing education firm was looking for a local practitioner to conduct a day-long workshop on effective clinical strategies for the treatment of borderline personality disorder. The administrator told the social worker that the firm was eager to hire someone who had extensive training experience and in-depth knowledge of the latest approaches to work with clients diagnosed with the disorder. The social worker found the training opportunity attractive, so he embellished his description of training he had conducted and exaggerated his knowledge of clinical strategies related to borderline personality disorder.

In addition to having appropriate knowledge and competence, social workers who serve as educators, field instructors, or trainers should provide instruction based on the most current information and theories available to the profession. Social work educators and trainers should keep current with the professional literature related to their teaching and training responsibilities. They should constantly update their knowledge by reviewing relevant books, journal articles, newsletters, videotapes, and any other sources, both published and unpublished, that provide current information (see standards 4.01[b] and [c] and 5.02[c]). Social work educators and trainers should not rely on or present outdated or antiquated theories, perspectives, or research, except to give students and training participants information about historical trends and changes in the field's knowledge base.

## STANDARD 3.02(b)

*Social workers who function as educators or field instructors for students should evaluate students' performance in a manner that is fair and respectful.*

This standard is similar to the standard concerning social work supervisors' evaluations of supervisees [standard 3.01(d)]. That is, any social worker who is in a position of authority and responsible for evaluating others must carry out those evaluations in a fair and respectful manner. This is particularly important for social work educators and field instructors, whose evaluations can have a profound effect on students' professional careers. As is the case for supervisors, social work educators and field instructors should not allow interpersonal clashes, personality conflicts, or honest and legitimate differences in ideological views to bias their evaluations of students. Such evaluations should be based entirely on the quality of students' academic work, performance in field settings, and ability to act in accord with the social work profession's ethical standards. Social work educators and field instructors should not be unjustly critical or unrealistic in their assessment of students' work. Below are examples of evaluations that do not comply with this standard:

- A social work instructor in an undergraduate social work education program was concerned about a student's attitudes expressed during discussions in a social policy class. During class discussion the student challenged many official NASW policy positions on welfare rights and reform. According to the instructor, the student had "remarkably conservative" views on the subject. The instructor gave the student a low grade on a written assignment in which the student summarized her views on the welfare issue. The instructor wrote a number of critical comments on the paper, including "How can you make such a ridiculous claim?" and "Are you serious about this? You've really been brainwashed." The student appealed the grade and, according to the committee (made up of faculty and students) that heard the appeal, the instructor's evaluation and comments were unduly harsh and unfair. The committee agreed that the quality of the writing and argumentation in the paper was satisfactory, albeit inconsistent with NASW policies, and consistent with the assignment. Committee members concluded that the low grade primarily reflected the instructor's profound disagreement with the student's views.

- A social worker employed at a nursing home provided field instruction to a social work graduate student. Over time the field instructor found himself attracted to the student. In the end-of-year evaluation, he gave the student unrealistically high ratings on her mastery of various knowledge areas and skills. Based largely on this evaluation, she was offered a prestigious and sought-after field placement in a major teaching hospital for the following academic year. The field instructor at the teaching hospital eventually complained to the school's director of field education that the student was not sufficiently knowledgeable or skilled to be able to handle the rigorous placement. The inflated first-year evaluation thus set the student up for difficulty in her second-year field placement.

## STANDARD 3.02(c)

*Social workers who function as educators or field instructors for students should take reasonable steps to ensure that clients are routinely informed when services are being provided by students.*

As a matter of principle, clients have the right to know about their social workers' professional experience, educational background, and credentials. Such information is important to many clients and is a key component in their consent to services. By extension clients also have the right to know when they are being served by students who, by definition, have not completed their formal social work education. Although many clients do not object to being served by students, some may have a strong preference for experienced practitioners—just as some medical patients insist that they be operated on by experienced surgeons and not by surgical residents. Although professionals in training must have access to clients and patients to develop their knowledge and skills, those clients and patients nonetheless have a right to express preferences with respect to the background and credentials of the professionals who assume primary responsibility for their care.

Consistent with this right, social workers who function as educators or field instructors for students should take reasonable steps to ensure that clients are routinely informed when services are being provided by students. Social work educators, field instructors, and the students themselves must be careful not to mislead clients or misrepresent the nature of students' background and credentials (see standard 4.06[c]). Agencies in which students conduct their field work should establish policies to ensure that clients are informed, either in writing or orally, that they are being served by students.

In one case, for example, a field instructor in a residential program for men with substance abuse problems told the social work graduate student she was supervising that the student was not to inform the clients that he was a student. The field instructor was concerned that disclosing this fact to the clients would undermine the student's credibility and effectiveness. The student, however, did not feel comfortable withholding this information. He told his supervisor, tactfully and diplomatically, that for two reasons he felt obligated to inform clients of his student status. First, as part of the informed consent process, he believed that clients had a right to know about his background and current status. Second, he believed it was important for him to model open and honest communication and avoid secrets in his interactions with the program's residents, because teaching such communication was one of the treatment program's principal goals. The field instructor relented and, ultimately, told the student that he had taught her an important lesson.

## STANDARD 3.02(d)

*Social workers who function as educators or field instructors for students should not engage in any dual or multiple relationships with students in which there is a risk of exploitation or potential harm to the student. Social work educators and field instructors are responsible for setting clear, appropriate, and culturally sensitive boundaries.*

Dual and multiple relationships between social work educators (whether classroom or field instructors) and students can occur in various ways. Examples include social work educators whose friends or relatives enroll in their program; social work educators or field instructors who are members of students' churches, synagogues, or other places of worship; and those who become close friends or sexually involved with students.

Some dual and multiple relationships between social work educators and students are unethical and some are not. As with any dual or multiple relationship, what distinguishes the ethical from the unethical is the risk of exploitation or potential harm to the person in the subordinate position in the relationship (in this case, the student). In one case a social work professor's close friend of many years enrolled in the master's degree program with which the professor was affiliated. The student's options were limited because this was the only MSW program within 150 miles. The professor and her friend talked openly and frankly about the need for them to avoid formal contact, as much as possible, at the school. They agreed that the friend should not sign up for any of the professor's classes (there were alternative sections available) and the professor should not serve as the friend's academic advisor. Both knew that it would be difficult for the professor to treat her close friend as a student and that it would be difficult for the friend to be under the professor's authority. Although the two were technically involved in a dual relationship because of their affiliation with the school of social work, they were able to establish firm boundaries at the school that virtually eliminated any risk of exploitation or potential harm to the student.

In another case a field instructor employed at a senior high school and her social work student discovered during the field placement that they were both members of the same church. The field instructor was a part-time administrative employee of the church and, shortly after the field placement began, the student was appointed to the church's board of trustees. The field instructor and the student talked frankly about their dual relationship: They agreed that the relationship might be challenging for them, particularly because the field instructor would be in a position of authority in the field placement setting, and the student would be in a position of authority in the church setting. The student said openly that she expected to feel uneasy being in a position of authority over her field instructor at the church; she speculated that this complicated relationship might affect her learning, even though she understood that the field instructor would handle the situation professionally and responsibly. Although both parties thought they could handle the situation, they decided together that it would be best for the student to pursue a new field placement.

In a case involving an inappropriate dual relationship, a woman returned to undergraduate school after an 18-year absence to re-enroll in the college's BSW program. The student took a human behavior course and spent considerable time talking to the professor during office hours about issues raised in the class. The professor and the student soon discovered that they had a number of common interests, including theater and dance. Throughout the semester they spent some time discussing local performances they had attended separately and decided to attend an upcoming dance performance together. After the performance the couple agreed that they would like to continue spending time together. Eventually the professor and the student began to date regularly and then began a sexual relationship. Despite this intimate relationship, the student continued to take courses from the professor.

This dual relationship was clearly unethical because of the likelihood that the professor would find it difficult to treat the student impartially in the educational context. In addition, it also was possible that the student's educational opportunities would be harmed if the relationship deteriorated over time. This dual relationship was unethical because of the potential harm to the student. The professor had an obligation to avoid entering into such a relationship while in a position of authority over the student.

## PERFORMANCE EVALUATION

### STANDARD 3.03

*Social workers who have responsibility for evaluating the performance of others should fulfill such responsibility in a fair and considerate manner and on the basis of clearly stated criteria.*

This standard is related to social work supervisors' obligation to evaluate supervisees' performance (standard 3.01[d]) and social work educators' obligation to evaluate students' performance in a fair and respectful manner (standard 3.02[b]). The same obligation applies to all social workers who are in a position to evaluate others.

In addition to supervision and education, there are several contexts in which social workers evaluate others' performance. For example, social workers who serve on accreditation site visit teams are ordinarily expected to assess the quality of services social workers provide in human services agencies that have applied for accreditation or reaccreditation. The same holds for social workers who serve on accreditation site visit teams assembled by the Council on Social Work Education to assess the quality of educational services provided by undergraduate and graduate social work faculty. In addition, social workers who are retained to conduct program evaluations are often in a position to evaluate the performance of social work staff, as are social work administrators who are charged with preparing annual personnel reports on their staff.

Whatever the context and purposes, social workers who are responsible for evaluating the performance of others should carry out their duties in a fair and respectful manner and on the basis of clearly stated criteria. Clearly stated criteria are especially important to ensure avoidance of arbitrary and capricious evaluations. Evaluations conducted by social workers should specify in behaviorally specific language what constitutes acceptable and unacceptable performance (what social work researchers refer to as "operational" definitions of variables). For example, a statement such as "the employee did not attend four of seven required staff meetings" is more clear and specific than "the employee has not complied with agency policy concerning attendance at required staff meetings." Similarly, a statement such as "discharge plans were missing from 13 percent of the randomly selected files reviewed by accreditation site visit team members" is more clear and specific than "accreditation site visit team members noted considerable gaps in the agency's case files." Below are examples of performance evaluations that are unfair or inconsiderate:

- A social worker was retained by a local foundation to evaluate a two-year substance abuse prevention program funded by the foundation. The program was administered by a community action agency. As part of the evaluation, the social worker interviewed the program's staff about intervention goals and methods and program outcomes. The social worker also interviewed a sample of the program's former clients about their satisfaction with services and personal progress.

  The social worker, who had considerable experience in the substance abuse field, disagreed with the treatment philosophy of the program staff. Even before he started the evaluation, he expected to be critical of the program's approach and effectiveness, and his final report was highly unflattering about the program, its staff, and its outcomes. The data presented by the social worker were, however, generally vague and did not substantiate the critical findings. Staff of the foundation that funded the program ultimately rejected the report and concluded that its findings were biased and unfounded. The foundation filed a lawsuit against the social worker to recover the costs of the contract and had to retain a new program evaluator.

- An accreditation site visit team consisting of three social workers was assigned to evaluate a family services agency that had applied for reaccreditation. During scheduled interviews with the agency's executive director, the chair of the site visit team, who was the director of a family services agency in another state, and the director engaged in several heated, contentious discussions. Their disagreements focused largely on resources and staff allocation. At one point the chair of the site visit team told the director that he felt "personally insulted by your haughty manner and arrogance."

  The site visit team's chair wrote a scathingly critical conclusion in the first draft of the report concerning the agency's application for reaccreditation. The other members of the site visit team told the chair that they thought he was being overly sensitive and unfairly critical in the report. They told him that they did not think there was evidence to support most of his critical comments and, therefore, they did not feel comfortable signing their names to the report. The team members were not able to resolve their disagreement. Consequently, the site visit team's chair and the other team members submitted separate reports. The accreditation organization's board of directors eventually refused to accept the site visit team chair's report because of its unfair criticism and removed him from its list of approved site visitors.

# CLIENT RECORDS

## STANDARD 3.04(a)

*Social workers should take reasonable steps to ensure that documentation in records is accurate and reflects the services provided.*

Documentation is one of the most important skills that social workers learn. Typically, undergraduate and graduate social work education programs teach students about the importance of recording, particularly to identify, describe, and assess clients' circumstances; define the purposes of services and interventions; document services goals, plans, activities, and progress; and evaluate the effectiveness of services and interventions (Kagle, 1991, 1995; Wilson, 1980).

It is important for social workers to include only accurate documentation in case records. Records should not be falsified, nor should inaccurate information be included intentionally. Such a practice is unethical, and including falsified or inaccurate information in case records can be detrimental to clients. Other services providers whose actions are based on false or inaccurate information in the case record may harm clients in the process. Below are several examples of unethical documentation in case records:

- A social worker in private practice provided services primarily to families with young children. A large percentage of these children were having behavioral problems in school.

  Technically, the formal *Diagnostic and Statistical Manual of Mental Disorders* (DSM) diagnosis for many of the children should have been "parent–child relational problem," "child or adolescent antisocial behavior," or "sibling relational problem." However, the social worker knew that most of the families' insurance carriers would not authorize payment for services to address these diagnoses. To qualify for reimbursement, the social worker exaggerated many clients' clinical symptoms when filling out their insurance claim forms, listing DSM diagnoses that were more serious than warranted by the children's symptoms. One of the insurance companies conducted a postservice audit and concluded that the social worker had defrauded the company. The insurance company cooperated with local law enforcement to prosecute the social worker, and the insurance company sued the social worker to recover the money it had paid her.

- A social worker employed by a residential substance abuse treatment program provided crisis counseling to a client who said he was deeply depressed because of the recent death of his mother. The client explained that his mother "was everything to me. I know I've really disappointed her and let her down with all I've done wrong in life. I'm not sure I can go on living." The social worker documented the crisis counseling but did not include explicit detail about the client's suicide-related comments. The staff who were on duty the next day were not aware of the suicide risk because of the incomplete documentation. Later that evening the client obtained a large quantity of illegal drugs and committed suicide. His sister and father subsequently filed an ethics complaint and lawsuit against the agency and the social worker, alleging that they had failed in their duty to prevent the suicide. The sister and father claimed that the social worker's failure to include thorough documentation of the client's suicide-related comments was the direct cause of the staff's subsequent failure to monitor the client closely. The plaintiffs argued that thorough documentation in the case record would have led to closer monitoring and supervision and thus would have prevented the client's suicide, and they retained two expert witnesses from the social work field who provided testimony supporting their claims. The case was ultimately settled before trial but at considerable cost to the social worker and his insurance company.

- A social worker for a public child welfare agency was responsible for monitoring foster placements. One of his cases involved a 13-year-old girl whose father was in prison and whose mother was in a long-term substance abuse treatment program. The social worker was expected to visit the home at least once every two weeks to assess the status of the placement and address any issues that had arisen (for example, behavioral problems, school issues, and relations between the foster family and the child). The social worker was having a number of personal problems primarily related to his marriage and alcohol abuse. As a result of his impairment, he neglected a number of his job responsibilities, including regular visits to this foster home. In his case notes, however, he indicated that he had made all of the required home visits; he also fabricated details related to the home visits to create the impression that he had actually conducted them.

  About three months after the girl had been placed with the foster family, she was sexually assaulted by her foster father and impregnated. The foster father was convicted of rape, and the social worker and the child welfare department were sued by the child's guardian ad litem (a guardian appointed by the court to represent a ward in legal proceedings) on the girl's behalf, alleging that the social worker's neglect was partly responsible for the rape. The complaint claimed that had the social worker conducted the home visits properly and not included inaccurate, misleading, and false documentation in the case record, he would have been able to identify serious problems in the foster home, the child welfare department would not have allowed the child to remain in the home, and the rape would have been prevented.

## STANDARD 3.04(b)

*Social workers should include sufficient and timely documentation in records to facilitate the delivery of services and to ensure continuity of services provided to clients in the future.*

As the cases presented in the discussion of standard 3.04(a) illustrate, accurate, thorough, and timely documentation is essential in social work. It is necessary to assess clients' circumstances; plan and deliver services appropriately; facilitate interstaff and interdisciplinary collaboration; facilitate supervision; provide proper accountability to clients, other services providers, funding agencies, insurers, utilization review staff, and the courts; evaluate services provided; and ensure continuity in the delivery of future services. Thorough documentation also can help protect social workers who are named in ethics complaints or lawsuits (for example, when documentation is needed to demonstrate that a social worker obtained a client's informed consent before releasing confidential information, assessed for suicide risk properly, consulted with knowledgeable experts about a client's clinical issues, or referred a client to other service providers when services were terminated). In clinical settings, documentation should ordinarily include a number of components (Austin et al., 1990; Kagle, 1995; Reamer, 1994; Schutz, 1982; Wilson, 1978):

- a complete social history, assessment, and treatment plan that states the client's problems, his or her reason for requesting services, objectives and relevant timetable, intervention strategy, planned number and duration of contacts, methods for assessment and evaluation of progress, termination plan, and reasons for termination

- informed consent procedures and signed consent forms for release of information and treatment

- notes on all contacts made with third parties (such as family members, acquaintances, and other professionals), whether in person or by telephone, including a brief description of the contacts and any important events surrounding them

- notes on any consultation with other professionals, including the date the client was referred to another professional for services

- a brief description of the social worker's reasoning for all decisions made and interventions provided during the course of services

- information summarizing any critical incidents (for example, suicide attempts, threats made by the client toward third parties, child abuse, family crises) and the social worker's response

- any instructions, recommendations, and advice provided to the client, including referral to and suggestions to seek consultation from specialists (including physicians)

- a description of all contacts with clients, including the type of contact (for example, in person or via telephone or in individual, family, couples, or group counseling), and dates and times of the contacts

- notation of failed or canceled appointments

- summaries of previous or current psychological, psychiatric, or medical evaluations relevant to the social worker's intervention

- information about fees, charges, and payment

- reasons for termination and final assessment

- copies of all relevant documents, such as signed consent forms, correspondence, fee agreements, and court documents.

A small number of social workers have preferred to include few detailed notes and little documentation in clients' case records, arguing that this is an effective way to protect clients in the event that social workers' records are subpoenaed in legal proceedings. This is a shortsighted view and contrary to prevailing ethical and practice standards in the profession. At a minimum, thorough documentation is essential for proper accountability and to enhance coordination and continuity of services. In addition, good documentation may help social workers protect themselves if they are named in an ethics complaint or a lawsuit. In one case a social worker provided counseling to a woman who had been sexually abused as a child. The social worker was sued by the client, who alleged that the social worker had engaged in an inappropriate dual relationship with the client and violated proper client–professional boundaries in a number of ways, including sending love letters to the client and giving her gifts, sharing a motel room with the client at a professional conference, going on a camping trip and dining with the client, and watching a video with the client in the social worker's bedroom. The social worker claimed that the activities she engaged in with the client were legitimate and professional as part of a reparenting therapeutic approach. During cross-examination the client's attorney asked the social worker to point to the documentation in her case notes indicating that each of these activities was provided as a professional service. The social worker responded by saying that she did not keep detailed case notes: "I don't believe in keeping lots of notes on clients. I don't record that sort of thing." The client's expert witness, another social worker, then testified as to the prevailing standards in social work with respect to documentation in case records. The court returned a verdict against the social worker and in its opinion was critical of her decision not to provide detailed documentation of her services.

## STANDARD 3.04(c)

*Social workers' documentation should protect clients' privacy to the extent that is possible and appropriate and should include only information that is directly relevant to the delivery of services.*

To protect clients' privacy, social workers should follow a number of guidelines when documenting information in case records. First, social workers should include information with the understanding that other parties may eventually have access to that information. In interdisciplinary settings, for example, other staff routinely have access to information in case records. In health care settings especially, utilization review and insurance company representatives may examine information in case records. In addition, social workers in all settings must realize that case records may be subpoenaed during legal proceedings. Although lawyers representing clients' or social workers' interests may convince judges to limit the disclosure of information in case records, social workers should include documentation as if the information were certain to be disclosed; one cannot guarantee that attorneys' attempts to limit the disclosure of information will always succeed.

Second, social workers who provide services to couples and families should consider preparing separate case notes for each individual to protect each person's privacy. For example, a social worker provided counseling to a married couple who then decided to divorce. The husband asked the social worker to allow him to read the case record—he wanted to see whether the case notes included any documentation of his wife's "emotional instability." The husband hoped to use such information against his wife to gain custody of their three children. Had the social worker recorded separate case notes for the parties, she would not have had to be as concerned about protecting the wife's privacy; without a court order, the husband would not have had access to the separate case record concerning his wife. Although the social worker was able to take steps to withhold information about the wife from the husband when he reviewed the case file (by omitting the portions of the record concerning the wife), the husband became agitated and contentious in the process. The strain in the relationship between the social worker and the husband might have been avoided if she had segregated the husband's and wife's files.

Third, social workers should not include any gratuitous or tangential information in the case record. Only information that is directly relevant to the clients' issues or problems and the services provided should be included. Practitioners should omit excessively subjective or speculative observations (for example, speculation concerning a client's extramarital affair or subjective impressions concerning a client's weight problem)—that is, observations for which there is little or no empirical evidence or documentation. Social workers also should avoid even temporary storage of process or narrative recordings in case records because of the possibility that this information could be used against clients if it were to be subpoenaed. The record also should not contain intimate information or gossip, derogatory language, or information about a client's political, religious, or other personal views, unless such details are directly relevant to treatment. Generally speaking, social workers should not include details of past crimes committed by clients or of crimes they are currently committing or details about people with whom clients have associated when they were engaged in illegal activity. Such information might be included, however, if doing so is required by law or the information is critical to the delivery of services (for example, when social workers who are probation or parole officers are required to report clients' illegal activities or a client has threatened to murder someone).

Some practitioners maintain separate sets of personal notes concerning clients, particularly to record subjective, impressionistic observations or intimate details about clients that other parties should not see. This is a risky practice. Although some jurisdictions have recognized therapists' right to maintain private notes, many experts strongly recommend against the practice because of the possibility that such personal notes could be subpoenaed (Austin et al., 1990). In one case a social worker in a family services agency provided counseling to a well-known elected official who wanted help in dealing with depression. The client disclosed to the social worker that he was also struggling with sexual orientation issues. He explicitly asked the social worker not to include details about the sexual orientation issues in the case notes, but the therapist recorded a separate set of personal notes that referred to them.

About two months after the counseling ended, the social worker's records were subpoenaed by a lawyer representing the client's former business partner. The lawyer was looking for evidence of the client's emotional instability because of a contractual dispute between the client and his former business partner, and he had worded the subpoena broadly to include the official agency case record and all other documents relevant to the client, including any correspondence, legal documents, and personal notes. Because the social worker practiced in a state that did not recognize a distinction between "official" and "personal" notes, he was obligated to turn over a copy of his personal notes to the former business partner's lawyer. The client was upset because the social worker had made notes about his sexual orientation issues without his client's knowledge, and he filed an ethics complaint against the social worker.

### STANDARD 3.04(d)

*Social workers should store records following the termination of services to ensure reasonable future access. Records should be maintained for the number of years required by state statutes or relevant contracts.*

There are many reasons why social workers should retain clients' records after termination of services. Some state statutes or licensing regulations stipulate that records must be retained for a specific period. This ensures that clients will have access to their records for a reasonable time and that the records will be available for use during any future legal proceedings involving the client. Also, contracts between social workers and, for example, insurance providers or employee assistance programs may stipulate that records be retained for quality assurance or utilization review purposes or for use during legal proceedings.

In the absence of statutory, regulatory, or contractual requirements, social workers should retain complete written records for at least three to five years, although many agencies and practitioners retain them for longer periods. For example, the American Psychological Association's *Specialty Guidelines for the Delivery of Services* suggests that when no statute addresses a specific time for retaining records, practitioners should retain full records for three years and either the full record or a summary of the record for 12 more years after termination of service. Counseling psychology's guidelines suggest that the full record be maintained for at least 14 years after completion of planned services or after the date of last contact with the client, whichever is later; that if a full record is not maintained, at least a summary be maintained for an additional three years; and that the record may be disposed of no sooner than seven years after the completion of planned services or after the date of last contact, whichever is later (Austin et al., 1990). Case records concerning minor children ordinarily should be kept longer, because in some states the statute of limitations does not begin to run until the child reaches the age of majority. To be especially cautious, some practitioners retain records indefinitely, beyond statutory, regulatory, or contractual requirements.

Sometimes clients ask social workers to destroy their case records, usually because they are concerned about possible privacy or confidentiality breaches, but social workers should not comply with such requests. Instead, they should explain to clients why they are obligated to store case records and discuss any particular concerns the clients might have about the records' confidentiality and security.

Social workers should also make special provisions for proper storage and maintenance of records in the event of their disability, incapacitation, termination of practice (because of retirement or disciplinary proceedings, for example), or death. As discussed with respect to standard 1.15, social workers should make reasonable efforts to ensure continuity of services. In addition to ensuring that responsible colleagues are available and willing to meet clients' needs, social workers should also take steps to make clients' records available when they are needed. Practitioners should consider working out agreements with colleagues who would be willing to assume responsibility for their records if they are unavailable because of relocation, illness, disability, death, or some other reason.

## BILLING

### STANDARD 3.05

*Social workers should establish and maintain billing practices that accurately reflect the nature and extent of services provided and that identify who provided the service in the practice setting.*

Social workers must avoid any intentionally misleading or fraudulent billing practices. In particular, clients' clinical symptoms or conditions should not be exaggerated to enhance reimbursement from third-party payers (see discussion of standard 3.04[a]). Practitioners should not provide misleading or fraudulent information concerning who provided the services being billed or the types or amount of services provided. In one case a clinical social worker in private practice had a contract with the state to provide counseling services to low-income people who were covered by the state's Medicaid program. According to the contract, she would be reimbursed at one hourly rate for individual counseling and at another, lower hourly rate for each client in family, couples, and group counseling (although the total the state would pay for each family, couples, or group counseling session would typically be higher when the fees for the participating clients were added together). The social worker believed that the reimbursement rates for family and group counseling were too low, but she agreed to the contract terms. Toward the end of the fiscal year, the social worker grew increasingly frustrated with the state's reimbursement rate. She began billing the state fraudulently for the services she provided—when she saw clients in a group, for example, she billed the state for individual counseling, which was reimbursed at a higher rate per hour. A financial audit by the state eventually uncovered the social worker's fraud. She was indicted by a grand jury, convicted in criminal court, and sentenced to one year in prison.

Practitioners also must include accurate information in their invoices concerning who provided the services being billed. An invoice should not indicate, for instance, that a social worker with a master's degree provided services to a client when, in fact, a bachelor's-degree-level practitioner—who would be reimbursed at a lower rate—actually worked with the client. In one case a family intervention program had a contract with a county child welfare department to provide home-based crisis intervention services. Agency staff provided counseling and case management services to families known to be a high risk because of previous problems with child abuse and neglect, substance abuse, and domestic violence. According to the program's contract, the child welfare department would reimburse the agency bimonthly for services rendered. Services provided by the program's master's degree practitioner were to be reimbursed at a higher hourly rate than services provided by the program's two practitioners with bachelor's degrees; the contract spelled out which services were to be provided by the social workers with the bachelor's degrees and which by the MSW social workers.

During the course of the contract, the agency began to have financial difficulties. To generate more revenue, the agency director, a social worker, billed the county welfare department for services provided by the program's MSW social worker when, in fact, the services had been provided by one of the BSW social workers. An audit by the county uncovered the billing fraud. The family services program was banned from entering into any future contracts with the child welfare department, was required to reimburse the funds that were paid to the agency inappropriately, and was fined, and the agency director was fired. The director also was charged with criminal theft of public funds and placed on probation by the court.

In another case a social worker in private practice was indicted for insurance fraud. According to the indictment, the social worker arranged for a psychiatrist to sign an insurance form indicating that he had provided clinical services to a client when, in fact, the services were provided entirely by the social worker. At his trial the social worker testified that such "signing off" is widespread in his community and occurs because some insurance companies refuse to pay for certain clinical services unless they are provided or supervised by a psychiatrist. He said that it is common for social workers to arrange for a psychiatrist who provided minimal supervision or consultation to sign an insurance form in exchange for part of the fee charged to the insurance company. These arguments exonerated neither the social worker nor the psychiatrist. The social worker was convicted, placed on probation, and ordered to make restitution to the insurer.

In a final example, a social worker was retained by a substance abuse treatment program to conduct a comprehensive program evaluation. The social worker's proposal stated that as part of the evaluation she would conduct interviews with staff and clients and would have staff routinely fill out a standardized "client progress" form. After work on the contract had begun, the agency's director asked the social worker to add a qualitative analysis of a sample of the agency's case records to the evaluation. The agency director wanted feedback on the records' contents, particularly with respect to their thoroughness and clarity. He agreed that for this addition to the program evaluation, the social worker would bill the agency for the number of hours she and her research assistant spent on the task (at an agreed-on hourly rate). At the end of the project, the social worker billed the agency for 84 hours of work in evaluating the sample of case records, but the task actually required only 51 hours. Although the fraudulent billing was never discovered, the added expense meant that the agency had less money available for other programs.

## CLIENT TRANSFER

### STANDARD 3.06(a)

*When an individual who is receiving services from another agency or colleague contacts a social worker for services, the social worker should carefully consider the client's needs before agreeing to provide*

> services. To minimize possible confusion and conflict, social work-
> ers should discuss with potential clients the nature of the clients'
> current relationship with other service providers and the implica-
> tions, including possible benefits or risks, of entering into a rela-
> tionship with a new service provider.

Individuals who are receiving services from agencies or practitioners in the community will sometimes contact a social worker for additional assistance. This may occur because the agencies or practitioners the individuals are currently seeing have advised them to seek specialized expertise from a so-cial worker. In other cases individuals approach social workers for services because they are not satisfied with their current providers.

To meet clients' needs and avoid conflict with colleagues, social workers should discuss with potential clients the nature of their current relationship with other services providers and the possible benefits and risks of receiving services from a new provider. It is important to avoid undermining or inter-fering with clients' relationships with other professionals and to avoid en-gaging in any activity that could be interpreted as an effort to lure clients away from other providers. For example, social workers should not exploit clients' disputes with other practitioners to advance their own interests. A social worker should accept a new client who is working with other pro-viders only when it is clear that the client is aware of the potential benefits and risks associated with entering into a new professional–client relation-ship and such a relationship appears to be in the client's best interest.

In one case Andrew, a social worker in private practice, was contacted by a woman who said she was "eager to locate a new counselor." Andrew met with the potential client and discovered during the first meeting that she was currently receiving services from another social worker, Brenda. The client told Andrew that she had been in counseling with his colleague for four months and lately had been feeling that "my counseling isn't going anywhere. I just don't feel like I'm connecting with her." Andrew asked the client about the issues she wanted to address in treatment and about the nature of her frustration and dissatisfaction with her relationship with the other social worker. The client told Andrew that she had not shared her concerns directly with Brenda, so Andrew explored with her the various as-pects of her tentative decision to terminate her relationship with her other therapist. Together they made lists of the possible benefits and risks in-volved. As a result of this discussion, the client decided to return to Brenda and discuss her concerns. Andrew suggested to the client that she might want to consider staying in treatment with his colleague "for a reasonable period of time after you tell her about your concerns" to see if the discus-sion of the issues makes a difference. Two months later the client called Andrew to tell him that "your strategy really worked. We cleared the air and since then I feel like I've made great progress. We're really connecting now." This is an example of a social worker's ethical and constructive at-tempt to help a client carefully consider the possible impact of establishing a relationship with a new provider. Although this approach will not always be successful in this way, it does help clients make thoughtful and informed choices about entering into relationships with new services providers.

In contrast, in another case a social worker in private practice was con-tacted by a potential client who said he was interested in "changing thera-pists." This social worker had worked for many years at a family services agency and was just beginning to build his private practice. He met with the client and spent most of the first session exploring the nature of the clinical issues the client wanted to address. He spent little time, however, asking the client questions about his relationship with his current therapist or exploring whether changing therapists was in the client's best interest. They then scheduled several appointments. When the client told his original social worker of his plans to change to a new therapist, she asked what had led to his decision. The client explained that he "was afraid to explore some of the issues about my past" that she had raised and that he thought she was "moving too fast" in his therapy. During this conversation the client admitted that he thought this social worker was very skillful and was "probably raising issues that needed to be raised, but that I was afraid to address." By the end of the meeting, he concluded that it would be best for him to continue seeing his original social worker and that his efforts to find a new therapist had reflected his anxiety about exploring a number of painful family-of-origin issues. The social worker explained to him that his choice of therapist ultimately was his own and no one else's.

In this case the social worker contacted by a potential client failed to take appropriate steps to help the client explore the reasons for changing therapists and the possible benefits and risks of doing so. As a result, the client was temporarily diverted from his relationship with his original therapist, which was both emotionally and financially costly to him. The social worker's concern about building up his client base in his new private practice seemed to cloud his judgment concerning the client's best interests.

## STANDARD 3.06(b)

*If a new client has been served by another agency or colleague, social workers should discuss with the client whether consultation with the previous service provider is in the client's best interest.*

Social workers' new clients often have received services from other professionals. In such cases practitioners should discuss with clients the appropriateness of consultation with the previous services provider. Such consultation is often appropriate to enhance the coordination and continuity of services. For example, a social worker was contacted by a couple who had been in marriage counseling with another practitioner. With the encouragement of their marriage counselor, the couple decided to have a social worker counsel their 10-year-old child, who was having difficulty in school and in dealing with the recent sudden death of his younger sister. The boy began seeing the social worker for individual psychotherapy. The social worker asked the child's parents if they thought it would be helpful for her to contact the social worker providing their marriage counseling for consultation about the family's problems and issues. She outlined the possible benefits (such as coordination of services) and risks (primarily the disclosure of private information) and explained to the parents that she would contact her colleague only with their informed consent (consistent with standards 1.03[a] and 1.07[b]). The couple agreed that it would be helpful for their son's social worker to consult with her colleague about family-related issues that were important for their child (for example, recent stressors in the family's life and the parents' behavior management approach). However, the couple explained to both social workers that they would like the consultation about their family to be limited to issues that were directly relevant to their son. They asked their marriage counselor to limit her disclosures and avoid talking about other issues the parents discussed in treatment (such as the father's criminal record and the couple's strained sexual relationship). This approach allowed for constructive consultation between the social workers to enhance the therapist's work with the couple's son, and it protected the couple's privacy to the greatest extent possible. This is consistent with the standards concerning clients' right to privacy (standard 1.07[a]) and social workers' obligation to "disclose the least amount of information necessary to achieve the purposes of the consultation" (standard 2.05[c]).

In another case, however, a social worker employed by a home health care agency failed to discuss properly with a client whether consultation with a previous services provider was in the client's best interest and failed to obtain the client's informed consent before consulting with the previous provider. The social worker who worked in the home health care agency provided counseling services to a retired judge, whose disability kept him homebound, to help him address issues related to his chronic disability. This social worker knew from the case record that about a year earlier, the client had received counseling from another social worker at a local family services agency. Without the client's knowledge, she contacted the other practitioner to discuss several clinical issues. During a subsequent conversation with the client, she mentioned some information that she had learned from her colleague. The client said he was "startled to learn that you spoke to my previous provider. I didn't know you were planning to do that. For some very personal reasons, I didn't want the two of you to talk. Aren't you supposed to get my permission for that?" The social worker apologized to her client and said, "I'm sorry I didn't tell you. I just assumed you wouldn't mind." The client told the social worker that he was deeply hurt and not sure he could continue to trust her. Although the client did not file an ethics complaint against his current provider, he did send a strongly worded complaint to the home health care agency director about the social worker's breach of confidentiality (standards 1.07[a], [b], [c], and [d]) and failure to obtain informed consent (standard 1.03[a]). He also sent a similar letter to the director of his previous provider's family services agency.

## ADMINISTRATION

### STANDARD 3.07(a)

*Social work administrators should advocate within and outside their agencies for adequate resources to meet clients' needs.*

By definition, a social work administrator is obligated to administer his or her organization's resources in a manner that enhances the organization's ability to meet client needs. This requires a wide range of skills related to planning, budgeting, and personnel management. However, in addition to managing the operation of human services organizations with existing resources, social work administrators must enhance the resources available to their organizations to pursue their goals. This obligation requires social work administrators to advocate within and outside their agencies for adequate resources to meet clients' needs.

Administrators' advocacy within their own organizations typically involves working with higher-level administrators and boards of directors to ensure that the organizations' budget allocations are sufficient to meet clients' needs. Social work administrators who believe that the programs and services for which they are responsible are not funded adequately have a duty to take steps to increase the relevant budgetary allocations. This may take the form of informal advocacy or more formal requests submitted as part of the organization's annual budget. For example, a social worker who served as assistant director of a state public welfare department was responsible for administering the agency's program for low-income immigrants and refugees. This program coordinated services related to public assistance benefits, health care, child care, and employment. During the past three years, however, the department director had reduced the program's budget—by 3 percent the first year, 6 percent the second year, and 8 percent the third year. The program director was distressed about the budget cuts because she had had to reduce the services delivered to the state's low-income refugees and immigrants and terminate contracts to outside service providers. In her view, the budget cuts were "severe and unconscionable in light of the immigrants' and refugees' compelling needs."

The program director held a long meeting with her staff to assess the implications of the latest round of budget cuts. However, instead of focusing primarily on how the staff could do more with less, as in past years, she asked the staff to brainstorm ways in which she might advocate within the department to restore the program's funds. The staff concluded that they should gather data documenting the magnitude of the immigrants' and refugees' social services needs and conduct a cost–benefit analysis to project the potential impact of the budget cuts. They hoped to produce data showing that an investment of the department's resources would be cost effective in the long run, and that their efforts to stabilize refugees and immigrants and enhance their employment and health ultimately would lead to lower public assistance and other expenditures required to assist this population. For three months the program staff worked feverishly to gather the data, working closely with a local economist who helped them conduct the cost–benefit analysis. The program director presented the study results to the department director and the department's chief budget officer, who were impressed with the analysis and convinced by the results. Consequently the department director rescinded the most recent budget cut and even modestly increased the program's budget.

Advocacy within an organization may not always be entirely successful or effective. In these circumstances social work administrators should advocate outside their organizations for additional resources. This form of advocacy requires social work administrators to have knowledge and skills related to "directly representing, defending, intervening, supporting, or recommending a course of action" (Mickelson, 1995, p. 95) to obtain additional resources for their programs. Such advocacy may involve contacting higher-level administrators who have funding authority (for example, appointed officials in federal, state, or local government), elected officials (members of Congress, state legislators, members of county boards or city councils) and their political aides, and foundation representatives. This form of advocacy also may require social workers to testify at legislative or administrative hearings.

Social workers who have administrative responsibility for inadequately funded programs often find themselves caught between their obligations to their employer and to the clients served by their agencies. Such divided loyalties can present social work administrators with daunting ethical choices. If administrators give precedence to their obligation to meet clients' needs and in the process challenge organizational policy or are critical of their superiors because of funding shortfalls, cutbacks, or recisions, they risk alienating their superiors and jeopardizing their careers. Those to whom social work administrators are accountable may resent their willingness to defy, protest, or dispute organizational policy and may accuse the administrators of insubordination. However, administrators who acquiesce and accept inadequate funding without protest then risk violating the social work profession's ethical standards concerning commitment to clients (standard 1.01). They also risk accusations from colleagues that they were co-opted by their organizations and "sold out" to administrative or political pressure. As a matter of principle, social work administrators are obligated to give precedence to their commitment to clients when they find themselves caught between clients' interests and organizational or professional self-interest.

In one case a social work administrator who directed a juvenile probation department was informed by the chief judge of the juvenile court, his boss, that the department's budget would be cut during the next fiscal year by 18 percent. The judge explained that the cut was necessary because of the county's grim revenue projections, due largely to a dramatic increase in unemployment and a declining income tax base. The social work administrator told the judge that with such a dramatic decline in funding, he would be forced to reduce the size of his staff and increase each remaining social worker's caseload size to an unmanageable number. In the administrator's opinion, the department's social workers could not possibly provide professional services in such conditions. He decided not to accept the cuts and engaged in advocacy in an effort to restore money to his department's budget. The administrator contacted members of the county's board of commissioners, the county executive, and staff from the governor's office. In the midst of the process, he was called by the county executive's chief of staff and told that "a number of important people are beginning to get annoyed with your demands" and he would be "well advised to begin behaving like a team player. Remember who signs your paycheck." The administrator believed that his advocacy efforts had failed and he was being pressured to abandon his commitment to his department's clients. He concluded that it would be unethical to continue working in such an environment and resigned his position.

The administrator's response to this situation was both ethical and honorable. He made a principled, albeit difficult, decision to sacrifice his job because of the unacceptable compromise he was being asked to accept. These are exceedingly difficult decisions that require social workers to weigh a number of compelling and competing factors that may involve both altruism and self-interest.

## STANDARD 3.07(b)

*Social workers should advocate for resource allocation procedures that are open and fair. When not all clients' needs can be met, an allocation procedure should be developed that is nondiscriminatory and based on appropriate and consistently applied principles.*

Social work administrators typically are responsible for distributing resources, such as agency funds, staff, office space, and nonmonetary compensation (for example, personal and educational leave time). Some resources are distributed to clients (such as food vouchers, emergency beds in a shelter, and access to staff), and others are distributed to staff (such as money for salaries, educational leave opportunities, and computers). In some cases—too few, it seems—social work administrators have ample resources to distribute. In many others, however, administrators struggle to locate and obtain resources in sufficient quantity to meet staff and client needs.

Social work administrators who are responsible for distributing resources, scarce or not, should attempt to implement resource allocation criteria and procedures that are open and fair. Whatever distribution mechanism administrators choose should be discussed openly among staff and clients. Resources should not be allocated in an arbitrary, capricious, or discriminatory manner. Rather, there should be a sound, fair, and conceptually based rationale for the criteria and mechanism used to allocate resources, to promote what philosophers call "distributive justice."

In one case a social worker was hired by a state housing agency to administer a program. The program's principal goal was to enhance the supply of affordable housing to low- and moderate-income people. This was accomplished through a variety of mechanisms, including working with nonprofit housing developers to build new housing, arranging below-market mortgages for first-time home buyers, and securing rent subsidies for low-income tenants.

One of the agency's programs involved construction of 120 townhouses for low-income families with three or more children. The families were expected to pay 30 percent of their income in rent; subsidies from federal, state, and private sources would make up the difference in the monthly housing costs (the debt service on the development's mortgage). Once the construction was under way, the program director issued a public announcement inviting eligible families (those who met the guidelines on income and family size) to submit applications for the units. Two hundred nineteen eligible families submitted applications for the 120 units. The program director held a meeting with his staff to decide how to allocate this resource.

In principle, the staff had several options. They could allocate the housing units by selecting 120 applicants at random, or they could accept the first 120 applications received in the office. Another option was to rank order the applications based on the applicants' level of need, financial or otherwise (for example, whether a family member had a physical or mental disability). The staff also could allocate the housing units based in part on affirmative action principles to ensure that ethnic subgroups and people of color received a certain number of units.

Historically, social workers and others have had difficulty reaching consensus about the fairest way to allocate resources. Some prefer allocation procedures that emphasize equality, but others favor criteria that give priority to those most in need or those who are victims of racism or discrimination (Dworkin, 1981; Krouse & McPherson, 1988; Rawls, 1971; Reamer, 1993c; Spicker, 1988). Given the lack of consensus in social work and elsewhere about the most appropriate mechanisms for distributing resources— and the likelihood that consensus will not be reached—social workers should strive to establish allocation procedures that are open, fair, nondiscriminatory, and based on consistently applied conceptual criteria. When appropriate, clients, staff, and members of the public should be invited to participate in the development of allocation criteria. Discussions of possible allocation criteria should draw on diverse schools of thought concerning distributive justice and the merits and demerits of various alternatives.

## STANDARD 3.07(c)

*Social workers who are administrators should take reasonable steps to ensure that adequate agency or organizational resources are available to provide appropriate staff supervision.*

Supervision is an essential component of social work practice. Social work administrators must ensure that sufficient agency or organizational resources are available to provide appropriate staff supervision. This is important for three reasons. First, competent supervision enhances the quality of social work services and social workers' ability to meet clients' needs. This form of quality control is especially important for less-experienced practitioners, for whom feedback from supervisors is an integral part of professional growth and development.

Second, the extent to which agencies and organizations provide quality supervision is assessed during licensing and accreditation reviews. Agencies and organizations that do not provide adequate supervision—that is, those that do not employ staff with the requisite skills and knowledge to provide supervision or do not schedule sufficient time for staff supervision—may be penalized when they are reviewed for licensure or accreditation. For example, a family services agency that sought re-accreditation from a national organization was sanctioned because it did not build in a sufficient amount of time per week for supervision of the agency's clinical staff.

Finally, administrators who do not devote sufficient resources for staff supervision expose themselves to considerable malpractice and liability risks. Under the doctrine of vicarious liability, social workers who provide flawed or inadequate supervision may be liable for the errors or omissions of their supervisees (see standard 3.01[a]). Thus, social work administrators must ensure that adequate agency or organizational resources are available to provide adequate staff supervision.

The nature of supervision varies from setting to setting and position to position. In many settings, supervision is primarily educational in nature (Shulman, 1995). According to Kadushin (1976), educational supervision occurs when "training is directed to the needs of a particular worker carrying a particular caseload, encountering particular problems and needing some individualized program of education" (p. 126).

Supervision also has an administrative function when the emphasis is on coordinating delivery of services and monitoring and assessing the quality of staff performance. Such administrative supervision can be especially helpful in regular personnel reviews and in facilitating interdisciplinary and interagency collaboration (for example, in health or mental health care settings where a supervisor is responsible for coordinating interdisciplinary staff or interagency involvement in cases). As Shulman (1995) observed,

> The administrative role of the supervisor contains a number of elements, all of which are designed to aid in the implementation of the mission. These elements include coordination of activities between

staff members and between one's unit or department and other parts of the organization, as well as between staff and the community (for example, other agencies). This . . . also involves working with staff and administration to design and implement policies and procedures for supporting the work of the setting. (p. 2375)

A third purpose of supervision involves the expressive–supportive function (Shulman, 1995). Here, a major goal of supervision is to provide support to social work staff, especially when they are feeling particularly overwhelmed and burdened. Supervision can be an important vehicle to help staff deal with job-related stress and trauma that may result from such phenomena as large caseload sizes and major crises that occur in clients' lives (for example, clients who attempt to commit suicide or who are sexually assaulted).

### STANDARD 3.07(d)

*Social work administrators should take reasonable steps to ensure that the working environment for which they are responsible is consistent with and encourages compliance with the NASW Code of Ethics. Social work administrators should take reasonable steps to eliminate any conditions in their organizations that violate, interfere with, or discourage compliance with the Code.*

Social work administrators should be familiar with the entire *NASW Code of Ethics*, but particularly as it pertains to their administrative duties. Administrators should assess the extent to which their agencies and organizations comply with the code's various provisions and attempt to develop policies and procedures designed to enhance compliance. They should take reasonable steps to ensure that their work settings—in actual practice and in policy and procedure—adhere to the code's ethical principles and standards in all areas of social work as discussed here.

In addition to developing and implementing policies and procedures that enhance agencies' and organizations' compliance with the *NASW Code of Ethics*, social work administrators also should attempt to eliminate any conditions in their work settings that violate, interfere with, or discourage compliance with the code. Below are several examples of administrators' efforts to address ethical problems in their organizations:

- A social worker was hired to serve as assistant director of a mentoring program in a women's residential substance abuse treatment program. The program's primary goal was to provide clients with volunteer mentors to help with discharge planning, employment counseling, and post-release support. To provide their services, program staff and volunteers often had to share confidential information with social services agencies and others in the community such as prospective employers, staff of substance abuse treatment programs, and mental health counselors. Shortly after she was hired, the social worker reviewed the program's informed consent procedures and forms for release of information. She was surprised to learn that the program's staff and volunteers often disclosed confidential information without properly obtaining clients' informed consent. In addition, the release form used did not include several critical pieces of information, including a description of the information to be released, the purpose of the release, a statement concerning the client's right to refuse to consent and to revoke consent, and an expiration date for the consent. The social worker met with the program director and shared her concerns, then she designed new forms and called a staff meeting to institute new informed consent and release procedures consistent with the *NASW Code of Ethics.*

- A social worker served as clinical director for a residential psychiatric program for adolescents. One of the program's case managers met with the social worker to share his concerns about a number of confidentiality breaches he had observed. In recent months the case manager had witnessed several members of the professional staff discussing confidential information in the program's hallways and cafeteria, within earshot of other staff and clients who should not have been privy to the information. In addition, the case manager said that, in his judgment, several of his colleagues "have gotten somewhat sloppy about leaving confidential material on their desks in a way that exposes the material to office visitors and custodial staff." As a result of the conversation, the social worker prepared written guidelines concerning protection of clients' privacy and confidentiality and conducted a short in-service training program to reiterate the program's policy.

- A social worker was the chief administrator of a sex offender treatment program in several state prisons. The program provided individual and group counseling to men who had been convicted of such sex offenses as child molestation and rape. As the number of inmates eligible for the program increased, the social worker hired another practitioner to work part-time in the program. The part-time staff member also had a large private practice in the community in which he counseled sex offenders who had been placed on probation or parole—the only such program in the community.

  Another social worker who served on the state parole board learned that the part-time staff member regularly recommended that certain inmates be paroled with the condition that they participate in a community-based sex offender treatment program. In effect, he was recommending that inmates be required to participate in his program. The social worker on the state parole board was concerned that this arrangement constituted a conflict of interest that violated standards in the *NASW Code of Ethics.* This social worker shared her concerns with the director of the prison system's sex offender treatment program, who agreed to replace the part-time social worker with another professional to avoid a conflict of interest.

- A social worker employed by a large, prominent policy institute was in charge of a major research project on national welfare reform. Over time the social worker noticed that a disproportionate number of promotions within the policy institute were granted to male employees. In his judgment, a number of highly qualified women were overlooked for promotions because they had taken leaves of absence or temporarily reduced their work hours after the birth or adoption of their children. This pattern disturbed the social worker, who believed that the organization was discriminating against women who chose to become parents while employed—a violation of standard 3.09(e). He raised the issue with several colleagues, who agreed with his perception, so he organized the group to bring the matter to the attention of the policy institute's chief executive officer (CEO). When the CEO did not respond satisfactorily, the group asked to meet with the institute's board of directors. This meeting led to a revision of the institute's policies and procedures on leaves of absences and reduced working hours after childbirth or adoption, which enabled women with infants and children or women considering parenthood to compete equally with all other staff who applied for or were considered for promotion.

- A client of a family services agency asked her social worker for a copy of her case record. After they discussed the reasons for the request, the social worker, who was recently hired by the agency, shared a copy of the record with the client. She explained the various pieces of information and answered the client's questions about them. During a meeting with her supervisor later that week, the social worker casually mentioned the client's request to see her record. The supervisor reprimanded the social worker, saying that "the agency has always had a policy that clients are not permitted to see their records." The social worker told her supervisor that she had learned in social work school that practitioners are obligated to provide clients with reasonable access to their records. The supervisor was not aware of the prevailing standards in the profession or the relevant standard in the *NASW Code of Ethics*. As a result of the meeting, the supervisor met with the agency director, who agreed that the agency should change its long-standing policy to comply with the code and widespread standards in the social work profession.

# CONTINUING EDUCATION AND STAFF DEVELOPMENT

*STANDARD 3.08*

---

*Social work administrators and supervisors should take reasonable steps to provide or arrange for continuing education and staff development for all staff for whom they are responsible. Continuing education and staff development should address current knowledge and emerging developments related to social work practice and ethics.*

One of the hallmarks of contemporary professions is the willingness of their members to continue their education throughout their careers. This is especially true in social work because the knowledge base of the profession has expanded dramatically since its inception in the late 19th century.

Continuing education in social work began to burgeon in the 1960s and 1970s. During this period there was ample federal funding to sponsor continuing education in nearly every social services setting, although it has since declined. Since then, the proliferation of state regulation and licensure for social workers has increased the demand for continuing education;

many states now require a quota of continuing education credits for registered and licensed social workers (Frumkin & Lloyd, 1995). Continuing education is now regularly offered by social services agencies, undergraduate and graduate social work education programs, NASW chapters and the national organization, licensing boards, private continuing education firms, and other national, statewide, and local professional organizations.

To provide continuing education for staff, administrators and supervisors should monitor the professional literature (books, journals, and relevant unpublished literature) and conference offerings to keep up-to-date with compelling topics and emerging knowledge to which their staff should be exposed. They also should allocate agency funds and release time for staff to attend continuing education and staff development workshops and lectures. Workshops and lectures may be provided in agencies and organizations by their own staff or outside experts, or staff may attend workshops or conferences in other settings.

The content of continuing education and staff development offerings should be determined by several factors, including the agency's or organization's mission, client population, staff's educational levels and professional experience, new developments in the field, and current important controversies. Depending on the setting, social workers should be provided with continuing education and staff development opportunities related to clinical and direct practice (such as assessment procedures, intervention approaches); human behavior (for example, new developments related to child development and aging); social welfare policies (important new laws, regulations, policies, and programs); social change (for example, how social workers can advocate for or organize clients and communities or lobby public officials); research and evaluation (such as new standardized measures that can be used to assess clients or monitor their progress, or program evaluation strategies); and social, cultural, and ethnic diversity (for example, knowledge related to working with gay and lesbian adolescents, resolving conflicts between health care institutions and clients who have emigrated from non-Western cultures, and strategies to empower women who are victims of domestic violence). Administrators and supervisors in community mental health settings might consider offering continuing education related to new treatment approaches for people with chronic mental illness, strategies for coping with mental illness in different cultural and ethnic groups, ways to evaluate client progress, new developments in the use of psychotropic and neuroleptic medication, and an overview of current mental health laws and regulations. Administrators and supervisors in school settings can consider continuing education opportunities in the treatment of specific disorders found among school-age children (such as attention deficit disorder, depression, eating disorders, developmental delays, and substance abuse); new developments in federal or state laws pertaining to special education; strategies for assisting children who are experiencing phenomena such as gender identity issues, sexual harassment, or the loss of a parent; strategies to prevent teacher burnout; and the use of empirically based tools to assess behavioral and emotional problems. Administrators and supervisors in policy settings (such as a governor's policy office, a social welfare policy institute, or the policy division of a privately funded charitable agency) might offer continuing education and staff development on such topics as new strategies for conducting cost–benefit analyses, models to promote public- and private-sector partnerships, the impact of welfare reform on refugees and immigrants, and programs and policies designed to address hunger and homelessness.

Social work administrators and supervisors also should be sure to provide opportunities for staff to attend continuing education and staff development offerings on the subject of professional social work ethics. First, social workers should be exposed to current knowledge about ethical dilemmas in practice—that is, circumstances when social workers must make difficult choices between and among competing duties or obligations (such as the choice between respecting a client's right to confidentiality and disclosing confidential information to protect a third party from harm, or the choice between respecting a client's right to self-determination and interfering with a client's attempt to engage in self-destructive behavior). Second, social workers should be exposed to current knowledge about ethical decision making. Social work literature now contains considerable discussion of such topics as the relevance of ethical and moral theory in ethical decision making, the use of institutional ethics committees and ethics "grand rounds," the use of professional codes of ethics (especially the *NASW Code of Ethics*), and the nature of ethics consultation (Loewenberg & Dolgoff, 1996; Reamer, 1995b, 1997a). Third, social workers should be exposed to current knowledge related to the problems of ethical misconduct and professional malpractice and liability. Practitioners should be aware of the forms that ethical misconduct takes, its various causes, and constructive ways to respond to unethical behavior. They also should be familiar with the nature of ethics complaints and lawsuits filed against social workers and useful prevention—risk management—strategies for sexual misconduct and other boundary violations, breach of confidentiality, defamation of character, inadequate supervision, and all other potential ethical problems (Barker & Branson, 1993; Besharov, 1985; Bullis, 1995; Houston-Vega et al., 1997; Reamer, 1994).

## COMMITMENTS TO EMPLOYERS

*STANDARD 3.09(a)*

*Social workers generally should adhere to commitments made to employers and employing organizations.*

For many reasons, social workers should support their employers' policies and honor their agreements with them. Organizational loyalty is important in promoting smooth functioning among staff, enhancing trust, and avoiding strife and conflict among personnel. Insubordination, for example, can be disruptive in an organization, interfere with the delivery of services, and ultimately undermine an organization's efforts to meet clients' needs. Renegade or subversive social workers who disregard commitments they have made to employers can damage social work's reputation as a profession.

However, social workers must realize that occasions sometimes arise in their practice when they may need to consider breaking commitments they have made to employers and employing organizations—when it is necessary to uphold the profession's values, ethical principles, and ethical standards. Organizations sometimes engage in unethical practices and enforce unethical policies. If this is the case, social workers have an obligation to challenge or break commitments they have made to employers. It is for this reason that standard 3.09(a) states that social workers "generally" should adhere to commitments made to employers and employing organizations.

The challenge for social workers, of course, is deciding how to determine when commitments to employers and employing organizations should and should not be honored. This broaches the broader subject of civil disobedience, that is, determining when active violation of laws, policies, and regulations is justifiable on ethical grounds. Most social workers acknowledge that certain extraordinary circumstances require civil disobedience. According to Campbell's (1991) definition that focused on deliberate violations of the law, *civil disobedience* involves "public and nonviolent violations of law to protest an actual or proposed law or practice in which the protesters are willing to submit to legal sanctions as punishment for their actions" (p. 169; see also Childress, 1971, 1986).

It is impossible to provide firm, clear, and unequivocal guidelines about when it is and is not ethical for social workers to break their commitments to employers. However, individuals should address several questions in their effort to determine whether civil disobedience is justifiable (Campbell, 1991). First, is the cause a just one? Is the policy at issue so unjust that civil disobedience is necessary? Social workers might argue that unjust policies that cause considerable human suffering—for example, the summary termination of health care benefits for legal immigrants—warrant civil disobedience (perhaps in the form of violating new laws or regulations to ensure that those in need get health care services), but unjust policies that have less grave consequences (such as agency regulations that limit the amount of overtime pay that social workers can earn) do not. There are times when a "higher good: the amelioration of suffering and the saving of lives" (Spiers, 1989, p. 34), and the vindication of rights wrongfully denied demand civil disobedience.

Second, is the civil disobedience a last resort? Have all other reasonable means to rectify unjust policies and procedures been pursued without success? It is unethical to jump to the option of civil disobedience, an extreme measure, without taking steps to pursue alternatives, such as negotiation, mediation, and other forms of dispute resolution. As Campbell (1991) argued with respect to civil disobedience to protest unjust laws,

> The functional and symbolic purposes of law in our society entail that its violation by acts of civil disobedience should be a last resort. That is, all other reasonable alternatives to redress wrongs and grievances, including appeals to political representatives, recourse through the courts, and legally permitted assemblies, protests, and demonstrations, should be exhausted before resort to civil disobedience is advocated. (p. 178)

Third, does the act of civil disobedience have a reasonable expectation of success? If not, the disruption and dissension that it may cause within an organization is difficult to justify. Without a reasonable expectation of success, civil disobedience seems simply gratuitous and provocative.

Fourth, do the benefits that are likely to result from the civil disobedience clearly outweigh possible negative outcomes, such as intraorganizational discord and erosion of staff respect for authority? Again, civil disobedience that is likely to rectify a grave injustice or wrong, although it generates some organizational chaos in the process, is more justifiable than civil disobedience that targets less compelling issues.

Finally, if civil disobedience is warranted, does it entail the least amount of disobedience required to rectify the targeted injustice? Widespread disobedience within an organization is not warranted when evidence suggests that more limited disobedience will be sufficient to address the pertinent issues. For example, refusing to book new clients, in violation of agency policy, to protest an agency's seriously inadequate funding may enable staff to draw attention to their concerns without paralyzing an agency completely by refusing to provide services to all clients.

Below are several examples of situations in which social workers struggled with their decisions about whether to adhere to their commitments to their employers and employing organizations.

- Soon after his graduation from social work school, a social worker was hired by a family services agency operated under the auspices of a prominent church. At the time he was hired, the social worker signed an agreement stating that he would not discuss abortion with clients as a legitimate option or refer clients for abortion services. About six months after he was hired he was contacted by a 15-year-old pregnant client who had been referred to his agency by the county human services department. This county department provided adolescents with information and referral services and referred clients to various local agencies for services on a rotating basis.

  The client told the social worker that she wanted to consider the possibility of having an abortion. After much thought and consultation with trusted colleagues, the social worker decided to try to persuade agency administrators of his client's right to receive abortion counseling or, at the very least, a referral to an agency providing abortion counseling. Agency administrators reprimanded the social worker and threatened to fire him if he discussed abortion with his client. He then decided that he was obligated to break his commitment to his employer and, contrary to agency policy and the agreement he had signed at the time of his employment, to refer the client to a local clinic providing abortion counseling and services. The social worker reasoned that the NASW Code of Ethics obligated him to promote his client's right to self-determination (standard 1.02) and respect her values and religious beliefs (standards 1.05[b] and [c]). Moreover, the social work profession generally supports women's right to choose whether to abort a pregnancy within legal limits (Figueira-McDonough, 1995). The social worker concluded that his cause was just, he had pursued reasonable alternatives before violating agency policy as a last resort (in his attempt to persuade agency administrators of the soundness of his position), his disobedience was likely to be successful (helping his client obtain the counseling services she needed), and the likely benefits (helping a client obtain counseling to consider her legal options) outweighed the possible negative outcomes (undermining the agency's authority).

- A social worker for a community action program administered a low-income housing plan. The agency managed 35 apartments for low-income families, and the social worker screened potential tenants to determine whether they met eligibility requirements. According to agency policy and federal regulations, she was not permitted to approve any applicant whose income and assets exceeded certain limits.

The social worker met with and reviewed an application submitted by a refugee family. The family had emigrated to the United States because of political persecution in their homeland. They were seeking subsidized housing because their public assistance benefits had just been terminated as a result of a controversial policy change.

The social worker discovered that the family's assets exceeded the limit set for eligibility. However, she believed that the family had been treated unjustly when its public assistance benefits were terminated. Consequently, she underreported the family's assets, contrary to agency policy, to qualify them for subsidized housing and to "help make up for their unconscionable treatment under the new public assistance policy."

This social worker concluded that the ends justified the means. However, she did not exhaust all reasonable alternatives before deciding to violate agency policy. She did not share her concerns with the agency administrators or explore whether there were any opportunities to petition or appeal for exceptions to the agency's policy. The social worker also did not engage in any advocacy in an effort to change the policy, either within or outside the agency. Although her cause was just, her decision to break her commitment was less defensible because of the failure first to pursue all reasonable alternatives.

- A social worker was hired to provide clinical supervision in a residential program for children with severe behavioral and emotional problems, many of whom were in state custody. At the time he was hired, the social worker signed an agreement that he would not talk to members of the media or officials from public child welfare or law enforcement agencies without the approval of the program's administration.

Over time the social worker became more and more concerned about the methods used to discipline children in the program and to modify their behavior. Child care workers regularly pinched children who were difficult to control, sprayed water in their faces, placed helmets on their heads that emitted a loud static noise, and restrained them by putting them in small closets. The social worker met with program administrators to express his concerns. He was told that the program only used empirically validated, effective treatment approaches and was not willing to change its methods. The social worker also met with the president of the program's board of directors, who deferred the matter to the chief administrator.

Frustrated in his attempt to address the program's apparently abusive behavior management and disciplinary methods, the social worker decided he was obligated to contact the state's child advocate's office, which monitored the treatment of children in county or state custody. The social worker concluded that his cause was just because his primary obligation was to the program's clients (standard 1.01), the likely benefits far outweighed possible negative outcomes (disrupting agency functioning), and he was required to take reasonable steps to ensure that his employer's practices did not conflict with the NASW Code of Ethics (standard 3.07[d]). He also believed he had taken steps to change the program's practices before resorting to notifying public child welfare officials, contrary to agency policy. The child advocate's office launched an investigation that eventually led to termination of the program's license to operate.

## STANDARD 3.09(b)

*Social workers should work to improve employing agencies' policies and procedures and the efficiency and effectiveness of their services.*

Social workers' ultimate aim always should be to enhance their employing organization's ability to meet clients' needs. One way to do this is to monitor organization policies and procedures to ensure that they are efficient and effective. Policies and procedures are efficient when they accomplish legitimate and appropriate goals in the most economical way possible, avoiding waste and extravagance. Social services agencies that spend their limited funds on unnecessarily expensive office quarters, furniture, and lavishly catered board meetings are inefficient, as are agencies whose administrators employ more staff than is necessary. Policies and procedures are effective when they accomplish their goals. Effectiveness is difficult to define and measure precisely, of course, but generally it means reaching specific objectives established by agency administrators, staff, and boards of directors. A home-based family intervention program, for example, might aim to reduce the number of children placed in foster care from client families by 25 percent by year's end. A community mental health center might aim to increase the amount of time, by 15 percent within a six-month period, that clients with serious chronic mental illness spend in the community between acute episodes requiring hospitalization. A community action program's goal could be to speed up application processing and approval to increase the number of low-income families for whom it locates affordable housing by 10 percent each year for a three-year period.

Social workers should always seek to improve their employing agencies' policies and procedures and the efficiency and effectiveness of their services, as in the following examples:

- A school social worker directed a counseling program, funded by the local United Way, for adolescents with substance abuse problems. During the school day the social worker met with eligible students individually and in groups.

  Part of the program included working with the students' families. The social worker regularly invited students' parents and occasionally siblings to meet with her to address family-related issues that might be linked to the students' substance abuse. She quickly discovered that few parents were able or willing to come to the school for meetings because they would have to take time off from work. Because the parents' lack of attendance was affecting the program's effectiveness, the social worker met with her supervisor and the school principal to explore possible remedies. They agreed that the social worker would rearrange her schedule so she could meet with parents in the late afternoon and early evening twice each week. To compensate for the new hours, she would begin work later in the morning on the two days she was scheduled to work late. Within one month after the scheduling change was implemented, parent participation in counseling increased from 6 percent of the clients for whom family counseling was recommended to 42 percent.

- For many years a family services agency sponsored an adoption program, counseling pregnant women who wanted to make an adoption plan for their children and placing their infants with adoptive families. All of the agency's adoptions were "closed, confidential, traditional adoptions," meaning that birth parents and prospective adoptive parents did not meet, exchange identifying information, or have contact with each other after the placement.

  One of the social workers on the staff became concerned because many adoptees, placed as infants through the agency, returned to the agency in adulthood to seek information about their biological heritage. A growing number of adoptive parents, responding to their children's distress over not having contact with their birth parents, also were approaching the agency to seek medical and other information on behalf of their adopted minor children. The social worker began to realize that traditional adoption practices—originally developed to protect adoptees, birth parents, and adoptive parents from shame, stigma, and intrusion—were experienced by many of the agency's clients as coercive, controlling, unhelpful, frustrating, and secretive. He reviewed recent literature and research on adoption and discovered that open adoptions—in which, if all parties agree, birth parents and prospective adoptive parents have the opportunity to meet, exchange identifying information, and have continuing contact—were becoming common practice in the field. After talking with colleagues at adoption conferences, the social worker concluded that many birth parents and adoptive parents prefer some form of open adoption because they believe that such arrangements are in the best interest of the children. As a result of the social worker's efforts, the family services agency changed its policies and procedures so that open adoption was offered as an option to birth parents and adoptive parents, and both parties could receive education about the adoptee's likely need for information about and perhaps contact with the birth family.

- A program for battered women offered a wide range of services, including shelter facilities for victims of domestic violence, a counseling program for battered and abused women living in the community, and an outreach program to educate the public. The social worker who directed the program was concerned about the consistently low census in the shelter. Although the demand for counseling in the community had increased slightly over the past three years, the demand for shelter services had declined substantially. After meeting with staff and consulting with knowledgeable colleagues in the community, the director concluded that the shelter's location, which was some distance from the nearest large population center, was a major reason for the low census. Because the money required to run the shelter consumed 48 percent of the program's budget, the director was determined to make dramatic changes. She convened the agency's staff and discussed the possibility of closing the shelter or moving it to a location closer to the nearby city. The director and staff ultimately concluded that the most efficient and cost-effective option was for the agency to close the shelter and use the savings to enhance the program's counseling and outreach programs. There would be adequate residential services available for local battered women because another agency operated a shelter in the nearby city. The reallocation of the agency's resources could be accomplished in a way that would enable the agency to retain all the staff who worked in the shelter; after receiving appropriate in-service training, they would be reassigned to positions in the agency's other programs.

## STANDARD 3.09(c)

*Social workers should take reasonable steps to ensure that employers are aware of social workers' ethical obligations as set forth in the* NASW Code of Ethics *and of the implications of those obligations for social work practice.*

Social workers sometimes find that their ethical instincts conflict with policies and procedures in their employment settings. This may occur especially when social workers are employed in a "host" setting (where social work is not the primary profession, such as in schools, correctional institutions, and the military) and administrators are not entirely familiar with social work values and ethical principles and standards. For example, social workers who serve as clinicians in a law enforcement agency or the military may find that administrators to whom they are accountable know relatively little about the social work profession, which could seem rather foreign or in conflict with the setting's norms. Social workers also may find that administrators in their employment settings are familiar with social work values, principles, and standards but fail to support them or may even actively reject them. In such cases, practitioners should take steps to ensure that their employers are familiar with social workers' ethical obligations and their specific implications, as in the following case examples:

- A social worker was hired to be the clinical supervisor in a school-based program that counseled adolescents at high risk for mental health and substance abuse problems. The social worker supervised three caseworkers and also carried her own caseload. Shortly after she started the job, she discovered that the school did not provide after-hours coverage for emergencies. Clients who called the office after regular school hours heard a recorded message that informed them of the program's hours and invited callers to leave a message. In the social worker's judgment, this arrangement violated the *NASW Code of Ethics* standard prohibiting client abandonment (standard 1.16[b]). She brought this problem to the attention of the school principal, who was not a social worker. After considerable discussion of the ethical issues and liability risks for the program staff and the school, the principal agreed that the program's caseworkers and the social worker should share after-hours coverage on a rotating basis. This change in procedures brought the agency into compliance with the code.

- A social worker in a juvenile correctional facility was asked by an assistant director to administer research interviews to a sample of residents. The purpose of the interviews was to gather data concerning the residents' self-esteem, substance abuse histories, and past delinquent activities. The data were gathered as part of the corrections department's study of the effectiveness of two different treatment approaches to institutionalized youths.

The administrator in charge of the study told the social worker to administer the interviews but did not mention anything about obtaining the residents' consent. When the social worker raised the issue, the administrator told her that consent was not necessary because the youths were in the corrections department's custody. The social worker, however, believed that she was obligated to explain to the youths what risks were involved in answering the interview questions and their right to refuse to consent to the interviews. The social worker told the administrator that according to the *NASW Code of Ethics*, when clients are receiving services involuntarily, social workers should provide information about the nature and extent of services and about the extent of clients' right to refuse service (standard 1.03[d]). In addition, she told the administrator, the code requires social workers to follow guidelines for the protection of evaluation and research participants (standard 5.02[d]), obtain research and evaluation participants' informed consent (standard 5.02[e]), and inform participants of their right to withdraw from evaluation and research without penalty at any time (standard 5.02[h]). The administrator read the code and, consequently, asked the social worker to chair a newly appointed committee charged with developing comprehensive guidelines for research and evaluation projects conducted at the juvenile correctional facility.

- A social worker in a junior high school provided counseling to students. Teachers often referred their students to him for assistance, sometimes because they were concerned that the students might be abusing drugs. The teachers usually shared their concerns with the school principal as well. On two occasions the school principal asked the social worker about particular students' progress in counseling, especially the status of their substance abuse problems. The social worker explained that, because of strict federal and state regulations concerning students' right to confidentiality, he was not permitted to disclose to the principal any information about the students he was counseling or their substance abuse issues. The principal had not been aware of the regulations prohibiting the disclosure of information. When the social worker had explained the regulations, their rationale, and his obligation to respect the students' right to confidentiality (standard 1.07[b]), the school principal stopped inquiring about individual students' status.

## STANDARD 3.09(d)

*Social workers should not allow an employing organization's policies, procedures, regulations, or administrative orders to interfere with their ethical practice of social work. Social workers should take reasonable steps to ensure that their employing organizations' practices are consistent with the NASW Code of Ethics.*

This standard is an extension of standard 3.09(c), which describes social workers' duty to bring to the attention of their employers any ethical issues and problems in their work settings, particularly as they pertain to matters addressed in the *NASW Code of Ethics*. Standard 3.09(c) exhorts social workers to ensure that their employers are aware of social workers' ethical obligations as set forth in the code and the implications of those obligations for social work practice, and standard 3.09(d) carries the obligation a step further in that it requires social workers to assert themselves and take reasonable steps to ensure that their employing organization's policies, procedures, regulations, or administrative orders comply with the values, ethical principles, and ethical standards contained in the code and do not interfere with the ethical practice of social work.

Social workers can address ethical issues and problems in their work setting in various ways. First, they can attempt to address the issue informally by discussing their concerns with appropriate colleagues and administrators. Informal efforts to resolve problematic policies, procedures, regulations, and administrative orders are often successful. When such informal efforts do not succeed, however, social workers should consider taking more formal steps within their agencies and organizations, perhaps by bringing their concerns to the attention of supervisors and administrators via memoranda or some other means that requests a formal response (for example, a formal request to change a policy or regulation or to appoint a committee or task force to address the matter). Approaching an agency or organization's board of directors, where they exist, also is an option. If these efforts fail, practitioners should consider whether the ethical issues or problems are sufficiently grave that they warrant bringing the matter to the attention of parties outside the employment setting. In extreme cases, social workers may need to consider notifying appropriate outside agencies (such as the governor's office, a public human services agency, an advocacy organization, law enforcement officials, or the media). Below are examples of social workers' efforts to address policies, procedures, regulations, and administrative orders that interfered with ethical practice:

- The clinical director of a state psychiatric hospital (who was not a social worker) issued a memorandum to all clinical staff about problems faced by patients who had difficulty understanding or speaking English. In recent months there had been several incidents involving language problems: patients had not understood explanations about their medication, instructions related to their treatment, or informed consent procedures. The memorandum instructed all staff to attempt to use an interpreter when they dealt with patients who had difficulties with English. The memorandum noted that several members of the hospital staff could serve as interpreters for Spanish-speaking patients, but clinical staff also might need to use other patients (or the friends or family of a patient) as interpreters when no one else able to speak the patient's primary language was available.

  A social worker at the hospital was concerned about this new policy. After she had observed staff using other patients as interpreters for non-English-speaking patients, the social worker concluded that the hospital's policy violated patients' informed consent and confidentiality rights (standards 1.03 [a], [b], [c], and 1.07[a]). Although some patients were sufficiently competent to be able to provide informed consent for use of other patients as interpreters, many were not. Consequently, sometimes patients who served as interpreters were privy to confidential information about other patients when the latter had not consented to such disclosures. The social worker shared her concern with the hospital's clinical director. The clinical director conceded that she had not thought about this problem, and she contacted the hospital's lawyer for an opinion. The lawyer agreed that the new procedures potentially violated patients' confidentiality rights. With the help of the lawyer, the hospital's chief administrator was convinced to allocate funds to retain interpreters from the community when hospital staff were not available to provide such services.

- Personnel policies in a county child welfare agency permitted staff to bid on open positions in the organization. Those who were eligible for open positions by virtue of their education typically were interviewed by appropriate supervisors, who then had the authority to select individuals to fill the positions. According to personnel regulations, supervisors were to give preferential consideration to applicants with seniority. Because seniority in the agency was a major consideration, several key positions were filled by staff who had been employed in the agency for many years but who had relatively little experience in the divisions that hired them. In one case, an employee with many years' experience conducting child abuse investigations was promoted to a supervisory position in the agency's foster care unit although she had almost no experience in the foster care field. A number of staff were working in positions that required them to oversee the work of subordinates who had more experience and were more knowledgeable than the supervisors.

  A social worker in the agency believed that this practice was unethical because services were being administered or delivered by individuals who lacked the necessary competence. In the social worker's judgment, this practice violated the standards in NASW Code of Ethics concerning practitioners' competence (standards 2.10[a] and [b] and 4.01[a]). She first brought her concern to the attention of her supervisor, who said he agreed but "you're gearing up for a union fight. You realize, don't you, that this is something the union negotiated with administration? I don't think you'll be able to do much about it." Despite this discouraging response, the social worker met with union officials, who said they were reluctant to propose a change in the personnel rules to their members. The social worker then organized a meeting of union members and spoke about the union's "shortsighted approach to this critically important issue. Our clients and our integrity are at stake here. It may not be entirely in our self-interest, but I think we're obligated to do the right thing and change the personnel rules to ensure that the most qualified staff fill the open positions, not just those with the most seniority." After much discussion and debate, the group voted two to one to request that the union begin negotiations with the administration to revise the personnel guidelines to ensure that substantive experience was weighed more heavily than seniority in promoting staff.

- A social worker who was assistant director of a community action agency was responsible for administering the agency's food assistance program. The program operated a soup kitchen and pantry for low-income residents in the area. Each month the social worker prepared a utilization report for the agency director that summarized the number of meals served by the soup kitchen and the volume of food dispensed by the pantry. The director used the reports to compile a year-end summary for submission to the state agency that funded the program.

At the end of the fiscal year, the social worker who administered the food assistance program asked the agency director's secretary for a copy of the year-end report. He was surprised to see that the agency director had inflated by approximately 20 percent the number of meals served and the volume of food dispensed. The social worker was concerned about this overreporting of the statistics for two reasons. First, his name was on the fraudulent report. Second, he believed that the overreporting was unethical and violated the *NASW Code of Ethics* standard concerning dishonesty, fraud, and deception (standard 4.04).

The social worker shared his concern with the agency director, who said, "Are you really that naive? Don't you realize that our funding for next year is based on our statistics for this year? The more people we serve and the more services we provide, the more money we get."

The social worker was disturbed by the director's response and realized that his informal attempt to address the matter would not succeed. He then contacted the chair of the agency's board of directors and informed her of the problem. The chair confronted the agency's director, who admitted that he had falsified the statistics in the report. She reported this information to the entire board, which asked for and received the agency director's resignation.

## STANDARD 3.09(e)

*Social workers should act to prevent and eliminate discrimination in the employing organization's work assignments and in its employment policies and practices.*

Social workers sometimes encounter or observe discriminatory practices in their work settings, whether in hiring, promotion, disciplinary, or termination-of-employment decisions or in work assignments. For example, a social work supervisor employed in a residential program for children interviewed applicants for a clinical position in the program. The job description stated that the social worker hired for the position would provide individual, group, and crisis intervention counseling to the program's clients. The social work supervisor interviewed one candidate who noted during the interview that he was gay. The supervisor, whose religious beliefs condemned homosexuality, rejected the applicant because of his sexual orientation, a clear violation of standard 4.02.

In a case involving discriminatory practices related to gender and promotion, a social worker was the director of a vocational training program. He interviewed two staff members who were finalists for the position of assistant director. One candidate was a middle-aged man and the other was a young woman. Both candidates had extensive experience in the field and at the agency. The director offered the position to the male employee because, as he confided to a colleague, "I just can't handle investing all this time and energy into training a woman who's just going to get pregnant and ask for a leave of absence. I'm tired of that routine."

Discrimination also can occur in relation to work assignments. In a case involving gender- and disability-based discrimination, a social work supervisor in the military needed to assign a staff member to gather data on the use of services from case files for the office's annual report, a job that staff considered to be burdensome and boring. At a staff meeting the supervisor asked for a volunteer to gather the data, but no one offered to assume the task. The supervisor finally assigned the task to a new civilian employee with paraplegia who used a wheelchair. According to the supervisor, who discussed the dilemma with a trusted colleague, "That little gal wouldn't turn me down. She needs this job too much. Who else would hire her in her condition? Besides, she doesn't have the chutzpah to take me on. Thank goodness I can dump this on her."

In another case a social worker who was the clinical director of a community mental health center started a new fee-for-service outpatient counseling program. He offered several clinical staff at the agency the option to work extra hours for additional income. He also hired several part-time clinical social workers from the community to work in the fee-for-service program. The agency staff who were offered the opportunity to work overtime were all men; the part-time social workers from the community were all women (most wanted to work part-time so they could be at home with their children). The clinical director paid all the staff hourly wages for their work in the fee-for-service program, but he paid the male (full-time) employees considerably more per hour than the female (part-time) employees, even though the two groups had similar levels of clinical experience and expertise.

Discrimination in the workplace is as unacceptable as discrimination in any other domain. Social workers need to be vigilant in their efforts to prevent and eliminate discrimination in the work setting. They should challenge colleagues who discriminate and attempt to change any discriminatory policies, procedures, regulations, or administrative orders. This may be done informally by consulting with colleagues, supervisors, and administrators when discriminatory practices become evident and, when necessary, through more formal means (urging agency administrators to change such discriminatory policies and practices). This obligation is consistent with standard 4.02 as well as the values, principles, and standards concerning social workers' obligation to engage in social change and promote social justice (see the code's mission statement, the section on ethical principles, and standard 6.04).

## STANDARD 3.09(f)

*Social workers should accept employment or arrange student field placements only in organizations that exercise fair personnel practices.*

Social workers should not accept employment or arrange student field placements in organizations that have been shown to discriminate against job applicants, staff, or employees; exploit employees; or otherwise violate the values, ethical principles, and ethical standards contained in the *NASW Code of Ethics*. It would be hypocritical for social workers to accept employment or arrange field placements in organizations with personnel policies and procedures that violate fair labor laws or regulations or are in any way inconsistent with the social work profession's values and ethical principles and standards. Of course, this may be easier said than done. It may take enormous self-restraint on the part of a social worker to refuse a very attractive job offer because of evidence that the potential employer has treated employees unfairly. Similarly, directors of field instruction in social work education programs, who sometimes struggle and scramble to find suitable field placements for their students, may find it difficult to pass up a potentially valuable field placement because the organization has treated some employees unfairly. However, social workers have an obligation to take a principled stand when there is compelling evidence that a potential employer or field placement site has engaged in unfair personnel practices.

In one case a social worker applied for an attractive supervisor's position at a prominent hospital. After applying for the job, the social worker learned that several members of the hospital's social work staff had filed a complaint concerning unfair personnel practices. The complaint alleged that the hospital had failed to provide its clinical social work staff with adequate supervision and in-service training. The job applicant checked with one of the complainants and learned that an arbitrator found that the hospital had, indeed, violated its own personnel standards and had not yet rectified the situation. Based on the information available to him, the social worker decided to withdraw his application.

In another case the director of field instruction at a graduate school of social work asked a community-based juvenile justice program to provide two students with field placements. The program employed a large number of staff who were responsible for monitoring youths at high risk for delinquency in the community, who were referred to the program by the local juvenile court as a condition of probation and as an alternative to incarceration. However, shortly after contacting the director of the juvenile justice program about possible field placements, the director of field instruction learned from another faculty member that the program had been sued successfully by two former staff, who had claimed that they were wrongfully fired from their jobs. According to the lawsuit, the program had a history of terminating the employment of staff just before they were eligible for a pay increase; the plaintiffs alleged that the program fired competent staff to avoid having to pay them higher wages and enable the program to hire new staff at an entry-level wage.

After he learned of the lawsuit, the director of field instruction contacted the juvenile justice program director to discuss the agency's personnel practices in the wake of the lawsuit. The program director told the field instruction director that the agency was appealing the verdict and had not made any changes in its personnel practices. Because of this information and the verdict against the program, the field instruction director stopped exploring the possibility of placing students at the program.

## STANDARD 3.09(g)

*Social workers should be diligent stewards of the resources of their employing organizations, wisely conserving funds where appropriate and never misappropriating funds or using them for unintended purposes.*

Social workers often have control over certain resources in their employing organizations. These can include personnel agency funds and office equipment and supplies. Social work administrators and supervisors have considerable authority to decide how resources will be used by staff for whom they are responsible.

All social workers, whether staff, supervisors, or administrators, are obligated to use agency resources for their intended purpose. Practitioners should avoid two specific forms of misuse or abuse of agency resources. First, social workers should not waste resources; squandering resources leaves fewer means available to deliver services to clients, organize meetings, sponsor relevant conferences, advocate for clients, evaluate programs, or meet other important goals. In one case, for example, a social worker who directed the social services component of a neighborhood health clinic, which served a low-income population, used funds from the budget that were designated for office furniture to purchase expensive window curtains, lighting fixtures, and waiting room furniture. When the agency's board of directors learned of the unapproved expenditures, they reprimanded the social worker. The board said the purchases were obviously inappropriate, particularly because no one else on the staff believed that anything more than modest, relatively inexpensive improvements needed to be made in the facility's decor. Moreover, the social worker had not obtained competitive bids before making the purchases. Both the staff and the board of directors were upset because of the wasteful use of the agency's limited funds. As the letter of reprimand from the chair of the board of directors to the social worker stated, "For years we have struggled to balance our budget and ensure that the agency's funds are spent responsibly on our vitally important mission. Your unilateral decision to spend funds as you did was irresponsible."

In another case a social worker who was an assistant dean of a social work school administered a federal grant used to train public-sector child welfare professionals. Near the end of the fiscal year, the dean realized that he had thousands of unspent dollars left in the budget, although the project was nearly complete and had achieved all of its major goals. Rather than return the funds to the federal agency that issued the grant, the assistant dean decided to spend the money on office supplies for the school's general use.

In addition to avoiding wasteful expenditures and misuse or abuse of agency resources, social workers also must avoid any corrupt use of agency resources—for example, when a social worker misappropriates funds to benefit himself or herself or others in a dishonest, self-serving, or unauthorized way. In one case a social worker was an assistant director of a large vocational training program and was responsible for conducting a comprehensive needs assessment. She was authorized to spend agency funds to hire part-time workers to interview the professional staff about their perceptions of clients' needs, the agency's goals, and the strategies and resources needed to reach those goals. The social worker estimated that she needed three part-time workers to carry out the task, but she decided to hire four because she wanted help in completing a program evaluation she was conducting on her own time as a paid consultant for another agency. The social worker never disclosed to her supervisors that she was using agency funds to pay someone to help her conduct work that was unrelated to her position with the vocational training program, as well as unrelated to the needs assessment conducted for the agency.

In another case involving the corrupt use of agency funds, a social worker employed by a home health care agency provided counseling and casework services to homebound patients. Each month the social worker was expected to submit a request for reimbursement of travel expenses. During an 18-month period he inflated his travel expenses and received a large sum to which he was not entitled.

To be diligent stewards, social workers should request agency funds and resources only when necessary and use them only for intended and legitimate purposes. In addition, practitioners should keep detailed and accurate records to account for their expenditure of agency funds and use of agency resources.

## LABOR–MANAGEMENT DISPUTES

### STANDARD 3.10(a)

*Social workers may engage in organized action, including the formation of and participation in labor unions, to improve services to clients and working conditions.*

Social workers have always recognized the importance of organized labor. Throughout the profession's history, social workers have been involved extensively in the formation and operation of unions. Some social workers have been employed in unions that work on behalf of organized groups, such as factory or municipal workers. Others have organized and participated in labor unions representing their profession.

The union movement in social work began in earnest during the Great Depression. In 1931 a small group of practitioners (most of whom were caseworkers in private social services agencies) formed the Social Worker's Discussion Club, which addressed, among other issues, problems related to employment and unemployment insurance (Karger, 1988). Also noteworthy during this period was the formation of a labor association, the Association of Federation Social Workers (AFSW) by practitioners facing salary cuts at the New York Federation for the Support of Jewish Philanthropic Societies. AFSW conducted the first strike in social work in 1934 (Fisher, 1980).

Collective bargaining rights for social workers are governed by federal and state laws that cover employees in public and private agencies. Social workers form and join unions for many reasons, which include advocating for reasonable wages, benefits, job security, and working conditions. About one-fourth of the social work labor force are union members, mostly in public-sector agencies (Tambor, 1995).

There has been some debate within the social work profession about whether there is inherent conflict between union goals and professional mission (Karger, 1988; Shulman, 1978). Some practitioners argue that unions sometimes place members' self-serving interests (for example, concerning wages, benefits, and working conditions) above clients' interests. As Tambor (1995) observed:

> A recurring theme in the professional literature has been the compatibility of unionization with professionalization. . . . Administrators

have viewed collective bargaining as inappropriate for the non-profit community service enterprise . . . and as inevitably promoting conflict between the agency's norm of serving the clients and the union's norm of serving the members' interests. . . . Unionization also has been seen as a responsible and logical means of dealing with power and decision making within the social agency workplace. (p. 2421)

The majority of social workers acknowledge that unions perform an important function in the profession by helping maintain worker morale and, ultimately, promoting working conditions that enhance social workers' ability to meet clients' needs. At various points in its history, NASW has recognized and endorsed social workers' right to organize and participate in labor unions. In 1967, for example, NASW adopted a policy acknowledging the right of members to "participate in the formulation of personnel policies and procedures through whatever instruments they choose" (Karger, 1988, p. 33). This policy was revised in 1971 and 1975 to encourage management in human services settings to "accept and work with whatever means of representation is chosen by the employee group" (Cole, 1977, p. 1559). Since 1968 NASW Standards for Social Work Personnel Practices (1991) have affirmed the right of social work employees to collective bargaining concerning wages and working conditions. Since 1975 staff in NASW's national office, with the exception of those in management and supervisory positions and those considered to be confidential employees, have been union members (Tambor, 1995). The 1996 NASW Code of Ethics is the first of the profession's codes to directly address social workers' right to form and participate in labor unions.

### STANDARD 3.10(b)

> The actions of social workers who are involved in labor–management disputes, job actions, or labor strikes should be guided by the profession's values, ethical principles, and ethical standards. Reasonable differences of opinion exist among social workers concerning their primary obligation as professionals during an actual or threatened labor strike or job action. Social workers should carefully examine relevant issues and their possible impact on clients before deciding on a course of action.

Social workers' decisions about whether to support or participate in an actual or threatened labor strike or job action are among the most difficult they face. On one hand, social workers are obligated to uphold their commitment to clients, whose needs might go unmet or neglected during a labor strike or job action. On the other hand, exercising the right to strike and engage in job actions may be necessary to sustain worker morale and promote working conditions that enhance social workers' ability to meet clients' needs. As I have said elsewhere (Reamer, 1988),

> The debate is old, yet it persists because of its intractability. Moreover, while the arguments are familiar, they are hardly hackneyed. From one vantage point, social workers are public servants and thus occupy positions of trust and obligation. It would be unconscionable for social workers to betray the poor, mentally ill, infirm, abused, and neglected in order to advance their own interests. Granted, their

claims may be legitimate, but, like police officers and fire fighters, the job comes with certain strings attached—strikes are not acceptable. (p. 136)

Critics, on the other hand, argue that social workers are particularly vulnerable to abuse. The presumption of altruism invites managers to take advantage of social workers' benevolent instincts. To counter such temptation, social workers must retain the right to strike. (p. 136)

As Bertha Capen Reynolds (1956), one of social work's pioneers and early social activists, put it, "In the history of unionization in social work it is impossible to separate the two notions of protecting one's own condition as a worker and safeguarding the right to treat clients ethically" (p. 237).

Social workers have always been ambivalent about job actions and strikes in their workplaces. In one well-known study of reactions to a work stoppage by psychiatric aides in a large metropolitan state hospital, social work staff were evenly divided as to whether they should have joined the walkout (Bohr, Brenner, & Kaplan, 1971). Rehr (1960) found a similar split in social workers' reactions to a strike of nonprofessional workers at Mount Sinai Hospital in New York City; half the staff remained on the job, but the other half refused to cross the picket line. Fisher (1987) reported similar disagreement among social workers at Mount Sinai Hospital during a second strike 25 years later. In one other prominent study, Lightman (1983) reported considerable disagreement among social workers about the legitimacy of a strike.

NASW historically has supported social workers' right to strike. For example, in 1969 the NASW Ad Hoc Committee on Advocacy published a statement asserting that "one cannot arbitrarily write off any action that may temporarily cause his clients hardship if he believes the ultimate benefits of his action will outweigh any initial harm" (p. 19). Further, the *NASW Standards for Social Work Personnel Practices* (1991) explicitly oppose laws or policies that prohibit strikes by employees.

Because of persistent disagreement among social workers concerning when job actions and labor strikes are appropriate, the *NASW Code of Ethics* Revision Committee did not take a position for or against such actions. Rather, the committee's standard recognizes that reasonable differences of opinion exist among social workers concerning their primary obligation and that practitioners should carefully examine the profession's values and ethical principles and standards as they make their decisions. In the end, social workers' decisions about their participation in job actions and labor strikes are matters of conscience.

# CHAPTER
## 5
# ETHICAL RESPONSIBILITIES AS PROFESSIONALS

The standards in this section of the code concern social workers' ethical responsibilities as professionals. They focus on issues related to professional competence; discrimination; private conduct; dishonesty, fraud, and deception; social worker impairment; misrepresentation; solicitation of clients; and acknowledgment of work done by social workers and others.

## COMPETENCE

### STANDARD 4.01(a)

*Social workers should accept responsibility or employment only on the basis of existing competence or the intention to acquire the necessary competence.*

Social workers should seek only those employment and professional opportunities for which they have proper education, training, knowledge, and skills. To do otherwise would undermine social workers' and their employers' efforts to meet clients' needs. Practitioners should have at least minimally acceptable competence to perform the duties required by their agencies, the prevailing practice and ethical standards in the profession, licensing requirements, and relevant regulations and laws. In one case, for example, an unemployed social worker responded to an advertisement recruiting a family therapist for a child guidance clinic. His prior experience had been exclusively in community mental health agencies that provided individual counseling to people diagnosed with chronic mental illness. After coping with several months of unemployment and financial strain, the social worker was eager to be hired for the position. In his interview, he intimated that he had studied family therapy and provided considerable family therapy in his previous jobs, but neither of these claims was true. The social worker was hired and, after a six-month probationary period, terminated from his position when it became clear that his family therapy skills were not up to the clinic's requirements.

In another case a social worker for a public welfare agency was summoned by the department's director and asked whether she would be willing to assume responsibility for overseeing the department's evaluation of a major welfare-to-work program that was attracting considerable local and national attention. The director had considered retaining an outside evaluator but decided to designate someone from his own staff to save funds. The social worker was particularly eager to win the department director's favor because she hoped to be considered for future promotions. Unfortunately, she had little formal training in program evaluation and data analysis beyond the basic courses required in graduate school. In addition, she did not contact any colleagues with expertise in the area before she designed the program evaluation and data analysis.

The social worker's final report was harshly criticized by welfare reform experts and by the research methodologists who reviewed it. She had made a number of serious errors in sample selection, questionnaire design, and statistical analyses. Because of the way the study was conducted and the data were gathered, most of the more important mistakes could not be rectified, and the program evaluation was considered a wasted effort. The agency director had to reallocate scarce program funds to contract with an outside evaluator to conduct a new study. Much to his chagrin and embarrassment, the director also had to apply to the federal agency that funded the program for an extension of the deadline for submitting the evaluation's final report.

In some cases it may be permissible for social workers to accept responsibility or employment based on their intention to acquire the necessary competence. Sometimes a social worker is qualified to perform most of the tasks associated with a particular position but lacks the knowledge or skills for certain aspects of the job. In such cases it may be permissible for social workers to accept the responsibility or position if they inform those in authority about the gaps in their knowledge and skills and their plans to acquire the necessary competence. For example, the director of social work in a large hospital wanted to hire a social worker to supervise the department's oncology program. The program included two clinical social workers who provided services to adult and child cancer patients and their families. The most attractive applicant for the position had extensive experience working in oncology programs for adults, but she told the director of social work that she did not have experience working with children diagnosed with cancer. Nonetheless, the department director was eager to hire her for the position. Together they developed a continuing education plan for the first nine months of the social worker's employment so she would acquire the knowledge she needed about working with children with cancer. The director hired the social worker because of her impressive professional background and references and because she had a clear plan to acquire the other competence she would need for the job.

In another case a social worker applied for a faculty position in an undergraduate social work education program. The social worker was enrolled in a doctoral program at a nearby university but had not yet completed her degree. The faculty position required a completed doctorate or explicit plans to complete a doctorate. The head of the social work department and the applicant worked out a detailed plan that would enable the applicant to teach in the department and complete his doctorate within two years, including leave time to permit completion of course work and the dissertation. The social worker was hired based on his plan to acquire the necessary competence for the position.

## STANDARD 4.01(b)

*Social workers should strive to become and remain proficient in professional practice and the performance of professional functions.*

*Social workers should critically examine and keep current with emerging knowledge relevant to social work. Social workers should routinely review the professional literature and participate in continuing education relevant to social work practice and social work ethics.*

Like all professionals, social workers should hone, enhance, and upgrade their knowledge and skills throughout their careers. Although social workers may have acquired extensive knowledge by the time of their graduation from undergraduate or graduate school, even the best social work education programs can provide students with only foundation-level knowledge and skills and a modest amount of advanced learning in the profession. The relatively limited amount of time social workers spend in formal social work education programs precludes acquisition of the breadth and depth of knowledge and skills required for competent practice throughout a career. In addition, social workers can expect new conceptual models, novel intervention approaches, and other innovations to emerge during the course of their careers.

As discussed under standard 3.08, social workers can acquire new knowledge and skills and become acquainted with important developments in the field by attending continuing education workshops and seminars sponsored by professional organizations, schools and departments of social work, state licensing boards, social services agencies and organizations, and private continuing education firms. Depending on their work setting, social workers can choose continuing education offered in clinical and direct practice; human behavior; social welfare policies; social change; research and evaluation; social, cultural, and ethnic diversity; and professional ethics.

Practitioners also should make a diligent effort to keep up with the professional literature, including books, professional journals, government documents and publications, encyclopedias, monographs published by private agencies and organizations, and unpublished material (such as evaluation reports, position papers, and dissertations). It is important to be familiar with techniques used to locate useful journal articles, especially published abstracts such as those in *Social Work Abstracts, Psychological Abstracts, Sociological Abstracts, Women's Studies Abstracts, Public Affairs Information Service Bulletin, Index Medicus, Child Development Abstracts and Bibliography,* and *ERIC.* Also, sophisticated computer technology has given today's social workers access to a great range of literature through the Internet. Practitioners who have not had an opportunity to learn how to conduct literature searches by computer or find citations and the full text of documents on the Internet should arrange for instruction in these techniques. Computer access to information and new knowledge has provided social workers with remarkably convenient and efficient ways to keep up with the professional literature relevant to their areas of expertise and interest.

Social workers should be familiar with publications issued by federal, state, and local government agencies, which can be enormously helpful in social work practice. Social workers involved in welfare reform efforts, for example, may want to update their information on the numbers and characteristics of people living in poverty. Practitioners who provide services to people with chronic diseases may want to monitor epidemiological data relevant to their client populations. Those who work in the area of drug and alcohol abuse prevention may want to check federal publications on demonstration projects or statistics concerning the incidence of drug and alcohol abuse among various demographic groups. College and university libraries, as well as public libraries, often employ reference librarians who can be helpful to social workers who are not familiar with this substantial resource. In addition, monographs and unpublished documents issued by private agencies and organizations can be useful in social work. Unfortunately, there is no master catalog of these documents, but often they can be found by colleagues' recommendations or references to them in the published literature.

A wide range of specialized encyclopedias written for professionals are also helpful. The most relevant for many social workers is the *Encyclopedia of Social Work*, published by NASW Press. This regularly updated reference work includes good introductory and overview articles on a wide range of subjects related to social work, including adoption, assessment, community organization, developmental disabilities, ethics and values, hospital social work, mental health, social workers in politics, and women in social policy. In addition, social workers may want to consult such encyclopedias as the *Encyclopedia of Psychology*, the *Encyclopedia of Applied Ethics*, the *Encyclopedia of Bioethics*, and the *Encyclopedia of Crime and Justice*.

## STANDARD 4.01(c)

*Social workers should base practice on recognized knowledge, including empirically based knowledge, relevant to social work and social work ethics.*

One of the characteristics of professionalism is the willingness to draw on relevant bodies of knowledge. Social workers have a responsibility to consult the literature pertinent to their practice areas. Consistent with their obligation to become and remain proficient in the profession (standard 4.01[b]), social workers should base their professional activities on knowledge available in social work and allied fields.

There are two general bodies of knowledge relevant to social work: nonempirical and empirical. Nonempirical knowledge includes theoretical and conceptual discussions of subjects such as social policy, intervention theories and approaches, human development, discrimination and oppression, cultural and social diversity, and professional ethics. These discussions are organized around and explore ideas, concepts, and constructs. They do not include analyses of data based on observation or experience of the subject matter. In contrast, empirical knowledge draws on and presents data or statistics pertaining to the subject matter. The data may be qualitative or quantitative and are obtained by means of such techniques as interviews, questionnaires, observation, formal psychometric assessments, and paper-and-pencil tests.

Social workers should base practice on recognized knowledge because professionals should have a sound rationale, as evidenced in the profession's evolving body of knowledge and standards, for their intervention approaches (whether they focus on clinical, administrative, community, programmatic, or policy issues). Social workers who act without consulting the profession's knowledge base or who dismiss its relevance and value are negligent and unethical.

Some social workers may worry that the requirement to base practice on recognized knowledge discourages innovation and creativity and promotes counterproductive conformity in the profession. To the contrary, practitioners should be encouraged to innovate and explore alternatives to conventional wisdom and practice. Standard 4.01(c) does not require social workers to adhere to or agree with the contents of the profession's extant knowledge base: They should feel free to challenge, critique, and reject prevailing beliefs and intervention approaches—remaining mindful, however, of the value of existing knowledge and their reasons for exploring alternatives. This kind of creative intellectual tension promotes healthy debate and growth in a profession and prevents stagnation.

In one case, for example, a social worker in private practice provided counseling to a young man who manifested anxiety and panic symptoms. The social worker had read an article in a general-interest magazine that advocated the use of certain herbs to reduce such symptoms. He gave his client a copy of the article and encouraged the client, for whom conventional therapeutic interventions had been unsuccessful, to consider the approach. Before doing so, however, the social worker did not attempt to locate any other articles (in professional journals or otherwise) on the approach or documentation of its effectiveness. This intervention was thus unprofessional and unethical (and may have bordered on practicing medicine without a license).

In a second case a social worker was hired by a mental health agency to provide clinical services to children who had been sexually abused. The social worker had considerable experience working with children in schools but relatively little experience counseling sexually abused children, so she wanted to learn more about clinical techniques and strategies used with this population. She arranged with her supervisor to allocate time during the first month of the job to researching the empirical and nonempirical literature on clinical interventions with sexually abused children. The social worker found a great deal of information in professional books and journals, as well as several unpublished documents, and a number of the discussions of clinical approaches were helpful and appealing, although she was critical of some of what she read. After sorting out her preferences and discussing them with her supervisor, the social worker developed an intervention repertoire to guide her practice with sexually abused children. She also attended several continuing education seminars and workshops to enhance her knowledge and skill (consistent with standard 4.01[b]).

Standard 4.01(c) also highlights social workers' obligation to base their practice on recognized knowledge relevant to social work ethics. Much of the social work literature on ethical dilemmas, decision making, misconduct, and professional malpractice and liability has been published since the late 1970s and especially since the mid-1980s. Many practicing social workers completed their formal social work education at a time when knowledge pertaining to social work ethics was nascent at best. It is important for practitioners to make a frequent special effort to update their knowledge on the broad subject of social work ethics.

# DISCRIMINATION

## STANDARD 4.02

*Social workers should not practice, condone, facilitate, or collabo-rate with any form of discrimination on the basis of race, ethnicity, national origin, color, sex, sexual orientation, age, marital status, political belief, religion, or mental or physical disability.*

Social workers have an obligation to prevent and eliminate discrimination in employing organizations' work assignments and employment policies and practices (standard 3.09[e]). Standard 4.02 broadens this requirement by prohibiting social workers from engaging in discrimination in any form.

Social work has a strong record of involvement in antidiscrimination efforts. Jane Addams, for example, was a founding member of the National Association for the Advancement of Colored People (NAACP). Social workers were especially involved in the civil rights campaigns and protests of the 1960s.

The concept of civil rights in the United States, which is at the root of efforts to prevent and discourage discrimination, is rooted in English laws pertaining to the protection of the individual from abuses by the state (Pollard, 1995). When English barons compelled King John to sign the Magna Carta in 1215, that document provided the foundation for the Anglo American legal system and many of the civil liberties that ultimately emerged in the United States.

Most of the civil rights gains in the United States for oppressed minorities were achieved in the 20th century as a result of major court decisions and legislation. Notable among the court decisions were the Supreme Court's decision in 1948 in *Shelly v. Kraemer*, which held that private arrangements to maintain racial segregation in housing patterns was unconstitutional; the 1954 Supreme Court decision in *Brown v. Board of Education of Topeka*, which overruled the "separate but equal" doctrine that had been in effect since 1896 and concluded that segregation of school children on the basis of race was unconstitutional, even if the facilities were of equal quality; the 1963 Supreme Court decision in *Gideon v. Wainright*, which asserted that poor people who have been accused of a criminal offense have the right to a lawyer; and the 1973 Supreme Court decision in *Roe v. Wade* granting women the right to abortion (Pollard, 1995). Important federal legislation pertaining to discrimination included the Civil Rights Act of 1957, which established the U.S. Commission on Civil Rights and strengthened federal enforcement powers (for example, programs receiving federal funding were prohibited from discriminating on the basis of race, color, religion, or national origin); the Civil Rights Act of 1964, which strengthened voting rights and mandated equal access to programs that receive federal funding; the Education for All Handicapped Children Act of 1975, which required free public education for all children with disabilities; the Americans with Disabilities Act of 1990, which enhanced access to employment and various other settings for people with disabilities; and the Civil Rights Act of 1991, which provided additional protections to women and people of color in the workplace.

Below are examples of unacceptable and unethical forms of discrimination in social work:

- A social worker at a school subscribed to strong religious beliefs that condemn homosexuality. He tried to convince one of the students he was counseling that it was immoral for the student to explore his homosexual feelings.
- A social work supervisor employed in a private residential program for boys at high risk for delinquency was not willing to hire social workers of color or Jewish social workers. When he was a young adult, often in trouble with the law, the social worker had been a member of the Ku Klux Klan. Although he resigned his membership in the organization long before enrolling in social work school, he still supported some of the Klan's discriminatory beliefs and practices.
- A social worker who directed a substance abuse treatment program hired a secretary who had been in a serious automobile accident and required the use of a wheelchair. The social worker fired the secretary after learning that she would have to pay to build a ramp to enable the secretary to enter their office building, as well as widen doorways and move furniture within the office to accommodate the wheelchair and remodel the restroom to make it accessible.
- A social work educator frequently facilitated discussions among students in his classes, but he consistently called on male students more frequently than female students when students volunteered to speak in class.

It is not enough for social workers personally to oppose discrimination and avoid engaging in any form of it. Social work's obligation to promote social justice requires its practitioners to work actively to change discriminatory practices and policies and implement fair and just practices and policies in the profession.

## PRIVATE CONDUCT

### STANDARD 4.03

*Social workers should not permit their private conduct to interfere with their ability to fulfill their professional responsibilities.*

In most cases what social workers do in their private time is their own business. They should certainly have the freedom to pursue their social, business, religious, and recreational interests unencumbered. However, social workers must draw the line at behavior or activities that interfere with their ability to carry out their professional duties and fulfill their professional obligations.

Social workers' private conduct can be problematic primarily in two ways. First, practitioners' affiliations sometimes can affect their ability to perform their professional duties. In one case, for example, a social worker who was an administrator of an outpatient clinic in a private psychiatric hospital volunteered as the campaign director for a candidate for public office who was widely regarded as a racist. Many members of the social services community became concerned about the social worker's close affiliation with the candidate and endorsement of his racist views. Two of the staff at the outpatient clinic resigned in protest, and a number of practitioners in the community refused to refer clients to the clinic. The social worker's supervisor at the hospital became concerned that the social worker's private conduct was harming the hospital's reputation and interfering with her ability to perform her duties.

Second, social workers' illegal or unethical conduct in their private lives can have a detrimental effect on their professional functioning. For example, a social worker employed by a residential program for children was convicted of third-degree sexual assault of a child in the community, and the judge placed him on supervised probation. The social worker could not continue to function effectively or with any credibility in the residential program for children, and the program's administrators could not continue allowing him to have access to children in the facility. In a similar case a social worker who served as a counselor in a substance abuse treatment program was arrested at her home after she tried to sell a small amount of illegal drugs to an undercover police officer. The social worker was convicted, placed on probation, and forced to resign her position with the substance abuse treatment program.

In some cases the relevance of practitioners' private conduct to their professional responsibilities is less clear; social workers may disagree about the extent to which their private conduct is germane to their profession. In one case a clinical social worker employed by a nursing home was indicted in federal court for income tax evasion. According to the indictment, for eight years the social worker had underreported his income from his former private practice and falsified a number of deductions. After learning of the indictment, administrators and supervisors at the nursing home disagreed about whether they should ask for his resignation. The social worker was highly respected by staff and residents, and the indictment was completely unrelated to his responsibilities at the nursing home. In another case a social worker who was an administrator at a child welfare agency was arrested for attempting to solicit a prostitute. The social worker was dismissed from his position and later appealed the dismissal, arguing that the crime with which he was charged had no bearing on his professional duties. Agency administrators disagreed among themselves about the relevance of the arrest to his work. After an administrative hearing, the social worker was reinstated to his position.

It is difficult to prescribe strict criteria for determining when practitioners' private conduct interferes with their ability to perform their professional duties. Although the relevance of private conduct is sometimes obvious—as when a social worker who counsels sexually abused children is convicted of molesting a child—it is not so obvious in other situations. As a guiding principle, social workers should attempt to distinguish between private conduct that directly interferes with the performance of professional functions and private conduct that, while perhaps distasteful, disturbing, or distracting, is tangential to professional obligations. The former cannot be permitted; the latter may need to be tolerated.

# Dishonesty, Fraud, and Deception

## STANDARD 4.04

*Social workers should not participate in, condone, or be associated with dishonesty, fraud, or deception.*

Social workers must avoid any knowingly dishonest, fraudulent, or deceptive activities. Such activities not only undermine individual practitioners' reputations and credibility, they also damage the entire profession's reputation and integrity.

Dishonest, fraudulent, and deceptive activities can take many forms. Examples of dishonesty include social workers who lie to potential employers or clients about their professional education and credentials (see standard 4.06[c]), falsify records (see standard 3.04[a]), or provide supervisees with less than candid feedback about the quality of their work (see standard 3.01[d]). In one case a social worker who worked in a city's subsidized housing program received a telephone call from a newspaper reporter who was investigating reports that some of the housing units did not have heat during a bitter cold spell. The social worker told the reporter that she was "on top of the situation" and had several staff members doing their best to rectify the problem, but in fact, she had done nothing to address the problem. In another case a social worker employed by a hospital provided services to an elderly man who needed a nursing home placement. The patient repeatedly asked the social worker if she had found any suitable nursing homes. The social worker told the patient that she had contacted three different nursing homes, all of which were filled or unable to care for the patient's unique medical needs. In fact, the social worker had not yet contacted any nursing homes.

There are social workers who believe that some forms of dishonesty may be permissible in extraordinary circumstances. Examples include social workers who give vulnerable clients false information (for example, about a prognosis or progress in treatment or the health of a loved one) because the clients would have difficulty handling or be harmed by truthful information, or social work administrators who knowingly provide staff with inaccurate information about their agency's financial status in an effort to preserve organizational morale. Such displays of dishonesty—"white lies"—are both controversial and risky (Dworkin, 1971; Reamer, 1983a).

Fraudulent activities also can take various forms. Examples include social workers who deliberately submit embellished insurance forms or vouchers for travel expenses, forge supervisors' signatures on official forms, falsify statistics on use of services, or complete informed consent forms after clients have signed them. In one case a social worker was sued by a former client who claimed that the social worker had him sign a blank consent form and subsequently filled in details concerning the nature and purpose of the consent. The consent form was then used to release information to another services provider, who shared the information with the lawyer for the client's estranged wife. The information ultimately was used against the client during a custody dispute with his estranged wife. In another case involving fraud a social worker submitted invoices to the state for clinical services allegedly provided to individuals when, in fact, all services had been provided to groups of clients and were supposed to have been reimbursed at a lower hourly rate.

Deceptive activities also can include elements of dishonesty and fraud. Examples include social workers who deliberately mislead clients about the likely expense involved in treatment or embellish program evaluation results. For example, a social worker who was director of a social services program for senior citizens submitted a grant proposal to a state agency in which he stated that the program would provide a range of services the agency could not provide. In another case a social worker who was a community organizer deliberately withheld information from community residents about a potential conflict of interest stemming from her part-time work with a housing developer that wanted to construct a number of low-income housing units in the community.

## IMPAIRMENT

### STANDARD 4.05(a)

*Social workers should not allow their own personal problems, psychosocial distress, legal problems, substance abuse, or mental health difficulties to interfere with their professional judgment and performance or to jeopardize the best interests of people for whom they have a professional responsibility.*

Standards 2.09(a) and (b) concern social workers' obligation to assist colleagues who manifest evidence of impairment and, when colleagues have not taken adequate steps to address the impairment, to take action through appropriate channels. Standard 4.05(a) also concerns impairment, but it focuses on social workers' obligation to ensure that their own personal problems do not affect their practice effectiveness.

No precise estimates of the extent of impairment among social workers are available.* No comprehensive surveys have been conducted. Only rough estimates of the extent of the problem have been made. For example, in the foreword to the *Impaired Social Worker Program Resource Book*, published by the NASW Commission on Employment and Economic Support (1987), the commission's chair stated, "Social workers have the same problems as most working groups. Up to 5 to 7 percent of our membership may have a problem with substance abuse. Another 10 to 15 percent may be going through personal transitions in their relationships, marriage, family, or their work life" (p. 4). The resource book concluded, however, that "there is little reliable information on the extent of impairment among social workers" (p. 6).

Research on impairment has been conducted in professions allied with social work, such as psychology and psychiatry, but prevalence rates for social workers cannot be inferred directly on the basis of data from these professions; the available data suggest that social workers should be particularly alert to several possible forms and causes of impairment. Surveys concerning

---

*Parts of this discussion are adapted from Reamer (1994).

stress in clinicians' lives suggest diverse sources, including their jobs, the illness or death of family members, marital or relationship problems, financial difficulties, midlife crises, physical or mental illness, legal problems, and substance abuse (Deutsch, 1985; Guy, Poelstra, & Stark, 1989; Millon, Millon, & Antoni, 1986; Pope, 1988; Thoreson, Miller, & Krauskopf, 1989). Lamb et al. (1987) argued that professional education itself can produce unique forms of stress and impairment, primarily as a result of the close clinical supervision to which students are typically subjected, the disruption often caused in their personal lives by the demands of schoolwork and internships, and the general pressures of academic programs. Commonly reported sources of impairment are personality disorders, depression and other emotional problems, marital problems, and physical illness.

In general, the literature has suggested that distress among clinical professionals falls into two categories: environmental stress, which is a function of employment conditions (actual working conditions and the broader culture's lack of support of the human services mission), and professional training and personal stress, caused by problems with marriage, relationships, emotional and physical health, and finances. Research suggested that psychotherapists and counseling professionals, in particular, encounter special problems that are a result of the extension of their therapeutic role into the nonwork aspects of their lives (such as relationships with friends and family members), the absence of reciprocity in relationships with clients (therapists are always the ones who give), the often slow and erratic nature of the therapeutic process, and personal issues that emerge as a result of their work with clients (Wood, Klein, Cross, Lammers, & Elliott, 1985). As Kilburg, Kaslow, and VandenBos (1988) concluded,

> [The] stresses of daily life—family responsibilities, death of family members and friends, other severe losses, illnesses, financial difficulties, crises of all kinds—quite naturally place mental health professionals, like other people, under pressure. However, by virtue of their training and place in society, such professionals face unique stresses. And although they have been trained extensively in how to deal with the emotional and behavioral crises of others, few are trained in how to deal with the stresses they themselves will face. . . . Mental health professionals are expected by everyone, including themselves, to be paragons. The fact that they may be unable to fill that role makes them a prime target for disillusionment, distress, and burnout. When this reaction occurs, the individual's ability to function as a professional may become impaired. (p. 723)

A distressingly recurrent theme in cases involving practitioner impairment is the problem of professional boundaries (see standards 1.06[b] and [c]; 1.09[a], [b], [c], and [d]; 1.10; 2.07[a] and [b]; and 3.01[c]). Particularly in cases of sexual involvement with clients, practitioners often are confused about what constitutes appropriate boundaries between themselves and their clients and the need to clearly delineate the practitioner's and client's involvement in each other's lives (Landers, 1992). Both parties can be confused about or will simply ignore warning signs and risks related to inappropriate involvement that may take the form of sexual contact, socializing, or business relationships unrelated to treatment.

*Social workers whose personal problems, psychosocial distress, legal problems, substance abuse, or mental health difficulties interfere with their professional judgment and performance should immediately seek consultation and take appropriate remedial action by seeking professional help, making adjustments in workload, terminating practice, or taking any other steps necessary to protect clients and others.*

Social workers who become aware of their own personal impairment have an obligation to take steps to remedy the situation. Unfortunately, little is known about the extent to which impaired social workers voluntarily seek help for their problems. One of the few empirical studies of impaired practitioners' efforts to seek help (Guy et al., 1989) found that 70 percent of the "distressed" clinical psychologists surveyed sought some form of therapeutic assistance, whether individual psychotherapy, family therapy, or group therapy. A small percentage of the practitioners were placed on medication or hospitalized or terminated their professional practice.

Thoreson, Nathan, Skorina, and Kilburg (1983) noted that impaired professionals sometimes find it difficult to seek help because of their mythical belief in their infinite power and invulnerability. The growth in the number of psychotherapists in private practice exacerbates the problem because there is reduced opportunity for colleagues to observe each other's unethical, impaired, or incompetent practice. In a valuable study by Deutsch (1985), a diverse group of therapists, including social workers, who admitted to personal problems gave a variety of reasons for not seeking professional help. These included believing that an acceptable professional was not available, seeking help from family members or friends as an alternative, fearing exposure and the disclosure of private or confidential information, concern about the amount of effort required and the cost, having a spouse who was unwilling to participate in treatment, failing to admit the seriousness of the problem, believing they should be able to solve their problems by themselves, and believing that therapy would not be effective in their particular case.

Social workers should make diligent efforts to raise the profession's awareness of the problem of impairment. Particular attention should be paid to any signs suggesting that a practitioner's personal problems, psychosocial distress, legal problems, substance abuse, or mental health difficulties are interfering with his or her professional judgment and performance. When such signs appear, a social worker should immediately seek consultation and take appropriate remedial action.

As social workers intensify their attention to impairment in the profession, they must be careful to avoid reductionist explanations of the problems they observe. Although emphasizing psychotherapeutic and other rehabilitative efforts in cases that call for them is certainly appropriate, practitioners must not lose sight of the environmental stresses that often lead to such disabilities. Distress experienced by social workers often is the result of unique professional challenges for which available resources are inadequate. Every day social workers face such problems as poverty, hunger, homelessness, domestic violence, child abuse and neglect, substance abuse, crime, mental illness—among many others—and so are prime candidates for stress and burnout. Inadequate funding, undependable political support, and public criticism of social workers' efforts often combine to produce low morale and high stress in the profession (Jayaratne & Chess, 1984; Johnson & Stone, 1986; Koeske & Koeske, 1989). In addition to responding to the private troubles of impaired colleagues, social workers must simultaneously confront the public issues and environmental flaws that can produce impairment.

# MISREPRESENTATION

## STANDARD 4.06(a)

*Social workers should make clear distinctions between statements made and actions engaged in as a private individual and as a representative of the social work profession, a professional social work organization, or the social worker's employing agency.*

Social workers are often in a position to express authoritative opinions, whether in work with clients, during meetings with colleagues, in giving public lectures or presentations at workshops or conferences, while teaching social work students, or in interviews with media representatives. Social workers who make statements, offer opinions, or provide advice in their role as professionals are likely to influence their audience in some way, in large part because they are viewed as well-educated, experienced experts. Because of the weight that is often attached to their professional opinions, practitioners must be careful to distinguish between statements they make as private individuals and those they make as representatives of the profession, a professional organization, or an employer. Care must be taken to avoid giving any misleading impression that a personal opinion, expressed by someone speaking as a private individual, represents an official position. In one case, for example, a social worker who was the executive director of a state chapter of NASW worked as a senior official on the campaign of a candidate for statewide political office. Because he split his time between his NASW duties and his work on the political campaign, the social worker needed to be exceedingly careful to distinguish between his statements as a private individual—in relation to his work on the campaign—and his statements as executive director of the NASW chapter. When he performed duties in his role in the NASW chapter, he was careful to state that his opinions were on behalf of the organization and its board of directors; when he performed duties in his role as a campaign official, he deliberately avoided mentioning his affiliation with NASW. Whenever a member of the public who attended a campaign event mentioned the social worker's affiliation with NASW, he acted responsibly and was careful to point out that he was acting only in his capacity as a member of the campaign staff and none of his comments should be construed as official NASW policies or positions. Although the social worker's simultaneous positions were challenging, he managed to distinguish between his two roles effectively throughout the course of the political campaign.

In contrast, a social worker employed as a caseworker in a private, nonsectarian senior high school was actively involved in abortion rights debates in her community. The social worker adamantly opposed abortion and was outspoken on the subject in various public forums, such as church-sponsored protests and legislative hearings. When she spoke in public on abortion issues she identified herself as someone with professional familiarity with teenage pregnancy issues and mentioned her professional title and the school where she was employed. She did not routinely explain to her audiences that her views were strictly her own and did not represent the views of her employer or the social work profession. As a result, some members of the social worker's audiences assumed that she was an official representative of her school or her profession.

In another case a social worker was an assistant director in a state welfare agency responsible for administering the state's public assistance program. The social worker was upset about a number of changes in the program that had been proposed by the governor. He published a strongly worded critique of the governor's proposal as an editorial in the state's most widely read newspaper in which he accused the governor of being "a brutish, insensitive politician who caved in to the draconian politics of the state's self-serving elite" and lambasted the governor for being "a pawn in a well-orchestrated national effort to create an archaic caste system in the United States." The social worker identified himself as a high-ranking official in the state agency, thereby creating the impression that he was speaking in his official capacity as a representative of the agency. After reading the editorial, the governor's chief of staff called the director of the state welfare agency and insisted that the social worker be disciplined for misrepresenting the department's position on the governor's proposed changes. The social worker was reprimanded severely by the agency director for failing to distinguish between his views as a private individual and the official position of his employer. In addition, the director passed over the social worker for promotion in his department, although previously he was being considered seriously for the new position.

## STANDARD 4.06(b)

*Social workers who speak on behalf of professional social work organizations should accurately represent the official and authorized positions of the organizations.*

Social workers sometimes function as spokespersons for professional organizations, such as the national office of NASW, state chapters of NASW, state social work licensing boards, social work education programs, and specialty groups within the profession (for example, the American Association of State Social Work Boards, the National Association of Black Social Workers, the National Federation of Societies for Clinical Social Work, the National Association of Oncology Social Workers, the National Indian Social Workers Association, or the National Network for Social Work Managers). They may speak on behalf of such organizations as paid staff members or as volunteers who serve as officers or assist with various organizational duties and activities. When speaking on behalf of professional social work organizations, practitioners should not misrepresent or distort the official positions of the organizations.

A social worker may misrepresent an organization's official position for self-serving reasons or altruistic ones. In one case that apparently involved both types of motives, a social worker chaired a state licensing board. The board had been profiled in the state's major newspaper because of its involvement in the widely publicized adjudication of a complaint against a clinical social worker who had been accused of sexually abusing a client. In an interview with the reporter who wrote the article, the chair said, "The public should be reassured that this licensing board is determined to raise the ethical standards to which social workers in this state will be held and increase the sanctions against those who violate the board's ethical standards." Although this statement reflected the chair's view, the licensing board members as a group had taken no such action and had not reached any consensus about raising standards or increasing sanctions. The chair, however, decided to take advantage of her interview with the reporter to create the impression among the public that the board had already taken a position on the issue. She hoped that her widely publicized, but inaccurate and misleading, statement would force her colleagues on the board to fall into line with her view. She also hoped that the other board members would not want to appear to be "soft" on ethical misconduct and thus would not want to challenge the chair's position as it was articulated in the newspaper article.

In another case a social worker chaired the clinical issues committee of the state NASW chapter. The committee agreed that the chair should testify at a legislative hearing on a bill that would require mental health professionals to report to the state licensing board any incidents of a client disclosing that he or she had been sexually abused by another mental health professional (if the client was willing to consent to the disclosure). The social worker identified herself as chair of the NASW chapter's clinical issues committee. She spoke in favor of the bill and claimed that the chapter supported the bill wholeheartedly, but only the clinical issues committee had discussed the bill and voted to support it. The chapter's board of directors had never discussed the issue or voted on whether the chapter should support it. The social worker's statement before the legislative panel did not accurately represent the NASW chapter's official position. Shortly after her testimony, which was summarized in a newspaper article on the bill's aims and its prospects in the legislature, two members of the NASW chapter's board of directors who were concerned about several of the bill's provisions contacted the social worker and reprimanded her for misrepresenting the organization's views.

### STANDARD 4.06(c)

*Social workers should ensure that their representations to clients, agencies, and the public of professional qualifications, credentials, education, competence, affiliations, services provided, or results to be achieved are accurate. Social workers should claim only those relevant professional credentials they actually possess and take steps to correct any inaccuracies or misrepresentations of their credentials by others.*

Social workers should not mislead clients, the public at large, colleagues, or employers about their backgrounds, skills, and areas of expertise. Their representations should not be embellished or exaggerated and should be accurate in each of the following areas:

- *Qualifications:* descriptions of particular areas of expertise and skill, specialized training, and experience. Social workers who do not have specialized background in specific areas of professional practice should not represent themselves as experts in those areas.
- *Credentials:* licenses from state or other public bodies and certifications granted by professional organizations. Social workers should claim only those licenses and certifications they actually possess.
- *Education:* degrees granted by accredited educational institutions. Social workers should claim only those educational degrees they have earned for completion of academic work.
- *Competence:* specialized areas of expertise. Social workers should represent themselves as competent only in those areas for which they have demonstrated and recognized expertise, including sufficient education and training.
- *Affiliations:* memberships in or involvement with professional organizations. In their public statements and biographical material, social workers should cite only those professional affiliations that they actually maintain.
- *Services provided:* services the practitioner is qualified to provide to clients. Social workers should not create the impression that they provide services that they are not educated or trained to provide.
- *Results to be achieved:* expected outcomes of social work interventions and services. Social workers should not exaggerate the likely results of their interventions and services or guarantee inappropriately that their interventions or services will achieve specific results. Clients and the public should be provided with realistic appraisals and estimates of likely results.

Standard 4.06(c) also states that social workers should claim only those relevant credentials they actually possess. Thus, social workers who have obtained educational degrees that are not directly relevant to social work should not cite those degrees in any misleading way. In one case, for example, a social worker obtained her MSW after her doctorate in biology. After she received her degree in social work, she was hired as a caseworker in a family services agency and later started a private practice. In her marketing materials and on her letterhead, the social worker listed herself as "Dr." or "Ph.D." and referred to herself as a "doctor" in conversations with clients and others. She thus created the impression that she had doctoral-level education that was directly relevant to her clinical social work, which was not the case.

Social workers should be sure to correct any inaccuracies or misrepresentations of their credentials by others. When qualifications, credentials, education, competence, affiliations, or services provided are cited or described inaccurately in, for example, marketing or advertising materials, practitioners should take immediate steps to correct the inaccuracies and avoid misleading clients, employers, colleagues, or the public.

# SOLICITATIONS

## STANDARD 4.07(a)

*Social workers should not engage in uninvited solicitation of potential clients who, because of their circumstances, are vulnerable to undue influence, manipulation, or coercion.*

The 1979 *NASW Code of Ethics* prohibited social workers from soliciting clients (principle II.F.2). However, the 1986 Federal Trade Commission (FTC) inquiry concerning this prohibition (see chapter 1) asserted that the principle possibly constituted restraint of trade. As a result of the inquiry, NASW entered into a consent agreement with the FTC and in 1990 removed the code's reference to solicitation of clients.

In 1996, the *NASW Code of Ethics* Revision Committee concluded that a standard should be included in the revised code to stipulate that solicitations, whether subtle or direct, are unethical when they are uninvited and involve potential clients who are vulnerable to exploitation or undue influence, manipulation, or coercion. According to Gifis (1991), undue influence is established by

> excessive importunity, superiority of will or mind, the relationship of the parties (e.g., priest and penitent or caretaker and senior citizen) or by any other means constraining the donor or testator to do what he is unable to refuse. . . . In such a case, the influencing party is said to have an unfair advantage over the other based, among other things, on real or apparent authority, knowledge of necessity or distress, or a fiduciary or confidential relationship. (p. 508)

Below are examples of unacceptable solicitation:

- A social worker was preparing to leave his position with a community mental health center to develop his private practice. At the community mental health center, he had worked exclusively with trauma victims in acute crisis (for example, victims of recent domestic violence or sexual assault). He told his clients about his impending departure and encouraged a number of them to leave the community mental health center and transfer to his private practice. The social worker did not explain to the clients that they also had the option to continue receiving services from another clinician at the center or seek another services provider (see standard 1.16[f]).
- A social worker at a public child welfare agency provided casework services to families whose children had been placed in foster care after allegations of abuse and neglect. She also maintained a small private practice. The social worker told a couple she worked with at the child welfare agency that they would need to obtain long-term counseling if they hoped to regain custody of their child. She mentioned that she had a private practice outside the agency, gave the couple her business card, and said, "It might be in your best interest to see me regularly for counseling." The couple felt coerced but nonetheless agreed to see the social worker privately to increase their chances of regaining custody of their child.

- A social worker heard a news bulletin announcing that a bus carrying school children had run off the road and tumbled down a steep hill, killing or seriously injuring all the passengers. The social worker, who had just started in private practice, drove to the local hospital where many of the dead and injured children had been brought and began talking informally with a number of the children's parents. He gave his business card to several of the parents whose children had died and encouraged them to contact him if they needed "some help dealing with this crisis."

Social workers may legitimately publicize their skills and services to attract clients. However, it is unethical for social workers to engage in uninvited solicitation of clients who are in a state of crisis or otherwise vulnerable.

## STANDARD 4.07(b)

---

*Social workers should not engage in solicitation of testimonial endorsements (including solicitation of consent to use a client's prior statement as a testimonial endorsement) from current clients or from other people who, because of their particular circumstances, are vulnerable to undue influence.*

Some social workers advertise or market their services, but a practitioner should never ask any current client for a testimonial concerning his or her skills or expertise. Clients may experience being asked for such an endorsement as manipulative or exploitative, and they may feel obligated to consent to avoid jeopardizing the relationship with the social worker. For example, a social worker provided counseling to a woman who had been diagnosed with a serious eating disorder. The social worker was invited to speak about the treatment of eating disorders at a meeting of Overeaters Anonymous. She accepted the invitation in part because she wanted to provide the group with useful information and in part because she saw this as an opportunity to recruit clients for her practice. She invited her client to attend the presentation with her and "describe your positive experience in treatment." The client was reluctant to talk about her problems in public but agreed to do so because of her gratitude to the social worker and her concern about offending her by refusing her request.

Standard 4.07(b) also prohibits social workers from soliciting testimonial endorsements from other people who, because of their particular circumstances, are vulnerable to undue influence. This would include, for example, former clients and colleagues who may feel manipulated or coerced into consenting to the use of their endorsement. Former clients may feel indebted to their social worker or consent to the use of their endorsement to obtain approval or because of some other complex transference phenomenon involved in the professional–client relationship. In approaching former clients for testimonials, social workers may establish an inappropriate dual relationship that could be harmful. The request could suggest to clients that the professional–client relationship is changing to a friendship or collegial relationship. As standard 1.06(b) states, "Social workers should not take unfair advantage of any professional relationship or exploit others to further their . . . business interests." Furthermore, standard 1.06(c) states, "Social workers should not engage in dual or multiple relationships with clients *or former clients* in which there is a risk of exploitation or potential harm to the client" [italics added].

It also can be inappropriate for social workers to approach colleagues for testimonial endorsements, especially when they are in a position of authority over their colleagues or when the colleagues are dependent on them in some way (for example, when social workers function as supervisors, administrators, or referral sources). Like current and former clients, colleagues can be susceptible to undue influence and may consent to the use of their testimonial because they have been manipulated or coerced. Colleagues who obtain referrals from social workers may feel obligated to consent to sustain their referral sources. Supervisees may feel obligated to consent to avoid alienating supervisors who are in a position to influence and shape their careers. In one case a social worker in private practice provided clinical supervision to a social worker who had not yet received her license. The supervisee was employed by a group home for children. The supervising practitioner learned that the social worker he was supervising occasionally made presentations to local school staff about the group home, its background and purpose, and its treatment approach. He asked her to "see if there are opportunities to mention my name and let the school staff know I'm available to provide clinical consultation. I hope you won't mind letting those folks know that I'm good at what I do and could be helpful to them." The supervisee felt pressured and manipulated by her supervisor, but she did not feel comfortable refusing his request.

## ACKNOWLEDGING CREDIT

*STANDARD 4.08(a)*

*Social workers should take responsibility and credit, including authorship credit, only for work they have actually performed and to which they have contributed.*

Social workers should not claim to have performed work that they did not actually do. This may include work related to, for example, a research project, clinical services or supervision, administering a program, writing a grant application, or lobbying. Social workers should take responsibility and credit that is in direct proportion to the work they have actually performed or to which they have contributed. For example, a professor of social work supervised a doctoral student's dissertation. When she had completed her dissertation, the student asked the professor for help in producing a summary and analysis of her results for submission to a professional journal. The professor helped the student highlight the major findings and organize the material for the manuscript, provided consultation on some additional data analysis, and provided feedback on and rewrote portions of the first draft. The professor and the student agreed that it would be appropriate to list the professor as the second author of the paper, because he had provided considerable technical assistance and support and had invested considerable time in helping the student prepare her manuscript. The professor claimed authorship credit that was in direct proportion to the work he actually performed. Listing him as the first author of the paper would be exploitative.

In contrast, in another case several staff members in a family services agency developed a treatment model for adolescents with major substance abuse problems. After working together for several years, the colleagues realized that they had developed an effective treatment approach that should be published. They gathered data demonstrating the treatment's effectiveness and spent much of a year writing a comprehensive manual for the treatment. When they informed their agency director of their plans to publish and disseminate the model, the director insisted that he be included among the authors because he was the agency administrator. The colleagues who had developed the treatment model and related materials resented the director's request and believed that he was taking unfair advantage of his administrative authority. They met with the chair of the agency's board of directors and explained their concerns. The board chair discussed the problem with the rest of the board, which concluded unanimously that the agency director had overstepped his authority in his effort to claim credit for work that he had not actually performed.

## STANDARD 4.08(b)

*Social workers should honestly acknowledge the work of and the contributions made by others.*

Consistent with standard 4.08(a), this standard requires social workers always to give proper credit to colleagues, supervisees, employees, and others who have contributed to work on any professional project. Social workers should not claim credit for work done by others and should acknowledge their efforts.

Social workers who have received assistance from others in activities such as administrative tasks, conference planning and operations, research projects, lobbying efforts, or social action events always should give credit where it is due. For example, a social worker who was the principal investigator of a research and demonstration project supervised the preparation of a final report on the two-year program. The final report was to be submitted to the foundation that funded the project. The social worker had relied heavily on two assistants, who helped with the data collection and analysis and wrote substantial sections of the final report. However, the final report listed the social worker as the sole author and made only brief, passing references to the two assistants in the acknowledgments section. The assistants were offended and believed that the social worker had not honestly acknowledged their contributions to the project's final product.

In a similar case a social worker who was an administrator at a rehabilitation center planned a statewide conference on social services provided in rehabilitation settings. She assembled a small group of colleagues who helped plan the conference, invite a keynote speaker and workshop leaders, and attend to the many logistical details. In the final conference brochure, however, the social worker listed only herself as the organizer. She did not acknowledge the work and contributions of her committee members. Although she briefly mentioned the committee members' efforts during her opening remarks at the conference, she did not acknowledge adequately her colleagues' substantial work and contributions.

It is equally important to acknowledge social workers' written work. Practitioners who prepare written documents, whether published journal articles or books or unpublished reports or monographs, should always accurately cite all their sources. They should not take credit for ideas that are not their own and must not plagiarize the work of others. In one case, for example, a social work student wrote a paper on the history of federal legislation related to public assistance and welfare benefits for a course on social policy. In the paper, the student copied, word for word and without any attribution, substantial passages from a prominent journal article on the subject. The professor recognized the passages and confronted the student, who admitted that she had plagiarized the material. The student was dismissed from her academic program because of her unethical conduct.

# CHAPTER

## 6

# ETHICAL RESPONSIBILITIES TO THE SOCIAL WORK PROFESSION

The standards in this section of the code concern social workers' ethical responsibilities to the profession. They concern issues related to the integrity of the social work profession and social work evaluation and research.

## INTEGRITY OF THE PROFESSION

### STANDARD 5.01(a)

*Social workers should work toward the maintenance and promotion of high standards of practice.*

High standards of practice enhance a profession's effectiveness, integrity, and credibility and are essential in all its domains. Standards of practice are based on widely respected and embraced schools of thought, research knowledge, and intervention approaches. Although such standards always should allow for minority opinions and critical views, the concept itself implies that there are established ways of thinking about and conducting practice. In legal terms, standards of practice constitute *standards of care*, which are uniform standards of behavior and that which would be done by a "reasonable person of ordinary prudence" (Gifis, 1991, p. 460).

The professional literature, particularly refereed documents such as journal articles and books that undergo peer review before publication, provides one of the most useful guideposts to social work's standards of practice. The peer review process builds in a useful system of checks and balances that, while not flawless, increases the likelihood that thoughtful and compelling opinions will enter social work's evolving body of knowledge and practice standards. Ideas and arguments that are not persuasive have less chance of surviving in social work's intellectual marketplace. In recent years especially, social workers have published extensive commentary on appropriate standards of care in all aspects of direct practice, including confidentiality and privacy, informed consent, assessment, boundary issues, billing practices, consultation, and documentation, among many others (Barker & Branson, 1993; Besharov, 1985; Bullis, 1995; Houston-Vega et al., 1997; Reamer, 1994; Saltzman & Proch, 1990).

Course content in social work education programs also demonstrates the prevailing standards in the profession. Educational curricula and syllabi are regularly and closely scrutinized by social work faculty. Content is added or deleted to reflect faculty members' opinions about current practice standards that need to be taught to social work students. In addition, accreditation procedures require that social work faculty continually monitor and update course content and curricula concerning standards of practice.

Standards published by recognized professional organizations, such as NASW and the Council on Social Work Education (CSWE), provide important guidance. Prominent professional organizations periodically appoint committees and task forces to establish practice standards in different domains of the profession. For example, CSWE regularly publishes its *Curriculum Policy Statement* that describes in detail the content that must be included in accredited social work education programs. NASW has developed a wide range of practice standards, such as *NASW Standards for School Social Work Services* (NASW, 1992), *NASW Standards for the Practice of Social Work with Adolescents* (NASW, 1993), *NASW Standards for the Practice of Clinical Social Work* (NASW, 1989), *NASW Standards for Social Work Practice in Child Protection* (NASW, 1981), and *Guidelines for Clinical Social Work Supervision* (NASW, 1994). Such standards are published only after considerable study and review by members of these organizations, which enhances the likelihood that the final product reflects prevailing standards of care. In addition, the standards are updated regularly to reflect changes in social workers' thinking and actual practice.

Social workers can work for maintenance and promotion of high standards of practice by involving themselves in committees, task forces, and organizations that assume responsibility for the development of practice standards. Vigorous study and debate about appropriate standards in the profession are always necessary, particularly when there is opportunity to be involved in the development of standards that will be disseminated among the entire profession. Social work administrators and supervisors should ensure that staff and supervisees are familiar with widely accepted standards of practice that appear in the professional literature and in guidelines developed by organizations such as NASW and CSWE.

## STANDARD 5.01(b)

*Social workers should uphold and advance the values, ethics, knowledge, and mission of the profession. Social workers should protect, enhance, and improve the integrity of the profession through appropriate study and research, active discussion, and responsible criticism of the profession.*

There are many ways in which social workers can comply with the requirements of this standard. First, they can study and research emerging issues in the profession, especially policy issues and debates concerning core values, ethical guidelines, and social work's mission. For example, since the late 1970s an increasing number of social work scholars and practitioners have devoted particular attention to ethical dilemmas in social work, conflicts among the profession's values, ethical decision making, and issues pertaining to ethical misconduct. Examples of further research in this area could include surveys of social workers' opinions about how specific ethical dilemmas should be addressed, the relative importance of competing values in the profession, the extent of practitioner misconduct, and social workers' familiarity with the profession's ethical guidelines.

Second, social workers can enhance the profession's integrity by engaging in active examination of compelling issues. Many opportunities arise for practitioners to participate in discussion about the profession's core values, ethical principles and standards, and mission. For example, for two years before the ratification of the 1996 NASW Code of Ethics, the revision committee sponsored a number of occasions for social workers to voice their opinions and participate in discussions about the new code. Through the NASW News, chapter newsletters, and invitations issued through other social work organizations, the revision committee solicited both written and oral testimony about possible changes in the code's content and structure from social workers throughout the United States. Social workers were also invited to comment on and discuss various drafts of the code. Members of the revision committee traveled around the country to give NASW members an opportunity to engage in frank discussion of the profession's ethical principles and standards. The process was enormously fruitful, and the many social workers who participated in it had the opportunity to influence the final version of the 1996 code. This process was a good illustration of the importance of active discussion in enhancing social work's integrity. Similar opportunities are often available with respect to many other critical issues facing the profession, such as NASW's position on welfare reform, abortion rights, end-of-life decisions, homelessness, and licensure requirements.

Finally, social workers should be encouraged to engage in responsible criticism of the profession. Social work's vitality and integrity can be sustained only by practitioners' willingness to continually monitor, examine and, when appropriate, criticize prevailing standards, practices, and ideological positions. Values, priorities, and opinions on key issues sometimes need to be changed over time as societal events and trends warrant. For example, the *Tarasoff* decision in 1976 required social workers to re-examine many long-standing assumptions about the limits of client confidentiality. Similarly, the HIV/AIDS crisis that emerged in the early 1980s posed fundamental challenges to social workers' beliefs about how they should balance their respect for clients' privacy rights and their obligation to protect third parties from harm. Such events generated considerable debate about and much responsible criticism of prevailing norms and practices in social work (Reamer, 1991b).

Social workers do not always agree on key policy issues. The letters to the editor in the NASW News and various professional journals, as well as debate on the floor of the NASW Delegate Assembly, demonstrate the legitimate and spirited disagreements about the profession's official positions on controversial issues such as transracial adoption, managed care, the role of religion in social work, welfare reform, end-of-life decisions, and various ethical standards. Responsible criticism of the profession—in the form of passionate but thoughtful, reasoned, and diplomatic debate and discourse—is a legitimate and essential part of maintaining social work's integrity, effectiveness, and development.

## STANDARD 5.01(c)

*Social workers should contribute time and professional expertise to activities that promote respect for the value, integrity, and competence of the social work profession. These activities may include*

*teaching, research, consultation, service, legislative testimony, pre-*
*sentations in the community, and participation in their professional*
*organizations.*

To the extent possible, social workers should devote time to activities that enhance the social work profession's integrity. Engaging in such activities is easier for some social workers than for others, depending on their workloads, family commitments, workplace autonomy, financial needs, and geographic location. Practitioners can contribute their time and professional expertise in various ways, including teaching and lecturing to social work students or serving as field instructors, conducting research, providing consultation to colleagues and members of the general public, providing services to the profession and community, giving legislative testimony on issues that are relevant to social work, making presentations in the community, and participating in professional organizations. Such activities can help promote respect among social workers, other professionals, and the public at large for the value, integrity, and competence of the social work profession.

- The director of social work services at a major hospital set aside time each year to deliver guest lectures on her area of expertise at the local school of social work.
- A social work professor who had considerable experience in conducting program evaluations provided pro bono technical assistance to a community nonprofit organization that offered social services to battered women.
- A social worker who served as assistant policy director for the mayor of a large city volunteered one evening each week at a homeless shelter.
- A social worker in private practice offered to serve on an NASW chapter committee that was developing continuing education guidelines for practitioners in his state.
- A school social worker was a member of an interagency task force that lobbied legislators to encourage them to vote in favor of a bill that would provide funds for a school breakfast program. The social worker offered to testify about the needs of local school children before a legislative subcommittee that was considering the bill.
- The vice president of an NASW chapter contacted local reporters and media outlets during Social Work Month to publicize the profession's mission and expertise. As a result of her efforts, two major newspapers in the state ran features about social workers, and a television station included a short profile of the profession during its daytime news program.

## STANDARD 5.01(d)

*Social workers should contribute to the knowledge base of social work and share with colleagues their knowledge related to practice, research, and ethics. Social workers should seek to contribute to the profession's literature and to share their knowledge at professional meetings and conferences.*

One of the defining features of a profession is the willingness of its members to explore and disseminate new knowledge, ideas, and intervention approaches and to share them with colleagues. There are two principal ways for social workers to contribute to the profession's knowledge base and disseminate information to colleagues. The first is to pursue opportunities to write journal articles, books, and monographs. Finding time to write for publication can be difficult for most social workers. Outside academic settings, most employers do not allot time in staff members' schedules for writing, and social workers in private practice may find it difficult to devote time to writing instead of revenue-generating activities. To the extent possible, however, social workers should try to make time to write for publication because findings and breakthroughs they make in their practice will be helpful to other professionals:

- A social worker and a psychologist collaborated on a project that provided intensive casework counseling to families of homeless adolescents. When referred to the program, the adolescents were living with their families in temporary housing, most of them in a local motel. The program helped families find permanent housing and addressed the adolescents' truancy problems. It also provided parent skills training, transportation, and advocacy support services. Project staff also gathered data on the program's effectiveness and published the results in a prominent social work journal (Twaite & Lampert, 1997).

- A social worker in private practice provided short-term, multiple-family group therapy for clients with bipolar disorder and their families that used a psycho-educational model developed for the treatment of schizophrenia. The treatment consisted of weekly two-hour sessions for 14 weeks, and educational information concerning bipolar disorder was shared with group members. The social worker wrote a journal article describing this novel treatment approach, including the setting, criteria for selection of clients, clinical issues, and a detailed overview of the content of the 14 treatment sessions (Brennan, 1995).

- A group of social workers provided clinical services to 115 survivors of childhood sexual abuse. Using a quasi-experimental design for a study of the effectiveness of group work intervention, they compared their clients with a group from their waiting list on measures of depression and self-esteem. The project results were published in a journal that showcases empirical evaluations of social work interventions (Richter, Snider, & Gorey, 1997).

- A social worker explored the impact of social support and network relationships among neglectful and non-neglectful single mothers with low incomes. The social worker who conducted the study gathered data through interviews, analyzed the extent of differences between the social networks and relationships of the two groups of mothers, and discussed the practical implications of the results (Beeman, 1997).

- A social worker who was special assistant to a U.S. senator published a journal article on ways to address childhood poverty. The social worker conducted a comprehensive review of the causes of childhood poverty (particularly for children in female-headed households on welfare), analyzed various proposals and programs to alleviate child-hood poverty, and proposed a novel approach to providing cash ben-efits to children in the form of a children's allowance (Jones, 1995).

Social workers also can contribute to the profession's knowledge base and share information with colleagues by making presentations at profes-sional meetings and conferences. Practitioners have many opportunities to submit proposals for presentations at national, state, and local conferences and seminars sponsored by professional social work organizations, colleges and universities, and private continuing education firms. Some social work-ers also disseminate information to colleagues via computerized bulletin boards, Internet Web sites, and e-mail.

## STANDARD 5.01(e)

*Social workers should act to prevent the unauthorized and unquali-fied practice of social work.*

Social work should be practiced only by men and women who have proper education and training and who possess the competencies, licenses, and credentials required for their areas of practice. Practitioners who are aware of individuals engaged in the unauthorized or unqualified practice of social work should take steps to prevent such practice. This may include notifying employers, agencies, NASW, licensing or regulatory boards, and other rele-vant professional organizations.

Unauthorized or unqualified practice can occur in three ways. The first involves individuals without formal social work education who represent themselves to be professionals with social work degrees, a form of misrepre-sentation (see standard 4.06[c]). In one case, for example, a social worker volunteered several hours each week at a local crisis intervention hotline. During one of his shifts at the hotline, he overheard another volunteer de-scribe herself to a caller as a trained social worker. The social worker knew that his hotline colleague had had no formal education in social work; she had a bachelor's degree in history, had received in-service training at the hotline, and had attended several workshops on crisis intervention and emergency services. The hotline operated in a state that required anyone calling himself or herself a social worker to have a social work degree from an accredited social work education program. (Not all states have such a requirement.) The social worker contacted the hotline's supervisor and tactfully explained his concern about his colleague's misrepresentation of her credentials. The supervisor circulated a memorandum clarifying how staff were to identify themselves to callers and spoke directly to the volun-teer who identified herself inappropriately.

A second form of unauthorized practice occurs when individuals, in-cluding trained social workers, claim qualifications and competence they do not possess. For example, a social worker with a bachelor's degree was employed as a caseworker in an emergency shelter. She spent most of her time arranging services and resources for shelter residents, such as mental health counseling, public assistance benefits, health care, and job counsel-ing and interviews. On occasion she also provided crisis counseling. After several months on the job, she began offering to provide "psychotherapy" to shelter residents who were experiencing emotional difficulty. She had had no formal education or training in psychotherapy, however, and thus was involved in the unqualified practice of social work.

The third form of unauthorized or unqualified practice occurs when trained social workers use unlicensed or unqualified employees to provide services. Social workers who use assistants improperly are engaged in what lawyers call "lending out a license," particularly when the employee is functioning in a way that leads reasonable people to mistake the employee for a licensed professional (Reamer, 1994). For example, a social worker had contracts with several school districts to provide counseling to students. He became so overwhelmed with referrals that he hired a part-time assistant to help him. The assistant had worked for many years as a child care worker in a residential program for adolescents but did not have any formal training in counseling. However, he began providing services to a 16-year-old girl who had run away from home. The assistant spent considerable time counseling the girl and eventually had sexual contact with her. The girl's parents filed suit against the assistant and the social worker who hired and supervised him. The lawsuit alleged that the social worker "lent out his license" improperly and enabled an unauthorized, unqualified individual to act as a trained social worker.

## EVALUATION AND RESEARCH

### STANDARD 5.02(a)

*Social workers should monitor and evaluate policies, the implementation of programs, and practice interventions.*

During the course of social work's history, practitioners have developed increasing appreciation for the relevance of research and evaluation.* During the era of the charity organization society, for example, many social workers believed that so-called "scientific philanthropy" would enable professionals to understand the nature and causes of pauperism and that the scientific method could be used to study and understand the treatment of individual clients (Reid, 1987; Zimbalist, 1977). Early 20th-century writings by such prominent social workers as Edith and Grace Abbott, Jane Addams, Gordon Hamilton, Florence Hollis, Florence Kelley, Julia Lathrop, Mary Richmond, and Virginia Robinson emphasized the importance of scientific study of social work practice (Orcutt, 1990; Tyson, 1995). Many social workers learned to use social science research methods (borrowing largely from disciplines such as sociology and psychology) to study social problems of professional interest, such as poverty, delinquency, casework effectiveness, and the impact of interventions.

In the late 1970s and early 1980s, social workers became increasingly interested in monitoring and assessing the implementation and effectiveness of policies, programs, and interventions, and a number of research texts written by and for social workers were published (Atherton & Klemmack, 1982; Bloom & Fischer, 1982; Grinnell, 1981; Jayaratne & Levy, 1979; Reid & Smith, 1981). These texts and other writings in the field

---

*Parts of this discussion are adapted from Reamer (1998a).

have had a substantial effect on social workers' current commitment to research and evaluation (Reamer, 1998a; Rubin & Babbie, 1997).

Research and evaluation to monitor and evaluate policies, the implementation of programs, and practice interventions enhance the social work profession's credibility and effectiveness. Policies should be monitored and evaluated primarily to assess the extent to which they achieve their goals and objectives. Although policies sometimes achieve their intended goals, even the best sometimes fall short of the mark, or the results achieved differ from those that policymakers originally had in mind. Data obtained from well-designed evaluation and research can provide policymakers with enormously useful feedback about the implementation and impact of policies. For example, a social worker served as the chief of staff for the director of a state mental health agency. Earlier in the year, the director had instituted a new policy intended to shift responsibility for many mental health services from the state agency to private-sector, community-based agencies. The chief of staff, who was responsible for overseeing the policy's implementation, conducted a study to assess both professionals' and clients' reactions to the new services delivery procedures. In another case a social work professor was concerned about the potential impact of changes in the state's welfare policy on legal immigrants and refugees. The professor worked with several graduate students to survey low-income immigrants and refugees about their living expenses, income, and ability to make ends meet, both before and after the policy changes.

Study of program implementation also is important. In one case a social worker designed and implemented a program to help pregnant and parenting teenagers remain in school. He raised a substantial amount of money from two local foundations and a state agency to administer the program. As a condition of the funding, he evaluated the program's impact by gathering data on dropout rates before and after the program.

Finally, social workers should monitor and evaluate practice interventions, especially clinical interventions with individuals, families, couples, and groups. Social workers have access to a wide range of research designs and tools to help them keep track of clients' progress and assess the impact of clinical interventions (Grinnell, 1997; Reamer, 1998a; Rubin & Babbie, 1997). Examples include single-case designs, group designs, easy-to-use clinical measures and assessment instruments, client logs (used by clients to record important daily events, behaviors, or feelings), and user-friendly computer software for data analysis. In one case a social worker in a family services agency provided counseling to an adolescent client who was having major problems in her relationship with her parents. The social worker used a standardized instrument to assess the quality of the client's relationship with her parents and a single-case design to monitor her progress over time. Similarly, a school social worker provided consultation to a third-grade teacher who was having difficulty managing a student's behavior. The social worker taught the teacher how to use several behavior management techniques based on principles of positive reinforcement. She also arranged for the teacher to collect daily data on the child's behavior by use of a simple instrument, both before and after the implementation of the intervention. This simple research design helped both the teacher and the social worker monitor and assess changes in the child's behavior.

## STANDARD 5.02(b)

*Social workers should promote and facilitate evaluation and research to contribute to the development of knowledge.*

Social workers who are in positions of authority, such as supervisors and administrators, should do as much as possible to enable those under their supervision to conduct evaluation and research. Supervisors and administrators in clinical or direct practice settings should encourage staff to use the wide variety of evaluation and research skills and techniques to monitor clients' progress and evaluate the effectiveness of interventions. In addition to generating information for large-scale studies and widespread dissemination in the field, these tools help social workers generate information that is directly useful in practice. For example, a social worker who served as clinical director in a family services agency asked a local social work professor to conduct a half-day workshop for staff about tools used to monitor and evaluate clinical interventions. The professor gave the staff an overview of commonly used research designs and data collection techniques. She also provided many case illustrations of the kinds of clinical issues that tended to come up at the family services agency. After the professor's presentation, the clinical director announced that the agency was hiring a new caseworker and reducing the size of each staff member's caseload to provide time for the staff to use research and evaluation tools to monitor and assess their work with clients.

In addition, social work supervisors and administrators should encourage staff to conduct needs assessments pertaining to their clients and programs. Evaluation and research skills can be valuable when social workers must assess the nature and extent of clients' needs, particularly when the information helps social workers plan and implement appropriate services, programs, and policies. In one case, for example, a social worker employed by a large United Way office was responsible for administering the program on emerging issues. Each year a portion of the United Way funds was set aside to support special projects on new and compelling issues that arose after the bulk of funds had been allocated to member agencies for the fiscal year. To gather information about new and compelling issues, the social worker conducted a needs assessment among agency directors. She designed a brief questionnaire that asked respondents about critical gaps in their services and requested information about emerging problems that the respondents' agencies would address if the resources were available. The social worker collated the information for use by a United Way committee in rank-ordering priorities for future funding.

Finally, supervisors and administrators should encourage social workers to conduct broad-based evaluations of social services programs. Such evaluations are essential elements in assessing the impact of interventions. For example, a social worker who administered a drug treatment program in a state prison obtained a grant to provide discharge planning services to inmates who required community-based drug treatment. As a condition of the grant, the social worker was required to conduct an evaluation of the program, so he used part of the grant funds to hire a social worker with program evaluation expertise. The program administrator used the results of the evaluation, which were largely positive, to modify some aspects of the discharge planning program and then was able to obtain an additional year of funding.

The results of clinical research and evaluation, needs assessments, and program evaluations can be useful to both those who collect the information and their colleagues and agencies or organizations throughout the profession. Social work supervisors and administrators should encourage and enable staff to present their findings at professional conferences and prepare written summaries and analyses for professional journals, books, and other publications (see standard 5.01[d]), even to the extent of allotting time during working hours for these activities when possible.

## STANDARD 5.02(c)

*Social workers should critically examine and keep current with emerging knowledge relevant to social work and fully use evaluation and research evidence in their professional practice.*

Social workers should do their best to keep up with the professional literature pertaining to their areas of expertise and responsibility (see standard 4.01[b]). When evaluation and research evidence is available, this knowledge should be used to inform social work practice (Myers & Thyer, 1997). For example, a social worker at a community mental health center provided counseling to a 15-year-old girl who manifested symptoms of an eating disorder. The social worker, who did not have experience in that area, set aside time to go to a local university library to gather research literature on the effectiveness of various treatment approaches for people with eating disorders. She also contacted two experts on eating disorders in the community and asked them to recommend empirically based studies for her to read.

Social workers and other professionals are increasingly aware that practitioners have an ethical responsibility to base their practice on empirical evidence of effectiveness. Curtis (1996) described four categories of empirical validation, with increasing levels of substantiation: (1) tentative or suggestive evidence, including anecdotal observations, single-case reports, or uncontrolled or open trials; (2) promising or interesting evidence, based on completion of several uncontrolled trials with fairly positive and consistent results; (3) probable effectiveness, when one rigorous controlled study or several less rigorous investigations have positive results; and (4) established effectiveness, only when several well-designed, controlled studies show the treatment to be superior to other accepted treatments. According to Curtis (1996), "Responsible practitioners are expected to know where various treatment plans stand in the research scheme and any limitations on their effectiveness . . . and have an obligation to disclose this information fully to their patients or clients" (p. 120). This sentiment is echoed further by the Task Force on Social Work Research (1991), sponsored by the U.S. National Institute of Mental Health, in its recommendations to CSWE. The task force suggested that social work education programs should

> require that all areas of the foundation curriculum, including practice methods, be based on knowledge derived to the fullest extent possible from research in social work and from related professions . . . require that textbooks for practice methods courses be based to the fullest extent possible on research-based knowledge from social work and

allied professions and disciplines (p. 82) . . . increase significantly the attention given to research-based knowledge in the teaching of practice methods and to the use of research methods to examine practice effectiveness (p. 89) . . . take increased responsibility for incorporating research-based information in the teaching of practice methods. (p. 90)

Empirically validated intervention approaches are available for many aspects of social work practice (Mullen & Magnabosco, 1997). Regrettably, however, a number of interventions—and potential interventions—currently lack such empirically validated evidence of effectiveness. Given this current state of knowledge, social workers should base their interventions on empirical evidence whenever possible. As Myers and Thyer (1997) concluded,

> There are clinical areas where effective treatments are developed but have not yet been validated and others where effective treatments have not been developed. Problems for which no treatment has been proved effective need further research and investigation. Social workers should, however, be ethically bound to provide empirically validated treatments to their clients when such are available. (p. 296)

## STANDARD 5.02(d)

*Social workers engaged in evaluation or research should carefully consider possible consequences and should follow guidelines developed for the protection of evaluation and research participants. Appropriate institutional review boards should be consulted.*

Ethical standards to protect evaluation and research participants have matured considerably, especially since the 1940s. Much of the effort to develop ethical protections began with the war crimes trials of Nazi doctors in Germany in 1945; the doctors were charged with conducting inhumane experiments on unconsenting prisoners. These legal proceedings documented and publicized the harm that can be caused by unethical research, and resulted in the establishment of various ethical standards to protect research participants.

Two other key events were the notorious Tuskegee and Willowbrook studies. The Tuskegee study was a 40-year project begun in 1932 by the U.S. Public Health Service to research the natural history of untreated syphilis. The subjects were low-income African American men from Alabama who were told that they had "bad blood," and research procedures such as spinal taps were provided in the guise of "free treatment." The study participants were given neither the then-standard treatment for syphilis nor penicillin when it became available in the 1940s. The men were not told of the research design and the risks to which they were exposed, and many of them died of causes attributable to the untreated disease. Unfortunately, the study's unethical practices did not come to light until 1972 (Levine, 1991).

The Willowbrook study investigated the natural history of untreated infectious hepatitis. In this study a group of children with mental disabilities, who lived at Willowbrook State Hospital in Staten Island, New York, were deliberately infected with hepatitis. The purpose of the studies was first to investigate the natural history of infectious hepatitis and later to test the effects of gamma-globulin in treating the disease. According to Levine (1991), "The major ethical criticisms concerned the deliberate infection of children (defended by the researchers because children were likely to get the disease in the institution anyway) and the inducement to parents to enroll their child in the study to gain admittance to the hospital, which was refusing new residents because of lack of space" (p. 79).

The most significant attempt to formulate public policy and regulations to prevent such research-related abuses occurred in 1966, when U.S. Surgeon General William Stewart issued the first Public Health Service directive on human experimentation. The surgeon general announced that the Public Health Service would not fund research unless the institution receiving the grant spelled out the procedures in place to ensure subjects' informed consent, the use of appropriate and ethical research procedures, adequate review of the risks and benefits of the study, and the general protection of research subjects' rights. Since then, the federal government has instituted a wide range of other regulations for protecting human research subjects. Most of the ethical principles underlying current regulations and standards are described in *The Belmont Report*, which was prepared by the National Commission for the Protection of Human Subjects of Biomedical and Behavioral Research (1978).

Another important requirement in standard 5.02(d) in the NASW code is consultation with appropriate institutional review boards (IRBs) by social workers engaged in evaluation or research. These boards provide a formal mechanism to examine the ethics of proposed research on human subjects and first came into wide use during the 1970s. Federal regulations require all organizations and agencies that receive federal funds for research to have an IRB, and its approval is required for a study or project to be carried out.

Not every research and evaluation activity proposed in social services agencies or academic settings requires formal IRB review. Some projects and activities may be exempt—for example, routine requirements of an educational or academic program, analysis of secondary or existing data, federal demonstration projects, or observation of public behavior.

## STANDARD 5.02(e)

*Social workers engaged in evaluation or research should obtain voluntary and written informed consent from participants, when appropriate, without any implied or actual deprivation or penalty for refusal to participate; without undue inducement to participate; and with due regard for participants' well-being, privacy, and dignity. Informed consent should include information about the nature, extent, and duration of the participation requested and disclosure of the risks and benefits of participation in the research.*

The six provisions of standard 1.03 delineate the concept of informed consent as it pertains to social work intervention. The concept of informed consent also is relevant to protection of the rights of evaluation and research participants (Gillespie, 1995). Various court decisions, regulations established by government and private-sector agencies, and scholarly inquiry have combined to produce a list of core points that should be included in informed consent procedures for evaluation and research:

- *Absence of coercion:* People invited by social workers to participate in evaluation and research should not be coerced. Practitioners must present a proposal for evaluation and research in a way that does not make potential participants feel pressured to consent. Social workers must be careful not to give participants any ultimatum—for example, suggesting that people must agree to participate in evaluation or research to receive social services or benefits to which they are entitled.
- *Competence:* Social workers who invite clients and others to participate in evaluation and research must be assured that these individuals are mentally competent to provide consent. People asked to consent to evaluation and research activities must be able to understand the project's purpose, possible benefits, and possible risks. Those who are not competent or whose competence is questionable should be excluded from evaluation and research activities that require formal consent, or consent should be obtained from their legally authorized representative, parent, or guardian.
- *Participants' consent to specific procedures or actions:* Social workers should provide potential participants with clear, detailed explanations of the study's purpose; the nature, extent, and duration of subjects' participation; possible benefits and risks; and alternatives or other options that they may want to consider. Broadly worded and vague explanations are not sufficient. In addition, the language used in consent forms should be clear and understandable, and individuals asked for consent should be offered ample opportunity to ask for clarification. Social workers should avoid using complex and technical jargon (for sample consent forms, see Houston-Vega et al., 1997; Reamer, 1998a).
- *Right to refuse or withdraw consent:* One of the key principles of informed consent is that all individuals have the right to refuse or withdraw consent. Refusal to give consent or withdrawal of consent may be based on, for example, concern about the amount of time participation would require, emotional or confidentiality risks, or lack of interest.

Having individuals sign a consent form is not in itself sufficient. Informed consent is a process that includes the deliberate, systematic disclosure of information and an opportunity for potential subjects to discuss and ask questions about the evaluation or research. As part of this process, social workers should be especially sensitive to clients' cultural and ethnic diversity as it concerns the meaning of such concepts as self-determination, autonomy, and consent (President's Commission, 1982). Special care should be taken with individuals whose primary language differs from that used in social workers' employment setting; when necessary, practitioners should use the services of an interpreter or translator. In addition, social workers should be certain that individuals who have auditory or visual impairments are provided with the assistance they need to provide informed consent.

## STANDARD 5.02(f)

*When evaluation or research participants are incapable of giving informed consent, social workers should provide an appropriate*

*explanation to the participants, obtain the participants' assent to*
*the extent they are able, and obtain written consent from an appro-*
*priate proxy.*

In general, two groups of people may be unable to provide informed consent: children and individuals who do not have the mental competence to do so. Although some evaluation and research participants may not be able to provide informed consent, social workers should offer a reasonable explanation consistent with their level of understanding whenever this is possible. Many children and many adults who have some form of brain dysfunction or impairment can understand certain aspects of informed consent procedures. Although they may not be competent to provide full informed consent, social workers should consider approaching these individuals for their agreement to participate.

When evaluation and research participants lack the capacity to provide informed consent, social workers should protect them by seeking written permission from an appropriate third party (parent, guardian, or legal representative). In such cases researchers should ensure that the proxy acts in a manner consistent with participants' wishes and interests. In one case, for example, a social worker in a program for children with developmental disabilities planned to videotape the children's interactions with each other for a research project on teaching social and communication skills. Although the social worker obtained informed consent from the children's parents and legal guardians, she also explained the videotaping to the children at a level consistent with their understanding. None of the children objected to the videotaping, although one child expressed some modest anxiety about the process. The social worker told the child additional details about the project and gave him an opportunity to ask questions about it. The child asked several questions and then said he was excited about being a "movie star."

Obtaining consent to involve children in evaluation or research activities can be particularly challenging. Social workers ordinarily obtain consent from children's parents or legal guardians, although it often makes sense to include children, especially older children, in the decision-making process. Also, sometimes it is not clear who is a particular child's legal guardian. Records may be inaccurate or missing, or a child's parents may be in the midst of a custody dispute. In such cases, social workers should obtain consent from any and all parties who might be the child's guardian. This can be burdensome, but it is the most prudent course of action. For example, a social worker employed by a residential program for children with psychiatric problems conducted a study concerning the relationship between children's history of sexual abuse and their tendency to engage in self-destructive behavior (suicide attempts, self-mutilation, substance abuse). The research project involved interviewing the children and examining their clinical records. The social worker obtained informed consent from each child's parent or guardian, but in the case of one child he was able to contact only the father, who was not the child's legal guardian and was no longer married to the mother. Although the father was functioning as the primary parent, the mother was the only parent legally authorized to provide informed consent. The social worker consulted with the program's lawyer about how to obtain consent properly, and the lawyer advised him to obtain the mother's informed consent, at the very least. The lawyer also advised the social worker to obtain the father's informed consent because the situation was ambiguous.

## STANDARD 5.02(g)

*Social workers should never design or conduct evaluation or research that does not use consent procedures, such as certain forms of naturalistic observation and archival research, unless rigorous and responsible review of the research has found it to be justified because of its prospective scientific, educational, or applied value and unless equally effective alternative procedures that do not involve waiver of consent are not feasible.*

In some extraordinary circumstances it may not be possible for social workers to obtain subjects' informed consent to participation in research and evaluation. For example, a social worker interested in documenting problems of homelessness wanted to gather data on the number of people in the community who slept outdoors at night (for example, under bridges, on heating grates, in alleys). Over a period of weeks, the social worker and two assistants traveled throughout the city during the evenings and recorded the numbers and locations of people sleeping outdoors. It was not necessary for the social worker to obtain the individuals' informed consent because the project exposed these people to only minimal risk and invasion of privacy (for example, the social worker did not wake them from their sleep, photograph them, or gather identifying information). In addition, alternative procedures that did not involve waiver of consent were not feasible.

In another case a social worker obtained permission from the director of a public child welfare agency to examine a sample of records from the past 10 years. The goal of the project was to read and analyze caseworkers' notes to determine whether their criteria and standards for substantiating child abuse and neglect had changed over time (as a function of, for example, increased in-service training, pressure from the public to respond to reports of abuse and neglect, or media scrutiny). Here, too, it was neither appropriate nor necessary for the social worker to obtain the former clients' informed consent. The research proposal had been reviewed by an IRB (see standard 5.02[d]), and the social worker had signed a confidentiality pledge attesting to her willingness to respect the confidentiality of the case records.

Some situations involving a social worker's request to waive informed consent requirements are less clear and more controversial. In these situations social workers struggle to balance the value of the information to be obtained from the evaluation or research with their obligation to obtain participants' informed consent. For example, sometimes disclosure of information to participants about the purposes, goals, and methods of the study is likely to affect the validity of the results. In one case a social worker employed by a large state prison was concerned about abusive treatment of inmates by some correctional officers. In the social worker's experience, correctional officers often verbally—and sometimes physically—abused inmates. For the final research project in his master's degree program in social work, he designed a study that involved observing interactions between correctional officers and inmates. The social worker planned to use this information to explore several hypotheses drawn from the professional literature about the exercise of authority by staff in institutional settings.

He assumed, however, that the correctional officers and inmates would temporarily improve their behavior if they knew they were being observed for a research project. The social worker submitted his proposal to the IRB at his university as well as to the IRB at the department of corrections. Both boards approved the project and found that its methodology was justifiable because of its potential educational value and because alternative procedures involving waiver of consent were not feasible.

## STANDARD 5.02(h)

*Social workers should inform participants of their right to withdraw from evaluation and research at any time without penalty.*

Standard informed consent procedures assume that evaluation and research participants have the right to refuse to participate and the right to withdraw from evaluation and research at any time without penalty. This condition is essential to ensure that evaluation and research participants are not coerced. Social workers should inform participants of these rights in writing on the informed consent form and should explain them orally as well. Prospective study subjects also should have an opportunity to ask questions about their right to refuse to participate or withdraw from evaluation and research. Below is a sample statement that can be included in an informed consent form:

> You are not under any obligation to participate in this project, and your decision will not affect your future relationship with [name of agency or provider]. If you decide to participate, you may stop participating at any time without penalty or negative consequences.

Projects involving mailed surveys or questionnaires may include a statement that tells prospective participants "Your completion and return of the enclosed survey/questionnaire will indicate your willingness to participate in this project and your consent to have the information used as described above."

In one case a social worker employed by a nursing home designed a study for her doctoral dissertation. The study involved collecting data from residents who participated in "reminiscence therapy" facilitated by the social worker. These groups provided residents with an opportunity to recall, describe, and reflect on the meaning of life events (Barker, 1995). The social worker planned to conduct content analyses of residents' reminiscences, particularly as they pertained to memories of traumatic life events, and to conduct follow-up interviews with group members to explore further the issues they raised during group discussion. She submitted her research proposal to the IRBs at the university and at the nursing home, and both boards approved the project. As part of the informed consent procedure, the social worker explained to the residents, both in writing and orally, that they had the right to refuse to participate in the research project and the right to withdraw from the project at any time without penalty. One of the reminiscence group's members consented to participate in the research project but later talked to the social worker about how upsetting it was for her to recall certain traumatic life events. The woman said she was suddenly having difficulty sleeping at night and was feeling more anxious than usual during the day. After discussing her feelings with the social worker, the woman decided to terminate her involvement with the reminiscence group and withdraw her consent to participate in the research. She was not penalized in any way for her decision to withdraw from the project.

In contrast, a school social worker designed a modest study to gather information from students who received services from him. The purpose of the study was to obtain information about students' feelings of anxiety and depression. (All of the youths who were to participate had been referred to the social services department by teachers and other staff who were concerned about the children's emotional state.) As part of the study, the social worker administered two standardized research instruments measuring anxiety and depression symptoms. He sought and obtained consent from the students' parents or guardians and also obtained the students' assent to participate (see standards 5.02[e] and [f]).

One student told the social worker that he did not want to continue filling out the research forms because he found the forms too tedious and irrelevant to complete. The social worker, who was eager to gather the data for presentation at a professional conference and possible publication in a professional journal, urged the student to complete the forms: "Come on, now. They're not all that bad, are they? It's really important for us to have this information so we can help you." The student later reported that he felt pressured by the social worker to complete the forms and that the social worker never informed him of his right to withdraw from participation.

## STANDARD 5.02(i)

---

*Social workers should take appropriate steps to ensure that participants in evaluation and research have access to appropriate supportive services.*

On occasion, social workers discover that evaluation and research participants are in need of supportive services such as counseling, crisis intervention, or emergency housing or health care. In the example given in the discussion of standard 5.02(h), the nursing home resident reported to the social worker that she was having considerable difficulty coping with some of the memories she had discussed during the reminiscence group. In that situation the social worker had an obligation to arrange appropriate counseling for the woman if she wanted assistance.

In another case a social worker interviewed a sample of women who had been sexually abused as children. During one of the interviews, the respondent broke into tears and began experiencing a panic attack. The social worker, who had considerable clinical skill and experience, stopped the interview immediately and provided crisis intervention services. He helped the woman calm down and then arranged for her to see her regular caseworker later that afternoon. The social worker was concerned about the woman's emotional vulnerability and told her that he was inclined not to complete the interview later. She agreed that the interview experience was too traumatic. Although the social worker was eager to have the data this respondent would have provided, he recognized that his primary responsibility was to protect her and provide her with access to appropriate supportive services (standard 1.01). Standard 5.02(i) also is consistent with social workers' obligation to refer clients to other professionals when their specialized knowledge or expertise is needed to serve clients fully (standard 2.06[a]).

## STANDARD 5.02(j)

*Social workers engaged in evaluation or research should protect participants from unwarranted physical or mental distress, harm, danger, or deprivation.*

This standard, consistent with standards 5.02(d–i), requires social workers to take whatever steps are necessary to protect participants from any avoidable or unnecessary emotional injury and physical danger. Practitioners can best accomplish this through careful design of evaluation or research projects. To the extent possible, study participants should not be subjected to research conditions that are likely to be stressful, embarrassing, traumatic, or intrusive. There may be times when a researcher needs to gather data on troubling or sensitive topics (such as substance abuse, domestic violence, loss, or mental illness) or to gather information in a way that intrudes upon participants' privacy (such as interview questions that address deeply personal, intimate issues or observation of subjects through a one-way mirror). However, social workers should avoid such methods whenever possible and, when they are necessary, seek participants' informed consent before they are used. Submitting an evaluation or research proposal to an IRB also provides considerable protection for all parties involved.

## STANDARD 5.02(k)

*Social workers engaged in the evaluation of services should discuss collected information only for professional purposes and only with people professionally concerned with this information.*

All information gathered as part of evaluation and research is confidential. To protect participants' privacy and confidentiality rights, social workers should discuss collected information only for professional purposes and only with people who are authorized to have access to such information. In one case, for example, a social worker in a family services agency mailed a questionnaire to former clients. The questionnaire asked the former clients for information about their current status, problems they had been experiencing, and their perceptions of the quality of services they had received from the agency. According to the cover letter sent to the former clients, only the social worker would have access to identifying information that could be linked with the confidential information on the questionnaires. The social worker collated the data and reported it in aggregate form (without identifying information) to the agency director, who planned to include the results in the agency's self-study for reaccreditation as documentation of efforts to provide follow-up services to clients and evaluate the quality of services provided. Soon after sharing the information with the agency director, the social worker discussed the project informally with a member of the agency board of directors, who expressed considerable interest in the data. The social worker then provided the board member with copies of the returned questionnaires (with the former clients' names attached) and discussed some of the results with the board member. The board member, therefore, had inappropriate access to confidential information.

In another case a social work student used a single-case design to evaluate her work with a client in her field placement—a day treatment program for people with substance abuse problems. Using a standardized data collection instrument, the student was able to generate data suggesting that the intervention had helped reduce the client's alcohol consumption over a six-month period. The student was so excited by the results that she showed the data summary and graph to her husband and explained both the intervention and the evaluation procedures. Two of the documents that the social worker showed her husband included the client's name. As a result, the social worker's husband, who had once worked with the client at a former job, was privy to confidential information obtained during the course of social work evaluation.

## STANDARD 5.02(l)

*Social workers engaged in evaluation or research should ensure the anonymity or confidentiality of participants and of the data obtained from them. Social workers should inform participants of any limits of confidentiality, the measures that will be taken to ensure confidentiality, and when any records containing research data will be destroyed.*

Social workers in positions of authority can take several steps to avoid inappropriate disclosures of confidential information obtained as part of evaluation or research activities. First, data can be gathered and recorded in a way that preserves participants' anonymity and protects confidentiality. Data collection forms can use identification numbers rather than names, and access to data stored in computer files can be limited by requiring authorized personnel to use passwords. Confidential data contained in such instruments as surveys, questionnaires, and clients' logs can be placed in locked, secure file cabinets. Final reports and summaries of results can be written so that only aggregate, nonidentifying information is included and descriptions of clients are thoroughly disguised.

Social workers in positions of authority should consider developing written guidelines for staff to follow. The guidelines might stipulate that staff involved in evaluation and research activities will not

- discuss confidential data or findings with any unauthorized individual
- disclose any identifying information about participants to any unauthorized party
- address evaluation and research participants by name when others are present
- leave evaluation or research reports or data unattended or where they can be seen by unauthorized parties (for example, on top of a desk or at home)
- display confidential information about participants on computer screens in a way that can be seen by others.

Information obtained as a result of evaluation and research should be treated as confidential, and social workers should be sure to inform participants of any limits of confidentiality. As in social work practice, however, extraordinary circumstances may arise that require social work evaluators and researchers to disclose confidential information without client consent (see standards 1.07[c], [d], and [e]). These may include instances when evaluation and research participants disclose that they have neglected or abused a child or senior citizen or threatened to harm a third party, or when legal regulations or court orders require the disclosure of confidential information. As Rubin and Babbie (1997) stated,

> Situations can arise in social work research where ethical considerations dictate that confidentiality not be maintained. Suppose in the course of conducting your interviews you learn that children are being abused or that respondents are at imminent risk of seriously harming themselves or others. It would be your professional (and perhaps legal) obligation to report this to the proper agency. Subjects need to be informed of this possibility, before they agree to participate in a study, as part of the informed consent process. (p. 63)

Clients and others participating in social workers' evaluation or research activities should know as early as possible what information will and will not be treated as confidential and the circumstances that would require the social worker to disclose confidential information without the clients' or other participants' permission (see standard 1.07[e]). Social workers also should inform evaluation and research participants of their plans to store and later destroy research data.

## STANDARD 5.02(m)

*Social workers who report evaluation and research results should protect participants' confidentiality by omitting identifying information unless proper consent has been obtained authorizing disclosure.*

Social workers report evaluation and research results in a variety of ways and contexts. Results may be reported to audiences attending professional conferences, members of the media, a board of directors, agency staff, or the general public. They may be presented in a lecture or in journal articles, monographs, and books.

However evaluation and research results are reported, investigators must protect participants' confidentiality. This is ordinarily accomplished by omitting identifying information (unless proper consent has been obtained to authorize disclosure). At professional conferences, for example, results should be presented in aggregate form and case material should be thoroughly disguised. When case material is presented in written form, authors typically include statements indicating that identifying information has been removed or altered to ensure anonymity and confidentiality. Case material can be disguised by changing details related to individuals' gender, age, ethnicity, occupation, employment setting, community of residence, marital status, and so forth. For example, a social worker employed by a community mental health center prepared a manuscript summarizing the results of clinical research with a depressed client who was male, age 32, a pharmacist, and single. For purposes of the paper, the social worker described the client as a 39-year-old married architect. The client's gender was relevant to the case and the intervention, so the social worker did not alter that detail.

In one disturbing case a social worker delivered a lecture at a local professional conference on mental health treatment approaches. During the lecture he presented a case study and discussed evaluation data gathered from a client about changes occurring over time in the client's severe clinical symptoms. The social worker disguised most of the identifying information, but a member of the audience recognized one key detail that the social worker had failed to disguise sufficiently (the client's former—and unusual—occupation). The audience member later told the social worker's client, who was an acquaintance, that the social worker had presented aspects of his case at the conference. The client was very upset, terminated his relationship with the social worker, and filed an ethics complaint against him.

### STANDARD 5.02(n)

---

*Social workers should report evaluation and research findings accurately. They should not fabricate or falsify results and should take steps to correct any errors later found in published data using standard publication methods.*

In recent years there have been a number of disturbing incidents of scientific misconduct and research fraud. The problem has been sufficiently serious that as part of the National Institutes of Health Revitalization Act of 1993, Congress required the secretary of health and human services to create a commission on research integrity (Palca, 1996).

Fortunately, there are relatively few incidents of documented fabrication or falsification of data in social work. Nonetheless, it is important to highlight social workers' obligation to report data accurately. Fabrication and falsification not only undermine the profession's credibility, they also lead social workers who base their practice on such evaluation and research results to intervene unnecessarily, inappropriately, and harmfully.

There could be several incentives for social workers to fabricate and falsify data. First, some social workers' careers, particularly in academic settings, may depend on publishing research results. Professional journals are more likely to publish thought-provoking, precedent-setting evaluation and research findings than findings that seem inconsequential, trivial, or insignificant. Some evaluators and researchers who feel pressure to publish may be tempted to exaggerate their findings to increase the chances of having their work accepted for publication.

Second, some social workers may feel the need to fabricate and falsify data to impress funding sources (for example, foundations or government agencies that finance demonstration projects). Social workers who are obligated to submit program evaluation results to funding sources and are requesting additional funds to extend their work may feel pressured to exaggerate their findings to increase their chances of being awarded additional grant or contract money.

Finally, some social workers may fabricate and falsify data to enhance professional reputation. Practitioners who claim to have created novel intervention approaches and who frequently consult with agencies, for example, may feel pressure to exaggerate evaluation and research findings to promote themselves and advance their careers.

Social workers should immediately correct any errors they discover in published or publicized results. In the case of results published in a journal, the social worker should contact the publisher and ask for an erratum or correction notice to be placed as soon as possible in that journal. In the case of results published in books, errata or corrections should be incorporated in the next edition. When results have been published informally (in agency-produced monographs, for example), social workers should attempt to notify recipients when possible and reissue the publication with the appropriate corrections.

To a great extent social workers must continue to depend on the "honor system" to minimize the fabrication and falsification of evaluation and research results. There is no foolproof mechanism to prevent this form of misconduct. As with much unethical conduct, social workers must hope that the profession's strong ethical foundation and its tradition of attracting morally decent practitioners will limit the incidence of scientific misconduct.

## STANDARD 5.02(o)

*Social workers engaged in evaluation or research should be alert to and avoid conflicts of interest and dual relationships with participants, should inform participants when a real or potential conflict of interest arises, and should take steps to resolve the issue in a manner that makes participants' interests primary.*

As in social work practice generally (see standards 1.06[a], [b], and [c]), social work evaluators and researchers should not engage in any conflicts of interests or dual relationships with participants when there is a risk of exploitation or potential harm to the participants. Conflicts of interest and dual relationships arising out of evaluation and research can occur in several ways. First, social workers should avoid engaging in evaluation or research activities that conflict with clients' social services needs. Social workers should not place their interest in evaluation or research above clients' needs when the two conflict. In one case, for example, a social worker was required to implement a single-case design to fulfill the requirements of a graduate school course. The social worker, who was employed by a residential program for children at high risk, used a reversal (ABAB) design for a client who had difficulty controlling his anger and was physically aggressive with other residents. The reversal design called for collecting baseline data before introducing the intervention (the A phase), introducing the intervention (the first B phase), withdrawing or reversing the intervention to see whether the behavior changed as a result (the second A phase), and reintroducing the intervention (the second B phase). The goal was to use the client as his own control to determine whether the intervention accounted for any behavior change that occurred (Grinnell, 1997; Reamer, 1998a; Rubin & Babbie, 1997). The intervention used positive reinforcement to change the client's behavior. During the baseline period, which lasted one week, the child was aggressive to the point of physically injuring several other residents on four occasions. During the first intervention phase, the aggressive behavior declined dramatically. The social worker and his colleagues decided that it would be unethical to withdraw the intervention because they did not want to risk an increase in the physically aggressive behavior. Although the research design was compromised and weakened (an AB design provides far less opportunity to control for extraneous factors that might account for the client's behavior change), the social worker decided that he had to place the client's (and other residents') interests above his own. He explained the situation to his course instructor, who fully supported his decision.

Second, social workers involved in evaluation or research should avoid dual relationships with participants when there is a risk of exploitation or harm to the participant or when the relationship might affect the validity of the evaluation or research results. For example, social workers who develop social or intimate relationships with evaluation or research participants may find it difficult to interpret objectively and impartially the data obtained from them. In addition, such dual relationships can lead to possible exploitation. In one case a social worker completing a doctoral dissertation conducted a longitudinal study of couples involved in marriage counseling. The study's purpose was to gather qualitative data from the couples about changes they experienced in their relationships over time and factors that might account for these changes and to gather quantitative data by use of standardized instruments about the nature of the couples' relationships. The research design called for the social worker to interview each couple in the sample six times over an 18-month period. After the third round of interviews, the investigator realized that he and one of the wives in the sample were attracted to one another. They eventually became sexually involved, although the wife did not separate from her husband. The social worker's dual relationship with the wife was unethical because of the potential for exploitation of and harm to the woman and her husband. In addition, the social worker's sexual relationship with the wife made it difficult for him to interpret objectively and impartially the research data he obtained from her.

Social workers also must avoid other forms of conflict of interest related to evaluation and research. In one case a social worker who served on an editorial board of a professional journal was asked to evaluate the quality of a manuscript submitted for publication. Although the manuscript did not contain the author's name, the reviewer was able to identify the author from some of the details and footnotes included in the paper. The manuscript reviewer and the author had once worked together on the research project that was discussed in the paper, but their relationship had ended after a bitter dispute. The reviewer knew that she could not provide a fair or impartial assessment of the paper. She returned the manuscript to the journal's editor and asked her to assign the paper to another reviewer.

In another case a social worker conducted a study of clients in a residential program for the treatment of eating disorders. To investigate the relationship between traumatic events in their lives and the onset of clients' eating disorders, in-depth interviews were conducted with clients about their trauma histories. The social worker discovered that one of the clients who was randomly selected to be in the sample was a neighbor with whom he had occasional, brief contact. He knew that it would not be appropriate for him to interview his neighbor about her personal and trauma history, so he removed the client from the sample and replaced her with another client.

Social workers should always inform evaluation and research participants when a real or potential conflict of interest arises. In addition, social
workers should take steps to resolve the issue in a manner that makes participants' interests primary. As the examples discussed above suggest, this
may require altering the research design to ensure that clients' needs are
met or recusing oneself from certain evaluation or research tasks.

## STANDARD 5.02(p)

*Social workers should educate themselves, their students, and their
colleagues about responsible research practices.*

Social workers can engage in a number of activities to educate themselves,
their students, and their colleagues about ethical issues related to evaluation and research. Review of the literature on the subject and attendance
at relevant continuing education workshops and seminars sponsored by social work organizations are always useful. With the increased emphasis in
the profession on empirically based practice, social workers should be sure
to acquaint themselves with ethical issues pertaining to the protection of
evaluation and research participants (for example, informed consent, confidentiality, research designs, data analysis, and the reporting of results).

Social work educators who teach evaluation and research courses should
be certain to include content, exercises, and assignments that help students
learn about and appreciate the importance of ethical issues. In addition to
mandatory course readings, social work educators should expect students to
address relevant ethical issues in their research proposals and reports.

Finally, social work supervisors and administrators in social services
agencies should sponsor in-service training to ensure that staff understand
relevant ethical issues. This is particularly important for social workers involved in clinical evaluation, program evaluation, and needs assessments.
Social work administrators should consider establishing IRBs to provide
feedback on ethical issues related to evaluation and research, review agency
guidelines for the protection of evaluation and research participants, and
sponsor relevant training on the subject.

# ETHICAL RESPONSIBILITIES TO THE BROADER SOCIETY

The standards in this section of the code concern social workers' ethical obligations to the general public. They concern issues related to the general welfare of society, promoting public participation in shaping social policies and institutions, social workers' involvement in public emergencies, and social workers' involvement in social and political action.

## SOCIAL WELFARE

### STANDARD 6.01

*Social workers should promote the general welfare of society, from local to global levels, and the development of people, their communities, and their environments. Social workers should advocate for living conditions conducive to the fulfillment of basic human needs and should promote social, economic, political, and cultural values and institutions that are compatible with the realization of social justice.*

Social work's most distinguishing quality is its enduring, earnest, and simultaneous commitment to both individual well-being and broad social welfare. The profession is rooted in and defined by the deep-seated belief that practitioners must couple their concern for individuals with concern about the broader culture and society in which people live (Hopps & Collins, 1995; Leiby, 1978; Lubove, 1965; Popple, 1995). Social workers understand that clients' problems in living are often shaped by cultural forces, societal events, and environmental influences. For example, a client who is physically disabled may struggle with chronic problems of underemployment and poverty in large part because of discriminatory employment practices, or a client may become clinically depressed because she was laid off when a major local industry relocated to a foreign country with lower labor costs.

In many cases the most effective way to prevent individual suffering is to address broad environmental conditions. For example, social workers' efforts to introduce legislation to create new jobs in a community may, through increased employment and family stability, prevent many individual problems related to substance abuse, domestic violence, child neglect, and depression. Attempts to increase domestic social services spending or foreign aid in underdeveloped countries may prevent many individual problems related to hunger and homelessness. Social workers, more than any other group of professionals, have understood the inexorable link between "case" (concern about individual welfare) and "cause" (the need to address structural, societal, and environmental determinants of individuals' problems). This overarching philosophy is reflected in the mission statement in the *NASW Code of Ethics* (1996): "A historic and defining feature of social work is the profession's focus on individual well-being in a social context and the well-being of society (p. 1). Fundamental to social work is attention to the environmental forces that create, contribute to, and address problems in living."

Social workers can promote the general welfare of society in various ways. First, they can address local issues, or matters that affect their immediate communities (Harrison, 1995; Weil & Gamble, 1995). These activities may take the form of community practice, organizing to increase the stock of affordable housing or augment funding for health care clinics in low-income neighborhoods, lobbying public officials for improved transportation services in underserved communities, promoting local economic development and job creation, building neighborhood coalitions to confront neighborhood crime, or organizing demonstrations to protest funding cuts in after-school programs for adolescents at high risk of delinquency and substance abuse. According to Harrison (1995),

> Community development practice often begins with helping communities realize that they can plan to make things better. The next step, after this realization, involves negotiating a joint vision about preferred outcomes and methods of reaching them. Thus, community development practice is the process of working with communities to help them recognize how they can improve community life and welfare both in the present and in the future. . . . Community development practice involves planned change. For social workers, planned change focuses not only on the use of professional expertise to enhance the interwoven fabric of social life but on enhancing the abilities (capacity building) of community members and including these people as participants in community development activities. (pp. 555–556)

Social workers can focus their efforts on national issues that have a bearing on the profession's goals and objectives. Examples include assisting political candidates who support social work values and policy positions, lobbying federal officials about relevant policies and legislation, and contributing to the efforts of national organizations that address issues of concern to social workers, such as organizations that focus on problems of poverty, discrimination, child abuse and neglect, and civil rights.

Practitioners also can become involved in international social welfare issues. They cannot afford to ignore suffering that exists outside their own political and geographic borders (Healy, 1995; Hokenstad & Kendall, 1995; Midgley, 1995). Social problems that traditionally have concerned social workers—poverty, homelessness, hunger, physical and mental illness, human rights violations, war—transcend politics and geography. Moreover, local social problems are often shaped or affected by international events. For example, domestic unemployment rates may be affected by conflict in oil-producing nations, and budget cuts in domestic federal spending may be caused by increases in defense spending to support allies involved in international conflict. Thus, social workers around the world should think globally as well as locally and seek opportunities to collaborate in addressing social problems. As Midgley (1995) asserted,

> A major direction for future activity in the professional domain requires the fostering of greater *mutual* collaboration among professionals in different parts of the world. The unidirectional transfer of professional ideas and practice methods from the industrial to the developing countries must be replaced by reciprocal exchanges in which professionals in many different societies learn from each other. The promotion of truly reciprocal exchanges requires a discerning attitude, the selective adaptation of practice approaches, and the careful testing and evaluation of innovations. (p. 1496)

Underlying social workers' broad-based efforts to promote the general welfare of society is their concern about oppression and social injustice (Gil, 1994). *Social justice* is an "ideal condition in which all members of a society have the same basic rights, protection, opportunities, obligations, and social benefits" (Barker, 1995, p. 354). Social workers' diverse efforts to enhance the general welfare of society—locally, nationally, and internationally—should concentrate on social, economic, political, and cultural values and institutions that attempt to eliminate oppression and social injustice, and promote equality with respect to people's basic rights, protection, opportunities, obligations, and social benefits (such as access to food, shelter, health care, and clothing). As Gil (1994) argued, "Understanding oppression and social injustice seems especially important for social workers, since the conditions that cause people to seek help from social services are usually direct or indirect consequences of oppressive and unjust social, economic, and political institutions, and since the profession of social work is ethically committed to promote social justice" (p. 232).

## PUBLIC PARTICIPATION

### STANDARD 6.02

*Social workers should facilitate informed participation by the public in shaping social policies and institutions.*

Throughout social work's history, practitioners have understood the importance of involving the public in efforts to address social problems. Mobilizing and empowering the public can be an effective way to bring about social change.

Social workers can facilitate and promote public participation in two ways. First, they can educate the public about important social concerns and problems through such activities as sponsoring debates on social issues among candidates for political office, giving lectures and workshops (for example, on the problems of malnutrition among children in the community, crime and delinquency, unemployment, or health risks), and working with media representatives to inform the public about social problems and ways to address them.

- A social worker employed by the United Way chaired a committee of human services professionals from the community concerned about the outcome of an upcoming gubernatorial election. The two candidates for governor embraced different views about public spending for social services. The social worker and her committee arranged for the two candidates to participate in a televised debate on human services and social policy issues.

- A social worker who was the executive director of a community mental health center was concerned about a pending bond referendum that would provide increased funding for community mental health services throughout the state. The social worker arranged to meet with the editorial board of the state's major newspaper in an effort to convince the board to write an editorial supporting the referendum.

- The mayor of a large city appointed a social worker to chair an advisory committee charged with making recommendations on human services needs, programs, and policies. The social worker persuaded the committee to sponsor a series of town meetings and public hearings to inform the public about major social problems in the city and solicit the public's advice and ideas about effective ways to address these problems. The committee incorporated many of the suggestions offered by city residents in its final report to the mayor.

Social workers can engage in efforts to increase public participation in shaping social policies and institutions. For example, social workers have been actively involved in organized attempts to promote voter registration, particularly among low-income people whose opinions often are not fully considered because of their historically low voting levels (Cloward & Piven, 1995). Social workers and other professionals and public activists created Human SERVE (for Human Service Employees Registration and Voter Education), an organization devoted to strengthening political efforts to maintain social spending and programs in the face of large-scale budget cuts. Ten years after Human SERVE's creation, Congress enacted the core of its plan in the form of the National Voter Registration Act of 1993.

Many social workers also are involved in efforts to organize clients and community groups to influence agency administrators, legislators, and other public officials who formulate and implement social policy. Examples include social workers who work with community groups to lobby public officials for changes in eligibility requirements for social services, circulate petitions to protest social services funding cuts, and identify neighborhood residents willing to testify before legislative panels reviewing pending legislation related to human services.

The concepts of empowerment and citizen participation are at the root of social workers' efforts to promote public participation. *Empowerment* is the process of helping individuals, families, groups, and communities increase their personal, interpersonal, socioeconomic, and political strength and influence to improve their circumstances (Barker, 1995; Gutierrez, 1990). This can occur through providing people and communities with information and tools (such as lobbying skills and voter participation) to influence individuals in positions of authority, particularly those responsible for the planning and implementation of social policy. Gamble and Weil (1995) described citizen participation as

the active, voluntary engagement of individuals and groups to change problematic conditions and to influence policies and programs that affect the quality of their lives or the lives of others. Citizen participation, the hallmark of a democratic society, takes place primarily through two types of structures: citizen-initiated groups that engage in a full range of social and economic problem areas, and government-initiated advisory and policy-setting bodies. (p. 483)

# PUBLIC EMERGENCIES

## STANDARD 6.03

*Social workers should provide appropriate professional services in public emergencies to the greatest extent possible.*

In addition to their obligations to their clients—whether individuals, families, groups, organizations, or communities—social workers have a responsibility to provide assistance to people and communities affected by public emergencies. This duty is part of social workers' role as responsible public citizens; it is an extension of the ethical principle in the 1996 *NASW Code of Ethics* that states, "Social workers' primary goal is to help people in need and to address social problems" (p. 5). Further, the code states in its summary of core ethical principles, "Social workers are encouraged to volunteer some portion of their professional skills with no expectation of significant financial return (pro bono service)" (p. 5).

Public emergencies can take many forms, including natural disasters such as floods, hurricanes, and tornadoes and other large-scale accidents such as airplane and train crashes. Whenever possible, social workers should offer their professional services to aid victims and surviving relatives and loved ones. Practitioners can offer a variety of services, including counseling and casework services (in the form of crisis intervention and grief counseling), community organizing (organizing volunteer assistance and soliciting emergency resources such as food, shelter, and relief funds), advocacy (lobbying public officials for needed resources), and planning (helping formulate recovery, rehabilitation, and services delivery plans).

- A local community was devastated by a severe hurricane. Hundreds of residents were homeless, hungry, and without electricity and water. The board of directors of the state's NASW chapter established a telephone tree to recruit NASW members as volunteers to work with the local Red Cross in providing emergency assistance. As a result, a group of NASW members volunteered to help coordinate emergency housing services and solicit food and monetary donations from NASW members throughout the state.

- An airplane crash killed 32 passengers and injured 47 others. Social workers from a nearby community mental health center contacted the local Federal Aviation Administration office and the state emergency management agency to offer their clinical expertise in crisis intervention and grief counseling. The executive director of the community mental health center provided several staff with paid leave to enable them to donate their assistance. Several of the social workers used a number of their own vacation days to provide additional assistance.

- A social worker employed in a major hospital learned of a deadly flood in a developing nation that killed hundreds of people and left thousands homeless and vulnerable to disease. The social worker arranged to take a leave of absence from her position to fly to the stricken area as part of an international relief organization's efforts to provide assistance. The hospital provided the social worker with a paid leave of absence for part of the time, and several social workers on staff donated some of their vacation days to the social worker to enable her to extend her stay.

The expectation that social workers will provide assistance during public emergencies must be tempered with a realistic understanding of the practical limitations all professionals face with respect to the time and energy they have available for such extra activities. Ideally, perhaps, social workers would be selfless altruists who are always available for all manner of crises and emergencies. Practically, however, social workers, like all human beings, have only a finite supply of time and energy and, by necessity, must make difficult decisions about which obligations should top their lists of priorities. Social workers must balance the competing professional and personal demands on their lives. It may not always be feasible for social workers to devote great amounts of time and resources to provide assistance during public emergencies; their family commitments, job obligations, and financial needs also must be taken into account. When possible, however, social workers should provide appropriate professional expertise and services during public emergencies.

## SOCIAL AND POLITICAL ACTION

### STANDARD 6.04(a)

*Social workers should engage in social and political action that seeks to ensure that all people have equal access to the resources, employment, services, and opportunities they require to meet their basic human needs and to develop fully. Social workers should be aware of the impact of the political arena on practice and should advocate for changes in policy and legislation to improve social conditions in order to meet basic human needs and promote social justice.*

Consistent with the profession's long-standing commitment to social justice, social workers have always recognized the importance of social action (Billups, 1992; Reamer, 1992c). Barker (1995) defined *social action* as a "coordinated effort to achieve institutional change to meet a need, solve a social problem, correct an injustice, or enhance the quality of human life" (p. 350). Social and political action can take many different forms, including lobbying public officials, organizing community residents to protest specific policies, boycotting discriminatory agencies or organizations, introducing legislation, testifying at legislative hearings, and campaigning for public office (Haynes & Mickelson, 1991). Throughout social work's history, practitioners have understood that social action to improve social policy and institutional responses to social problems has a direct bearing on the quality of people's lives and their efforts to cope with their problems in living (Gil, 1994; Mahaffey, 1987; Mahaffey & Hanks, 1982).

More specifically, social workers understand that to bring about meaningful social change, it is important for them to be actively involved in the political arena. Government institutions are profoundly influential, and social workers have always recognized that the profession needs a visible and vocal presence in politics. As Weismiller and Rome (1995) noted, "From the beginning, the experience of some social workers taught them that government action was often needed to protect and enhance the lives of people. They recognized the need to change public policies and private services delivery to meet the needs of the individuals and groups they served" (p. 2305).

Social work's involvement in political action dates back to the settlement house workers of the early 20th century. Jane Addams and Florence Kelley "quickly recognized that improving social conditions required challenging the existing power structure" (Weismiller & Rome, 1995, p. 2306) by forming coalitions, molding public opinion, lobbying government officials, and actively participating in partisan politics. Social workers became particularly active in politics during the 1930s, largely as a result of the devastating impact of the Great Depression. Since then, they have intensified their efforts to shape public policy and legislation through political action. Although social workers' political activities have been more visible during some periods than others (most notably during the 1960s and early 1970s), the profession continuously has strengthened its political involvement. For example, in 1972 "NASW concluded that merely having a Washington office was not sufficient and moved from New York to Washington, DC: The organization had to be in the seat of power" (Weismiller & Rome, 1995, p. 2308). Below are several examples of social workers' social and political action efforts.

- A school social worker was becoming increasingly concerned about various social problems that were affecting the lives of students and their families, including poverty, substance abuse, and domestic violence. The social worker, who had relatively little experience in politics, decided that it was time to become more actively involved in public life. She met with local leaders of her political party, read literature on political issues and campaigning, and decided to run for the state legislature. The social worker was elected and eventually became an influential voice in the legislature on human services issues.

- The executive director of an NASW state chapter recruited eight members to establish a political issues committee. The committee's purpose was to highlight major social problems and policy issues and identify legislative priorities for NASW. They reviewed all pending legislation relevant to social work and made recommendations to the chapter's board of directors as to whether NASW should support or oppose each bill. In addition, members of the committee lobbied legislators about critically important bills.

- The governor of a large state planned to drastically reduce funding for child care for low-income families. A group of students in the graduate social work program at the state university organized the student body, faculty, NASW members throughout the state, and community residents to sign petitions, write letters of protest to the governor, and stage a demonstration at the state house.

- A state legislator sponsored a bill that would close a number of health clinics in low-income neighborhoods. The directors of social work at several hospitals in the state met to discuss the potential impact of the legislation. They decided to contact NASW and ask for assistance in mobilizing the membership to oppose the bill. With NASW members' help, the hospital social work directors organized an extensive telephone tree to inform social workers throughout the state of the likely dire consequences of the legislation and ask them to contact their local legislators and urge them to vote against the bill.

Social workers' social and political action will not always be successful. However, the profession's history is filled with compelling examples of successful efforts. Social and political action can have a profound effect on society, and social workers' involvement in these endeavors helps fulfill their obligation to promote social justice. As Weismiller and Rome (1995) concluded,

> Within the profession, there is a growing recognition that the self-interest of social workers and clients can be served by effective political action. The transformation of society to meet the needs of its members can come about only through organizing and educating significant numbers of people so that they can work together. Individuals, including clients, need to see their situation within the larger context of society. (p. 2312)

## STANDARD 6.04(b)

*Social workers should act to expand choice and opportunity for all people, with special regard for vulnerable, disadvantaged, oppressed, and exploited people and groups.*

The code's preamble makes it clear that social work aims to meet the needs of *all* people. Whether rich or poor, young or old, people from all social, cultural, and ethnic groups experience problems in living—among them, mental illness, substance abuse, domestic violence, physical disabilities, or unemployment. Without question, social work has a legitimate role to play in efforts to help all people cope with life's challenges. Overwhelming emotional anguish experienced by an affluent client is as deserving of a social worker's attention as is a low-income hospital patient's need for a nursing home placement.

Social work, however, must maintain its fundamental commitment to serving those who are most at risk. As the *NASW Code of Ethics* states, "The primary mission of the social work profession is to enhance human well-being and help meet the basic human needs of all people, *with particular attention to the needs and empowerment of people who are vulnerable, oppressed, and living in poverty*" (p. 1, emphasis added). As a profession, social work cannot abandon its principal concern for low-income and oppressed people. This commitment is a defining feature of the profession, one that ultimately sets it apart from all other helping professions. As Siporin (1992) asserted,

"Social workers need to know clearly that they are agents of the community, with contractual obligations to represent the poor and disadvantaged, yet serving and mediating the interests of both poor and non-poor. . . . Social workers are also obligated to foster social integration for all, to see that the social welfare system serves all needy members of the community" (p. 87).

To fulfill their mission, social workers must have a solid understanding of the nature of oppression, injustice, and exploitation. According to Gil (1994),

> Oppression refers to relations of domination and exploitation—economic, social, and psychologic—between individuals; between social groups and classes within and beyond societies; and, globally, between entire societies. Injustice refers to discriminatory, dehumanizing, and development-inhibiting conditions of living (e.g., unemployment, poverty, homelessness, and lack of health care), imposed by oppressors upon dominated and exploited individuals, social groups, classes, and peoples. These conditions will often cause people to turn to social services for help.
>
> Oppression seems motivated by an intent to exploit (i.e., benefit disproportionately from the resources, capacities, and productivity of others), and it results typically in disadvantageous, unjust conditions of living for its victims. It serves as *means* to enforce exploitation toward the *goal* of securing advantageous conditions of living for its perpetrators. (p. 233)

Social workers must always keep in mind the profession's primary obligation to confront oppression and injustice. To this end, ideally social workers should devote at least a portion of their professional time and expertise to efforts to challenge oppression and injustice. The practitioner who chooses not to work exclusively with people who are economically, politically, or racially oppressed should consider dedicating some part of his or her career (for example, a period of months or years) or professional time (for example, a certain number of hours weekly or monthly) to helping people who are oppressed and exploited.

- A social worker spent the first seven years of her career working with low-income people diagnosed with chronic mental illness. Over time she found herself tiring of the struggle to obtain adequate funding and resources to meet her clients' substantial needs, and toward the end of this period, she was showing some signs of professional burnout. She decided to resign her position and work in a less stressful environment, providing mental health counseling to employees of a large financial investment corporation. Shortly after beginning her new job, she decided to volunteer several hours each week working with a local welfare rights organization.

- A social worker in private practice provided counseling services primarily to middle- and upper-income clients. He also set aside one half-day each week to offer counseling services pro bono to low-income clients referred to him by the pastor of his church.

- A social worker was the director of a large for-profit employee assistance program. She also spent considerable time each month volunteering her services as chair of a task force charged by her city's mayor with developing a comprehensive plan to meet the needs of battered and abused women.

- A social worker who owned a management consulting firm, which provided technical assistance to human services organizations, became actively involved in a coalition formed by several social services agencies concerned about the exploitation of immigrants and refugees living in their community. The coalition lobbied public officials for increased enforcement of fair-labor and housing discrimination laws.

## STANDARD 6.04(c)

*Social workers should promote conditions that encourage respect for cultural and social diversity within the United States and globally. Social workers should promote policies and practices that demonstrate respect for difference, support the expansion of cultural knowledge and resources, advocate for programs and institutions that demonstrate cultural competence, and promote policies that safeguard the rights of and confirm equity and social justice for all people.*

As stated in the provisions of standard 1.05, social workers should understand the relevance of cultural and social diversity to clients' lives and the delivery of social services. Standard 6.04(c) expands this beyond its direct relevance to social work practice, encouraging social workers actively to promote conditions that foster respect for cultural and social diversity among people generally. Such measures can help promote peaceful relations among peoples and avoid local and international conflict.

At the practical level, social workers can become involved in a variety of activities that promote respect for cultural and social diversity. Practitioners can enhance their own understanding by reading the professional literature and attending lectures, workshops, and seminars on the subject. Social work educators, supervisors, and administrators can sponsor instruction and in-service training on cultural and social diversity for students and staff. The Council on Social Work Education's (CSWE's) *Curriculum Policy Statements* (1994), for example, requires all social work curricula to include the subject of diversity:

> Professional social work education is committed to preparing students to understand and appreciate human diversity. Programs must provide curriculum content about differences and similarities in the experiences, needs, and beliefs of people. The curriculum must include content about differential assessment and intervention skills that will enable practitioners to serve diverse populations.
>
> Each program is required to include content about population groups that are particularly relevant to the program's mission. These include, but are not limited to, groups distinguished by race, ethnicity, culture, class, gender, sexual orientation, religion, physical or mental disability, age, and national origin.

Social workers also can become involved in various professional activities that promote respect for cultural and social diversity. Many local, state, and national organizations and coalitions work to educate the public about diversity, advocate for social and political change, and promote peaceful relations among various peoples and groups. Examples include the National Association for the Advancement of Colored People, National Conference, Southern Poverty Law Center, and American Jewish Committee. Social workers may become involved in these organizations' activities by volunteering for conferences, lectures, workshops, or fundraising campaigns, or by giving them financial support.

Social workers also can support and become involved with international organizations that promote respect for cultural and ethnic differences; promote policies that safeguard human rights; provide international aid; and seek to reduce international, interracial, and interethnic conflict. Examples of social work-related organizations include the International Federation of Social Workers, European Centre for Social Welfare Policy and Research, International Association of Schools of Social Work, Interuniversity Consortium on International Social Development, NASW International Activities Committee, NASW's Peace and International Affairs Program, and CSWE's International Commission. Other organizations with a broader focus include the Council on International Programs, Experiment in International Living, International Committee of the Red Cross, Amnesty International, CARE, Oxfam, Christian Children's Fund, American Jewish World Service, and Unitarian Universalist Service Committee (Healy, 1995).

- A social worker in private practice was concerned about human rights violations in developing countries governed by dictatorships. She believed that the social work profession's values obligated her to be concerned about social justice issues abroad as well as domestically. She joined Amnesty International and volunteered her time to chair a subcommittee responsible for contacting U.S. senators and representatives about international human rights violations.

- A social work professor conducted a study demonstrating that many social work students in the United States have only a modest understanding of various forms of exploitation and discrimination practiced outside their own countries. Based on information he gathered from various international organizations, he developed an elective course on the subject for students at his university. He also presented a workshop on the topic at the annual program meeting of CSWE and shared his course materials with other faculty interested in the topic.

- A school social worker was concerned about ethnic and racial conflict among students in her school system. She contacted staff at the local National Conference office to discuss ways to address the problem. As a result of her efforts, the National Conference staff organized a series of workshops for teachers and administrators on effective ways to work with students to minimize ethnic and racial conflict.

- A social worker who administered an economic development program in a major U.S. city was concerned about economic exploitation and poverty in developing countries. He decided to take a leave of absence to volunteer for three months with an international relief organization in a developing country. The social worker arranged to use his economic development skills to help individuals form small businesses and to support international collaboration. His employer agreed to pay 75 percent of his salary during the leave of absence.

### STANDARD 6.04(d)

*Social workers should act to prevent and eliminate domination of, exploitation of, and discrimination against any person, group, or class on the basis of race, ethnicity, national origin, color, sex, sexual orientation, age, marital status, political belief, religion, or mental or physical disability.*

Standard 4.02 states that social workers should not practice, condone, facilitate, or collaborate with any form of discrimination. Standard 6.04 takes this obligation a step further by requiring that social workers take affirmative steps to prevent and eliminate all forms of exploitation, discrimination, and oppression.

Exploitation, discrimination, and oppression have many targets, including low-income people; racial, ethnic, and sexual subgroups; women; and people living with disabilities. These groups and others have been subjected to such forms of persecution as employment and housing discrimination, derogatory language and epithets, harassment, and physical assault (Asch & Mudrick, 1995; Balgopal, 1995; Berger & Kelly, 1995; Black, 1994; Bricker-Jenkins & Hooyman, 1984; Davis & Proctor, 1989; Gottlieb, 1995; Gutierrez, 1990; Hooyman, 1994; Leashore, 1995; Lewis, 1995; Longres, 1995; Newman, 1994; Pinderhughes, 1994; Tully, 1995). As described in the examples below, social workers can help prevent and eliminate oppression by using their skills in direct practice, community organizing, supervision, consultation, administration, advocacy, social and political action, policy development and implementation, education, and research and evaluation.

- A clinical social worker at a residential program for male adolescents overheard an assistant administrator comment that he did not want to accept any new referrals from a particular outpatient treatment program because "all they've been sending us lately are troubled fags. They're just too much to handle." The social worker was disturbed by the administrator's homophobic, insensitive, and judgmental comment. After much thought, she decided to let the administrator know that she had overheard the comment and was upset by it. Although the administrator was defensive at first, at the end of their conversation he apologized for his inappropriate comment and assured the social worker that he would not make a similar one again.

- A social worker served as a community organizer in a mostly middle-income neighborhood. He spent most of his time working on issues related to affordable housing. The social worker met with a group of neighborhood residents who were concerned about a developer's plans to raze a number of deteriorated, low-income housing units and replace them with middle-income units. During the conversation one of the residents said, "Well, at least if the developer comes in here we'll be able to trade some niggers for some decent white folk." Several other residents nodded in agreement. The social worker felt exceedingly uncomfortable being part of a racist conversation. At the group's next meeting, he shared his feelings with the group, which led to a productive conversation about race relations in the community. The social worker and the residents' group eventually agreed that it would be helpful to consult with a race relations expert to improve the neighborhood's racial climate.

- A social worker was a program director at a family services agency. The agency administrator confided to the social worker that the agency was experiencing serious financial problems and would need to lay off several full-time staff and replace them with part-time employees who would be paid lower salaries and not receive benefits. The administrator said she planned to hire women "who are taking care of their kids and desperate for some part-time work. Those are the folks you can get to work for next to nothing. They don't exactly have a lot of bargaining power." The social worker was appalled by the administrator's explicitly exploitative plan. After expressing his concern to the administrator and being rebuffed, he convened a meeting of trusted colleagues at the agency—two of whom had overheard the administrator's comment—who decided to share their concerns with the chair of the agency's board of directors. As a result, the board reprimanded the administrator and developed a new hiring and personnel policy that ensured fair treatment of both full-time and part-time employees.

- A social worker who directed a community action program had gathered anecdotal evidence that several absentee landlords in the area were failing to fix lead-paint problems in the apartments of many low-income families and families of color, exposing the tenants to serious harm. The social worker was eager to gather empirical evidence of this exploitation to support a formal complaint that several area residents planned to file with the state's housing court. She contacted a social work researcher to help her design a data collection instrument, select a sample of families in the community, and gather the data. The social worker and several community residents collated the information and successfully argued their case before the court. As a result of this advocacy, the landlords involved were fined. In addition, a state legislator introduced legislation strengthening the state's fair housing laws.

Social workers must not become pawns or agents of oppression as they provide assistance to society's exploited victims. Practitioners continually should examine the extent to which they are enabling, facilitating, or reinforcing oppression and exploitation by providing aid and comfort to those who are injured by society. As Gil (1994) argued,

> Social work and social services would probably never have evolved at all unless oppression and injustice had become normal aspects of social life. The institutionalization of these dehumanizing phenomena undoubtedly preceded the emergence of social services and social work. For these latter may be understood as societal responses, designed to stabilize oppressive social orders by "fine-tuning" their unjust conditions in order to facilitate the survival of their victims and regulate their behavior, as well as to protect those social classes that benefit socially, psychologically, and economically from oppressive practices. . . . In this context, social work and social services seem

important components of an array of consciousness-shaping and social control mechanisms necessary for the maintenance of coercively
established, exploitative, and unjust systems of resource stewardship,
work, exchange, and distribution. (pp. 256–257)

Social workers are in an ideal position to confront exploitation, discrimination, and oppression. Their skills uniquely qualify them to identify
and assess the nature of exploitation, discrimination, and oppression, plan
and intervene meaningfully, and evaluate the outcomes of their efforts. Social work's enduring commitment to challenging social injustice is an essential element in the profession's noble mission. Most important, social
workers must make earnest attempts to identify and eradicate the principal
causes of exploitation, discrimination, and oppression as they continue to
give assistance to the victims of these phenomena.

# AFTERWORD

Social work is a remarkably diverse profession. Its practitioners use a wide array of professional skills and perspectives to provide services and assistance to a comparably wide range of people in various settings. The profession's core values, ethical principles, and ethical standards, as presented in the *NASW Code of Ethics*, are what bind social workers together.

Over the years, social workers, like all professionals, have struggled to define and understand their principal purpose and mission. The *NASW Code of Ethics* reflects social workers' vision of the profession's aims, values, ethical principles, and ethical standards. This vision draws from the profound legacy of the profession's pioneers and is informed by contemporary practitioners' understanding of their mission and ethical obligations. In this sense, the code is a living document, one that must be sensitive to social work's traditional commitments and purpose and to current exigencies, circumstances, and interpretations as well.

Social workers cannot expect their code of ethics to provide simple, quick, and formulaic solutions to all ethical problems and issues. Rather, they can expect it to acquaint them with compelling ethical issues and dilemmas and offer reasonable guidance in light of current knowledge. In the final analysis, social workers must rely on their own good judgment to discern the relevance of the code to their particular circumstances.

Some years ago, a colleague of mine observed that ethics is the "immune system of a humane society," in that ethical principles and standards provide an essential measure of protection. He was so right. Ethics also is the "immune system of a humane profession," which is what social work most certainly is.

# APPENDIX

# NASW CODE OF ETHICS

## PREAMBLE

The primary mission of the social work profession is to enhance human well-being and help meet the basic human needs of all people, with particular attention to the needs and empowerment of people who are vulnerable, oppressed, and living in poverty. A historic and defining feature of social work is the profession's focus on individual well-being in a social context and the well-being of society. Fundamental to social work is attention to the environmental forces that create, contribute to, and address problems in living.

Social workers promote social justice and social change with and on behalf of clients. "Clients" is used inclusively to refer to individuals, families, groups, organizations, and communities. Social workers are sensitive to cultural and ethnic diversity and strive to end discrimination, oppression, poverty, and other forms of social injustice. These activities may be in the form of direct practice, community organizing, supervision, consultation, administration, advocacy, social and political action, policy development and implementation, education, and research and evaluation. Social workers seek to enhance the capacity of people to address their own needs. Social workers also seek to promote the responsiveness of organizations, communities, and other social institutions to individuals' needs and social problems.

The mission of the social work profession is rooted in a set of core values. These core values, embraced by social workers throughout the profession's history, are the foundation of social work's unique purpose and perspective:

- service
- social justice
- dignity and worth of the person
- importance of human relationships
- integrity
- competence.

This constellation of core values reflects what is unique to the social work profession. Core values, and the principles that flow from them, must be balanced within the context and complexity of the human experience.

---

Adopted by the NASW Delegate Assembly, August 1996.

# Purpose of the *NASW Code of Ethics*

Professional ethics are at the core of social work. The profession has an obligation to articulate its basic values, ethical principles, and ethical standards. The *NASW Code of Ethics* sets forth these values, principles, and standards to guide social workers' conduct. The *Code* is relevant to all social workers and social work students, regardless of their professional functions, the settings in which they work, or the populations they serve.

The *NASW Code of Ethics* serves six purposes:

1. The *Code* identifies core values on which social work's mission is based.
2. The *Code* summarizes broad ethical principles that reflect the profession's core values and establishes a set of specific ethical standards that should be used to guide social work practice.
3. The *Code* is designed to help social workers identify relevant considerations when professional obligations conflict or ethical uncertainties arise.
4. The *Code* provides ethical standards to which the general public can hold the social work profession accountable.
5. The *Code* socializes practitioners new to the field to social work's mission, values, ethical principles, and ethical standards.
6. The *Code* articulates standards that the social work profession itself can use to assess whether social workers have engaged in unethical conduct. NASW has formal procedures to adjudicate ethics complaints filed against its members.* In subscribing to this *Code*, social workers are required to cooperate in its implementation, participate in NASW adjudication proceedings, and abide by any NASW disciplinary rulings or sanctions based on it.

The *Code* offers a set of values, principles, and standards to guide decision making and conduct when ethical issues arise. It does not provide a set of rules that prescribe how social workers should act in all situations. Specific applications of the *Code* must take into account the context in which it is being considered and the possibility of conflicts among the *Code*'s values, principles, and standards. Ethical responsibilities flow from all human relationships, from the personal and familial to the social and professional.

Further, the *NASW Code of Ethics* does not specify which values, principles, and standards are most important and ought to outweigh others in instances when they conflict. Reasonable differences of opinion can and do exist among social workers with respect to the ways in which values, ethical principles, and ethical standards should be rank ordered when they conflict. Ethical decision making in a given situation must apply the informed judgment of the individual social worker and should also consider how the issues would be judged in a peer review process where the ethical standards of the profession would be applied.

Ethical decision making is a process. There are many instances in social work where simple answers are not available to resolve complex ethical issues. Social workers should take into consideration all the values, principles,

---

*For information on NASW adjudication procedures, see *NASW Procedures for the Adjudication of Grievances*.

and standards in this *Code* that are relevant to any situation in which ethical judgment is warranted. Social workers' decisions and actions should be consistent with the spirit as well as the letter of this *Code*.

In addition to this *Code*, there are many other sources of information about ethical thinking that may be useful. Social workers should consider ethical theory and principles generally, social work theory and research, laws, regulations, agency policies, and other relevant codes of ethics, recognizing that among codes of ethics social workers should consider the *NASW Code of Ethics* as their primary source. Social workers also should be aware of the impact on ethical decision making of their clients' and their own personal values and cultural and religious beliefs and practices. They should be aware of any conflicts between personal and professional values and deal with them responsibly. For additional guidance social workers should consult the relevant literature on professional ethics and ethical decision making and seek appropriate consultation when faced with ethical dilemmas. This may involve consultation with an agency-based or social work organization's ethics committee, a regulatory body, knowledgeable colleagues, supervisors, or legal counsel.

Instances may arise when social workers' ethical obligations conflict with agency policies or relevant laws or regulations. When such conflicts occur, social workers must make a responsible effort to resolve the conflict in a manner that is consistent with the values, principles, and standards expressed in this *Code*. If a reasonable resolution of the conflict does not appear possible, social workers should seek proper consultation before making a decision.

The *NASW Code of Ethics* is to be used by NASW and by individuals, agencies, organizations, and bodies (such as licensing and regulatory boards, professional liability insurance providers, courts of law, agency boards of directors, government agencies, and other professional groups) that choose to adopt it or use it as a frame of reference. Violation of standards in this *Code* does not automatically imply legal liability or violation of the law. Such determination can only be made in the context of legal and judicial proceedings. Alleged violations of the *Code* would be subject to a peer review process. Such processes are generally separate from legal or administrative procedures and insulated from legal review or proceedings to allow the profession to counsel and discipline its own members.

A code of ethics cannot guarantee ethical behavior. Moreover, a code of ethics cannot resolve all ethical issues or disputes or capture the richness and complexity involved in striving to make responsible choices within a moral community. Rather, a code of ethics sets forth values, ethical principles, and ethical standards to which professionals aspire and by which their actions can be judged. Social workers' ethical behavior should result from their personal commitment to engage in ethical practice. The *NASW Code of Ethics* reflects the commitment of all social workers to uphold the profession's values and to act ethically. Principles and standards must be applied by individuals of good character who discern moral questions and, in good faith, seek to make reliable ethical judgments.

# Ethical Principles

The following broad ethical principles are based on social work's core values of service, social justice, dignity and worth of the person, importance of human relationships, integrity, and competence. These principles set forth ideals to which all social workers should aspire.

**Value:** *Service*

**Ethical Principle:** *Social workers' primary goal is to help people in need and to address social problems.*

> Social workers elevate service to others above self-interest. Social workers draw on their knowledge, values, and skills to help people in need and to address social problems. Social workers are encouraged to volunteer some portion of their professional skills with no expectation of significant financial return (pro bono service).

**Value:** *Social Justice*

**Ethical Principle:** *Social workers challenge social injustice.*

> Social workers pursue social change, particularly with and on behalf of vulnerable and oppressed individuals and groups of people. Social workers' social change efforts are focused primarily on issues of poverty, unemployment, discrimination, and other forms of social injustice. These activities seek to promote sensitivity to and knowledge about oppression and cultural and ethnic diversity. Social workers strive to ensure access to needed information, services, and resources; equality of opportunity; and meaningful participation in decision making for all people.

**Value:** *Dignity and Worth of the Person*

**Ethical Principle:** *Social workers respect the inherent dignity and worth of the person.*

> Social workers treat each person in a caring and respectful fashion, mindful of individual differences and cultural and ethnic diversity. Social workers promote clients' socially responsible self-determination. Social workers seek to enhance clients' capacity and opportunity to change and to address their own needs. Social workers are cognizant of their dual responsibility to clients and to the broader society. They seek to resolve conflicts between clients' interests and the broader society's interests in a socially responsible manner consistent with the values, ethical principles, and ethical standards of the profession.

**Value:** *Importance of Human Relationships*

**Ethical Principle:** *Social workers recognize the central importance of human relationships.*

> Social workers understand that relationships between and among people are an important vehicle for change. Social workers engage people as partners in the helping process. Social workers seek to strengthen relationships among people in a purposeful effort to promote, restore, maintain, and enhance the well-being of individuals, families, social groups, organizations, and communities.

**Value:** *Integrity*

**Ethical Principle:** *Social workers behave in a trustworthy manner.*

Social workers are continually aware of the profession's mission, values, ethical principles, and ethical standards and practice in a manner consistent with them. Social workers act honestly and responsibly and promote ethical practices on the part of the organizations with which they are affiliated.

**Value:** *Competence*

**Ethical Principle:** *Social workers practice within their areas of competence and develop and enhance their professional expertise.*

Social workers continually strive to increase their professional knowledge and skills and to apply them in practice. Social workers should aspire to contribute to the knowledge base of the profession.

# ETHICAL STANDARDS

The following ethical standards are relevant to the professional activities of all social workers. These standards concern (1) social workers' ethical responsibilities to clients, (2) social workers' ethical responsibilities to colleagues, (3) social workers' ethical responsibilities in practice settings, (4) social workers' ethical responsibilities as professionals, (5) social workers' ethical responsibilities to the social work profession, and (6) social workers' ethical responsibilities to the broader society.

Some of the standards that follow are enforceable guidelines for professional conduct, and some are aspirational. The extent to which each standard is enforceable is a matter of professional judgment to be exercised by those responsible for reviewing alleged violations of ethical standards.

## 1. SOCIAL WORKERS' ETHICAL RESPONSIBILITIES TO CLIENTS

### 1.01 Commitment to Clients

Social workers' primary responsibility is to promote the well-being of clients. In general, clients' interests are primary. However, social workers' responsibility to the larger society or specific legal obligations may on limited occasions supersede the loyalty owed clients, and clients should be so advised. (Examples include when a social worker is required by law to report that a client has abused a child or has threatened to harm self or others.)

### 1.02 Self-Determination

Social workers respect and promote the right of clients to self-determination and assist clients in their efforts to identify and clarify their goals. Social workers may limit clients' right to self-determination when, in the social workers' professional judgment, clients' actions or potential actions pose a serious, foreseeable, and imminent risk to themselves or others.

## 1.03 Informed Consent

(a) Social workers should provide services to clients only in the context of a professional relationship based, when appropriate, on valid informed consent. Social workers should use clear and understandable language to inform clients of the purpose of the services, risks related to the services, limits to services because of the requirements of a third-party payer, relevant costs, reasonable alternatives, clients' right to refuse or withdraw consent, and the time frame covered by the consent. Social workers should provide clients with an opportunity to ask questions.

(b) In instances when clients are not literate or have difficulty understanding the primary language used in the practice setting, social workers should take steps to ensure clients' comprehension. This may include providing clients with a detailed verbal explanation or arranging for a qualified interpreter or translator whenever possible.

(c) In instances when clients lack the capacity to provide informed consent, social workers should protect clients' interests by seeking permission from an appropriate third party, informing clients consistent with the clients' level of understanding. In such instances social workers should seek to ensure that the third party acts in a manner consistent with clients' wishes and interests. Social workers should take reasonable steps to enhance such clients' ability to give informed consent.

(d) In instances when clients are receiving services involuntarily, social workers should provide information about the nature and extent of services and about the extent of clients' right to refuse service.

(e) Social workers who provide services via electronic media (such as computer, telephone, radio, and television) should inform recipients of the limitations and risks associated with such services.

(f) Social workers should obtain clients' informed consent before audiotaping or videotaping clients or permitting observation of services to clients by a third party.

## 1.04 Competence

(a) Social workers should provide services and represent themselves as competent only within the boundaries of their education, training, license, certification, consultation received, supervised experience, or other relevant professional experience.

(b) Social workers should provide services in substantive areas or use intervention techniques or approaches that are new to them only after engaging in appropriate study, training, consultation, and supervision from people who are competent in those interventions or techniques.

(c) When generally recognized standards do not exist with respect to an emerging area of practice, social workers should exercise careful judgment and take responsible steps (including appropriate education, research, training, consultation, and supervision) to ensure the competence of their work and to protect clients from harm.

### 1.05 Cultural Competence and Social Diversity

(a) Social workers should understand culture and its function in human behavior and society, recognizing the strengths that exist in all cultures.

(b) Social workers should have a knowledge base of their clients' cultures and be able to demonstrate competence in the provision of services that are sensitive to clients' cultures and to differences among people and cultural groups.

(c) Social workers should obtain education about and seek to understand the nature of social diversity and oppression with respect to race, ethnicity, national origin, color, sex, sexual orientation, age, marital status, political belief, religion, and mental or physical disability.

### 1.06 Conflicts of Interest

(a) Social workers should be alert to and avoid conflicts of interest that interfere with the exercise of professional discretion and impartial judgment. Social workers should inform clients when a real or potential conflict of interest arises and take reasonable steps to resolve the issue in a manner that makes the clients' interests primary and protects clients' interests to the greatest extent possible. In some cases, protecting clients' interests may require termination of the professional relationship with proper referral of the client.

(b) Social workers should not take unfair advantage of any professional relationship or exploit others to further their personal, religious, political, or business interests.

(c) Social workers should not engage in dual or multiple relationships with clients or former clients in which there is a risk of exploitation or potential harm to the client. In instances when dual or multiple relationships are unavoidable, social workers should take steps to protect clients and are responsible for setting clear, appropriate, and culturally sensitive boundaries. (Dual or multiple relationships occur when social workers relate to clients in more than one relationship, whether professional, social, or business. Dual or multiple relationships can occur simultaneously or consecutively.)

(d) When social workers provide services to two or more people who have a relationship with each other (for example, couples, family members), social workers should clarify with all parties which individuals will be considered clients and the nature of social workers' professional obligations to the various individuals who are receiving services. Social workers who anticipate a conflict of interest among the individuals receiving services or who anticipate having to perform in potentially conflicting roles (for example, when a social worker is asked to testify in a child custody dispute or divorce proceedings involving clients) should clarify their role with the parties involved and take appropriate action to minimize any conflict of interest.

## 1.07 Privacy and Confidentiality

  (a)  Social workers should respect clients' right to privacy. Social workers should not solicit private information from clients unless it is essential to providing services or conducting social work evaluation or research. Once private information is shared, standards of confidentiality apply.

  (b)  Social workers may disclose confidential information when appropriate with valid consent from a client or a person legally authorized to consent on behalf of a client.

  (c)  Social workers should protect the confidentiality of all information obtained in the course of professional service, except for compelling professional reasons. The general expectation that social workers will keep information confidential does not apply when disclosure is necessary to prevent serious, foreseeable, and imminent harm to a client or other identifiable person or when laws or regulations require disclosure without a client's consent. In all instances, social workers should disclose the least amount of confidential information necessary to achieve the desired purpose; only information that is directly relevant to the purpose for which the disclosure is made should be revealed.

  (d)  Social workers should inform clients, to the extent possible, about the disclosure of confidential information and the potential consequences, when feasible before the disclosure is made. This applies whether social workers disclose confidential information on the basis of a legal requirement or client consent.

  (e)  Social workers should discuss with clients and other interested parties the nature of confidentiality and limitations of clients' right to confidentiality. Social workers should review with clients circumstances where confidential information may be requested and where disclosure of confidential information may be legally required. This discussion should occur as soon as possible in the social worker–client relationship and as needed throughout the course of the relationship.

  (f)  When social workers provide counseling services to families, couples, or groups, social workers should seek agreement among the parties involved concerning each individual's right to confidentiality and obligation to preserve the confidentiality of information shared by others. Social workers should inform participants in family, couples, or group counseling that social workers cannot guarantee that all participants will honor such agreements.

  (g)  Social workers should inform clients involved in family, couples, marital, or group counseling of the social worker's, employer's, and agency's policy concerning the social worker's disclosure of confidential information among the parties involved in the counseling.

  (h)  Social workers should not disclose confidential information to third-party payers unless clients have authorized such disclosure.

  (i)  Social workers should not discuss confidential information in any setting unless privacy can be ensured. Social workers should not discuss confidential information in public or semipublic areas such as hallways, waiting rooms, elevators, and restaurants.

                        ETHICAL STANDARDS IN SOCIAL WORK

(j) Social workers should protect the confidentiality of clients during legal proceedings to the extent permitted by law. When a court of law or other legally authorized body orders social workers to disclose confidential or privileged information without a client's consent and such disclosure could cause harm to the client, social workers should request that the court withdraw the order or limit the order as narrowly as possible or maintain the records under seal, unavailable for public inspection.

(k) Social workers should protect the confidentiality of clients when responding to requests from members of the media.

(l) Social workers should protect the confidentiality of clients' written and electronic records and other sensitive information. Social workers should take reasonable steps to ensure that clients' records are stored in a secure location and that clients' records are not available to others who are not authorized to have access.

(m) Social workers should take precautions to ensure and maintain the confidentiality of information transmitted to other parties through the use of computers, electronic mail, facsimile machines, telephones and telephone answering machines, and other electronic or computer technology. Disclosure of identifying information should be avoided whenever possible.

(n) Social workers should transfer or dispose of clients' records in a manner that protects clients' confidentiality and is consistent with state statutes governing records and social work licensure.

(o) Social workers should take reasonable precautions to protect client confidentiality in the event of the social worker's termination of practice, incapacitation, or death.

(p) Social workers should not disclose identifying information when discussing clients for teaching or training purposes unless the client has consented to disclosure of confidential information.

(q) Social workers should not disclose identifying information when discussing clients with consultants unless the client has consented to disclosure of confidential information or there is a compelling need for such disclosure.

(r) Social workers should protect the confidentiality of deceased clients consistent with the preceding standards.

### 1.08 Access to Records

(a) Social workers should provide clients with reasonable access to records concerning the clients. Social workers who are concerned that clients' access to their records could cause serious misunderstanding or harm to the client should provide assistance in interpreting the records and consultation with the client regarding the records. Social workers should limit clients' access to their records, or portions of their records, only in exceptional circumstances when there is compelling evidence that such access would cause serious harm to the client. Both clients' requests and the rationale for withholding some or all of the record should be documented in clients' files.

(b) When providing clients with access to their records, social workers should take steps to protect the confidentiality of other individuals identified or discussed in such records.

### 1.09 Sexual Relationships

(a) Social workers should under no circumstances engage in sexual activities or sexual contact with current clients, whether such contact is consensual or forced.

(b) Social workers should not engage in sexual activities or sexual contact with clients' relatives or other individuals with whom clients maintain a close personal relationship when there is a risk of exploitation or potential harm to the client. Sexual activity or sexual contact with clients' relatives or other individuals with whom clients maintain a personal relationship has the potential to be harmful to the client and may make it difficult for the social worker and client to maintain appropriate professional boundaries. Social workers—not their clients, their clients' relatives, or other individuals with whom the client maintains a personal relationship—assume the full burden for setting clear, appropriate, and culturally sensitive boundaries.

(c) Social workers should not engage in sexual activities or sexual contact with former clients because of the potential for harm to the client. If social workers engage in conduct contrary to this prohibition or claim that an exception to this prohibition is warranted because of extraordinary circumstances, it is social workers—not their clients—who assume the full burden of demonstrating that the former client has not been exploited, coerced, or manipulated, intentionally or unintentionally.

(d) Social workers should not provide clinical services to individuals with whom they have had a prior sexual relationship. Providing clinical services to a former sexual partner has the potential to be harmful to the individual and is likely to make it difficult for the social worker and individual to maintain appropriate professional boundaries.

### 1.10 Physical Contact

Social workers should not engage in physical contact with clients when there is a possibility of psychological harm to the client as a result of the contact (such as cradling or caressing clients). Social workers who engage in appropriate physical contact with clients are responsible for setting clear, appropriate, and culturally sensitive boundaries that govern such physical contact.

### 1.11 Sexual Harassment

Social workers should not sexually harass clients. Sexual harassment includes sexual advances, sexual solicitation, requests for sexual favors, and other verbal or physical conduct of a sexual nature.

## 1.12 Derogatory Language

Social workers should not use derogatory language in their written or verbal communications to or about clients. Social workers should use accurate and respectful language in all communications to and about clients.

## 1.13 Payment for Services

(a) When setting fees, social workers should ensure that the fees are fair, reasonable, and commensurate with the services performed. Consideration should be given to clients' ability to pay.

(b) Social workers should avoid accepting goods or services from clients as payment for professional services. Bartering arrangements, particularly involving services, create the potential for conflicts of interest, exploitation, and inappropriate boundaries in social workers' relationships with clients. Social workers should explore and may participate in bartering only in very limited circumstances when it can be demonstrated that such arrangements are an accepted practice among professionals in the local community, considered to be essential for the provision of services, negotiated without coercion, and entered into at the client's initiative and with the client's informed consent. Social workers who accept goods or services from clients as payment for professional services assume the full burden of demonstrating that this arrangement will not be detrimental to the client or the professional relationship.

(c) Social workers should not solicit a private fee or other remuneration for providing services to clients who are entitled to such available services through the social workers' employer or agency.

## 1.14 Clients Who Lack Decision-Making Capacity

When social workers act on behalf of clients who lack the capacity to make informed decisions, social workers should take reasonable steps to safeguard the interests and rights of those clients.

## 1.15 Interruption of Services

Social workers should make reasonable efforts to ensure continuity of services in the event that services are interrupted by factors such as unavailability, relocation, illness, disability, or death.

## 1.16 Termination of Services

(a) Social workers should terminate services to clients and professional relationships with them when such services and relationships are no longer required or no longer serve the clients' needs or interests.

(b) Social workers should take reasonable steps to avoid abandoning clients who are still in need of services. Social workers should withdraw services precipitously only under unusual circumstances, giving careful consideration to all factors in the situation and taking care to minimize possible adverse effects. Social workers should assist in making appropriate arrangements for continuation of services when necessary.

(c) Social workers in fee-for-service settings may terminate services to clients who are not paying an overdue balance if the financial contractual arrangements have been made clear to the client, if the client does not pose an imminent danger to self or others, and if the clinical and other consequences of the current nonpayment have been addressed and discussed with the client.

(d) Social workers should not terminate services to pursue a social, financial, or sexual relationship with a client.

(e) Social workers who anticipate the termination or interruption of services to clients should notify clients promptly and seek the transfer, referral, or continuation of services in relation to the clients' needs and preferences.

(f) Social workers who are leaving an employment setting should inform clients of appropriate options for the continuation of services and of the benefits and risks of the options.

## 2. SOCIAL WORKERS' ETHICAL RESPONSIBILITIES TO COLLEAGUES

### 2.01 Respect

(a) Social workers should treat colleagues with respect and should represent accurately and fairly the qualifications, views, and obligations of colleagues.

(b) Social workers should avoid unwarranted negative criticism of colleagues in communications with clients or with other professionals. Unwarranted negative criticism may include demeaning comments that refer to colleagues' level of competence or to individuals' attributes such as race, ethnicity, national origin, color, sex, sexual orientation, age, marital status, political belief, religion, and mental or physical disability.

(c) Social workers should cooperate with social work colleagues and with colleagues of other professions when such cooperation serves the well-being of clients.

### 2.02 Confidentiality

Social workers should respect confidential information shared by colleagues in the course of their professional relationships and transactions. Social workers should ensure that such colleagues understand social workers' obligation to respect confidentiality and any exceptions related to it.

### 2.03 Interdisciplinary Collaboration

(a) Social workers who are members of an interdisciplinary team should participate in and contribute to decisions that affect the well-being of clients by drawing on the perspectives, values, and experiences of the social work profession. Professional and ethical obligations of the interdisciplinary team as a whole and of its individual members should be clearly established.

(b) Social workers for whom a team decision raises ethical concerns should attempt to resolve the disagreement through appropriate channels. If the disagreement cannot be resolved, social workers should pursue other avenues to address their concerns consistent with client well-being.

### 2.04 Disputes Involving Colleagues

(a) Social workers should not take advantage of a dispute between a colleague and an employer to obtain a position or otherwise advance the social workers' own interests.

(b) Social workers should not exploit clients in disputes with colleagues or engage clients in any inappropriate discussion of conflicts between social workers and their colleagues.

### 2.05 Consultation

(a) Social workers should seek the advice and counsel of colleagues whenever such consultation is in the best interests of clients.

(b) Social workers should keep themselves informed about colleagues' areas of expertise and competencies. Social workers should seek consultation only from colleagues who have demonstrated knowledge, expertise, and competence related to the subject of the consultation.

(c) When consulting with colleagues about clients, social workers should disclose the least amount of information necessary to achieve the purposes of the consultation.

### 2.06 Referral for Services

(a) Social workers should refer clients to other professionals when the other professionals' specialized knowledge or expertise is needed to serve clients fully or when social workers believe that they are not being effective or making reasonable progress with clients and that additional service is required.

(b) Social workers who refer clients to other professionals should take appropriate steps to facilitate an orderly transfer of responsibility. Social workers who refer clients to other professionals should disclose, with clients' consent, all pertinent information to the new service providers.

(c) Social workers are prohibited from giving or receiving payment for a referral when no professional service is provided by the referring social worker.

### 2.07 Sexual Relationships

(a) Social workers who function as supervisors or educators should not engage in sexual activities or contact with supervisees, students, trainees, or other colleagues over whom they exercise professional authority.

(b) Social workers should avoid engaging in sexual relationships with colleagues when there is potential for a conflict of interest. Social workers who become involved in, or anticipate becoming involved in, a sexual relationship with a colleague have a duty to transfer professional responsibilities, when necessary, to avoid a conflict of interest.

## 2.08 Sexual Harassment

Social workers should not sexually harass supervisees, students, trainees, or colleagues. Sexual harassment includes sexual advances, sexual solicitation, requests for sexual favors, and other verbal or physical conduct of a sexual nature.

## 2.09 Impairment of Colleagues

(a) Social workers who have direct knowledge of a social work colleague's impairment that is due to personal problems, psychosocial distress, substance abuse, or mental health difficulties and that interferes with practice effectiveness should consult with that colleague when feasible and assist the colleague in taking remedial action.

(b) Social workers who believe that a social work colleague's impairment interferes with practice effectiveness and that the colleague has not taken adequate steps to address the impairment should take action through appropriate channels established by employers, agencies, NASW, licensing and regulatory bodies, and other professional organizations.

## 2.10 Incompetence of Colleagues

(a) Social workers who have direct knowledge of a social work colleague's incompetence should consult with that colleague when feasible and assist the colleague in taking remedial action.

(b) Social workers who believe that a social work colleague is incompetent and has not taken adequate steps to address the incompetence should take action through appropriate channels established by employers, agencies, NASW, licensing and regulatory bodies, and other professional organizations.

## 2.11 Unethical Conduct of Colleagues

(a) Social workers should take adequate measures to discourage, prevent, expose, and correct the unethical conduct of colleagues.

(b) Social workers should be knowledgeable about established policies and procedures for handling concerns about colleagues' unethical behavior. Social workers should be familiar with national, state, and local procedures for handling ethics complaints. These include policies and procedures created by NASW, licensing and regulatory bodies, employers, agencies, and other professional organizations.

(c) Social workers who believe that a colleague has acted unethically should seek resolution by discussing their concerns with the colleague when feasible and when such discussion is likely to be productive.

(d) When necessary, social workers who believe that a colleague has acted unethically should take action through appropriate formal channels (such as contacting a state licensing board or regulatory body, an NASW committee on inquiry, or other professional ethics committees).

(e) Social workers should defend and assist colleagues who are unjustly charged with unethical conduct.

## 3. SOCIAL WORKERS' ETHICAL RESPONSIBILITIES IN PRACTICE SETTINGS

### 3.01 Supervision and Consultation

(a) Social workers who provide supervision or consultation should have the necessary knowledge and skill to supervise or consult appropriately and should do so only within their areas of knowledge and competence.

(b) Social workers who provide supervision or consultation are responsible for setting clear, appropriate, and culturally sensitive boundaries.

(c) Social workers should not engage in any dual or multiple relationships with supervisees in which there is a risk of exploitation of or potential harm to the supervisee.

(d) Social workers who provide supervision should evaluate supervisees' performance in a manner that is fair and respectful.

### 3.02 Education and Training

(a) Social workers who function as educators, field instructors for students, or trainers should provide instruction only within their areas of knowledge and competence and should provide instruction based on the most current information and knowledge available in the profession.

(b) Social workers who function as educators or field instructors for students should evaluate students' performance in a manner that is fair and respectful.

(c) Social workers who function as educators or field instructors for students should take reasonable steps to ensure that clients are routinely informed when services are being provided by students.

(d) Social workers who function as educators or field instructors for students should not engage in any dual or multiple relationships with students in which there is a risk of exploitation or potential harm to the student. Social work educators and field instructors are responsible for setting clear, appropriate, and culturally sensitive boundaries.

### 3.03 Performance Evaluation

Social workers who have responsibility for evaluating the performance of others should fulfill such responsibility in a fair and considerate manner and on the basis of clearly stated criteria.

### 3.04 Client Records

(a) Social workers should take reasonable steps to ensure that documentation in records is accurate and reflects the services provided.

(b) Social workers should include sufficient and timely documentation in records to facilitate the delivery of services and to ensure continuity of services provided to clients in the future.

(c) Social workers' documentation should protect clients' privacy to the extent that is possible and appropriate and should include only information that is directly relevant to the delivery of services.

(d) Social workers should store records following the termination of services to ensure reasonable future access. Records should be maintained for the number of years required by state statutes or relevant contracts.

### 3.05 Billing

Social workers should establish and maintain billing practices that accurately reflect the nature and extent of services provided and that identify who provided the service in the practice setting.

### 3.06 Client Transfer

(a) When an individual who is receiving services from another agency or colleague contacts a social worker for services, the social worker should carefully consider the client's needs before agreeing to provide services. To minimize possible confusion and conflict, social workers should discuss with potential clients the nature of the clients' current relationship with other service providers and the implications, including possible benefits or risks, of entering into a relationship with a new service provider.

(b) If a new client has been served by another agency or colleague, social workers should discuss with the client whether consultation with the previous service provider is in the client's best interest.

### 3.07 Administration

(a) Social work administrators should advocate within and outside their agencies for adequate resources to meet clients' needs.

(b) Social workers should advocate for resource allocation procedures that are open and fair. When not all clients' needs can be met, an allocation procedure should be developed that is nondiscriminatory and based on appropriate and consistently applied principles.

(c) Social workers who are administrators should take reasonable steps to ensure that adequate agency or organizational resources are available to provide appropriate staff supervision.

(d) Social work administrators should take reasonable steps to ensure that the working environment for which they are responsible is consistent with and encourages compliance with the *NASW Code of Ethics*. Social work administrators should take reasonable steps to eliminate any conditions in their organizations that violate, interfere with, or discourage compliance with the *Code*.

### 3.08 Continuing Education and Staff Development

Social work administrators and supervisors should take reasonable steps to provide or arrange for continuing education and staff development for all staff for whom they are responsible. Continuing education and staff development should address current knowledge and emerging developments related to social work practice and ethics.

### 3.09 Commitments to Employers

(a) Social workers generally should adhere to commitments made to employers and employing organizations.

(b) Social workers should work to improve employing agencies' policies and procedures and the efficiency and effectiveness of their services.

(c) Social workers should take reasonable steps to ensure that employers are aware of social workers' ethical obligations as set forth in the *NASW Code of Ethics* and of the implications of those obligations for social work practice.

(d) Social workers should not allow an employing organization's policies, procedures, regulations, or administrative orders to interfere with their ethical practice of social work. Social workers should take reasonable steps to ensure that their employing organizations' practices are consistent with the *NASW Code of Ethics*.

(e) Social workers should act to prevent and eliminate discrimination in the employing organization's work assignments and in its employment policies and practices.

(f) Social workers should accept employment or arrange student field placements only in organizations that exercise fair personnel practices.

(g) Social workers should be diligent stewards of the resources of their employing organizations, wisely conserving funds where appropriate and never misappropriating funds or using them for unintended purposes.

### 3.10 Labor–Management Disputes

(a) Social workers may engage in organized action, including the formation of and participation in labor unions, to improve services to clients and working conditions.

(b) The actions of social workers who are involved in labor–management disputes, job actions, or labor strikes should be guided by the profession's values, ethical principles, and ethical standards. Reasonable differences of opinion exist among social workers concerning their primary obligation as professionals during an actual or threatened labor strike or job action. Social workers should carefully examine relevant issues and their possible impact on clients before deciding on a course of action.

# 4. SOCIAL WORKERS' ETHICAL RESPONSIBILITIES AS PROFESSIONALS

## 4.01 Competence

(a) Social workers should accept responsibility or employment only on the basis of existing competence or the intention to acquire the necessary competence.

(b) Social workers should strive to become and remain proficient in professional practice and the performance of professional functions. Social workers should critically examine and keep current with emerging knowledge relevant to social work. Social workers should routinely review the professional literature and participate in continuing education relevant to social work practice and social work ethics.

(c) Social workers should base practice on recognized knowledge, including empirically based knowledge, relevant to social work and social work ethics.

## 4.02 Discrimination

Social workers should not practice, condone, facilitate, or collaborate with any form of discrimination on the basis of race, ethnicity, national origin, color, sex, sexual orientation, age, marital status, political belief, religion, or mental or physical disability.

## 4.03 Private Conduct

Social workers should not permit their private conduct to interfere with their ability to fulfill their professional responsibilities.

## 4.04 Dishonesty, Fraud, and Deception

Social workers should not participate in, condone, or be associated with dishonesty, fraud, or deception.

## 4.05 Impairment

(a) Social workers should not allow their own personal problems, psychosocial distress, legal problems, substance abuse, or mental health difficulties to interfere with their professional judgment and performance or to jeopardize the best interests of people for whom they have a professional responsibility.

(b) Social workers whose personal problems, psychosocial distress, legal problems, substance abuse, or mental health difficulties interfere with their professional judgment and performance should immediately seek consultation and take appropriate remedial action by seeking professional help, making adjustments in workload, terminating practice, or taking any other steps necessary to protect clients and others.

### 4.06 Misrepresentation

(a) Social workers should make clear distinctions between statements made and actions engaged in as a private individual and as a representative of the social work profession, a professional social work organization, or the social worker's employing agency.

(b) Social workers who speak on behalf of professional social work organizations should accurately represent the official and authorized positions of the organizations.

(c) Social workers should ensure that their representations to clients, agencies, and the public of professional qualifications, credentials, education, competence, affiliations, services provided, or results to be achieved are accurate. Social workers should claim only those relevant professional credentials they actually possess and take steps to correct any inaccuracies or misrepresentations of their credentials by others.

### 4.07 Solicitations

(a) Social workers should not engage in uninvited solicitation of potential clients who, because of their circumstances, are vulnerable to undue influence, manipulation, or coercion.

(b) Social workers should not engage in solicitation of testimonial endorsements (including solicitation of consent to use a client's prior statement as a testimonial endorsement) from current clients or from other people who, because of their particular circumstances, are vulnerable to undue influence.

### 4.08 Acknowledging Credit

(a) Social workers should take responsibility and credit, including authorship credit, only for work they have actually performed and to which they have contributed.

(b) Social workers should honestly acknowledge the work of and the contributions made by others.

## 5. SOCIAL WORKERS' ETHICAL RESPONSIBILITIES TO THE SOCIAL WORK PROFESSION

### 5.01 Integrity of the Profession

(a) Social workers should work toward the maintenance and promotion of high standards of practice.

(b) Social workers should uphold and advance the values, ethics, knowledge, and mission of the profession. Social workers should protect, enhance, and improve the integrity of the profession through appropriate study and research, active discussion, and responsible criticism of the profession.

(c) Social workers should contribute time and professional expertise to activities that promote respect for the value, integrity, and competence of the social work profession. These activities may include teaching, research, consultation, service, legislative testimony, presentations in the community, and participation in their professional organizations.

(d) Social workers should contribute to the knowledge base of social work and share with colleagues their knowledge related to practice, research, and ethics. Social workers should seek to contribute to the profession's literature and to share their knowledge at professional meetings and conferences.

(e) Social workers should act to prevent the unauthorized and unqualified practice of social work.

## 5.02 Evaluation and Research

(a) Social workers should monitor and evaluate policies, the implementation of programs, and practice interventions.

(b) Social workers should promote and facilitate evaluation and research to contribute to the development of knowledge.

(c) Social workers should critically examine and keep current with emerging knowledge relevant to social work and fully use evaluation and research evidence in their professional practice.

(d) Social workers engaged in evaluation or research should carefully consider possible consequences and should follow guidelines developed for the protection of evaluation and research participants. Appropriate institutional review boards should be consulted.

(e) Social workers engaged in evaluation or research should obtain voluntary and written informed consent from participants, when appropriate, without any implied or actual deprivation or penalty for refusal to participate; without undue inducement to participate; and with due regard for participants' well-being, privacy, and dignity. Informed consent should include information about the nature, extent, and duration of the participation requested and disclosure of the risks and benefits of participation in the research.

(f) When evaluation or research participants are incapable of giving informed consent, social workers should provide an appropriate explanation to the participants, obtain the participants' assent to the extent they are able, and obtain written consent from an appropriate proxy.

(g) Social workers should never design or conduct evaluation or research that does not use consent procedures, such as certain forms of naturalistic observation and archival research, unless rigorous and responsible review of the research has found it to be justified because of its prospective scientific, educational, or applied value and unless equally effective alternative procedures that do not involve waiver of consent are not feasible.

(h) Social workers should inform participants of their right to withdraw from evaluation and research at any time without penalty.

(i) Social workers should take appropriate steps to ensure that participants in evaluation and research have access to appropriate supportive services.

(j) Social workers engaged in evaluation or research should protect participants from unwarranted physical or mental distress, harm, danger, or deprivation.

(k) Social workers engaged in the evaluation of services should discuss collected information only for professional purposes and only with people professionally concerned with this information.

(l) Social workers engaged in evaluation or research should ensure the anonymity or confidentiality of participants and of the data obtained from them. Social workers should inform participants of any limits of confidentiality, the measures that will be taken to ensure confidentiality, and when any records containing research data will be destroyed.

(m) Social workers who report evaluation and research results should protect participants' confidentiality by omitting identifying information unless proper consent has been obtained authorizing disclosure.

(n) Social workers should report evaluation and research findings accurately. They should not fabricate or falsify results and should take steps to correct any errors later found in published data using standard publication methods.

(o) Social workers engaged in evaluation or research should be alert to and avoid conflicts of interest and dual relationships with participants, should inform participants when a real or potential conflict of interest arises, and should take steps to resolve the issue in a manner that makes participants' interests primary.

(p) Social workers should educate themselves, their students, and their colleagues about responsible research practices.

## 6. SOCIAL WORKERS' ETHICAL RESPONSIBILITIES TO THE BROADER SOCIETY

### 6.01 Social Welfare

Social workers should promote the general welfare of society, from local to global levels, and the development of people, their communities, and their environments. Social workers should advocate for living conditions conducive to the fulfillment of basic human needs and should promote social, economic, political, and cultural values and institutions that are compatible with the realization of social justice.

### 6.02 Public Participation

Social workers should facilitate informed participation by the public in shaping social policies and institutions.

### 6.03 Public Emergencies

Social workers should provide appropriate professional services in public emergencies to the greatest extent possible.

### 6.04 Social and Political Action

(a) Social workers should engage in social and political action that seeks to ensure that all people have equal access to the resources, employment, services, and opportunities they require to meet their basic human needs and to develop fully. Social workers should be aware of the impact of the political arena on practice and should advocate for changes in policy and legislation to improve social conditions in order to meet basic human needs and promote social justice.

(b) Social workers should act to expand choice and opportunity for all people, with special regard for vulnerable, disadvantaged, oppressed, and exploited people and groups.

(c) Social workers should promote conditions that encourage respect for cultural and social diversity within the United States and globally. Social workers should promote policies and practices that demonstrate respect for difference, support the expansion of cultural knowledge and resources, advocate for programs and institutions that demonstrate cultural competence, and promote policies that safeguard the rights of and confirm equity and social justice for all people.

(d) Social workers should act to prevent and eliminate domination of, exploitation of, and discrimination against any person, group, or class on the basis of race, ethnicity, national origin, color, sex, sexual orientation, age, marital status, political belief, religion, or mental or physical disability.

# REFERENCES

Alexander, R., Jr. (1997). Social workers and privileged communication in the federal legal system. *Social Work, 42*, 387–391.

Americans with Disabilities Act of 1990, P.L. 101-336, 104 Stat. 327.

Appelbaum, P. S., Lidz, C. W., & Meisel, A. (1987). *Informed consent: Legal theory and clinical practice*. New York: Oxford University Press.

Asch, A., & Mudrick, N. R. (1995). Disability. In R. L. Edwards (Ed.-in-Chief), *Encyclopedia of social work* (19th ed., Vol. 1, pp. 752–761). Washington, DC: NASW Press.

Atherton, C. R., & Klemmack, D. L. (1982). *Research methods in social work*. Lexington, MA: D. C. Heath.

Austin, K. M., Moline, M. E., & Williams, G. T. (1990). *Confronting malpractice: Legal and ethical dilemmas in psychotherapy*. Newbury Park, CA: Sage Publications.

Balgopal, P. R. (1995). Asian Americans overview. In R. L. Edwards (Ed.-in-Chief), *Encyclopedia of social work* (19th ed., Vol. 1, pp. 231–237). Washington, DC: NASW Press.

Barker, R. L. (1995). *The social work dictionary* (3rd ed.). Washington, DC: NASW Press.

Barker, R. L., & Branson, D. M. (1993). *Forensic social work*. New York: Haworth Press.

Barry, V. (1986). *Moral issues in business* (3rd ed.). Belmont, CA: Wadsworth.

Bayles, M. (1986). Professional power and self-regulation. *Business and Professional Ethics Journal, 5*, 26–46.

Bayles, M. D. (1981). *Professional ethics*. Belmont, CA: Wadsworth.

Beauchamp, T. L. (1982). *Philosophical ethics: An introduction to moral philosophy*. New York: McGraw-Hill.

Beckett, J. O., & Johnson, H. C. (1995). Human development. In R. L. Edwards (Ed.-in-Chief), *Encyclopedia of social work* (19th ed., Vol. 2, pp. 1385–1405). Washington, DC: NASW Press.

Beeman, S. K. (1997). Reconceptualizing social support and its relationship to child neglect. *Social Service Review, 71*, 421–440.

Berger, R. M., & Kelly, J. J. (1995). Gay men overview. In R. L. Edwards (Ed.-in-Chief), *Encyclopedia of social work* (19th ed., Vol. 2, pp. 1064–1075). Washington, DC: NASW Press.

Bernstein, S. (1960). Self-determination: King or citizen in the realm of values? *Social Work, 5*(1), 3–8.

Besharov, D. J. (1985). *The vulnerable social worker: Liability for serving children and families*. Silver Spring, MD: National Association of Social Workers.

Billups, J. O. (1992). The moral basis for a radical reconstruction of social work. In P. N. Reid & P. R. Popple (Eds.), *The moral purposes of social work* (pp. 100–119). Chicago: Nelson-Hall.

Black, R. B. (1994). Diversity and populations at risk: People with disabilities. In F. G. Reamer (Ed.), *The foundations of social work knowledge* (pp. 393–416). New York: Columbia University Press.

Bloom, M., & Fischer, J. (1982). *Evaluating practice: Guidelines for the accountable professional*. Englewood Cliffs, NJ: Prentice Hall.

Bohr, R. H., Brenner, H. I., & Kaplan, H. M. (1971). Value conflicts in a hospital walkout. *Social Work, 16*, 33–42.

Boyd-Franklin, N. (1989). *Black families in therapy*. New York: Guilford Press.

Brennan, J. W. (1995). A short-term psychoeducational multiple-family group for bipolar patients and their families. *Social Work, 40*, 737–743.

Bricker-Jenkins, M., & Gottlieb, N. (Eds.). (1991). *Feminist social work practice in clinical settings*. Newbury Park, CA: Sage Publications.

Bricker-Jenkins, M., & Hooyman, N. (1984). Feminist pedagogy in education for social change. *Feminist Teacher, 2*(2), 36–42.

Brown v. Board of Education of Topeka, Kansas, 347 U.S. 483, 74 S. Ct. 686 (1954).

Buchanan, A. E., & Brock, D. W. (1989). *Deciding for others: The ethics of surrogate decision making*. Cambridge, England: Cambridge University Press.

Bullis, R. K. (1995). *Clinical social worker misconduct*. Chicago: Nelson-Hall.

Callahan, D., & Bok, S. (Eds.). (1980). *Ethics teaching in higher education*. New York: Plenum Press.

Campbell, C. S. (1991). Ethics and militant AIDS activism. In F. G. Reamer (Ed.), *AIDS and ethics* (pp. 155–187). New York: Columbia University Press.

Chau, K. (1991). Social work with ethnic minorities: Practice issues and potentials. *Journal of Multicultural Social Work, 1*(1), 29–39.

Chestang, L. (1972). *Character development in a hostile environment* (Occasional Paper No. 3). Chicago: University of Chicago, School of Social Service Administration.

Childress, J. F. (1971). *Civil disobedience and political obligation: A study in Christian social ethics*. New Haven, CT: Yale University Press.

Childress, J. F. (1986). Civil disobedience. In J. F. Childress & J. Macquarrie (Eds.), *The Westminster dictionary of Christian ethics* (pp. 94–95). Philadelphia: Westminster Press.

Civil Rights Act of 1957, P.L. 85-315, 71 Stat. 634.

Civil Rights Act of 1964, P.L. 88-352, 78 Stat. 241.

Civil Rights Act of 1991, P.L. 102-166, 105 Stat. 1071.

Cloward, R. A., & Piven, F. F. (1995). Voter registration. In R. L. Edwards (Ed.-in-Chief), *Encyclopedia of social work* (19th ed., Vol. 3, pp. 2491–2498). Washington, DC: NASW Press.

Cohen, C. B. (1988). Ethics committees. *Hastings Center Report, 18*, 11.

Cohen, R. J. (1979). *Malpractice: A guide for mental health professionals*. New York: Free Press.

Cohen, R. J., & Mariano, W. E. (1982). *Legal guidebook in mental health*. New York: Free Press.

Cole, E. P. (1977). Unions in social work. In J. B. Turner (Ed.-in-Chief), *Encyclopedia of social work* (17th ed., Vol. 2, pp. 1559–1563). Washington, DC: National Association of Social Workers.

Compton, B. R., & Galaway, B. (1994). *Social work processes* (5th ed.). Belmont, CA: Brooks/Cole.

Conrad, A. P. (1989). Developing an ethics review process in a social service agency. *Social Thought, 15*(3–4), 102–115.

Conte, A. (1990). *Sexual harassment in the workplace: Law and practice*. New York: John Wiley & Sons.

Council on Social Work Education. (1992). *CSWE curriculum policy statements*. Alexandria, VA: Author.

Council on Social Work Education. (1994). *CSWE curriculum policy statements* (rev. ed.). Alexandria, VA: Author.

Cowles, J. (1976). *Informed consent*. New York: Coward, McCann & Geoghegan.

Cranford, R. E., & Doudera, E. (Eds.). (1984). *Institutional ethics committees and health care decision making*. Ann Arbor, MI: Health Administration Press.

Curtis, G. C. (1996). The scientific evaluation of new claims. *Research on Social Work Practice, 6*, 117–121.

Davis, L. E., & Proctor, E. K. (1989). *Race, gender, and class: Guidelines for practice with individuals, families, and groups*. Englewood Cliffs, NJ: Prentice Hall.

Deutsch, C. (1985). A survey of therapists' personal problems and treatment. *Professional Psychology: Research and Practice, 16*, 305–315.

Devore, W., & Schlesinger, E. G. (1987). *Ethnic-sensitive social work practice* (2nd ed.). Columbus, OH: Charles E. Merrill.

Dickson, D. T. (1995). *Law in the health and human services*. New York: Free Press.

Dickson, D. T. (1998). *Confidentiality and privacy in social work*. New York: Free Press.

Dworkin, G. (1971). Paternalism. In R. A. Wasserstrom (Ed.), *Morality and the law* (pp. 107–126). Belmont, CA: Wadsworth.

Dworkin, R. (1981). What is equality? Part 2: Equality of resources. *Philosophy and Public Affairs, 10*, 283–345.

Education for All Handicapped Children Act of 1975, P.L. 94-142, 89 Stat. 773.

Fausel, D. F. (1988). Helping the helper heal: Co-dependency in helping professionals. *Journal of Independent Social Work, 3*(2), 35–45.

Figueira-McDonough, J. (1995). Abortion. In R. L. Edwards (Ed.-in-Chief), *Encyclopedia of social work* (19th ed., Vol. 1, pp. 7–15). Washington, DC: NASW Press.

Fisher, D. (1987). Problems for social work in a strike situation: Professional, ethical, and value considerations. *Social Work, 32*, 252–254.

Fisher, J. (1980). *The response of social work to the Depression*. Cambridge, MA: Schenkman.

Fletcher, J. (1986). The goals of ethics consultation. *Biolaw, 2*, 36–47.

Fletcher, J. C., Quist, N., & Jonsen, A. R. (1989). *Ethics consultation in health care*. Ann Arbor, MI: Health Administration Press.

Flexner, A. (1915). Is social work a profession? In *Proceedings of the National Conference of Charities and Correction* (pp. 576–590). Chicago: Hildman.

Foster, L. W. (1995). Bioethical issues. In R. L. Edwards (Ed.-in-Chief), *Encyclopedia of social work* (19th ed., Vol. 1, pp. 292–298). Washington, DC: NASW Press.

Francis, D. D., & Chin, J. (1987). The prevention of acquired immunodeficiency syndrome in the United States. *JAMA, 257*, 1357–1366.

Frankena, W. K. (1973). *Ethics* (2nd ed.). Englewood Cliffs, NJ: Prentice Hall.

Freedom of Information Act, P.L. 89-487, 80 Stat. 250.

Freeman, E. M. (1990). The black family's life cycle: Operationalizing a strengths perspective. In S.M.L. Logan, E. M. Freeman, & R. G. McRoy (Eds.), *Social work practice with black families* (pp. 55–72). New York: Longman.

Freudenberger, H. J. (1986). Chemical abuse among psychologists: Symptoms, causes, and treatment issues. In R. R. Kilburg, P. E. Nathan, & R. W. Thoreson (Eds.), *Professionals in distress: Issues, syndromes, and solutions in psychology* (pp. 135–138). Washington, DC: American Psychological Association.

Frumkin, M., & Lloyd, G. A. (1995). Social work education. In R. L. Edwards (Ed.-in-Chief), *Encyclopedia of social work* (19th ed., Vol. 3, pp. 2238–2247). Washington, DC: NASW Press.

Gamble, D. N., & Weil, M. O. (1995). Citizen participation. In R. L. Edwards (Ed.-in-Chief), *Encyclopedia of social work* (19th ed., Vol. 1, pp. 483–494). Washington, DC: NASW Press.

Gambrill, E., & Pruger, R. (Eds.). (1997). *Controversial issues in social work ethics, values, and obligations*. Needham Heights, MA: Allyn & Bacon.

Germain, C. B., & Gitterman, A. (1980). *The life model of social work practice*. New York: Columbia University Press.

Gewirth, A. (1978). *Reason and morality*. Chicago: University of Chicago Press.

Gideon v. Wainwright, 83 S. Ct. 792 (1963).

Gifis, S. H. (Ed.). (1991). *Law dictionary* (3rd ed.). Hauppauge, NY: Barron's.

Gil, D. G. (1994). Confronting social injustice and oppression. In F. G. Reamer (Ed.), *The foundations of social work knowledge* (pp. 231–263). New York: Columbia University Press.

Gil, D. G. (1998). *Confronting injustice and oppression: Concepts and strategies for social workers*. New York: Columbia University Press.

Gillespie, D. F. (1995). Ethical issues in research. In R. L. Edwards (Ed.-in-Chief), *Encyclopedia of social work* (19th ed., Vol. 1, pp. 884–893). Washington, DC: NASW Press.

Gorovitz, S. (Ed.). (1971). *Mill: Utilitarianism*. Indianapolis: Bobbs-Merrill.

Gottlieb, N. (1995). Women overview. In R. L. Edwards (Ed.-in-Chief), *Encyclopedia of social work* (19th ed., Vol. 3, pp. 2518–2529). Washington, DC: NASW Press.

Gray, L. A., & Harding, K. (1988). Confidentiality limits with clients who have the AIDS virus. *Journal of Counseling and Development, 66*, 219–223.

Green, J. (Ed.). (1982). *Cultural awareness in the human services*. Englewood Cliffs, NJ: Prentice Hall.

Greenwood, E. (1957). Attributes of a profession. *Social Work, 2*(3), 45–55.

Grinnell, R. M., Jr. (Ed.). (1981). *Social work research and evaluation*. Itasca, IL: F. E. Peacock.

Grinnell, R. M., Jr. (Ed.). (1997). *Social work research and evaluation* (5th ed.). Itasca, IL: F. E. Peacock.

Grossman, M. (1978). Confidentiality: The right to privacy versus the right to know. In W. E. Barton & C. J. Sanborn (Eds.), *Law and the mental health professions* (p. 137). New York: International Universities Press.

Gutierrez, L. (1990). Working with women of color: An empowerment perspective. *Social Work, 35*, 149–153.

Guy, J. D., Poelstra, P. L., & Stark, M. (1989). Personal distress and therapeutic effectiveness: National survey of psychologists practicing psychotherapy. *Professional Psychology: Research and Practice, 20*, 48–50.

Hall, R. H. (1968). Professionalization and bureaucratization. *American Sociological Review, 33*, 92–104.

Harrison, W. D. (1995). Community development. In R. L. Edwards (Ed.-in-Chief), *Encyclopedia of social work* (19th ed., Vol. 1, pp. 555–562). Washington, DC: NASW Press.

Hartman, A. (1994). Social work practice. In F. G. Reamer (Ed.), *The foundations of social work knowledge* (pp. 13–50). New York: Columbia University Press.

Haynes, K., & Mickelson, J. (1991). *Affecting change: Social workers in the political arena* (2nd ed.). New York: Longman.

Healy, L. M. (1995). International social welfare: Organizations and activities. In R. L. Edwards (Ed.-in-Chief), *Encyclopedia of social work* (19th ed., Vol. 2, pp. 1499–1510). Washington, DC: NASW Press.

Hidalgo, H., Peterson, T., & Woodman, N. (Eds.). (1985). *Lesbian and gay issues: A resource manual for social workers*. Silver Spring, MD: National Association of Social Workers.

Ho, M. K. (1987). *Family therapy with ethnic minorities*. Newbury Park, CA: Sage Publications.

Hogan, D. B. (1979). *The regulation of psychotherapists: Volume I—A study in the philosophy and practice of professional regulation*. Cambridge, MA: Ballinger.

Hokenstad, M. C., & Kendall, K. A. (1995). International social work education. In R. L. Edwards (Ed.-in-Chief), *Encyclopedia of social work* (19th ed., Vol. 2, pp. 1511–1520). Washington, DC: NASW Press.

Hooyman, N. R. (1994). Diversity and populations at risk: Women. In F. G. Reamer (Ed.), *The foundations of social work knowledge* (pp. 309–345). New York: Columbia University Press.

Hopps, J. G., & Collins, P. M. (1995). Social work profession overview. In R. L. Edwards (Ed.-in-Chief), *Encyclopedia of social work* (19th ed., Vol. 3, pp. 2266–2281). Washington, DC: NASW Press.

Houston-Vega, M. K., Nuehring, E. M., & Daguio, E. R. (1997). *Prudent practice: A guide for managing malpractice risk*. Washington, DC: NASW Press.

Jacobs, C., & Bowles, D. D. (Eds.). (1988). *Ethnicity and race: Critical concepts in social work*. Silver Spring, MD: National Association of Social Workers.

Jaffe v. Redmond, 116 S. Ct. 1923 (1996).

Jamal, K., & Bowie, N. (1995). Theoretical considerations for a meaningful code of ethics. *Journal of Business Ethics, 14*, 703–714.

Jayaratne, S., & Chess, W. A. (1984). Job satisfaction, burnout, and turnover: A national study. *Social Work, 29*, 448–455.

Jayaratne, S., & Levy, R. (1979). *Empirical clinical practice*. New York: Columbia University Press.

Johnson, A. (1955). Educating professional social workers for ethical practice. *Social Service Review, 29*(2), 125–136.

Johnson, M., & Stone, G. L. (1986). Social workers and burnout. *Journal of Social Work Research, 10*, 67–80.

Jones, R. M. (1995). The price of welfare dependency: Children pay. *Social Work, 40*, 496–505.

Joseph, M. V. (1989). Social work ethics. Historical and contemporary perspectives. *Social Thought, 15*(3–4), 4–17.

Kadushin, A. (1976). *Supervision in social work*. New York: Columbia University Press.

Kadushin, A. (1977). *Consultation in social work*. New York: Columbia University Press.

Kadushin, A. (1992). *Supervision in social work* (3rd ed). New York: Columbia University Press.

Kagle, J. D. (1991). *Social work records* (3rd ed.). Belmont, CA: Wadsworth.

Kagle, J. D. (1995). Recording. In R. L. Edwards (Ed.-in-Chief), *Encyclopedia of social work* (19th ed., Vol. 3, pp. 2027–2033). Washington, DC: NASW Press.

Kagle, J. D., & Giebelhausen, P. N. (1994). Dual relationships and professional boundaries. *Social Work, 39*, 213–220.

Kain, C. D. (1988). To breach or not to breach: Is that the question? *Journal of Counseling and Development, 66*, 224–225.

Karger, H. J. (Ed.). (1988). *Social workers and labor unions.* Westport, CT: Greenwood Press.

Kass, L. R. (1990). Practicing ethics: Where's the action? *Hastings Center Report, 20*(1), 5–12.

Keith-Lucas, A. (1963). A critique of the principle of client self-determination. *Social Work, 8*(3), 66–71.

Keith-Lucas, A. (1977). Ethics in social work. In J. B. Turner (Ed.-in-Chief), *Encyclopedia of social work* (17th ed., Vol. 1, pp. 350–355). Washington, DC: National Association of Social Workers.

Kilburg, R. R., Kaslow, F. W., & VandenBos, G. R. (1988). Professionals in distress. *Hospital and Community Psychiatry, 39*, 723–725.

Kilburg, R. R., Nathan, P. E., & Thoreson, R. W. (Eds.). (1986). *Professionals in distress: Issues, syndromes, and solutions in psychology.* Washington, DC: American Psychological Association.

Koeske, G. F., & Koeske, R. D. (1989). Work load and burnout: Can social support and perceived accomplishment help? *Social Work, 34*, 243–248.

Kopels, S., & Kagle, J. D. (1993). Do social workers have a duty to warn? *Social Service Review, 67*, 101–126.

Krouse, R., & McPherson, M. (1988). Capitalism: "Property-owning democracy" and the welfare state. In A. Gutmann (Ed.), *Democracy and the welfare state* (pp. 79–105). Princeton, NJ: Princeton University Press.

Kultgen, J. (1982). The ideological use of professional codes. *Business and Professional Ethics Journal, 1*, 53–69.

Lamb, D. H., Clark, C., Drumheller, P., Frizzell, K., & Surrey, L. (1989). Applying *Tarasoff* to AIDS-related psychotherapy issues. *Professional Psychology: Research and Practice, 20*, 37–43.

Lamb, D. H., Presser, N. R., Pfost, K. S., Baum, M. C., Jackson, V. R., & Jarvis, P. A. (1987). Confronting professional impairment during the internship: Identification, due process, and remediation. *Professional Psychology: Research and Practice, 18*, 597–603.

Landers, S. (1992, October). Ethical boundaries easily trespassed. *NASW News,* p. 3.

La Puma, J., & Schiedermayer, D. L. (1991). Ethics consultation: Skills, roles, and training. *Annals of Internal Medicine, 114*, 155–160.

Leashore, B. R. (1995). African Americans overview. In R. L. Edwards (Ed.-in-Chief), *Encyclopedia of social work* (19th ed., Vol. 1, pp. 101–115). Washington, DC: NASW Press.

Leiby, J. (1978). *A history of social work and social welfare in the United States.* New York: Columbia University Press.

Levine, C. (1991). AIDS and the ethics of human subjects research. In F. G. Reamer (Ed.), *AIDS and ethics* (pp. 77–104). New York: Columbia University Press.

Levy, C. S. (1972). The context of social work ethics. *Social Work, 17*, 488–493.

Levy, C. S. (1973). The value base of social work. *Journal of Education for Social Work, 9*(1), 34–42.

Levy, C. S. (1976). *Social work ethics.* New York: Human Sciences Press.

Lewis, M. B. (1986). Duty to warn versus duty to maintain confidentiality: Conflicting demands on mental health professionals. *Suffolk Law Review, 20*(3), 579–615.

Lewis, R. G. (1995). American Indians. In R. L. Edwards (Ed.-in-Chief), *Encyclopedia of social work* (19th ed., Vol. 1, pp. 216–225). Washington, DC: NASW Press.

Lightman, E. S. (1983). Social workers, strikes, and service to clients. *Social Work*, 28, 142–148.

Lindeman, E. (1947). *Social work matures in a confused world*. Albany: New York State Conference on Social Workers.

Lister, L. (1987). Curriculum building in social work education: The example of ethnocultural content. *Journal of Social Work Education*, 23(1), 31–39.

Loewenberg, F., & Dolgoff, R. (1996). *Ethical decisions for social work practice* (5th ed.). Itasca, IL: F. E. Peacock.

Logan, M. L., Freeman, E. M., & McRoy, R. G. (Eds.). (1990). *Social work practice with families*. New York: Longman.

Longres, J. (1991). Toward a status model of ethnic sensitive practice. *Journal of Multicultural Social Work*, 1(1), 41–56.

Longres, J. F. (1995). Hispanics overview. In R. L. Edwards (Ed.-in-Chief), *Encyclopedia of social work* (19th ed., Vol. 2, pp. 1214–1222). Washington, DC: NASW Press.

Lubove, R. (1965). *The professional altruist: The emergence of social work as a career*. Cambridge, MA: Harvard University Press.

Lum, D. (1986). *Social work practice and people of color*. Monterey, CA: Brooks/Cole.

Lum, D. (1992). *Social work practice and people of color* (2nd ed.). Belmont, CA: Brooks/Cole.

Mahaffey, M. (1987). Political action in social work. In A. Minahan (Ed.-in-Chief), *Encyclopedia of social work* (18th ed., Vol. 2, pp. 283–293). Silver Spring, MD: National Association of Social Workers.

Mahaffey, M., & Hanks, J. (Eds.). (1982). *Practical politics*. Washington, DC: National Association of Social Workers.

McCann, C. W., & Cutler, J. P. (1979). Ethics and the alleged unethical. *Social Work*, 24, 5–8.

McDermott, F. E. (Ed.). (1975). *Self-determination in social work*. London: Routledge & Kegan Paul.

McMahon, M. O. (1992). Responding to the call. In P. N. Reid & P. R. Popple (Eds.), *The moral purposes of social work* (pp. 173–188). Chicago: Nelson-Hall.

Meyer, R. G., Landis, E. R., & Hays, J. R. (1988). *Law for the psychotherapist*. New York: W. W. Norton.

Mickelson, J. S. (1995). Advocacy. In R. L. Edwards (Ed.-in-Chief), *Encyclopedia of social work* (19th ed., Vol. 1, pp. 95–100). Washington, DC: NASW Press.

Midgley, J. (1995). International and comparative social welfare. In R. L. Edwards (Ed.-in-Chief), *Encyclopedia of social work* (19th ed., Vol. 2, pp. 1490–1499). Washington, DC: NASW Press.

Miller, I. (1987). Supervision in social work. In A. Minahan (Ed.-in-Chief), *Encyclopedia of social work* (18th ed., Vol. 2, pp. 748–756). Silver Spring, MD: National Association of Social Workers.

Millon, T., Millon, C., & Antoni, M. (1986). Sources of emotional and mental disorder among psychologists: A career development perspective. In R. R. Kilburg, P. E. Nathan, & R. W. Thoreson (Eds.), *Professionals in distress: Issues, syndromes, and solutions in psychology* (p. 119). Washington, DC: American Psychological Association.

Mullen, E. J., & Magnabosco, J. L. (Eds.). (1997). *Outcomes measurement in the human services*. Washington, DC: NASW Press.

Myers, L., & Thyer, B. A. (1997). Should social work clients have the right to effective treatment? *Social Work, 42,* 288–298.

National Association of Social Workers. (1960). *NASW code of ethics.* Washington, DC: Author.

National Association of Social Workers. (1967). *NASW code of ethics.* Washington, DC: Author.

National Association of Social Workers. (1979). *NASW code of ethics.* Silver Spring, MD: Author.

National Association of Social Workers. (1981). *NASW standards for social work practice in child protection.* Washington, DC: Author.

National Association of Social Workers. (1989). *NASW standards for the practice of clinical social work.* Washington, DC: Author.

National Association of Social Workers. (1991). *NASW standards for social work personnel practices.* Washington, DC: Author.

National Association of Social Workers. (1992). *NASW standards for school social work services.* Washington, DC: Author.

National Association of Social Workers. (1993). *NASW standards for the practice of social work with adolescents.* Washington, DC: Author.

National Association of Social Workers. (1994a). *Guidelines for clinical social work supervision.* Washington, DC: Author.

National Association of Social Workers. (1994b). *NASW procedures for the adjudication of grievances* (3rd ed.). Washington, DC: Author.

National Association of Social Workers. (1996). *NASW code of ethics.* Washington, DC: Author.

National Association of Social Workers, Ad Hoc Committee on Advocacy. (1969). The social worker as advocate: Champion of social victims. *Social Work, 14*(2), 19.

National Association of Social Workers, Commission on Employment and Economic Support. (1987). *Impaired social worker program resource book.* Silver Spring, MD: Author.

National Commission for the Protection of Human Subjects of Biomedical and Behavioral Research. (1978). *The Belmont Report: Ethical principles and guidelines for the protection of human subjects of research.* Washington, DC: Author.

National Voter Registration Act of 1993, P.L. 103-31, 107 Stat. 77.

Newman, B. S. (1994). Diversity and populations at risk: Gays and lesbians. In F. G. Reamer (Ed.), *The foundations of social work knowledge* (pp. 346–392). New York: Columbia University Press.

Orcutt, B. A. (1990). *Science and inquiry in social work practice.* New York: Columbia University Press.

Palca, J. (1996). Scientific misconduct: Ill-defined, redefined. *Hastings Center Report, 26*(5), 4.

Perlman, H. H. (1965). Self-determination: Reality or illusion? *Social Service Review, 39,* 410–421.

Pernick, M. S. (1982). The patient's role in medical decisionmaking: A social history of informed consent in medical therapy. In President's Commission for the Study of Ethical Problems in Medicine and Biomedical and Behavioral Research (Ed.), *Making health care decisions: The ethical and legal implications of informed consent in the patient–practitioner relationship* (Vol. 3, pp. 28–29). Washington, DC: U. S. Government Printing Office.

Pinderhughes, E. (1989). *Understanding race, ethnicity, and power.* New York: Free Press.

Pinderhughes, E. (1994). Diversity and populations at risk: Ethnic minorities and people of color. In F. G. Reamer (Ed.), *The foundations of social work knowledge* (pp. 264–308). New York: Columbia University Press.

Pollard, W. L. (1995). Civil rights. In R. L. Edwards (Ed.-in-Chief), *Encyclopedia of social work* (19th ed., Vol. 1, pp. 494–502). Washington, DC: NASW Press.

Pope, K. S. (1988). How clients are harmed by sexual contact with mental health professionals: The syndrome and its prevalence. *Journal of Counseling and Development, 67*, 222–226.

Popple, P. R. (1992). Social work: Social function and moral purpose. In P. N. Reid & P. R. Popple (Eds.), *The moral purposes of social work* (pp. 141–154). Chicago: Nelson-Hall.

Popple, P. R. (1995). Social work profession: History. In R. L. Edwards (Ed.-in-Chief), *Encyclopedia of social work* (19th ed., Vol. 3, pp. 2282–2292). Washington, DC: NASW Press.

President's Commission for the Study of Ethical Problems in Medicine and Biomedical and Behavioral Research. (1982). *Making health care decisions: The ethical and legal implications of informed consent in the patient–practitioner relationship* (Vol. 3). Washington, DC: U.S. Government Printing Office.

Proposal: Revision of the Code of Ethics. (1996, January). *NASW News*, pp. 19–22.

Psychologist–patient privilege prevents counselor from testifying at divorce trial. (1991). *Mental Health Law News, 6*(6), 5.

Pumphrey, M. W. (1959). *The teaching of values and ethics in social work education.* New York: Council on Social Work Education.

Rawls, J. (1971). *A theory of justice.* Cambridge, MA: Harvard University Press.

Reamer, F. G. (1980). Ethical content in social work. *Social Casework, 61*, 531–540.

Reamer, F. G. (1982). Conflicts of professional duty in social work. *Social Casework, 63*, 579–585.

Reamer, F. G. (1983a). The concept of paternalism in social work. *Social Service Review, 57*, 254–271.

Reamer, F. G. (1983b). Ethical dilemmas in social work practice. *Social Work, 28*, 31–35.

Reamer, F. G. (1984). Enforcing ethics in social work. *Health Matrix, 2*(2), 17–25.

Reamer, F. G. (1985). The emergence of bioethics in social work. *Health & Social Work, 10*, 271–281.

Reamer, F. G. (1986). The use of modern technology in social work: Ethical dilemmas. *Social Work, 31*, 469–472.

Reamer, F. G. (1987a). Ethics committees in social work. *Social Work, 32*, 188–192.

Reamer, F. G. (1987b). Informed consent in social work. *Social Work, 32*, 425–429.

Reamer, F. G. (1987c). Values and ethics. In A. Minahan (Ed.-in-Chief), *Encyclopedia of social work* (18th ed., Vol. 2, pp. 801–809). Silver Spring, MD: National Association of Social Workers.

Reamer, F. G. (1988). Social workers and unions: Ethical dilemmas. In H. J. Karger (Ed.), *Social workers and labor unions* (pp. 131–143). Westport, CT: Greenwood Press.

Reamer, F. G. (1989a). Liability issues in social work supervision. *Social Work, 34*, 445–448.

Reamer, F. G. (1989b). Toward ethical practice: The relevance of ethical theory. *Social Thought, 15*(3–4), 67–78.

Reamer, F. G. (1990). *Ethical dilemmas in social service* (2nd ed.). New York: Columbia University Press.

Reamer, F. G. (Ed.). (1991a). *AIDS and ethics.* New York: Columbia University Press.

Reamer, F. G. (1991b). AIDS, social work, and the duty to protect. *Social Work, 36*, 56–60.

Reamer, F. G. (1992a). The impaired social worker. *Social Work, 37*, 165–170.

Reamer, F. G. (1992b). Should social workers blow the whistle on incompetent colleagues? Yes. In E. Gambrill & R. Pruger (Eds.), *Controversial issues in social work* (pp. 66–78). Needham Heights, MA: Allyn & Bacon.

Reamer, F. G. (1992c). Social work and the public good: Calling or career? In P. N. Reid & P. R. Popple (Eds.), *The moral purposes of social work* (pp. 11–33). Chicago: Nelson-Hall.

Reamer, F. G. (1993a). AIDS and social work: The ethics and civil liberties agenda. *Social Work, 38*, 412–414.

Reamer, F. G. (1993b). Liability issues in social work supervision. *Administration in Social Work, 17*(4), 11–25.

Reamer, F. G. (1993c). *The philosophical foundations of social work.* New York: Columbia University Press.

Reamer, F. G. (1994). *Social work malpractice and liability.* New York: Columbia University Press.

Reamer, F. G. (1995a). Ethics and values. In R. L. Edwards (Ed.-in-Chief), *Encyclopedia of social work* (19th ed., Vol. 1, pp. 893–902). Washington, DC: NASW Press.

Reamer, F. G. (1995b). Ethics consultation in social work. *Social Thought, 18*(1), 3–16.

Reamer, F. G. (1995c). Malpractice claims against social workers: First facts. *Social Work, 40*, 595–601.

Reamer, F. G. (1995d). *Social work values and ethics.* New York: Columbia University Press.

Reamer, F. G. (1997a). Ethical issues for social work practice. In M. Reisch & E. Gambrill (Eds.), *Social work in the 21st century* (pp. 340–349). Thousand Oaks, CA: Pine Forge/Sage Publications.

Reamer, F. G. (1997b). Ethical standards in social work: The NASW *Code of Ethics.* In R. L. Edwards (Ed.-in-Chief), *Encyclopedia of social work* (19th ed., 1997 Suppl., pp. 113–123). Washington, DC: NASW Press.

Reamer, F. G. (1997c). Managing ethics under managed care. *Families in Society, 78*(1), 96–101.

Reamer, F. G. (1998a). *Social work research and evaluation skills.* New York: Columbia University Press.

Reamer, F. G. (1998b). Social work. In R. Chadwick (Ed.-in-Chief), *Encyclopedia of applied ethics* (Vol. 4, pp. 169–180). San Diego: Academic Press.

Reamer, F. G., & Abramson, M. (1982). *The teaching of social work ethics.* Hastings-on-Hudson, NY: Hastings Center.

Rehr, H. (1960). Problems for a profession in a strike situation. *Social Work, 5*(2), 22–28.

Reid, P. N., & Popple, P. R. (Eds.). (1992). *The moral purposes of social work.* Chicago: Nelson-Hall.

Reid, W. J. (1987). Social work research. In A. Minahan (Ed.-in-Chief), *Encyclopedia of social work* (18th ed., Vol. 2, pp. 474–487). Silver Spring, MD: National Association of Social Workers.

Reid, W. J., & Smith, A. (1981). *Research in social work.* New York: Columbia University Press.

Rennie v. Klein, 462 F. Supp. 1131 (D. N. J. 1978).

Reynolds, B. C. (1956). *Uncharted journey.* New York: Citadel.

Rhodes, M. L. (1986). *Ethical dilemmas in social work practice*. London: Routledge & Kegan Paul.

Richter, N. L., Snider, E., & Gorey, K. M. (1997). Group work intervention with female survivors of childhood sexual abuse. *Research on Social Work Practice*, 7(1), 53–69.

Rieman, D. (1992). *Strategies in social work consultation*. New York: Longman.

Robertson, H. W., & Jackson, V. H. (1991). *NASW guidelines on the private practice of clinical social work*. Silver Spring, MD: National Association of Social Workers.

Roe v. Wade, 93 S. Ct. 705 (1973).

Rozovsky, F. A. (1984). *Consent to treatment: A practical guide*. Boston: Little, Brown.

Rubin, A., & Babbie, E. (1997). *Research methods for social work* (3rd ed.). Pacific Grove, CA: Brooks/Cole.

Salgo v. Leland Stanford Jr. University Board of Trustees, 317 P. 2d 170 (Cal. Ct. App. 1957).

Saltzman, A., & Proch, K. (1990). *Law in social work practice*. Chicago: Nelson-Hall.

Schlesinger, E. G., & Devore, W. (1995). Ethnic-sensitive practice. In R. L. Edwards (Ed.-in-Chief), *Encyclopedia of social work* (19th ed., Vol. 1, pp. 902–908). Washington, DC: NASW Press.

Schloendorff v. Society of New York Hospital, 211 N.Y. 125 (1914).

Schoener, G. R., & Gonsiorek, J. (1988). Assessment and development of rehabilitation plans for counselors who have sexually exploited their clients. *Journal of Counseling and Development*, 67, 227–232.

Schutz, B. M. (1982). *Legal liability in psychotherapy*. San Francisco: Jossey-Bass.

Shelly v. Kraemer, 68 S. Ct. 836 (1948).

Shulman, L. (1978). Unionization and the professional employee: The social service director's view. In S. Slavin (Ed.), *Social administration: The management of the social services* (pp. 460–468). New York: Haworth Press.

Shulman, L. (1995). Supervision and consultation. In R. L. Edwards (Ed.-in-Chief), *Encyclopedia of social work* (19th ed., Vol. 3, pp. 2373–2379). Washington, DC: NASW Press.

Singer, T. L. (1995). Sexual harassment. In R. L. Edwards (Ed.-in-Chief), *Encyclopedia of social work* (19th ed., Vol. 3, pp. 2148–2156). Washington, DC: NASW Press.

Siporin, M. (1992). Strengthening the moral mission of social work. In P. N. Reid & P. R. Popple (Eds.), *The moral purposes of social work* (pp. 71–99). Chicago: Nelson-Hall.

Skeel, J. D., & Self, D. J. (1989). An analysis of ethics consultation in the clinical setting. *Theoretical Medicine*, 10, 289–299.

Slovenko, R. (1978). Psychotherapy and informed consent: A search in judicial regulation. In W. E. Barton & C. J. Sanborn (Eds.), *Law and the mental health professions* (p. 51–62). New York: International Universities Press.

Smart, J.J.C., & Williams, B. (1973). *Utilitarianism: For and against*. Cambridge, England: Cambridge University Press.

Sonnenstuhl, W. J. (1989). Reaching the impaired professional: Applying findings from organizational and occupational research. *Journal of Drug Issues*, 19, 533–539.

Spicker, P. (1988). *Principles of social welfare*. London: Routledge.

Spiers, H. R. (1989). AIDS and civil disobedience. *Hastings Center Report*, 19(6), 34–35.

Tambor, M. (1995). Unions. In R. L. Edwards (Ed.-in-Chief), *Encyclopedia of social work* (19th ed., Vol. 3, pp. 2418–2426). Washington, DC: NASW Press.

Tarasoff v. Board of Regents of the University of California, 33 Cal. 3d 275 (1973), 529 P. 2d 553 (1974), 17 Cal. 3d 425 (1976), 551 P. 2d 334 (1976), 131 Cal. Rptr. 14 (1976).

Task Force on Social Work Research. (1991). *Building social work knowledge for effective services and policies*. Washington, DC: National Institute of Mental Health.

Teel, K. (1975). The physician's dilemma: A doctor's view: What the law should be. *Baylor Law Review, 27*, 6–9.

Thoreson, R. W., Miller, M., & Krauskopf, C. J. (1989). The distressed psychologist: Prevalence and treatment considerations. *Professional Psychology: Research and Practice, 20*, 153–158.

Thoreson, R. W., Nathan, P. E., Skorina, J. K., & Kilburg, R. R. (1983). The alcoholic psychologist: Issues, problems, and implications for the profession. *Professional Psychology: Research and Practice, 14*, 670–684.

Towle, C. (1965). *Common human needs*. Washington, DC: National Association of Social Workers.

Tully, C. T. (1995). Lesbians overview. In R. L. Edwards (Ed.-in-Chief), *Encyclopedia of social work* (19th ed., Vol. 2, pp. 1591–1596). Washington, DC: NASW Press.

Twaite, J. A., & Lampert, D. T. (1997). Outcomes of mandated preventive services programs for homeless and truant children: A follow-up study. *Social Work, 42*, 11–18.

Tyson, K. (1995). *New foundations for scientific social and behavioral research*. Needham Heights, MA: Allyn & Bacon.

U.S. National Center on Child Abuse and Neglect. (1981). *National study of the incidence and severity of child abuse and neglect*. Washington, DC: U.S. Department of Health and Human Services.

VandeCreek, L., & Knapp, S. (1993). *Tarasoff and beyond*. Sarasota, FL: Professional Resource Press.

VandeCreek, L., Knapp, S., & Herzog, C. (1988). Privileged communication for social workers. *Social Casework, 69*(1), 28–34.

Van Den Bergh, N., & Cooper, L. (1986). *Feminist visions for social work*. Silver Spring, MD: National Association of Social Workers.

VandenBos, G. R., & Duthie, R. F. (1986). Confronting and supporting colleagues in distress. In R. R. Kilburg, P. E. Nathan, & R. W. Thoreson (Eds.), *Professionals in distress: Issues, syndromes, and solutions in psychology* (p. 211). Washington, DC: American Psychological Association.

Weick, A., Rapp, C., Sullivan, W. P., & Kristhardt, W. (1989). A strengths perspective for social work practice. *Social Work, 34*, 350–354.

Weil, M. O., & Gamble, D. N. (1995). Community practice models. In R. L. Edwards (Ed.-in-Chief), *Encyclopedia of social work* (19th ed., Vol. 1, pp. 577–594). Washington, DC: NASW Press.

Weismiller, T., & Rome, S. H. (1995). Social workers in politics. In R. L. Edwards (Ed.-in-Chief), *Encyclopedia of social work* (19th ed., Vol. 3, pp. 2305–2313). Washington, DC: NASW Press.

Wigmore, J. H. (1961). *Evidence in trials at common law* (rev. ed., Vol. 8, J. T. McNaughton, Ed.). Boston: Little, Brown.

Wilson, S. J. (1978). *Confidentiality in social work*. New York: Free Press.

Wilson, S. J. (1980). *Recording: Guidelines for social workers*. New York: Free Press.

Wood, B. J., Klein, S., Cross, H. J., Lammers, C. J., & Elliott, J. K. (1985). Impaired practitioners: Psychologists' opinions about prevalence, and proposals for intervention. *Professional Psychology: Research and Practice, 16*, 843–850.

Woodman, N. (1985). Parents of lesbians and gays: Concerns and interventions. In H. Hidalgo, T. Peterson, & N. Woodman (Eds.), *Lesbian and gay issues: A resource manual for social workers.* Silver Spring, MD: National Association of Social Workers.

Zimbalist, S. E. (1977). *Historic themes and landmarks in social welfare research.* New York: Harper & Row.

# INDEX

# T

# U

# V

# W

# ABOUT THE AUTHOR

**Frederic G. Reamer, PhD,** is professor at the School of Social Work, Rhode Island College. Dr. Reamer has served as a social worker in mental health, correctional, and housing agencies, and in a governor's office. He was chair of the *NASW Code of Ethics* Revision Committee, and he lectures nationally and internationally on the subjects of social work and professional ethics. Dr. Reamer's books include *Social Work Values and Ethics, Ethical Dilemmas in Social Service, Social Work Malpractice and Liability, The Philosophical Foundations of Social Work, The Foundations of Social Work Knowledge, AIDS and Ethics, Rehabilitating Juvenile Justice* (with Charles Shireman), and *Social Work Research and Evaluation Skills.*

# ETHICAL STANDARDS IN SOCIAL WORK
## A CRITICAL REVIEW OF THE NASW CODE OF ETHICS

Cover design by The Watermark Design Office

Composed by UpperCase Publication Services, in Goudy Old Style

Printed by Graphic Communications, Inc.